Proselytization
and Communal
Self-Determination
in Africa

Religion and Human Rights Series

Series Editors
John Witte Jr.
Abdullahi Ahmed An-Na'im
Emory University

Board of Advisors
Azizah al-Hibri, University of Richmond
Donna Arzt, Syracuse University
Irwin Cotler, McGill University
Frances Deng, The Brookings Institution
Jean Bethke Elshtain, University of Chicago
David Little, United States Institute of Peace
Ann Elizabeth Mayer, University of Pennsylvania
José Míguez Bonino, Facultad Evangélica, ISEDET, Buenos Aires
Chandra Muzzafar, University of Malaysia
John T. Noonan Jr., U.S. Court of Appeals
Kusumita Pedersen, St. Francis College
Lamin Sanneh, Yale University
Max Stackhouse, Princeton Theological Seminary
M. Thomas Thangaraj, Emory University

Other Books Published in the Series

Proselytism and Orthodoxy in Russia: The New War for Souls
   John Witte Jr. and Michael Bourdeaux, editors

Religious Freedom and Evangelization in Latin America: The Challenge of Religious Pluralism
   Paul E. Sigmund, editor

RELIGION AND HUMAN RIGHTS SERIES

Proselytization and Communal Self-Determination in Africa

Abdullahi Ahmed An-Na'im
Editor

ORBIS BOOKS

Maryknoll, New York 10545

The Catholic Foreign Mission Society of America (Maryknoll) recruits and trains people for overseas missionary service. Through Orbis Books, Maryknoll aims to foster the international dialogue that is essential to mission. The books published, however, reflect the opinions of their authors and are not meant to represent the official position of the Society. To obtain more information about Maryknoll and Orbis Books, please visit our website at www.maryknoll.org.

Published by Orbis Books, Maryknoll, New York, U.S.A.

Manufactured in the United States of America.

Manuscript editing and typesetting by Joan Weber Laflamme.

Library of Congress Cataloging-in-Publication Data

Proselytization and communal self-determination in Africa / Abdullahi Ahmed An-Na'im, editor.
    p. cm. — (Religion & human rights series)
    Includes bibliographical references and index.
    ISBN 1-57075-261-3 (pa.)
    1. Proselytizing—Africa.   2. Self-determination, National—Africa.   I. Na'īm, 'Abd Allāh Ahmad,   1946–   . II. Series.
BL2400.P76   1999
291.7'2'096—dc21   99-37929
                                                                        CIP

CONTENTS

THE RELIGION AND HUMAN RIGHTS
SERIES PREFACE

The relationship between religion and human rights is both problematic and unavoidable in all parts of the world. Religion, broadly defined to include various traditional, cultural, and customary institutions and practices, is unquestionably a formidable force for violence, repression, and chauvinism of untold dimensions. But religion is also a natural and necessary ally in the global struggle for human rights. For human rights norms are inherently abstract ideals—universal statements of the good life and the good society. They depend upon the visions and values of human communities to give them content, coherence, and concrete manifestation. Religion is an inherent condition of human lives and human communities. Religion invariably provides the sources and scales of dignity and responsibility, shame and respect, restitution and reconciliation that a human rights regime needs to survive and to flourish.

This book series explores the interaction of religious ideas and institutions with human rights principles and practices. It seeks to discover the religious sources of human rights—both their cultivation and their corruption in the discourse of sacred texts, the activism of religious organizations, and the practices of religious polities. It seeks to uncover the legal sources of human rights—both their protection and their abridgment in international human rights instruments and in domestic constitutions, statutes, and cases. It seeks to address some of the cutting edge issues of religion and human rights in theory and practice.

This series is made possible, in part, by the generous funding of The Pew Charitable Trusts, Inc. and the Ford Foundation. Pew's support came through its funding of a three year project on "Soul Wars: The Problem and Promise of Proselytism in the New World Order." Ford's support came through its funding of a three-year project on "Cultural Transformation in Africa: Legal, Religious, and Human Rights Perspectives." Several of the early volumes in this series are parts and products of these two projects. They provide pilots and prototypes for the type of rigorous interdisciplinary and interreligious analysis that the subject of religion and human rights requires.

We wish to express our gratitude to our friends at the two foundations for their generous support of this effort. We also wish to thank the Maryknoll

vii

Fathers and Brothers and Bill Burrows and Bernadette Price of Orbis for their sage stewardship of this series.

— JOHN WITTE JR.
ABDULLAHI AHMED AN-NA'IM
EMORY UNIVERSITY, ATLANTA

PREFACE

This collection of essays on issues of proselytization and communal self-determination in Africa is one of the first titles to appear in a new book series entitled Religion and Human Rights, a joint venture between the Law and Religion Program of Emory University School of Law and Orbis Books. The Law and Religion Program is dedicated to scholarly research and teaching on the religious dimensions of law, the legal dimensions of religion, and the interaction of legal and religious ideas and methods in different parts of the world. The program is decidedly ecumenical and comparative in perspective, combining an emphasis on Christianity, Judaism, and Islam in North America, Europe, and the Middle East, with growing engagement of other religious traditions and legal systems in Africa, Asia, and Latin America.

The new series, Religion and Human Rights, helps the Law and Religion Program meet a growing demand for interdisciplinary scholarship on the problematic, yet unavoidable, relationship between religion and human rights throughout the world. Besides addressing questions of freedom of religion and belief in relation to different religious and cultural traditions, this series also seeks to examine the interaction between public policy and civic activism within a broad and dynamic human rights framework. As an occasional series, Religion and Human Rights will feature monographs, anthologies, and source books reflecting a variety of scholarly and cultural/religious perspectives.

This book on Africa is part of a wider project, "The Problem of Proselytism in the New World Order," which focuses on aspects of the emerging global dynamics of competition, confrontation, and/or mutual accommodation between and within religious belief systems in selected regions of the world. Work on the Africa sub-project began with a meeting of the project team in January 1996 at Emory University in Atlanta. Various studies were commissioned by that meeting for presentation and discussion at a workshop co-organized with the Council for the Development of Social Science Research in Africa (CODESRIA) in Dakar, Senegal, in May 1997. Another workshop on proselytization in Southern Africa was also organized in collaboration with the University of Stellenbosch and convened earlier in Franschoek, South Africa, in March 1997.

I wish to gratefully acknowledge the original work of Professor John Witte Jr., assisted by Professor Johan van der Vyver, in developing the concept of this project on issues of proselytization. As the director of the Law and Religion Program of Emory University School of Law, Professor Witte was able to secure funding for the whole project and to guide all aspects of its practical implementation. He has also been a constant source of moral and intellectual support to me personally throughout the implementation of the Africa sub-project, in addition to his own work on all other aspects of the project as a whole.

The preparation of this volume for publication would not have been possible without the valuable assistance of Professor Rosalind I. J. Hackett of the University of Tennessee, Knoxville, and Ms. Amy Wheeler of Emory University School of Law. Dr. Hackett not only translated from French to English the paper by Chabha Bouslimani, and revised the translation of the paper by T. K. Biaya, but also closely reviewed and commented on all the chapters in this book. Her outstanding expertise in religious studies, especially in relation to Africa, has been an indispensable resource throughout the implementation of this sub-project. Ms. Wheeler's assistance in following through with authors and preparing the manuscript in its final form has also been equally indispensable. I am truly grateful to Professor Hackett and Ms. Wheeler.

As indicated earlier, this book series is a joint venture between Orbis Books and the Law and Religion Program. On behalf of my colleagues in the Law and Religion Program, I would like to express our deep gratitude to Dr. William R. Burrows and his colleagues at Maryknoll for establishing this series. As co-editor of the series and editor of this book, I particularly appreciate the patience and courtesy of Dr. Burrows and his colleagues during various stages of editing and production.

The implementation of all aspects of the proselytization project, including the part on Africa that is the focus of this book, would not have been possible without a generous grant from The Pew Charitable Trusts. We are truly grateful for that indispensable support.

—ABDULLAHI A. AN-NA'IM

1.

INTRODUCTION

Competing Claims to Religious Freedom and Communal Self-Determination in Africa

——————— ◆ ———————

Abdullahi Ahmed An-Na'im

INTRODUCTION

This book on proselytization in Africa is part of a wider project addressing issues of conflict between competing claims to religious freedom, on the one hand, and "communal" self-determination,[1] on the other, in the context of three regions of the world: Eastern Europe, Latin America, and Africa.[2] This primarily geographical focus of the project as a whole is intended to highlight contextual factors, without underestimating the role of cross-regional dynamics. Those making competing claims to religious freedom and communal self-determination neither perceive their claims in exclusively regional terms, nor do they act or react in isolation of actors and factors in other parts of the world. While opting for specific regional scope in the interest of depth of analysis, the project seeks to bring a variety of perspectives to bear on the issues through the multidisciplinary composition of its project team and researchers, as reflected in the chapters of this volume.

Another distinguishing feature of this project is that it seeks to apply a human rights paradigm to the mediation of competing claims over proselytization and its implications. A discussion of how that paradigm might apply, and what difference it is likely to make, will follow an explanation of the nature, context, and dynamics of proselytization in general, and with reference to Africa in particular. It should be noted from the outset, however, that proselytization should not be equated with conversion, as the latter may or may not follow from the former. Conversion may also be an unintended consequence of commercial, social, or other forms of interaction that cannot be characterized as proselytization in the usual sense of the term.

On any given day, one can point to numerous religious conflicts and tensions within and between communities around the world as a primary or contributory cause of broader persistent strife that sometimes leads to massive violence and destruction. Regarding each situation, observers will probably disagree about such issues as the underlying causes of the conflict; the role of religion as such; and the identity, motivation, objectives and relative importance of various internal and external actors. Efforts to explain or understand these situations may recall histories of religious and ethnic rivalries or hostilities, highlight current economic difficulties and political frustrations, emphasize demographic and geopolitical factors, cite the role of charismatic leaders with their complex motivations, and so forth. Prescriptions for resolution of such conflicts will also vary with the analysis and orientation of the parties in relation to particularities of specific context, as well as pragmatic possibilities of implementation. Proselytization is often an explicit or implicit element of religious conflict in all parts of the world, usually overlapping and interacting with other factors. However, the two phenomena should not be taken as synonymous. This project is concerned with proselytization in particular, and not with religious conflict and tension in general.

Part of the impetus for this choice arose out of concerns about what Martin Marty, the leading American scholar of religion, has called a "new war for souls" among churches and religious groups competing among themselves over numerical membership and social and political influence, in addition to more conventionally understood forms of proselytization in the sense of seeking new converts. While those initial concerns were confirmed in subsequent studies within the framework of the project as a whole, it also became clear that the concept of proselytization and its manifestations should not be confined to such preconceived notions. In this project, this concept conveys a range of meanings and methods of communication of religious ideas. Similar issues are raised by the numerous possibilities of "conversion" within the same tradition or sub-tradition in response to internal and/or external stimuli. For example, Muslim proselytizers not only seek to convert non-Muslims to Islam, or from Sunni to Shi'i Islam, or from one Sufi group to another, but may also endeavor to motivate and mobilize members of their own sub-tradition of Islam into a more active mode in support of local political and economic objectives or in response to perceptions of "external" threat, whether identifiable as Islamic or otherwise. Evangelical, Pentecostal, and charismatic forms of Christianity, which have gained momentum in the last two decades in Africa, are also predicated on the spirit of revival within the same religion.

The basic rationale of the project's focus is the paradox of greater risks of proselytization in the modern context coupled with apparently improved possibilities of peaceful mediation of conflict. On the risks side, recent global and technological developments dramatically enhance the frequency and efficacy of proselytizing initiatives, thereby raising the threat of consequential confrontation and conflict. The ease of international travel and communication and the increased availability of material resources lead to more diverse and potentially conflictual proselytizing initiatives than ever before, thereby raising the political and security stakes for all concerned. What may have been far-fetched scenarios of effective proselytization are now easily implemented (from North America and East Asia into Eastern Europe and Russia, from the Middle East and South Asia into central Asia or sub-Saharan Africa), and are therefore more threatening to their opponents. The hold of formally or informally established churches over their membership and territories is fast diminishing in some places, while resurgent religious groups seek to control or influence the state in order to enforce their own models of governance or policy. Massive financial resources, media campaigns, technical expertise, and political influence on powerful states can now easily be mounted in support of co-believers around the world, whether in support of their right and efforts to proselytize, or to "protect" them from proselytization by others. Like many aspects of domestic and international affairs after the Cold War, previously established patterns of religious (sometimes including ethnic) power relations no longer apply, with consequent possibilities of political fragmentation or reorganization of existing states in pursuit of old or new rivalries and alliances. In other words, the same conditions of democratization and economic liberalization often provide the conditions for increased religious pluralization and proselytization activities.

On the mediation side, the same dynamic of increased possibilities of confrontation and conflict may enhance the prospects of negotiations and peaceful settlement precisely because the stakes can become too high for all concerned to pursue hostile means. In other words, the plausibility of violent secession and separate statehood with transnational support and encouragement may force all sides to a conflict to reconsider their options for just and peaceful cooperation within an existing state (An-Na'im and Deng 1996). That is to say, deadlock or stalemate resulting from relatively matched power and resources of proselytizers and target groups may propel both sides to seek peaceful mediation for their competing claims.[3]

The key question to be addressed later in this chapter is whether the modern human rights paradigm, and the notion of communal self-determination in particular, may provide a theoretical framework for mediation between these competing claims. It is important to note here that such a framework should also be assessed as a possible source of policy directions, as well as practical guidelines for the mediation of these competing claims. As I will argue later in this Introduction, the possibility of a human rights paradigm should be explored and developed in this context because it is already part of the foundation of freedom of religion, which includes the right to proselytize, on the one hand, and self-determination, which can be the basis of resistance to proselytization efforts, on the other.

Prevailing conceptions of democracy stipulate that the state should foster religious pluralism without undue preference for a particular religion over others. These conceptions of democracy require religions to sustain themselves and thrive on the cogency and validity of their message to believers without coercion or undue advantage over unbelievers and their beliefs or lifestyle.[4] This religious "neutrality" of the state is supposed to be enshrined in the constitution and legal system of the state, which protect religious rights as well as related freedoms of association, assembly, and expression for all, in addition to safeguarding the autonomy of civil society organizations engaged in the provision of educational, health, or social and charitable services. These ideas are also associated with the modern human rights paradigm and the principle of self-determination, though with some conceptual difficulty as discussed later.

Unfortunately, it seems that the emerging democracies of Eastern Europe and the former Soviet Union, and the recent wave of democratization in Africa have failed to live up to these ideals. In Eastern Europe and the former Soviet Union, older "established" churches and communities seek to dominate or eliminate local religious and cultural rivals. Yet the same older churches feel threatened by, and even besieged by, foreign religious groups deploying vast material resources and human expertise in attempting to attract converts away from their present religious and community affiliations. Unable to match the educational, health, and other advantages of the foreign proselytizers, local religious groups appeal to the state for protection of their traditional status and membership. Yet, the recent veneer of constitutional protection of religious rights and other freedoms is often being subverted by overt state favoritism of some religious groups and oppression of others. Rival local and foreign religious groups in many parts of the world are now locked in a "new war for souls" of mutual defamation, manipulation of political power, and deployment of constitutional norms and legal mechanisms for purported religious advantage, with consequent religious fragmentation and fundamentalism. Before highlighting some aspects of the context and processes of this phenomenon in relation to Africa in particular, it might be helpful to briefly clarify the nature of proselytization in general.

THE DYNAMICS OF PROSELYTIZATION

Perceptions of the nature and role of proselytization are often conditioned or influenced by such factors as personal experience or religious orientation, and disciplinary or professional perspectives. Such perceptions can also be affected by the desire to seek or promote pragmatic approaches to resolving acute political or security problems in specific situations. Existing scholarship on the subject in English reflects this diversity of perceptions and perspectives, but mainly in relation to Christianity (Macmullen 1984; Marty and Greenspan 1988), with little on Islam, which is the other proselytizing religion relevant to the African context (Goodman 1994). Moreover, as observed by Christopher Clark, the largest amount of literature on proselytization is "in house histories," followed in volume by material from a theological and church historical perspective, with works which take account of political context and social/cultural factors taking third place (Clark 1995, 5). Some studies deal with the nature and process of "conversion" and related religious experiences from the perspectives of social science theory or psychology (Festinger 1957; Goodman 1994, 173; Rambo 1993; Hefner 1993).[5] The following remarks are not intended to review or discuss this wide variety of literature. Rather, my purpose here is to offer some general reflections on proselytization with a view to addressing the issues in relation to the mediation of competing claims within a human rights framework in particular.

To its proponents, proselytization is about people's freedom to propagate their own religious commitments in an effort to reach out and share with others the merits and benefits that the religion is held to generate and sustain in the individual and communal life of believers. Proselytization is also represented as a religious imperative for believers to pursue for their own personal salvation and self-realization. The sacred history of Christianity or Islam, for example, is cited to illustrate the transforming power of religious commitment—how the very few powerless and oppressed early believers managed to transform their own lives and to infuse the values and institutions of their religion into many other communities. The underlying claim is that target groups would probably "see the light" if only they were allowed to hear the message or observe the living example of the believers. That is, proselytization is said to be for the "good" of intended target groups as much as it is for the benefit of those who seek to proselytize others.

Such perceptions of proselytization are premised on two claims: The first claim is that the members of the target group are free to accept or reject the message of the proselytizer once they have had a chance to hear it from the believers themselves. The second claim is that proselytizers are entitled "as of right" to reach the target group with their religious message, regardless of the declared or presumed response of that group. Both propositions are problematic because in the majority of cases the target group is unlikely to be truly free to accept or reject the message of the proselytizer, nor is the demand of access by the proselytizers independent from the material and political interests and concerns of both sides. *Proselytization is hardly ever simply and exclusively about the communication of a religious message, to be accepted or rejected on its own terms.* Interaction over a religious message is necessarily embedded in the cultural and ideological context of the proselytizers and their community of believers, on the one hand, and of the target individuals of proselytization and their community, on the other. Throughout human history, religious interaction has always been as much about material interests and power relations as it has been about spiritual insights and moral values. Proselytization is by definition the effort of believers in one religion to change the spiritual and material conditions of perceived unbelievers. Otherwise, the social, economic, and political transformation of convert communities may not occur as claimed in the sacred histories of proselytizing religions.

As a consequence of this, the opponents of proselytization perceive it as a challenge to the individual and collective self-identity of target groups—a threat to their political independence and material well-being. From this perspective, proselytization is inherently dangerous and offensive to its actual or potential target group precisely because it seeks to radically change people's identities and lifestyle. As discussed in the chapters by Francis M. Deng, Makau Mutua, and Benjamin F. Soares below, this is especially the case when indigenous groups are targeted because their religious beliefs and practices are central to their cultural identity. That is to say, the objection is to the very nature and objectives of the process, and is only confirmed by the prospects of its success, regardless of the "fairness" of its methods. At this level, proselytization is rejected for the implicit, if not explicit, assumption of the proselytizer that the target group needs changing, and that the religion of the proselytizer offers a better alternative. This implication of religious and cultural superiority is therefore integral to the very notion of proselytization, regardless of the methods used or the power relations of the two sides.

Moreover, opponents of proselytization claim that experience everywhere shows that it has consistently been used throughout history to spearhead or legitimize local domination or imperialist expansion by foreign powers. They dispute the facts and implications of the sacred history of Christianity and Islam, and challenge claims about the cultural and ideological content of those religions, as well as the material objectives of their proselytizing agents. In so doing, these opponents emphasize that in the early history or recent experience of their communities the issue was never simply about spiritual insights or moral values that were to be freely accepted or rejected as such. The objection here is twofold: First, that the issue is never simply a matter of a "free market of religious ideas" competing on a "level playing field," where only the inherent validity of one set of religious beliefs is seeking to expose the invalidity of the other in order to simply "persuade" believers in the latter religion to freely accept the former. The second and related objection is that serious and systematic proselytization is unlikely to be attempted, or to be successful, except when the proselytizers are encouraged and supported by extra-religious material advantages over the target group.

This analysis of the all-important *dynamics* of proselytization can be further clarified by highlighting the two aspects of *agency* and *self-determination*. First, advocacy of and opposition to proselytization are usually done by individuals who claim to speak on behalf of their community of believers or the target group, respectively. While the moral and material support of the general public of each community is actively sought by those elites, the community at large is rarely involved in the actual discourse of competing religions, cultures, and ideologies. Second, and regardless of the apparent terms of the debate, these competing claims are necessarily about communal self-determination. On the one hand, the proponents of proselytization demand the possibility of converting others as matter of exercising their individual freedom of religion—in collaboration with other members of their own religious community, but the process also involves an attempt to transform the other community. On the other hand, opponents reject the intrusion in the name of protecting the existing expression of the self-determination of their community, in material as well as ideological terms, often without substantiating their claim to speak for the community or justifying the assumptions they are making about the practical content of self-determination for that community.

In the polemics of proselytization the proponents tend to avoid acknowledging its wider implications and seek to challenge the right of their opponents to speak on behalf of the target group. That is, the proponents may insist that their objective is purely religious and claim that the target group would be freely willing to listen and perhaps accept the message if only their own elites allowed them to hear it. Paradoxically, that denial of wider political, economic, and cultural agendas is usually coupled with a sense of assertive self-confidence that proselytizers derive from their own material advantage over the target group. In so doing, proselytizers are appropriating the agency of their own religious communities by claiming to discharge its obligation of "a mission of salvation." Since those communities at large are unlikely to agree at least on the wider implications of proselytization, there may be problems of agency between the claims of the individual proselytizers (and their religious organizations) on the one hand, and the wider home communities which fund and support them through the use of (or the threat of the use of) economic and even military power, on the other. Whatever the private motives of proselytizers may be, they are unlikely to be identical to those of the national communities on whose strength and resources they draw in seeking to proselytize others. For example, while missionaries for specific religious communities in the United States draw on the material and diplomatic resources of their country in pursuit of proselytization, other American religious communities and the public at large may not be in agreement with that objective as such, though they may accept the wider material and political benefits of missionary work.

In contrast, opponents tend to emphasize the wider implications of proselytization by believers in another religion and may avoid acknowledging the real nature and internal contradictions of their claim to protect the existing expression of self-determination of the target community. While presenting the proselytizer as simply and purely the agent of an imperial or colonial power, opponents tend to claim that they are only protecting the beliefs or religious identity of their community without admitting the ramifications of that claim. Even to the extent that opponents of proselytization might acknowledge the latter, they are unlikely to recognize that the status quo they are defending may not be a true and valid expression of self-determination by the community at all. In other words, opposition to proselytization is premised on an alleged communal (even national) consensus on the religious beliefs and material conditions of the community (or country at large) that must be defended against external intrusion by the proselytizers and the imperial powers they serve. Internal disagreement about that, they would assert, must be suppressed in the interest of unity against the greater external alleged danger of proselytization and its purportedly detrimental consequences.

In my view, a more plausible position between these two polarized claims is to acknowledge the positive aspects of proselytization while trying to guard against its risks and/or excesses. Notwithstanding the absolutist claims of proponents and opponents, proselytization initiatives can have positive consequences for both sides of the relationship. The challenge proselytization represents can invigorate the religious, social, and political life of the target group as it attempts to better articulate its own beliefs and enhance the individual and communal life of its members in order to more effectively resist that external threat. The reality of open contestation forces the community to seek to demonstrate to its own members the validity of its claims about their religious and material well-being under the status quo. In the process, significant positive change can occur in practice, if only in an effort to match or do better than the benefits the proselytizers claim to bring to the religious and material life of the community in question. It is also reasonable to expect these processes to generally promote the political awareness and organization of the target community. Similar consequences can also be expected to occur within the religious community represented by the proselytizers, as it will be challenged to live up to its claims of religious enlightenment and social and personal well-being. The fact that the religious community of the proselytizer is presented as a model for other communities to follow will in itself attract scrutiny and criticism by others, thereby generating internal efforts to address social, political, and economic, as well as religious, problems. In other words, it is true that competition in a "free market" of religious ideas can be beneficial to both (all) sides, even though this market is hardly ever as free as its proponents claim.

In light of these remarks, I would conclude that despite its problematic nature and negative associations, proselytization is actually a vital part of the dynamism of spiritual and intellectual development of individual persons, as well as the social, political, material, and artistic life of communities and societies at large. Proselytization is too integral and important to people's lives for it to be suppressed altogether, yet it is too problematic to leave totally unregulated for the powerful to manipulate and exploit at will. Accordingly, the question is not only how can proselytization be practiced subject to appropriate limitations, but also how can such regulation be effectively implemented in an orderly and peaceful manner? In order to address this question properly, the issues should be placed in the present African context.

CONTEXT AND PROCESSES OF PROSELYTIZATION IN AFRICA

Like many other issues of public policy in Africa today, the mediation of competing claims to religious freedom and communal self-determination should be considered against the background of two related phenomena, namely, European colonialism and globalization. Though African societies were certainly not isolated from each other or insulated from external influence in the past, various types of European colonialism have had the most far-reaching and enduring impact by the sheer scale and magnitude of the changes they introduced in the continent. For the purposes of this chapter in particular, I would emphasize that it was colonialism that primarily determined the nature of the postcolonial states which continue to rule African societies and control their interactions with the rest of the world in this age of growing globalization. What does this mean, and how is it relevant to the mediation of competing claims about proselytization?

Present states in Africa are direct successors of the colonies established by agreements among European powers (especially the Berlin Conference of 1884-85) regardless of the wishes of local groups. The borders of the colonies which African states came to inherit were established by European continental partition and occupation rather than by African political realities or geography. Colonial governments were organized according to European colonial theory and practice, as modified by expediency; their economies were managed with imperial and/or local colonial considerations primarily in mind; and their legal systems reflected the interests and values of European imperial powers. The vast majority of the African populations of those colonies had little or no constitutional standing in them (Jackson and Rosberg 1986, 5-6).

When independence came, it usually signified the transfer of control over authoritarian power structures and processes of government from colonial masters to local elites (Ayoade 1988, 104). With few exceptions, the postcolonial state in Africa, was

> both overdeveloped and soft. It was overdeveloped because it was erected, artificially, on the foundations of the colonial state. It did not grow organically from within civil society. It was soft because, although in theory all-powerful, it scarcely had the administrative and political means of its dominance. Neither did it have an economic basis on which to rest political power (Chabal 1986, 13).[6]

Since independence, the preservation of juridical statehood and territorial integrity, rather than promotion of the ability and willingness of the state to live up to the practical requirements of sovereignty, became the primary concern of African states.

To make matters worse, the vast majority of first constitutions were either suspended or radically altered by military usurpers or single-party states within a few years of independence (Okoth-Ogendo 1991; Shivji 1991). For decades after independence, successive cycles of civilian and military governments, alike in the majority of African countries, maintained the same colonial legal and institutional mechanisms to suppress political dissent to their policies and to deny accountability for their own actions (Young 1994, 287).[7] Lacking any sense of "ownership," expectation of protection and service, or a general belief in their ability to influence its functioning, African societies often regard the postcolonial state with profound mistrust. They tend to tolerate its existence as an unavoidable evil but prefer to have the least interaction with its institutions and processes (Young 1994, 5). Nevertheless, the postcolonial state is supposed to be firmly in control of the formulation and implementation of public policy at home and the conduct of international relations abroad. In other words, it is the primary framework within which African societies seek to realize their right to self-determination in an increasingly globalized world.

As a working definition, I take *globalization* to refer to, inter alia, transformation of the relations between states, institutions, groups, and individuals; the universalization of certain practices, identities, and structures; and the global restructuring of economic relations within the modern capitalist framework (Falk 1995, 71). Mlinar defines the term as "extending the determinative frameworks of social change to the world as a whole" and suggests the following five dimensions of the process: (1) increasing global interdependence whereby the activities of people in specific areas have repercussions that go beyond local, regional, or national borders; (2) the expansion of domination and dependence; (3) homogenization that tends to emphasize uniformity rather than mutual exclusivity; (4) diversification within "territorial communities" as they open to the wealth of diversity of the world as a whole; and (5) overcoming temporal discontinuities by, for example, temporal inclusiveness resulting from the functioning of particular services to global spaces (Mlinar 1992, 20-22).

In my view, a crucial element of such definitions for our purposes here is the fact that globalization is simply a more effective and comprehensive vehicle or instrument of perpetuating existing power relations within the same country, as well as in its relationship to other countries at the regional and international level. As Tade Akin Aina rightly observed, commonly cited definitions of globalization fail to address "the importance of notions such as coercion, conflict, polarization, domination, inequality, exploitation and injustice. . . . There is little or nothing about monopolies, disruption and dislocation of the labor and other markets, the emergence of a global regulatory chaos and possible anomie and how these are being exploited for gain" (Aina 1997, 11). Accordingly, one would expect globalization to facilitate and intensify neocolonial relations between African and developed countries (Bach 1993; Othman 1993); the domination of civil society by the state within African countries themselves, as well as any hegemonic or conflictual relations that may exist within African societies themselves.

Against this background, I will now briefly review available literature on proselytization in Africa. As with the earlier review of literature about proselytization in general, my purpose here is only to highlight aspects that are pertinent to the subject of this chapter, namely, the mediation of competing claims to religious freedom and communal self-determination. For this reason, I am concerned with works that take into account historical and political context, sociocultural factors, and so forth, as opposed to material produced by religious groups for their own internal use or from a theological perspective.[8] Even for this "social science" type of literature, it is not surprising to find nothing specifically on the subject of mediation of competing claims as such, because this formulation of the issue brings together different disciplinary approaches of scholars who have not been open to possibilities of collaboration. In other words, while scholars of religion rarely consider human rights aspects of their work, lawyers and political scientists who are concerned with human rights issues tend to have a secular perspective.

Available works can be reviewed under the following headings: "conversion" and related religious experiences; Islamic proselytization; Christian proselytization; and works that consider relations between these two proselytizing religions.

An example of the first type is the dialogue between Robin Horton and Humphrey Fisher regarding the nature and circumstances of conversion from "traditional" to "world" religions. Horton began (in a book review of John Peel's study of two Aladura or "prayer healing" churches in Nigeria) by asserting that both Islam and Christianity have achieved only conditional acceptance, suggesting that beliefs and practices of the so-called world religions are only accepted where they happen to coincide with the responses of traditional cosmology to other, non-missionary factors of the modern situation. He saw Islam and Christianity as catalysts which trigger reactions in which they do not always appear among the end products, and he asserted that the success of these two religions as institutions depends on the extent of their willingness to accept these roles (Horton 1971, 104-5). Fisher responded by suggesting that Horton has "overestimated the survival . . . of original African elements of religion; and more important, has under-estimated the willingness and ability of Africans to make even rigorous Islam and Christianity their own" (Fisher 1973, 27). Following other exchanges, Fisher subsequently defined their disagreement as between Horton's view that "the essential patterns of religious development in black Africa are determined by the enduring influence of a traditional cosmology which arises from the ashes of colonialism and conversion," on the one hand, and Fisher's view that "a genuine religious transference is possible," on the other (Fisher 1986, 153; Horton 1975; Hackett 1989).[9]

Recent scholarship, however, reflects concern about the analytical utility of the term *conversion*, even within the framework of a single religion like Christianity. Noting the European connotations of the term, John and Jean Comaroff wonder whether it oversimplifies the real process it purports to describe: "How does it grasp the highly variable, usually gradual, often implicit and demonstrably 'syncretic' manner in which social identities, cultural styles, and ritual practices of African peoples were transformed by the evangelical encounter?" (Comaroff 1991, 250). According to K. F. Morrison, "It is a confusion of categories to use the word *conversion* as though it were an instrument of critical analysis, equally appropriate to any culture or religion. . . . The word is more properly a subject, rather than a tool of analysis" (Morrison 1992, xiv). Talal Asad comments that "it would be better to say that in studying conversion, one was dealing with the narratives by which people apprehend and describe a radical change in the significance of their lives. Sometimes these narratives employ the notion of divine intervention; at other times the notion of a secular teleology" (Asad 1996, 266).

On Islamic proselytization, J. Spencer Trimingham provides a historical analysis in which he divides Africa into seven culture zones and treats each as a historical unity to provide data on the processes and consequences of "Islamization" in each region (Trimingham 1968, 5).[10] He discusses factors that affected the spread of Islam and suggests that it has always followed the routes of traders (Trimingham 1968, 38-39). A deeper and more focused historical analysis of the spread of Islam in West Africa is presented by Mervyn Hiskett, who offers detailed critical examination of proselytization in the context of specific case studies. For example, he describes the roles of several ethnic groups who differed in their Islamic emphasis and discusses the role of Islamic education (Hiskett 1984, 44, 55-58, respectively). Reiterating that conversion takes place on a continuum between military conquest and peaceful persuasion, he suggests that although the military means have been labeled less effective, the change in political and social institutions by the conquerors often forces ideological change. Distinguishing between "trade" as an institution and "traders" as people using that structure, he insists that it was the institution which was the most influential factor in spreading Islam in the region (Hiskett 1984, 303-5). He also further asserts that literacy is often the impetus that propels a society through the stages of conversion and concludes by saying that the unbroken thread throughout the history of Islam in West Africa is "a triumph for the power of literate ideas" (Hiskett 1984, 305, 319; Banwo 1995).[11]

Regarding Christian proselytization, Ruth Rouse represents an early precursor to what has since become an important point in discussions of proselytization; namely, the role of the motive of the missionaries in understanding their beliefs and actions, and their relationship to the proselytized (Rouse 1936). More recent and broader analyses include the work of Thomas O. Beidelman from a social anthropology and colonial history perspective in which he suggests six basic themes or principles for organizing field and theoretical data, namely, secular aspects of missionaries, religious beliefs and missionary activities, theories of conversion and associated beliefs, careers in mission work, compartmentalization of sacred and secular affairs, and parallels in colonial structure (Beidelman 1982, 9; 1981, 73; 1974, 235). Elizabeth Isichei's work on the growth of Christianity in Africa includes analysis of missionaries as "agents of change" and examines the wide variety of their economic and educational backgrounds and the differing roles of missionary women. She also discusses the relationship of the missions to commerce and imperial expansion (Isichei 1995, especially chap. 3). Lamin Sanneh makes the point that "by their root conviction that the gospel is transmissible in the mother tongue, missionaries opened the way for the local idiom to gain ascendancy over assertions of foreign superiority" (Sanneh 1993, 19). A few other works address issues of proselytization, either in specific case studies or general overview, while others include responses to questions of religious pluralism, including the documents of Vatican II (Yates 1994; Isichei 1970, 209-27; McCracken 1977).

The few works which discuss Christianity and Islam together in relation to Africa fail to address the issues most pertinent to this chapter. For example, Noel King traces the growth of both religions since the fifteenth century, but he does not address their methods of proselytization (King 1971). Johaanes Haafkins asserts that "Christian authenticity" warrants a pan-African view which accepts Africa's rich linguistic, cultural and religious pluralism and suggests that Christians will have to accept the nondifferentiation of sacred and secular, including Muslim belief in *Shari'a* as divinely inspired law. But he does not address issues on which Islam and Christianity conflict (Haafkins 1995; Haafkins 1994).[12] Craig Bartholomew raised the question of how Muslims and Christians can live together in a pluralistic society in Africa, but he does not mention proselytization except to criticize Muslim "fundamentalists" for not allowing religious evangelism (Bartholomew 1994). More recently, however, serious scholarly attention is being given to issues of proselytization and Christian-Muslim relations in Africa (Sanneh 1997).

My purpose in presenting this brief review is to show that even social-science scholarship tends to study Islam and Christianity as universal proselytizing religious "actors" transforming their African "subjects" without being affected by them except in terms of adapting the proselytizer's methods of operation to local conditions. Proselytization is presented as an exclusively "one-way" flow of influence and change from the propagators of the two "world religions" to local communities, with implicit assumptions of freedom of choice, "fair play," and the occasional plea for mutual understanding in the interest of coexistence. In light of the available literature, it seems clear to me that the following conclusions are warranted regarding the context and process of proselytization in Africa:

1. The actual process of proselytization in Africa is an inherently hegemonic, unilateral process that seeks to transform local communities.
2. The assumptions of well-informed freedom of choice and fair play of matched protagonists on a "level playing field" are difficult to verify and apply in practice.
3. Even if verifiable and applicable, these assumptions are inappropriate for the nature and dynamics of the process of proselytization in the African context because they envisage autonomous *individual* action in a profoundly *communal* situation. Individual decisions to convert, even if one assumes them to be well-informed and freely made, tend to undermine and erode communal identity and institutions (without allowing the community opportunity of response.)

It is in this context that I see a vital role for the state not only as mediator of competing claims of proselytizers according to some basic "ground rules," but also as protector of the interests of the target groups. To the extent that the postcolonial state is unable and/or unwilling to perform this regulatory function, the so-called right to proselytize would be open to serious abuse without the prospects of redress. As globalization simply intensifies existing power relations, it is likely to enhance any hegemonic or conflictual relations that may exist within the same African society, both among competing proselytizers, and between them and their "subjects." Nothing in the existing literature addresses the general question of mediation of competing claims, in particular from a human rights perspective.

THE MODERN HUMAN RIGHTS PARADIGM

Historically, and up to the present time, disputes about proselytization were often settled by the use or threat of force or other form of coercion, rather than through negotiations and agreement as a matter of principle. Proselytizers were sometimes able to compel access to the target group, while at other times they were successfully resisted by their opponents, with religious rationale being used by both sides to legitimate their actions or mobilization of people and resources in support of their cause. The question raised by this chapter is whether it is possible and useful to cast these issues in human rights terms, for both proselytizers and target groups: Why and how is a human rights paradigm relevant? What difference is it likely to make to the mediation of conflicts and tensions over proselytization? How can the potential of a human rights paradigm in this regard be realized?

The realm of what is presently known as human rights can be traced to ancient beginnings of normative attempts to define human relationships in ways that are conducive to peaceful resolution of conflict and tension under the rule of law (Steiner and Alston 1996, 117-65). The rule of law can also be traced to similar beginnings and long evolution. Those early normative definitions evolved in content and mechanisms of implementation with the development of each community. As European models of states gradually prevailed throughout the world, national governments became responsible for regulating human relationships through the normative systems and mechanisms of implementation of each country. This function continues today under constitutional schemes of rights as discussed in the present African context in J. D. van der Vyver's chapter in this book.

While it is supposed to have undergone drastic transformation since the adoption of the Charter of the United Nations in 1945, the modern concept of human rights remains bound to domestic frameworks for its practical specification and implementation, including questions of competing claims of religious freedom. On the one hand, under the United Nations system,[13] as well as the regional systems it inspired,[14] normative propositions about human relationships are now made on behalf of all human beings as such, rather than as citizens of particular states. On the other hand, the international law framework which gives binding force to all treaties, including the Charter of the United Nations itself and the human rights conventions adopted under its auspices (as well as those adopted under regional systems), presupposes the sovereignty and exclusive territorial jurisdiction of the state. Not only must a state freely ratify a treaty in order to be bound by its terms, but the international legal obligations assumed by a state under such treaties are supposed to be implemented by the state itself through its own domestic jurisdiction.

Moreover, the purported transition of certain norms from domestic civil liberties into universal human rights of all human beings retains some of the features of that conceptual origin. For example, a key feature of the "universalization" of the domestic civil liberties paradigm is the notion that human rights can only be claimed against the state and its official agents, rather than against whoever might challenge or violate them. Two corollaries of this conception are particularly relevant to the analysis of this chapter: the persistence of the notion that human rights can only be held by individual persons, and the realities of a hierarchy of rights despite repeated claims of the interdependence and indivisibility of all human rights. While the first feature tends to frustrate possibilities of articulating and implementing rights for groups or collective entities (herein called collective rights),[15] the second gives priority to civil and political rights over economic, social, and cultural rights, such as the right to food, shelter, health care, and education.

It is true that a people's right to self-determination is recognized under the United Nations system, but this right is generally believed to mean the right of a people to political independence from foreign or colonial rule, rather than the collective right of groups and communities to cultural survival and integrity within an existing state (short of secession and separate statehood). I will return to the question of the meaning and scope of self-determination in the next section of this chapter. Other examples of what might be called collective rights under international law can be cited,[16] but strong opposition to the concept itself persists among human rights scholars and activists.

Under what has become the established framework after the adoption of the Universal Declaration of 1948, proselytization is generally understood as a matter of freedom of religion of individual persons and their human rights of expression and association as individuals practicing their religion in community with others. While a right to proselytize was taken for granted, the primary concern was with the ability of an individual person to adopt a religion, or change it, according to his or her own free will, without compulsion or coercion. I believe that this conception of individual freedom of religion remains vitally important throughout the world and could certainly be used to achieve some degree of protection for both the proselytizer and individual members of the target group. But I also believe that this conception of individual freedom of religion cannot adequately address the concerns of communities about proselytization, and its consequences, as indicated earlier in this chapter. Individual religious choices, however freely made, do affect communal interests, especially in view of the dynamic of proselytization as highlighted above. For example, apostasy as a capital crime under traditional Islamic law (*Shari'a*) should be seen in light of the linkages between religious faith and "citizenship" in early Islamic states, and the consequences of individual choices for the community. For a Muslim to abandon belief in Islam, it has been argued by some modern Islamic scholars, was tantamount to treason in the modern sense of the term (Al-Mubarak 1981, 24-28; An-Na'im 1990, 86-87, 109).

In view of such linkages between individual choices and communal concerns, I suggest that the present human rights paradigm should include a dynamic and creative understanding of *collective rights* in order to address those concerns, as well as individual rights to safeguard freedom of belief. But in suggesting adoption of collective rights, I see them as *complementing,* not replacing, individual rights. In fact, individual rights will always remain necessary for the definition and implementation of any collective right. For example, the protection of individual freedoms of expression and association is extremely important for the integrity of the process of regulating questions of membership, political representation, equality, and justice within the group. Without valid resolution of such questions, a group cannot be entitled to claim collective human rights. This thesis will be further explained and substantiated in the next section of this chapter as it applies to issues of proselytization. What I propose to do here by way of introduction is to develop a general argument in support of the *possibility* of the inclusion of collective rights within the human rights framework. I say "possibility" because I am calling for the careful examination of the *candidacy* of each claim for a collective right and not a blanket inclusion of every assertion of such a right.

My first point is to question the present conceptual opposition to the idea of collective rights as human rights simply because it does not fit the individual human rights paradigm. In my view, this objection not only mocks the universality of human rights but also contributes to the growing isolation and irrelevance of the international human rights movement. Since a collective framework for the realization of rights is essential for the majority of human societies and communities around the world, rejection of any possibility of collective rights undermines the assumption that universal human rights are accepted and applicable everywhere. Moreover, the categorical exclusion of this perspective from the human rights paradigm is making this paradigm increasingly less relevant to the daily lives of many societies. As emphasized by one author, the Western liberal perspective

> acknowledges the rights of the individual on the one hand, and the sovereignty of the total social collective on the other, but it is not alive to the rich variety of intermediate or alternative associational groupings actually found in human cultures, nor is it prepared to ascribe to such groups any rights not reducible either to the liberties of the citizen or to the prerogative of the state (Anaya 1995, 326).

In my view, the exclusion of any possibility of collective rights is untenable for two reasons: (1) the actual interdependence of individual and collective rights; and (2) the inadequacy of an individual-rights paradigm in certain situations. Regarding the first reason, I suggest that neither can individual rights be fully realized without collective rights, nor can the latter be ensured without the protection of the former (Shepherd 1981, 215). This is particularly true, I believe, because of the need for structural change and long-term solutions, as opposed to the piecemeal, case-by-case approach of individual rights, as explained below. This combination of an acceptance of interdependence of rights and appreciation of the need for long-term structural approaches is clearly reflected in Article 5 of the International Convention for the Elimination of All Forms of Discrimination against Women (1979),[17] which provides that "States Parties shall take all appropriate measures: (a) To modify the social and cultural patterns of conduct of men and women, with a view to achieving the elimination of prejudices and customary and all other practices which are based on the idea of the inferiority or the superiority of either of the sexes or on stereotyped roles for men and women." The presumed objective of this Convention is to protect the human rights of individual women, yet it is clear that a more structural approach is needed to eliminate root causes of the violation of these rights. In imposing this obligation under Article 5, the Convention is clearly envisaging men and women as groups, rather than as individual persons.

As to the inadequacy of an individual-rights approach in some situations, we should recall the assumptions and nature of the process by which these rights are supposed to be protected in everyday life. It is commonly asserted that the main advantage of individual human rights from a practical application perspective is their "justiciability," which signifies the ability of a court of law to identify an individual victim, a violator, and to prescribe a remedy for the violation. The way this is supposed to work is that when a person or group of persons believe that one of their individual human rights has been violated by a state policy or administrative action, or the behavior of a state official, the aggrieved party or parties can sue for redress (or prosecute if criminal charges are warranted, as in a torture case) before a court of law. If the issue is not settled out of court, a trial may follow whereby the court will determine whether a violation has occurred and direct the implementation of appropriate remedy.

It is therefore clear that this conception of legal protection of individual human rights presupposes that the violation of rights is the exception rather than the rule, because no system for the legal enforcement of rights can have the resources and political will to cope with massive violations. This conception also assumes that potential victims have access to and can afford to pay for legal services, that the judiciary is independent and effective, that government officials will comply with court orders, and so forth. As such, this model is not only limited, exclusive, expensive, and inaccessible to most Africans whose human rights are routinely violated by officials as well as nonofficial actors, but it is also incapable of redressing the type and scope of violations most frequently suffered by Africans. Recent experiences with genocide and ethnic cleansing, massive forced population movements, increasingly unequal economic and political power relations, unpayable national debt, and coercive structural adjustment programs in Africa make an exclusive focus on individual human rights unrealistic, if not counterproductive.

Finally, I believe it is important to recognize the possibility of collective rights as human rights (Van Dyke 1985), rather than as part of domestic or constitutional structures, or under international law in general (Thornberry 1991; Kymlicka 1995; Anaya 1996). The special value of the modern human rights paradigm is that it provides an external normative frame of reference to which victims can appeal for redress against their own governments in accordance with universal standards applicable to all human beings without distinction on grounds such as race, gender, belief, or national origin.

While drawing on previous and existing experiences, the proposed approach to the development of collective rights can be distinguished as follows. Treaty-based regimes for the protection of religious and ethnic minorities can be seen as one of the antecedents of the present human rights paradigm in that they imposed obligations under international law. But those minority-rights regimes offered only specific protections for discrete minorities, rather than as a matter of general principles of international human rights law applicable to all groups throughout the world. In any case, the whole system ended with the collapse of the League of Nations and was deliberately rejected at the time of the drafting of the Universal Declaration of Human Rights (Steiner and Alston 1996, 86-89). Domestic constitutional regimes not only vary with the peculiar historical, economic, and political context of each country but are also supposed to operate only within the domestic constitutional framework of the country in question (McDonald 1991). In other words, domestic regimes as such do not permit the possibility of challenging their own scope and/or implementation in terms of internationally established norms and institutions. My point here is that, while constitutional regimes of rights should certainly be maintained and improved, they should not be seen as an adequate substitute for the development of an internationally recognized regime of collective human rights which brings the benefits of the above-mentioned external, international frame of reference.

It is true that the notion of collectivities as bearers of rights is problematic because of ambiguities of the nature and dynamics of membership, as well as agency and representation, as will be briefly discussed in the next section of this paper (Johnston 1995). But it should be noted that the notion of individual human rights as entitlement of all human beings by virtue of their humanity and without distinction on such grounds as race, gender, belief, or national origin also had its problems. That is, the present concept of individual human rights is the product of a long historical process of contestation and negotiation. The practical implementation of individual human rights continues to be hampered by entrenched notions of sovereignty and exclusive territorial jurisdiction, weak acceptance of economic, social, and cultural rights, and so forth. In addition to facing similar difficulties of implementation, the notion of collective rights remains conceptually problematic precisely because it has not yet received serious consideration by human rights scholars and activists. What is important is that when collective rights are considered, they should not be expected to fit the same conceptual framework and implementation strategies of individual rights (Abi Sab 1980, 163).

In conclusion of this section, I suggest that the same dynamics that have transformed the rights of citizens into universal rights of all human beings will probably continue to propel further evolution of the concept, as well as its content and implementation mechanisms. The initial transformation of the concept of domestic constitutional rights into the paradigm adopted by the Universal Declaration of Human Rights of 1948 was produced by a sequence of local and global developments culminating in the catastrophic events leading to and including the Second World War, which exposed the drastic inadequacy of exclusive national jurisdictions for the protection of civil liberties. The political will to combat a state's oppression of its own citizens generated the conceptual and institutional instruments of the modern movement for the promotion and protection of universal human rights. While much needs to be done to realize that vision, significant progress in the protection of individual civil and political rights has already been achieved around the world. The same drive must continue today, I suggest, to expand the conceptual and institutional limits of the present framework in response to new threats to the protection of human rights arising from local and global developments. This possibility is particularly important for the application of a human rights paradigm to issues of proselytization.

THE MEDIATION OF COMPETING CLAIMS
OF PROSELYTIZATION AND SELF-DETERMINATION

In the section on the dynamics of proselytization above I have attempted to highlight the basic dilemma presented by such activities, especially in the present African context. For one thing, the issue is hardly ever simply and exclusively a matter of communicating a religious message to be accepted or rejected on its own terms. As a deliberate effort to change the spiritual and material conditions of target groups, proselytization is by definition offensive and hegemonic—it is premised on the assumption of proselytizers that the belief systems and institutions of target groups need to change, and that those of the proselytizer offer a better alterative. Moreover, the claims of proselytizers that they have a "right" to propagate their beliefs, while their target groups have the "freedom" to accept or reject the message, overlook the role of power relations. Without a power differential in their favor, proselytizers would not have the self-confidence and resources needed in seeking to convert others. Yet, without redressing that differential, the freedom of the target community to accept or reject the message cannot be realized. Nevertheless, I have concluded, proselytization is too integral to people's lives to be suppressed altogether, yet it is too problematic to leave totally unregulated.

In response, I suggested that a human rights paradigm should be applied to mediate competing claims about proselytization and its consequences. However, given the communal nature and implications of the interaction, especially in the African context, the proposed human rights paradigm should include collective or group rights as well as the rights of individual persons. The primary reason for the need for collective rights is that communal concerns are necessarily those of the community at large, rather than of some of their specific individual members. Otherwise, certain self-appointed elites will claim to speak on behalf of the whole community without credible accountability to that community. That is precisely what the human rights paradigm is supposed to prevent. In other words, for the human rights paradigm to play its mediatory role, it has to include collective rights as well as individual rights. Without the former, communal concerns cannot be properly formulated; and without the latter, there is the risk of elite appropriation of the voice of the community.

Assuming that the case made earlier for collective rights is accepted, how will these rights operate in practice without violating the rights of individual persons in the community? In particular, how will questions of membership, agency, and representation be resolved and by whom? For example, who is to decide on the existence and termination of the membership of a person in a specific community? To address these questions in proper context, it might be helpful to briefly specify some of the problems raised by the competing claims of proselytization and self-determination.

If the conclusions made earlier about the context and process of proselytization in Africa are to be formulated as problems to be overcome, they may read as follows:

1. How does one reduce, and eventually eliminate, the hegemonic, unilateral nature of proselytization in Africa? What is that rationale as agreed among all parties? Moreover, since that presupposes that all sides must understand and appreciate the concerns of one another, how can this prerequisite be realized?

2. If the validity of the assumptions of well-informed freedom of choice and fair play of matched protagonists on a "level playing field" is part of the answer to the above question, how can that be achieved and verified in practice? Would a voluntary "code of conduct" be sufficient without independent verification of compliance? If such verification is entrusted to a judicial or quasi-judicial institution of the state, what will safeguard against other forms of state interference for ulterior motives?

3. If another part of the answer is for proselytizers to respect the apprehensions of communities about the profound communal conditions of presumably autonomous individual action, how can that be achieved? Can proselytizers accept the proposition that individual decisions to convert, even if they were well-informed and freely made, undermine and erode communal identity and institutions, and yet still maintain the vigor of their "mission"? Doesn't such vigor require disrespect, if not contempt,

for the communal identity and institutions of the communities they seek to convert, which are probably based on the religion the proselytizers wish to replace with their own?

The approach I propose for addressing these questions in the African context is the process of mediation of competing claims rather than an attempt to prescribe specific solutions in advance. It is in this context that I see a vital role for the state not only as mediator of competing claims of proselytizers according to some basic "ground rules," but also as protector of the interests of the target groups. As noted earlier, given the inability and/or unwillingness of the state in Africa to perform this regulatory function, the so-called right to proselytize would be open to serious abuse without the prospects of redress. It was also noted above that since globalization simply intensifies existing power relations, it is likely to exacerbate any hegemonic or conflictual relations that may exist within the same African society, both among competing proselytizers, and between them and their "subjects."

But despite the importance of its role, the state is only one party to the process of mediation I am proposing. Other parties include existing religious institutions within the communities, other civil society organizations (whatever form or manner of operation they may actually take in the community), as well as representatives of proselytizing organizations or groups. Moreover, the external constituencies of those non-state actors also have their role. One of the consequences of globalization is that the increasing ease of communication and expanding reach of the media enable groups and communities throughout the world to cooperate in pursuit of shared objectives. As recently shown by the cases of Ogoni of Nigeria and Sabbistas of Mexico, apparently isolated local communities can now attract much attention and support for their cause among human rights organizations, environmental groups, and other constituencies from around the world.

Much of the success of the proposed process of mediation will depend, in my view, on the effectiveness of educating all parties about the concerns of the others. A related but slightly different requirement is the need to inspire or persuade all sides to positively respond to the concerns of the others. But first of all, there has to be an appreciation of the need for the mediation of competing claims. It is hoped that this book will contribute to the generation of such appreciation and the education of all the parties about each others' concerns, as well as inspire or persuade them to respond positively. If the proselytizers are true to their claims of moral commitment, they should understand and appreciate the concerns of the communities about the survival of their identity and institutions. Should that happen, then the communities would have no justification for refusing to allow proselytizing activities. But if either or both parties fail to live up to these mutual expectations, then the state should act as arbiter. The state in turn should be held accountable to civil society institutions for its performance of its role as arbiter. In this way, the mediation process acts as its own guardian.

REVIEW OF CHAPTERS

This volume moves from broader theoretical analysis to specific case studies that attempt to develop their own frameworks out of the concrete experiences of particular African countries or communities within a certain time frame. The two approaches clearly overlap. While theoretical analysis should draw on practical experience, case studies should lead to theoretical conclusions. Besides this introductory chapter, general theoretical analyses are also offered in the chapters by Farid Esack, J. Paul Martin and Harry Winter, and Lamin Sanneh. Political, theological, and legal aspects of proselytization in Africa are discussed in the chapters by Makau Mutua and J. D. van der Vyver. Specific case studies are presented by Tshikala K. Biaya, Chabha Bouslimani, Francis M. Deng, Rosalind I. J. Hackett, Hannah W. Kinoti, and Benjamin F. Soares.

The issue of definition is taken up by Martin and Winter in their analysis of the processes and dynamics of proselytization. Van der Vyver discerns a range of components of proselytization in terms of constitutional regulation in Africa. Deng compares modes of religious intervention in Sudan, identifying the varying elements of coercion and persuasion therein. Biaya examines new forms of popular proselytization whereby rival religious groups address each other through oral dialogue in the public sphere. Hackett argues that the increase in the use of modern media technologies has reshaped proselytizing techniques. Coupled with the growth in revivalist activity, this has aggravated Christian-Muslim relations in Nigeria especially.

Several of the authors address the question of proselytization within wider contexts, whether that of relations between religion and the state, constitutional law, religious freedom, or religious growth and pluralization. The latter is particularly salient in the African context. Countries such as Kenya (Kinoti), Nigeria and Ghana (Hackett), and Congo-Zaire (Biaya) have experienced remarkable religious development and diversification in the postcolonial phase. Even predominantly Muslim countries such as Mali (Soares) and Algeria (Bouslimani) are characterized by a variety of Muslim groups with considerable diversity in religious discourses and practices. This type of development receives its impetus from both local and international agents.

In several of the chapters, the historical dimension of proselytization is emphasized. Soares compares the efforts of Malian Muslims in the nineteenth century to persuade others to abandon traditional practices such as spirit possession with the proselytization campaigns of a contemporary Muslim religious leader. Sanneh discusses how debates in precolonial Muslim Africa sowed the seeds for the separation of the religious and political spheres, despite subsequent fundamentalist attempts to join the two. He also compares the separation debate in Islam to the long history of discussions on church-state relations in the Christian West. Martin and Winter note the evolution of attitudes in Christian theological and missionary circles with regard to religious pluralism and interreligious dialogue. Bouslimani traces the interweaving of intra-Islamic strands of Algeria's historical experience with the significant emergence of Islamist tendencies at present. Biaya describes the changing interreligious configurations and political manipulations of religious constituencies against the backdrop of the history of Zairian nationalism and the secularization of the postcolonial state.

Issues of identity and cultural self-determination recur in several papers. Mutua links the problems of the modern African state to persistent efforts by colonial, missionary, and present-day political leaders to propagate ideas that were antithetical to African values and identity. Deng demonstrates, through his exposition of Dinka religious thought, the importance of preserving cultural identity and continuity, and of resisting self-denying assimilation without excluding the possibility of integrating traits and ideas from other cultures. Bouslimani analyzes the complex interplay of religious, cultural, political, and ethnic forces which constitute the continually negotiated matrix of Algerian identity.

A number of authors analyze the conditions which give rise to or hinder proselytizing activities. These may be external and/or internal forces, viz. colonialism (Sanneh); the development of the modern African state (van der Vyver, Mutua, Sanneh); changing economic patterns (Kinoti); political manipulation (Biaya, Mutua); introduction of new actors, such as humanitarian agencies (Martin and Winter); new religious organizations, or influences, such as Christian and Islamic revivalist movements (Hackett, Soares, Bouslimani, Biaya, Kinoti); or Eastern mystical movements (Kinoti).

The chapters display the range of agents involved in proselytization—whether individuals (rulers, missionaries), groups (youth and women's groups, religious organizations, professional associations), institutions (mission agencies), nation-states, or world bodies (transnational religious associations). The state emerges as the primary actor in many cases (Mutua, van der Vyver, Deng, Sanneh, Bouslimani, Biaya). Yet, importantly, the covert and creative strategies employed by non-state actors (Soares, Biaya) in their efforts to proselytize and enjoy freedom of religious expression and association—even when constrained by political ideologies and institutions—are brought out.

Suggestions for resolving tensions created by excessive or coercive proselytizing are discussed by Hackett, Sanneh, Deng, and Kinoti. Several of the authors show, through their specific or more general examples, how the rights of (usually minority) religious groups to operate in the public sphere are shaped not just by official public or religious policy, but also by popular perceptions which circulate through the print and broadcast media, as well as more informally. A number of the chapters describe the effects of more sustained and militant forms of proselytization (Bouslimani, Soares, Hackett, Kinoti), which are often highlighted by news organizations and campaigners for religious liberty.

It is hoped that this book will provide a more nuanced and enhanced understanding of the complexity of proselytization in the present African context. The various contributions in this volume underscore both the pressing need for, as well as the potential of, the type of mediation model proposed above. They also explicitly or implicitly indicate the complex relationship between proselytization and self-determination, and hence individual and group rights. All of these issues call for careful and well-informed reflection from different perspectives. In any case, it is hoped that the following chapters will show that proselytization is a much more compelling, challenging, and multifaceted subject for analysis than has been appreciated to the present time.

NOTES

[1] The term *communal* here indicates, as elaborated below, that the right to self-determination should not be confined to achieving political independence and separate statehood.

[2] This project builds directly on two preceding projects of the Law and Religion Program of Emory University. The first project was "Christianity and Democracy" (1989-92), and the second "Religious Human Rights" (1992-95). The themes of the extensive program of discussion and publication generated by those two projects clearly indicated that issues of proselytization and its implications are intimately connected to conceptions, institutions, and processes of democratization, as well as to the definition and protection of religious human rights in all parts of the world.

[3] While proselytization efforts usually target individuals, rather than the whole group as such all at once, I am here using the notion "target group" as the operational term to indicate the strategic use of individuals in transforming the status of the community as a whole. Reference to groups is also appropriate for the purposes of this chapter in particular because conflicts generally occur between communities (whether religiously, culturally, or politically conceived), rather than isolated and autonomous individuals.

[4] The term *beliefs* is used instead of *faith* throughout this Introduction because the latter term is normally used to refer to so-called world religions to the exclusion of indigenous traditions, which are particularly important in the African context.

[5] For example, as a cognitive psychologist, Leon Festinger sought to develop a theory of why and how proselytization occurred. Goodman draws on variations of this theory in arguing that the early Christians could not agree on certain important theological questions, so they focused on proselytizing new members to calm the movement's internal disagreement. For social-science analysis, see Rambo 1993 and Hefner 1993.

[6] On the crisis of the postcolonial state and the search for explanation, see Young 1994, 2-12.

[7] Young calls the postcolonial state in Africa the "integral state," which he defines as "a design of perfected hegemony, whereby the state seeks to achieve unrestricted domination over civil society."

[8] I am referring here to the classification made by Clark 1995, 5.

[9] On page 170 of this article, Fisher characterized his disagreement with Horton as a matter of focal point in the consideration of religious development. See also Hackett's discussion of different types of "conversion."

[10] This book is useful as a historical overview, though somewhat dated. For example, he does not address Islamic political movements, and his use of the term "Islamization" is not nuanced in the modern sense of the term.

[11] Hiskett supports Humphrey Fisher's three stages of conversion to Islam—quarantine, mixing, and reform—but stresses that they cannot be applied rigidly. For another example of specific case studies on the spread of Islam, see Banwo 1995.

[12] This second source includes a statistical table of Muslims and Christians in Africa.

[13] When the Universal Declaration of Human Rights was adopted in 1948, it was envisaged that binding treaties would follow. In due course, the two main human rights treaties—International Covenant on Economic, Social, and Cultural Rights, and the International Covenant on Civil and Political Rights—were adopted in 1966. The International Convention on the Elimination of All Forms of Racial Discrimination already had been adopted in 1965. Others followed, such as the Convention on the Elimination of All Forms of Discrimination against Women of 1979; Convention against Torture and Other Cruel, Inhuman, or Degrading Treatment or Punishment of 1984; and Convention on the Rights of the Child of 1989. On the UN human rights system, see Steiner and Alston 1996, 347-455.

[14] Namely, the European Convention for the Protection of Human Rights and Fundamental Freedoms of 1950; The American Convention on Human Rights of 1969; and the African Charter on Human and Peoples' Rights of 1981. There is no regional system for Asia yet. On these regional systems, see Steiner and Alston 1996, 563-705.

[15] On the concept of "collective rights" and its relation to ideas of individual rights see, for example, Van Dyke 1982, 21-40; Garet 1983, 1001-75; MacDonald 1989, 117-36; Sanders 1991, 217-419.

[16] See, for example, the International Labour Organization's Convention concerning the Protection and Integration of Indigenous and Other Tribal and Semi-Tribal Populations in Independent Countries (ILO, No. 107) of 1957 and the Convention concerning Indigenous and Tribal Peoples in Independent Countries (ILO, No. 169) of 1989. The European regional system is also beginning to tentatively explore the possibility of collective rights, as can be seen in the 1994 document "Framework Convention for the Protection of National Minorities." However, the most far-reaching formulations of collective rights so far are to be found under the African Charter of Human and Peoples' Rights of 1981.

[17] This Convention was adopted 18 December 1979 and entered into force 3 September 1981. At the time of writing, the Convention has been ratified by more than 150 states, reflecting a truly remarkable consensus across regional, cultural, political, and economic boundaries.

BIBLIOGRAPHY

Abi Sab, Georges. 1980. "The Legal Formulation of a Right to Development," *Le droit au developpement au plan international: colloque*, La Haye, 16-18 Octobre 1979 (The Right to Development at the International Level: Workshop. The Hague, October 16-18, 1979). Hague Academy of International Law. 159-75.

Aina, Tade Akin. 1997. *Globalization and Social Policy in Africa: Issues and Research Directions*. Dakar, Senegal: CODESRIA Working Paper Series 6/96.

Al-Mubarak. 1981. *Nizam al-Islam fi al-Hukm wa al-Dawla* (The Islamic Order for Governance and the State). Beirut: Da al-Fikr.

Anaya, S. James. 1995. "The Capacity of International Law to Advance Ethnic or Nationality Rights Claims," in Kymlicka 1995.

———. 1996. *Indigenous Peoples in International Law.* Oxford: Oxford University Press.

An-Na'im, Abdullahi A. 1990. *Toward an Islamic Reformation: Civil Liberties, Human Rights and International Law.* Syracuse, N.Y.: Syracuse University Press.

An-Na'im, Abdullahi A., and Francis M. Deng. 1996. "Self-Determination and Unity: The Case of Sudan," *Law & Policy* 18, 199-233.

Asad, Talal. 1996. "Comments on Conversion," in *Conversion to Modernities: The Globalization of Christianity,* edited by Peter van der Veer. New York: Routledge.

Ayoade, John A. A. 1988. "States without Citizens: An Emerging African Phenomenon," in *The Precarious Balance: State and Society in Africa,* edited by Donald Rothchild and Naomi Chazan, 100-18. Boulder, Colo.: Westview Press.

Bach, Daniel C. 1993. "Reappraising Postcolonial Geopolitics: Europe, Africa and the End of the Cold War," in *Legitimacy and the State in Twentieth-Century Africa: Essays in Honour of A. H. Kirk-Greene,* edited by Terence Ranger and Olufemi Vaughan, 247-57. London: Macmillan.

Banwo, Adeyinka. 1995. "The Nineteenth Century Ilorin Wars and the Growth of Islam in Yorubaland: A Re-Assessment," *Hamdard Islamicus* 18, 85-97.

Bartholomew, Craig. 1994. "The Challenge of Islam in Africa," *Journal of Interdisciplinary Studies* 6, 129-46.

Beidelman, Thomas O. 1974. "Social Theory and the Study of Christian Missions in Africa," *Africa* 44, 235-49.

———. 1981. "Contradictions between the Sacred and the Secular Life: The Church Missionary Society in Ukaguru, Tanzania, East Africa, 1876-1914," *Comparative Studies in Sociology and History* 23, 73-95.

———. 1982. *Colonial Evangelism: A Socio-historical Study of an East African Mission at the Grassroots.* Bloomington, Ind.: Indiana University Press.

Chabal, Patrick. 1986. "Introduction: Thinking about Politics in Africa," in *Political Domination in Africa: Reflections on the Limits of Power,* edited by Patrick Chabal. Cambridge: Cambridge University Press.

Clark, Christopher. 1995. *The Politics of Conversion: Missionary Protestantism and the Jews in Prussia 1728-1941.* Oxford: Clarendon Press.

Comaroff, Jean, and John Comaroff. 1991. *Of Revelation and Revolution.* 2 volumes. Chicago: University of Chicago Press.

Falk, Richard. 1995. "Regionalism and World Order after the Cold War," *St. Louis-Warsaw Transatlantic Law Journal,* 71-88.

Festinger, Leon. 1957. *A Theory of Cognitive Dissonance.* Stanford, Calif.: Stanford University Press.

Fisher, Humphrey. 1973. "Conversion Reconsidered," *Africa* 43, 27-40.

———. 1986. "The Juggernaut's Apology: Conversion to Islam in Black Africa," *Africa* 55, 153-73.

Garet, Ronald. 1983. "Communality and Existence: The Rights of Groups," *Southern California Law Review* 56, 1001-75.

Goodman, Martin. 1994. *Mission and Conversion: Proselytization in the Religious History of the Roman Empire.* Oxford: Clarendon Press.

Haafkins, Johaanes. 1994. *Claiming the Promise: African Churches Speak.* New York: Friendship Press.

———. 1995. "The Christian Muslim Encounter in Sub-Saharan Africa," *Church and Society* (March/April), 66-78.

Hackett, Rosalind I. J. 1989. *Religion in Calabar.* New York: Mouton de Gruyter.

Hefner, Robert, ed. 1993. *Conversion to Christianity: Historical and Anthropological Perspectives on a Great Transformation.* Berkeley and Los Angeles: University of California Press.

Hiskett, Mervyn. 1984. *The Development of Islam in Western Africa.* New York: Longman.

Horton, Robin. 1971. "African Conversion," *Africa* 41, 85-108.

———. 1975. "On the Rationality of Conversion," *Africa* 45, 219-35, and 373-99.

Isichei, Elizabeth. 1970. "Seven Varieties of Ambiguity: Some Patterns of Igbo Response to Christian Missions," *Journal of Religion in Africa* 3, 209-27.

———. 1995. *A History of Christianity in Africa.* London: The Society for Publishing Christian Knowledge.

Jackson, Robert H., and Carl G. Rosberg. 1986. "Sovereignty and Underdevelopment: Juridical Statehood in the African Crisis," *The Journal of Modern African Studies* 24, 5-6.

Johnston, D. "Native Rights as Collective Rights: A Question of Group Self-Preservation," in Kymlicka 1995, 179-201.

King, Noel. 1971. *Christians and Muslims in Africa.* New York: Harper & Row.

Kymlicka, Will, ed. 1995. *The Rights of Minority Cultures.* Oxford: Oxford University Press.

McCracken, John. 1977. *Politics and Christianity in Malawi 1875-1940.* Cambridge: Cambridge University Press.

MacDonald, Ian. 1989. "Group Rights," *Philosophical Papers* 28, 117-36.

McDonald, M., ed. 1991. *Collective Rights,* special issue of the *Canadian Journal of Law and Jurisprudence* 4, 217-419.

Macmullen, Ramsay. 1984. *Christianizing the Roman Empire.* New Haven: Yale University Press.

Marty, Martin, and Frederick E. Greenspan, eds. 1988. *Pushing the Faith: Proselytism and Civility in a Pluralistic World.* New York: Crossroad.

Mlinar, Zdravko. 1992. "Individuation and Globalization: The Transformation of Territorial Social Organization," in *Globalization and Territorial Identities,* edited by Zdravko Mlinar, 15-34. Brookfield, Vt.: Avebury.

Morrison, K. F. 1992. *Understanding Conversion.* Charlottesville, Va.: University of Virginia Press.

Okoth-Ogendo, H. W. 1991. "Constitutions without Constitutionalism: Reflections on an African Political Paradox," in *State and Constitutionalism: An African Debate on Democracy,* edited by Issa G. Shivji, 3-25. Harare, Zimbabwe: Southern African Political Economy Series (SAPES) Trust.

Othman, Shehu. 1993. "Postscript: Legitimacy, Civil Society and the Return of Europe," in *Legitimacy and the State in Twentieth-Century Africa: Essays in Honour of A. H. Kirk-Greene,* edited by Terence Ranger and Olufemi Vaughan, 258-62. London: Macmillan.

Rambo, Lewis. 1993. *Understanding Religious Conversion.* New Haven, Conn.: Yale University Press.

Rouse, Ruth. 1936. "The Missionary Motive," *International Review of Missions* 25, 250-58.

Sanders, Douglas. 1991. "Collective Rights," *Human Rights Quarterly* 13, 217-419.

Sanneh, Lamin. 1993. *Encountering the West—Christianity and the Global Cultural Process: The African Dimension.* Maryknoll, N.Y.: Orbis Books.

———. 1997. *The Crown and the Turban: Muslims and West African Pluralism.* Boulder, Colo.: Westview Press.

Shepherd Jr., George W. 1981. "Transnational Development of Human Rights: The Third World Crucible," in *Global Human Rights: Public Policies, Comparative Measures and NGO Strategies,* edited by V. P. Nanda, J. R. Scarritt, and G. W. Shepherd Jr. Boulder, Colo.: Westeview Press.

Shivji, Issa G. 1991. "State and Constitutionalism: A New Democratic Perspective," in *State and Constitutionalism: An African Debate on Democracy,* edited by Issa G. Shivji, 27-54. Harare, Zimbabwe: Southern African Political Economy Series (SAPES) Trust.

Steiner, Henry, and Philip Alston. 1996. *International Human Rights in Context: Law, Politics, Morals.* Oxford: Clarendon Press.

Thornberry, Patrick. 1991. *International Law and the Rights of Minorities.* Oxford: Clarendon Press.

Trimingham, Spencer. 1968. *The Influence of Islam upon Africa.* New York: Frederick A. Praeger Publishing.

Van Dyke, Vernon. 1982. "Collective Rights and Moral Rights: Problems in Liberal Democratic Thought," *Journal of Politics* 44, 21-40.

———. 1985. *Human Rights, Ethnicity and Discrimination.* Westport, Conn.: Greenwood Press.

Yates, Timothy. 1994. *Christian Mission in the Twentieth Century.* Cambridge: Cambridge University Press.

Young, Crawford. 1994. *The African Colonial State in Comparative Perspective.* New Haven, Conn.: Yale University Press.

2.

Religious Proselytization

*Historical and Theological Perspectives
at the End of the Twentieth Century*

————◆————

J. Paul Martin and Harry Winter, O.M.I.

INTRODUCTION

In *The Clash of Civilizations and the Remaking of World Order* Samuel P. Huntington identifies religion as the primary determinant in his division of the contemporary world into nine different civilizations (Huntington 1996, 47). At the end of the twentieth century, religion, and, unfortunately especially religiously defined conflicts, have returned to center stage in world politics. Huntington's analysis reinforces popular perceptions of the dangers posed by Islam, which together with China, are portrayed by him as the two major challenges to "European" civilization (Huntington 1996, 102). After years of neglect, other academics are also returning to the study of the role religious beliefs and practices play in the lives of large segments of the earth's population and in the decisions of many of their leaders. Modern communications and increasing population movements are bringing about an unprecedented inter-mingling of religions, eliminating, virtually everywhere, religiously homogeneous communities. The resulting tensions are aggravated by religious recruiting.

Proselytization[1] has been coterminous with the history of the Christian and Muslim religions. Today, Muslims and Christians are increasingly living in greater numbers in the same spaces, if not also competing for the same souls. The long history of competition, among Christians themselves as well as with Islam, has come to be characterized by the negative term *proselytism*. To avoid this connotation of their missionary work, some Christian groups are refor-mulating their theologies of mission to talk about witness, dialogue, and co-operation. Increasing pluralism is bringing segments in both traditions to lobby for religious tolerance as public policy and for rules to govern proselytization (Nelson 1995, 5).

The purpose of this essay is to reach beyond stereotypic views of religious proselytization, to delineate the social components that are obscured by popular images of proselytization as inherently coercive or deceptive, and to examine the possibility of standards more reflective of the modern understanding of human rights and the pluralism that increasingly reflects the societies of the modern world.

In this essay *proselytization* is defined neutrally rather than pejoratively as implied in *proselytism;* namely, as activities by one religious group to promulgate its particular views and to recruit new members. The words *missionary* and *proselytizer* are used interchangeably. As the means used to convert others can vary so considerably, means are not included in the definition. Equally a problem, but equally varied in its relationship to proselytization in practice, the role of the state or secular power is also excluded from the definition. A major consequence of proselytization, which is also not part of the definition, is competition among religious groups to recruit third parties, if not one another's members. This frequently aggravates sensitive religious, political, economic, and even diplomatic relations. This essay seeks to show that day-to-day missionary activities are more complex than can be subsumed under either the old label of proselytism or the new ones of witness and dialogue.

Religious missionary activity is always intermingled with other social forces and interests, making its analysis a challenge not only for social scientists and those who sponsor missionary work but also for public officials responsible for social order. Implicit in the analysis of this essay is the assumption that the secular authority is not in a position to evaluate the truth or validity of a particular religious tradition. On the other hand, it is necessarily the supreme arbiter of social order and thus of many of the components of religious proselytization. It is the task of the civil authorities to identify ways in which religious recruiting, which we take to be inevitable and a legitimate form of expression, might take place with a degree of fairness, tolerance, and avoidance of conflict. In playing this role, it is assumed that the civil power must act even though it can never be in a position to determine authoritatively the truth of one religion over another. With recent historical experiences and the other essays in this volume in mind, we are seeking a normative model that would better describe the process and reconcile the rights of both the missionaries or proselytizers and the people they would recruit, and, at the same time, assure general social order. It is further assumed that international human rights standards have a major role to play because they represent the broadest consensus both on religious freedom and questions of social justice in general.

The primary components in the proselytization process are:

1. the principal actors, namely, the missionaries or proselytizers, their target groups, and the significant others, notably public officials, competing religions, and any nonreligious sponsors of the missionaries;
2. the goals and methods used by the missionaries;

3. the social environment and factors influencing and being influenced by the missionaries, including various secondary actors such as commercial and other forces of change;
4. the resulting processes of accommodation, adaptation, interaction, etc., on all sides;
5. the eventual outcomes of the missionary work;
6. the normative systems governing each of the above; and
7. the remedial actions (if any) taken by the state or the public power.

While the methods used by the missionaries are the prima facie point of concern, the process and its consequences are more complicated. To evaluate outcomes all seven components need to be taken into consideration.

Religious freedom has long been a concern of law, both international and domestic. Rules governing religious observance were enacted in many societies in the centuries before the common era. Generally they were expressions of the will (and faith) of the ruler, and religion was frequently used to serve political purposes. As nations grew in size and diversity, provisions were made to protect religious and other minorities. Governments took it upon themselves to protect the religious freedom of their coreligionists in other countries. Christendom signed such treaties with Islam over one thousand years ago. More recently, the treaties of Paris after World War I sought to protect religious minorities in the new countries in Eastern Europe. Today international treaties and declarations define religious freedom as a human right.

Article 18(1) of the International Covenant on Civil and Political Rights reads:

Everyone shall have the right to freedom of thought, conscience and religion. This right shall include freedom to have or to adopt a religion or belief of his choice, and freedom, either individually or in community with others and in public or private, to manifest his religion or belief in worship, observance, practice and teaching.

This statement is further expanded in the 1981 Declaration on the Elimination of All Forms of Intolerance and of Discrimination Based on Religion or Belief. To these specific standards can be added the more generic, internationally defined rights of nondiscrimination; freedom of expression, assembly, and conscience; as well as certain, still debated, group rights based on ethnic and linguistic heritage. Unlike in the case of other human rights, the international community has not yet been able to draft a convention or treaty encompassing and imposing basic standards of religious freedom on the states who would ratify it. International agreement remains at the level of Article 18 and the Declaration and is likely to remain that way for the immediate future. There is neither the political will nor the degree of necessary consensus to achieve a full treaty.

Against this background of a very skimpy consensus in international law, the problems associated with recruiting and the ideal of religious freedom are treated diversely in the domestic law of the world states, ranging from tolerance and the promotion of religious diversity to proscription and even persecution of religious groups actively recruiting new members. On the other hand, some religions impose such recruiting as a daily commitment on all their members, and others require years of service consecrated to it. Recruits who change their religious affiliation must often accept major changes in their moral principles, worldview, and social status as well as belief structure. Religious affiliation defines social relationships and personal identity. It can also bring material benefits, such as freedom from persecution or a more advantageous tax system. The rules set by each state, diverse though they are, can have a major impact on the outcome of missionary work. Moreover, the spread and maintenance of both Christianity and Islam was, and continues to be, influenced by the interests of secular powers, if not also by the sword. The state is rarely a neutral force.

PROSELYTIZATION: THE AGENTS

In seeking to recruit new members, religious organizations seek to strengthen themselves, to bring benefits to others, and to fulfill a task that is often seen as essential to their own salvation. Proselytizing is thus seen by religious agents as both their right and their major duty. Most religions, and logically the individual believers, see their religion, if not as absolute truth, at least as the best understanding of life and afterlife available and attainable on earth. Both Christianity and Islam claim to be the ultimate revelation from God. Tolerance of other religions is thus easily portrayed as tolerance of falsehood. Both Islam and Christianity are universalist religions, appealing and welcoming all human beings and decrying all forms of discrimination on grounds of gender, nationality, ethnic origin, etc.

Religious missionaries are part of a more general cultural and economic flow. Today, Russia and the former socialist countries, for example, face numerous forces from the outside seeking to change or help change their societies (Witte and Bourdeaux 1999). Among these "evangelists" are those who would promote democracy, "open society," rule of law, and market economies. They include well-financed agents of economic change, working with both private corporations and local and national governments—and supported by outside governments and private businesses—to promote certain patterns of economic growth. The religious organizations that have come to Russia from East and West with diverse religious creeds are merely some of many newcomers. Their relationship to the other invading forces varies from the intimate to the hostile. They have come to a country where the Orthodox church is seeking to reestablish its authority and influence as the "soul" of Russia after seventy-five years of persecution and manipulation by the secular power. Just as in the last century in Africa and Asia, the religious missionaries in Russia cannot be understood unless they are seen as part of that larger group of external actors and social forces.

Missionaries from different denominations are usually competitors among themselves and with preexisting religious institutions. For example, Catholic and Protestant missionaries from France working among the Sotho in Southern Africa interacted more with their target groups and the civil authorities than they did with their religious competitors, even when the latter came from the same country. In Lesotho the original Catholic-Protestant religious split closely coincides with today's two major political parties. Religious affiliations often reinforce other social divisions and can in turn be aggravated by subsequent economic developments tied to the original divide. In other words, religious competition born through proselytization is often reflected in other aspects of the social fabric.

The first need of missionaries is access to their target population. International law does not grant anyone the right to enter a country, only the right to flee. Once they have access to their target population, missionaries can exercise rights common to all human beings, such as freedom of expression, association, etc. If they are noncitizens, they might be subject to special restrictions common to other non-citizens. In practice, the situation becomes contentious when others—citizens, the public authorities, or other religious groups—object to their actions and seek to prevent them. At that point the civil authorities are called, or at least need to intervene, putting to the test existing rules and practices that protect individual rights and balance them against the requirements of public order. The issue is therefore not so much that conflict arises but rather the capability of a given system to solve it with a degree of fairness. Ultimately the rights of the missionaries are determined by the domestic law of the country in which they are working.

PROSELYTIZATION: THE TARGET GROUPS

The target group can be anyone that a given missionary group does not consider fully converted, ranging from fallen-away members of its own community and members of other interpretations of a common tradition to members of completely different faiths. Both Christianity and Islam have used, and to a lesser extent continue to use, the concept of "heathen" or "infidel" to describe their target groups, as if they were without religion and thus fair game. Neither give much recognition to the targets' prior beliefs. This has been especially true in Africa, where traditional religions were often relegated by European missionaries to the realm of mere superstition, devoid of any rights or claims. The net effect was to demonize the members of those traditions. Some of the chapters in this volume (Deng, Mutua) address the enduring values of traditional African religions, and others (Sanneh) indicate how some Africans saw, and some missionaries sought to portray, Christianity as a logical sequel to their own beliefs in a single God and an afterlife. These quite different attitudes to one another, ranging from seeing the unconverted as inherently evil to seeing them as on the same path but only not so far along, explain some of the diverse outcomes of missionary work.

The responses of the target groups are strongly determined by their primary group loyalties and their attitude toward their leaders, political and otherwise. Typically, missionaries found the more receptive groups to be those with weaker loyalties, among the socially inferior and the more disenfranchised. Through education they would then often recast them to become the socially advantaged in the new dispensation. In the case of Africa those most responsive to missionaries usually fared better than the others under the colonial regimes seeking local officials and collaborators. In addition to adopting a new faith, converts respond to explicit and implicit inducements such as opportunities to change undesired social status or conditions. Africans saw education as an opportunity for social advancement. The more enterprising among them moved from faith to faith to obtain the education available to them at the various levels. Missionaries in Africa provided many other services as diverse as liaison with colonial authorities to developing orthographies and assuring a language's survival. The benefits of some services were obvious at the time; others, such as developing an orthography, only became visible with time.

While often underestimated by the missionaries, traditional religion always played a role in the target group's definition of itself. Traditional religions were intimately integrated into the life of the societies the missionaries first found in Africa. Traditional beliefs structured group identity and emphasized the link between the living and their ancestors. Becoming a Christian was seen to break this link. Converts feared that when they died they would enter an afterlife with fellow Christians and Europeans, not with their own people.

Missionary work at the interfaces between Christianity and Islam is as complex as the diversity of the two religions' various histories in the many different regions and periods that make up their respective experiences. With missionary work at the core of their message and practiced from their earliest years, both groups have had a major impact on world history, with alternating periods of collaboration, tolerance, and competition. Jews and Christians, the other "People of the Book," enjoy a somewhat protected status in Muslim societies, as compared with other human beings who are considered "pagan" and to be converted. Christians have rarely considered Muslims a privileged category. Colonial governments were willing to make use of Islamic law and institutions to govern sub-units within their jurisdictions. Islamic family laws were generally enforced by colonial authorities in the interest of social peace. The activities of their European Christian missionaries were sometimes restricted by colonial administrators in such heavily Muslim areas as the northern parts of Sudan and Nigeria. Historically, this was not in consideration of the rights of the populations but rather to assure the peace. One negative effect, however, seems to have been to postpone the tension, as those two countries are now undergoing the worst tensions between Islam and Christianity in

Africa. This is in considerable contrast to Burkina Faso, Kenya, Mali, Tanzania, Senegal, and others that also lie along the line of Christian and Muslim interaction but are not experiencing major tensions.

PROSELYTIZATION: THE PUBLIC AUTHORITY

Some Christian missionaries penetrated Africa ahead of any colonial administration, forcing the former to accept the social order of the preexisting society. Those nineteenth-century African societies that welcomed missionaries did so for a variety of reasons. Some chiefs invited them for prestige, access to new learning and services, linkage to the encroaching new powers, or even as protection from a superior foe. Equally compelling for other chiefs were contrary reasons to justify keeping the missionaries at a distance, principally, that they represented potential challenges to their authority, in order to preserve the traditions of their people, and for fear of opening their society to other foreign forces.

The role of the public authority with regard to missionary work in precolonial and colonial societies is complex, with both long- and short-term points of reference. African societies took positions all along the spectrum from welcoming to hostile persecution. Some, like the Sotho, welcomed the missionaries as a way to help them adjust to the encroaching Western forces. Others, like the Zulu, preferred to rely on their own resources and traditions. Once they accepted missionaries, all these societies, African and colonial, had to mediate conflicts among the missionary groups and their converts as well as between the missionaries and traditional political and religious authorities. The processes were ad hoc in the African societies but were formalized through laws under the colonial powers. In general, as occurred with land settlement in Southern Africa, the available political space and the quite different patterns of religious practice on the part of traditional and Christian religions meant that a considerable amount of symbiosis was possible before conflicts became overt. Religious conflicts were rare, and the public authority was able to play a benign role.

Over a hundred years of interaction between religious traditions in Africa have resulted today in thousands of independent churches, many of which have memberships extending into the millions (Barrett 1968). Their identities combine elements of Christianity with traditional and regional loyalties. The possibility of such accommodation is another reason why African governments have had to play a minimal role in religious conflicts. The main exceptions are a handful of states, such as Nigeria and Sudan, along the Islam-Christianity divide. Following the Western European model, modern African states do not have public officials or ministries in charge of religious affairs. The relationship between organized religions and the civil authorities is more complex elsewhere. Under Communism, Eastern European governments enforced socialist atheism and closely controlled religious activities. The present Sudanese government imposes elements of Islamic law on Christians and other non-Muslims and seeks to recruit new members to Islam in ways that clearly violate basic human freedoms (Human Rights Watch 1991). Governments have at their disposal many instruments to control religious organizations and their members: taxation, property and inheritance laws, use of public property and institutions, access to press, print and other media, control of public and private assemblies and associations, as well as other powers that can enable the civil authority to act in a less than neutral fashion. Typically calls for the use of these powers come into question especially in situations where one or the other group objects to proselytizing by another.

PROSELYTIZATION: THE METHODS

History reveals multiple approaches to promulgating religious tradition. Indirect action has taken forms ranging from simple witness and lifestyle, without any attempt to preach or harangue, to the provision of health, education, and other social services. Education and health services have always been a major component of Christian missions around the world. More recently, Islamic groups have increased their humanitarian work both within Islamic countries and in countries undergoing or recovering from major social upheavals. Other religious organizations adopt a purely direct form; namely, the "I am here to convert you" message. The issue as far as methods are concerned is the fear that actions conceal, deceive, or are coercive.

From the human rights point of view, the issue is the need to protect the freedom of choice on the part of members of the target group. A second consideration is the claims of local, preexisting religious organizations who feel challenged by the recruiters. The latter are often from the outside, are more affluent, and can buy more in the way of attractions and access to the media. Methods of persuasion have also been criticized for being manipulative, disrespectful, fraudulent, or invasive. How does one decide which are legitimate methods of persuasion? Who decides? Inevitably it falls to the public authority, which has its own interests and has no criterion by which to judge the innate truth of any religion. In the absence of more than a few basic principles and institutions in international law, it is domestic law and domestic institutions that must make these decisions.

PROSELYTIZATION: THE SIGNIFICANT OTHERS

Activism does not take place in a vacuum. Religious missionaries, like other activists, need to make allies and choose the social forces and individuals with goals other than their own with whom they are willing to work. These alliances can often be more implicit and informal than explicit. In addition to those in positions of local authority and leaders of other religions there are likely to be other persons with whom the missionaries feel cultural and other bonds or allegiances. Today, such groups would include the various development agencies, many of which are creatures of other governments or intergovernmental organizations (IGOs). Muslim missionary activity in the south of the former Soviet Union appears to enjoy support from governments as varied as Turkey and Iran. Christian missionary activity all over the world benefits from the support of Western governments in addition to their own congregations at home. On the other hand, some development agencies, such as the Open Society Institute, maintain a strictly secularist approach in their promotion of open, democratic societies.

Human rights rhetoric pervades the work of the American and European development groups, often under the rubrics of democracy, rule of law, and good governance. To them, Western missionaries are natural allies. They are viewed more ambiguously by the international business concerns trying to set themselves up in the newly independent countries. Conversely, as the missionaries seek to protect their own access to these democratizing countries, they look to these external influences to ensure that local legislatures do not turn back to nationalist and religious protectionism. Where once missionaries enjoyed the support of colonial regimes in Africa, in the former socialist countries of today they enjoy the assistance of the international aid organizations working alongside them.

THE PROCESSES OF ADAPTATION

The insertion of the range of new elements into a society that can come with even the simplest of religious messages sets in motion processes of interaction, adaptation, and accommodation as preexisting systems adjust or resist. This very complex interactive process puts virtually every element of a society in question: values, mores, worldviews, economic structures, level of political, economic independence, etc. This is as true in an African village in the nineteenth century as it is in a Russian one today as the Orthodox church seeks to regain moral authority in the face of missionaries from Europe and Asia.

History shows that groups and individuals who respond to religious messages calling for conversion reflect a degree of dissatisfaction with their immediate social environment or prospects. They are ready for change, and religion offers the opportunity. Celibacy as a nun, for example, quickly proved an attractive option for young Sotho women unhappy with the marriage patterns and practices of their society, offering them, in addition, higher social status. Proselytization takes place within a wider process of social change, but it also sets off its own process of social change. As has been argued frequently in this text, the acceptance of new beliefs is a social statement that usually brings with it many other changes, impinging on a person's and a group's social loyalties, needs, and interests. In both nineteenth- and twentieth-century Africa and the turn-of-the-century former socialist countries, massive social transformations coincide with missionary activity or proselytization. Although at very different stages of relative development, both of these incursions have come from the West.

The relatively simple forms of presence—whether as colonial administrators, local shopkeepers, or religious missionaries that Africa faced in the last century—have now been supplemented or replaced by the presence of a very wide range of change-oriented forces: governmental and intergovernmental aid, development and humanitarian agencies, corporations ranging from extractive industries to commodity producers in search of cheap labor, and nongovernmental organizations (NGOs) of all sizes with a myriad of goals and interests, many of which extend their influence through consultancies with and grants to local NGOs and governments. The Coca-Cola executive, committed to a profit margin for Atlanta, is no less a missionary than the American Baptist who teaches science in a high school in Nigeria or Armenia. On the positive side is the fact that religious missionaries, with their focus on people, often help the people to interpret and adapt to the powerful external forces.

Either way, both in Africa and in present-day Eastern Europe, the missionaries are a very small component of the external change forces faced by these societies. It is thus very hard to single out and evaluate their influence, especially when one relies on stereotypes of coercive and deceptive missionary tactics and ignores their wider impact and that of the many other, often much more pervasive and energetic, forces.

FROM PROSELYTISM TO WITNESS AND DIALOGUE

Reflection on this history is persuading many Christian groups to reformulate their conceptualization of missionary work. A distinction is now made between proselytism on one hand, and witness and dialogue on the other. This new thinking is having an impact on the way Christian groups work with one another and with non-Christian religions. Within Christianity, the movement began at the beginning of the century with the Protestant churches that formed the International Missionary Council (IMC), and later the World Council of Churches (WCC), calling for a reexamination of religious freedom. The 1928 Jerusalem meeting of the IMC focused on religious liberty in response to the call of the ecumenical patriarch of Constantinople for an interfaith discussion (among Christians) on Protestant missionary efforts in Orthodox lands (Nelson 1995, 5). Recruiting of members, which often includes recruiting members from other Christian denominations, was perceived then and still remains the most dangerous ignition point in inter-religious relations.

The 1948 Universal Declaration on Human Rights, with its Article 18 on freedom of thought, conscience, and religion, gave new global impetus to discussions among the churches that formed the WCC (Koshy 1996, 137-55; Joint Working Group 1970, 82-92; Joint Working Group 1980; WCC 1982, 17, 37-45; Joint Working Group 1995; Cooney 1996, 283-89).[2] In 1971, the

Joint Working Group between the Roman Catholic Church and the WCC produced a study document entitled *Common Witness and Proselytism*, which concisely defines *proselytism* as "improper attitudes and behavior in the practice of Christian witness. Proselytism embraces whatever violates the right of the human person, Christian or non-Christian, to be free from external coercion in religious matters, or whatever, in the proclamation of the Gospel, does not conform to the ways God draws free men to himself in response to his calls to serve in spirit and truth."

Since 1971, the preference for using *proselytism* as negative and *witness* as positive has grown. But the ambiguity is not totally absent. *Proselytization*, as used in this essay, is more neutral and more descriptive of the goal of the exercise; namely, to witness with a view to recruiting.

What do *witness, mission, evangelism,* and other allied terms that believers of many faiths use mean in practice? According to the Study Document, the ability of individuals or religious communities to "proclaim," manifest, and especially to defend "human rights," to promote "religious freedom," and to eradicate "economic, social and racial injustice" (Articles 5, 6, 7, 14) are all part of witness to the gospel.

The Roman Catholic Church's understanding of religious freedom was articulated in the Second Vatican Council's *Declaration on Religious Freedom* (1965). An analysis of this document was carried in the symposium on *Dignitatis Humanae* held at Catholic University of America, Washington, D.C., in June 1993. After the meeting the Methodist theologian J. Robert Nelson observed: "We can all recognize its front-line importance for all churches and, beyond them, for civil orders and societies in many cultures and nations" (Nelson 1995, 3/67; Brown 1969, 244-66). This document had an enormous influence in Roman Catholic countries such as Italy and Spain, where the Catholic church was part of the fabric of society and where other religions were allowed very little public visibility. By 1997, for all intents and purposes, in these countries other religions had been given legal rights.

Within evangelical, and to a certain extent, fundamentalist Christianity, the Lausanne Covenant of 1974 marks a development for such Christians with regard to religious freedom and pluralism: after confessing in no. 12 that we have "manipulated our hearers through pressure techniques," the signers dealt in no. 13 with freedom and persecution:

> It is the God-appointed duty of every government to secure conditions of peace, justice and liberty in which the church may obey God, serve the Lord Jesus Christ, and preach the gospel without interference. We therefore pray for the leaders of the nations and call upon them to guarantee freedom of thought and conscience, and freedom to practice and propagate religion in accordance with the will of God and as set forth in The Universal Declaration of Human Rights. We also express our deep concern for all who have been unjustly imprisoned, and especially for our brethren who are suffering for their testimony to the Lord Jesus. We

promise to pray and work for their freedom. At the same time we refuse to be intimidated by their fate. God helping us, we too will seek to stand against injustice and to remain faithful to the gospel, whatever the cost. We do not forget the warnings of Jesus that persecution is inevitable.[3]

In 1981, 102 Christian leaders (mostly Catholic, but including a few Protestants from the WCC) met near Rome as "The SEDOS Seminar on the Future of Mission." Section 6 (of eight sections) was titled "Religious Freedom and the Local Church's Responsibility for Mission" (443-88). In many places in the proceedings the issue of reconciling mission and human rights is developed (Motte and Lang 1982, esp. 679). More recently, the entire January 1996 issue of the *International Bulletin of Missionary Research* was devoted to the question "Evangelize or Proselytize?" The editorial observed: "Proselytism has been characterized as 'the corruption of witness.' But as Cecil Robeck observes in the lead article, 'One group's evangelization is another group's proselytism.'" The entire issue of *Missiology* for April 1996 was devoted to "Missionaries, Anthropologists and Human Rights."

In an attempt to expand communication with the Christian groups, Pope John Paul II has promoted the use of the word *dialogue*. First developed within the Roman Catholic Church, it has quickly spread to other branches of Christianity, and to interreligious relations as a whole. Perhaps the most informative document is the Vatican's *Dialogue and Proclamation,* authored by both the Pontifical Council on Interreligious Dialogue and the Congregation for the Evangelization of Peoples. The former is charged with developing dialogue with religions outside Christianity; the latter, with missionary activity. The document shows a certain tension, explaining that interreligious dialogue and proclamation "though not on the same level, are both authentic elements of the Church's evangelizing mission. Both are legitimate and necessary. They are intimately related, but not interchangeable" (Burrows 1993, 93-118, quotation at 114). Dialogue received a strong boost at Assisi on October 27, 1986, when the Vatican organized an event at which representatives of different religions prayed together for peace. Until this event the Vatican had carefully avoided taking part in gatherings that could suggest equality among faiths. This initiative of Pope John Paul (Zago 1987, 96-106) continues both on the Vatican level and in many countries. Its goal is to promote religious cooperation in reducing war and promoting social justice.

A number of other outcomes of the dialogue initiative have been visible. In the United States, following bloodshed between Presbyterians and Roman Catholics in Mexico, a series of dialogues took place between North American Evangelicals and Catholics that resulted in the statement "Evangelicals and Catholics Together for Mission: Towards the Third Millennium." Drawing a great deal of comment from the evangelical community, and surprisingly little from Roman Catholics, the statement inspired three Evangelicals and three Roman Catholics to publish a book edited by Charles Colson and Richard

Neuhaus entitled *Evangelicals and Catholics Together* (Colson and Neuhaus 1995, xv-xxxiii). The original statement noted:

> In many parts of the world, the relationship between these communities is marked more by conflict than cooperation, more by animosity than by love, more by suspicion than by trust, more by propaganda and ignorance than by respect for the truth. This is alarmingly the case in Latin America, increasingly the case in Eastern Europe, and too often the case in our own country.[4]

The authors admit their continuing differences but find areas of cooperation and convergence. The statement also unequivocally asserts: "Any form of coercion—physical, psychological, legal, economic—corrupts Christian witness and is to be unqualifiedly rejected" (ibid., xxx).

Scholars of religion note that the breakup of the three major Christian faiths (Roman Catholics and Orthodox in 1054, Roman Catholics and Protestants in the 1520s) was part of a general breakup of society and culture. Beginning in the mid-1850s, some scholars observe a coming together of societies, with Christian religions sharing and contributing to that movement. It is no coincidence, they argue, that the great ecumenical effort that culminated with the establishment of the World Council of Churches in 1947 and the Vatican Council II from 1962 to 1965 took place at the same time as the United Nations was born and developed. Today there is considerable evidence to show that the leaders of the different Christian traditions are working more closely than in the past, but the overall picture is more complex when we look at their memberships as a whole.

Relations between the Christian churches and other traditions have also changed in recent years, albeit more at the higher administrative rather than at the level of ordinary members. While both the Vatican and the World Council of Churches prefer to restrict the word *ecumenical* to dialogue among Christians and use *interfaith* or *interreligious* for contact with other religions, other Christian groups tend to avoid the word *ecumenical,* and to use *interfaith* or *interreligious* for all such contacts. These mainline relationships have been complicated by the successes of missionary groups as diverse as Jehovah Witnesses, Hare Krishna, and the Church of the Latter Day Saints, who sponsor worldwide missions, especially to the former Soviet Bloc, and do not fit into traditional categories. Sometimes called sects or cults, these religious groups pose a special challenge to the older denominations, particularly in their enthusiasm for converts, and the reaction of governments which find that such enthusiasm offends and aggravates both older religions, and those who profess no religious belief. But with more and more contact with other religions, the sects and cults tend to become domesticated (Niebuhr 1967).[5]

When Friedrich Schleiermacher (1768-1834) wrote his classic *On Religion, Speeches to Its Cultured Despisers*, he coined a phrase that has been used ever since. Not only Christians but also Jews and Muslims today are taking the offensive against secularism and those called the "cultured despisers" of religion. After the Second Vatican Council (1962-65) many local and national ecumenical organizations expanded to include Roman Catholics. Special commissions were established by Christians to work with Jews; new groups were formed which included first Jews and, most recently, Buddhists and Hindus.[6] These local, state, national, and regional organizations address issues such as proselytism, racial and ethnic prejudice, and economic injustice. Contact among religions now exists on a level never before attained; cooperation, which stresses both matters of mutual interest and growth in self-identity, is growing.

One of the most sensitive relationships for Christians is their relationship with Jews. Separation from Judaism was at the root of Christianity. The subsequent relationships between the two groups have been characterized by a long history, often of anti-Semitism, and most recently, by the Holocaust. On the positive side, the only condemnation issued by the Second Vatican Council was its condemnation of anti-Semitism. Its strong statement in the *Declaration on the Relationship of the Church to Non-Christian Religions* came as a surprise because the council had previously agreed not to search out errors and heresies. It said: "The Church repudiates all persecutions against any man. Moreover, mindful of her common patrimony with the Jews, and motivated by the gospel's spiritual love and by no political considerations, she deplores the hatred, persecutions, and displays of anti-Semitism directed against the Jews at any time and from any source" (Abbott 1996, no. 4, esp. notes 26, 27, and 31) (Brown 1969, 267-95; Hargrove 1997).

Discussions during the council moved some Roman Catholics to go further and join members of the World Council of Churches in questioning any witness to Jews. The American Paulist priest Michael McGarry argues against all witness to Jews in *Christology after Auschwitz* (McGarry 1977; Brown 1969, 289-95).[7] On the other hand, some Catholics of Jewish background take a very different viewpoint: not to witness, they say, would be to discriminate by denying to Jews the most precious gift Christians have to offer—the love of Jesus Christ (Neuman 1990, 323-26; Donohue 1983, 145-49; 1997, 8-9).[8] The approach of the year 2000 has brought many Christians to newer forms of cooperation. But one Jewish response to note is that whenever Christians have cooperated, Jews have suffered. Special efforts are being made to include Jews and other faiths in the religious and spiritual preparation for the third millennium. The signs remain ambiguous on both sides of Jewish-Christian relations. In January 1997, when Israeli Prime Minister Benjamin Netanyahu met for the first time with Pope John Paul II, he presented him with a book, noting that it was "a copy of my father's last book about the history of Jews in Spain." The book documents how Roman pontiffs acted on behalf of Jews in Spain during the period in which they were persecuted by the monarchy (reported in the Catholic press, for example, *The Florida Catholic*, January 2, 1997, A-5. The book was reviewed, for example, in *America*, December 30, 1995, 26-27). A major question for Catholics and Jews is the future status of

Jerusalem, with the church interested both in the holy sites and in the well-being of Palestinian Christians. Historically, Jews have feared cooperative activity with Christians, fearing that it leads to assimilation or greater alienation and anti-Semitism. In the meantime, dialogue is seen to mean that Jews and Christians be committed to deepening their own identity and to working with each other for a better world.

With the expansion of Islam into the West and visibility of its fundamentalist movements, there are many points of friction between Christians and Muslims. Not only in the Middle East and sub-Saharan Africa, but in countries such as France, there are increasing conflicts. The wearing of Muslim dress to public schools in France, for example, is a contentious issue. Yet not only scholars but also missionaries call for dialogue and note areas of mutual interest (Ryan 1994, 13-17). The founder of the Focolare Movement, Chiara Lubich, for example, was recently invited to speak (in her own language, Italian), in "perhaps the most historical mosque in the U.S., the Malcolm Shabass Mosque, in Harlem, New York City" (*PIME World* 1997, 2). Theologians such as Hans Küng suggest many areas of dialogue with Islam (Küng 1993). Some Catholic orders, such as the Little Brothers and Little Sisters of Charles de Foucauld, carry out their work among the Muslims through a form of silent presence rather than through direct preaching. In practice, most Christians see Islam as competitor and even persecutor, pointing to such countries as Sudan and Pakistan.

Among the other groups emerging to promote dialogue among members, if not exactly among the religions themselves, is the Council for Research in Values and Philosophy based in Washington, D.C., and directed by Father George McLean, O.M.I. This is a network of philosophers and theologians on every continent, many of whom have attended annual seminars at the Catholic University of America. Under its auspices, Soviet Communists, Chinese Communists, African Christians, European atheists, and other scholars have lived under the same roof for ten weeks, creating a remarkable blend of scholarship, personal contact, and social bonding. Their discussions focus on themes relating to person, society, and culture. Between 1975 and 1987 the council held annual colloquia with the Institutes of Philosophy of the Academies of Science in Central and Eastern Europe, and later included scholars from China. These encounters resulted in more than fifty joint publications on value-related questions in the participants' home countries, such as *Abrahamic Faiths, Ethnicity, and Ethnic Conflicts*, a collection of articles by Christian, Islamic, and Jewish scholars (Peachey et al. 1997). A second work, *Civil Society and Social Reconstruction*, contains articles by the Dutch Catholic missiologist Joseph G. Donders and the Filipino scholar Florencio Riguera; the latter explores the role of Hinduism, Islam, and Buddhism with respect to civil society (McLean 1997). From this work a distinct philosophical interpretation is emerging: discerning the Divine—the Holy Spirit in Christian terms—at work in the world. In some contrast to the earlier religious focus upon the divine as transcendent and communicating to a nonreligious humankind from without, there is now a greater appreciation of the Holy Spirit at work within the hearts of *all* persons and cultures. In this tradition the goal of evangelization is defined as assisting the Spirit, to help avoid unwarranted tension between its diverse manifestations in various groups or peoples, by seeing them as the work of the same Spirit, and to facilitate their convergence through the pilgrimage of the many peoples to the Holy Mountain. As each of the religions bears its gift or unique combination of gifts—prophetism, salvation, harmony, contemplation— all are enriched, God is praised, and God's creative work of life is fulfilled.

The net result is that religious pluralism is now hailed. The evangelical scholar George R. Hunsberger, based at Western Theological Seminary, Holland, Michigan, sponsors conferences of missiologists and a quarterly newsletter, *The Gospel and Our Culture*, which is now in its ninth year. One of the figures especially admired by Hunsberger is the Scottish missionary bishop of the Church of South India, Lesslie Newbigin, who promoted a positive attitude toward religious pluralism among Christians (Newbigin 1989). More and more Christians are posing for the first time the possibility that pluralism is also a benefit for their own religion (Carpe 1995, 2; Institute for Ecumenical and Cultural Research 1995). Convergence is taking place within Christianity, and Christian cooperation with the world religions is on a change course. Church authorities are therefore seeking to ensure that their missionaries' work does not appear coercive, manipulative, and deceptive. The question is how and when these ideas will percolate down to local communities.

EVALUATING MISSIONARY ACHIEVEMENTS: IN WHOSE EYES, FOR WHAT PURPOSES?

With this growing convergence among Christians and interest in rapprochement with Islam, is it possible to develop a common analytical and a normative framework which would set mutually acceptable or common criteria and then rules for tolerance? This is not yet and may never be possible. There are so many theological perspectives, and religious missionary work is always intermingled with other forces and interests. What is a success or beneficial for some is a failure or harmful for others. Religious missionaries evaluate their work primarily in otherworldly terms. This was highlighted in the discussions that followed the death of Mother Teresa in Calcutta. She was criticized on the grounds that she did not seek social change but rather sought to console the poor in their poverty. Success for many missionaries is not defined in terms of secular law or even interfaith relations. Their goal is not to seek a balance between religious teaching and social action, or to change their attitude to local cultures, or to improve their relationship with local authorities, let alone focus on economic development and well-being. The goal of the most aggressive, fundamentalist, and most visible activists, whether they are Muslim or Christian, is primarily conversion and salvation. At best all other activities are means to this goal. Clearly it is beyond human capacity to evaluate their success in achieving conversion and salvation in the afterlife. The missionaries do bring about, however, other more tangible changes, and we can focus on these. The purpose of this section is to delineate some of the other key reference points that can be used to evaluate missionary work in order both to avoid juxtaposing different criteria and to encourage a more comprehensive, non-stereotypical view of their activities.

In the modern world most societies have moved toward accepting increasing levels of religious and other forms of pluralism. Geographically defined units are increasingly more heterogeneous. Few are the countries like Saudi Arabia and China that impose severe restrictions on the exercise of religion. As can be seen from other essays in this book, the outcomes of missionary work go far beyond internal spiritual conversion. The social consequences are enormous, whether or not the missionaries share the same culture with their new converts. The impact is greater when there is a marked prior difference between the two cultures and the converts' society is undergoing a more general political and cultural invasion. The outcomes, any of which can be used as indicators of achievement or success, will involve in varying degrees combinations of the following (listed without suggesting priorities):

- the formation of new social groupings, the adoption of new normative reference groups and of new worldviews and visions that reorient the next generations, typically with a more inclusive, universalist vision;
- the adoption of new social practices which challenge previous practices and put in question the social institutions that supported them;
- the establishment of new relationships with the world beyond the immediate local community, reaching to Mecca, Rome, or other religious centers, but also to other economies;
- the incorporation of new cultural traits and institutions ranging from words, music, art, social practices and ceremonies, to eating patterns and economic structures, new positive and/or negative relationships with external actors inside and outside the community;
- the impact of the missionaries' work and resources (funding, health and education services, communications equipment, etc.) on the physical well-being of the local community (educational and health services and standards, economic structures and systems of wealth, etc.);
- the impact of the missionaries as mediator vis-à-vis the other forces of change; and lastly,
- the tangible aspects of the spiritual and moral impact of the missionaries, which they consider the essence of their work, namely, public behavior of converts, participation in religious activities, etc.

Writings on the work of religious missionaries and external influence in general use these various categories to evaluate the missionary impact. Using these diverse categories permits studies that go beyond stereotypical images of missionaries as the arms of imperialism or paternalism. The very diversity and arbitrariness in their selection and use as indicators of justice and moral standards point to the need for more basic common indicators. We recommend the use of the human rights standards enunciated in documents such as the Universal Declaration of Human Rights. These are the only standards of social justice that have received the approval of the world community—as represented by the world's governments at the United Nations. These standards have been promulgated as applicable to and can be claimed by all human beings on the planet whatever their religious, geographical, or gender status. Violations of religious and personal freedoms on the part of those who would recruit members to their view of life can be protected by national institutions, but they need national legislation that adapts general human rights principles of freedom of association, speech, belief, etc. to the circumstances of each society.

The above analysis suggests that the groups most in need of protection are target groups who are at risk because of their relative weakness vis-à-vis outside forces. This weakness can stem from many reasons ranging from pressing needs, such as hunger, physical plight, and outright coercion, to such desires for advancement as education or interest in the larger world. At what point do they need protection? At what point are their rights being violated? What generally acceptable criteria ought to be used to evaluate their situation? This task of normative analysis is yet to be undertaken even by scholars. It is a necessary prelude to formal international standards on freedom of religion and belief. In international law, and many domestic laws, religious convictions enjoy special protection, ultimately because they cannot be proven or disproved by the secular authority and because they reflect deep personal and social commitments. The concept of religious freedom grew up in common law as a way to restrict governments from trying to impose religious beliefs. This reasoning is visible in John Locke, and one could argue that this was the first step leading to his development of the wider theory of rights (Bloom et al. 1996).

On the other hand, the state has many interests at stake in the whole issue of proselytization, including its own legitimate interest in the well-being of its people, their language, and their culture, but also such traditional concerns as public order and safety. Each of these provides the state with a potentially legitimate rubric for restricting missionary activity. Some governments use these prerogatives to exclude missionaries. More often than in the case of most other human rights violations, religious missionary activity has an in-built international dimension; namely, the fact that the missionaries come from another country and are the concern of that country's officials. Anything that happens to Western missionaries quickly becomes international news. The task of the state is to assure a reduction in tension and conflict and peaceful coexistence among religious groups, which presumably translates into mutual tolerance. Human rights practice and international law have made these activities subject to international scrutiny.

CONCLUSION

The purpose of this essay has been to lay out some of the elements that make up the process of religious missionary activity, proselytization and recruitment.

Using international human rights as the only widely accepted standards that can be applied across countries, we have focused on the impact of the methods used by the missionaries on the rights of the target group as the ones most likely to be violated. In recent years Christian missions have tended to become more responsive to the rights of other religions and consequently to those of their target groups. As established religions both Islam and Christianity have often fought hard, in word and through politics, to exclude other religions from their territories. While states have the primary responsibility to regulate this process, the complex political and legal interests involved mean that state action can not go unexamined. Given the role that religion, as personal conviction and as institutional heritage, still plays in personal and national identity and the danger outlined in Huntington's book that such social identities easily become lines of conflict, the resolving of tensions with religious dimensions ought to be a high priority for all public authorities.

States are not in a position to rank one religion against another in their essential spiritual terms. Religion is part of the political process, making it hard to differentiate between religion as basic inspiration, religion as pretext, religion as mobilizing tool, and religion as demarcation of different interests. Each situation exhibits a different and often evolving balance among these aspects. The positive news is that most religions advocate a world of peace and human solidarity. On the other hand, can they promote such a world if the effective political apparatus is neutral? This transposes into a question of political order, the most appropriate place being along the spectrum between the position of the United States (maximum separation of religion and state) and the position of those that have instituted elaborate government controls to prevent conflict based on religious grounds. As each system has its merits, it would be impossible here to advocate either model or one of the many possible intermediates.

Our conclusions, therefore, are (1) that while domestic and international legislation may help, the critical factors in religious harmony are the secular and religious administrative and educational institutions which, on a day-to-day basis, can assure social peace, and (2) that to achieve this, a strong commitment on the part of both people and government to equal treatment and effective and appropriate rules and institutions must be cultivated. In the final analysis, each society needs its own formal and informal social structures to protect the rights of all individuals, and in this case to mediate between potentially competing religious groups based on principles of tolerance and equal treatment. Such structures could be either designed specifically for religious institutions, or the religious institutions could make use of more generic structures as they do in the United States, where there are no government offices of religious affairs.

Notes

[1] *Proselytism* and *religious missionary work* are used interchangeably in this chapter. In their most generic form they consist primarily in "witnessing and recruiting

new members to the beliefs and practices of a particular religious or other tradition." The focus of the essay is on the actions of the recruiting agents rather than on the conversion experienced by members of the target population.

[2] Koshy's article appears in the *Journal of Church and State*. This journal is a quarterly of the J. M. Dawson Institute of Church-State Studies of Baylor University (Waco, Texas) and lists doctoral dissertations in church-state relations, as well as a "Calendar of Events in Church and State." In a footnote this document (Joint Working Group 1970) states: "In certain linguistic, cultural and confessional contexts, the term 'proselytism,' used without qualification has acquired this pejorative sense. In these other languages and contexts in which the term still retains its more original meanings of 'zeal in spreading the faith,' it will be necessary always to use proselytism in the pejorative sense, or some phrase which denotes defective attitudes and conduct."

[3] The covenant was published in *Christianity Today* 18, no. 22 (August 16, 1974), 22-24 (1244-46), and is available with some bibliography in Gerald H. Anderson and Thomas F. Stransky, eds., *Mission Trends 2* (Paulist/Eerdmans, 1975), 239-48. Recently many American Christians joined in promoting legislation which would create an Office of Religious Persecution Monitoring; see, for example, *Catalyst* (Journal of Catholic League for Religious and Civil Rights) 24, no. 6 (July-August 1997): 13.

[4] The statement, which was issued in March 1994, is on pages xv-xxxiii, quotation at xvi. *Proselytizing* is a very frequent entry in the index (see page 234).

[5] Niebuhr explains how sects become denominations. For how one major religion treats the concrete challenge of the sects, see the Vatican Secretariat (now Council) for Promoting Christian Unity et al., *Reports on Sects, Cults and Religious Movements*, May 4, 1986. *The Washington Post*, June 8, 1996, in the religion section, accurately describes how the Hare Krishna have evolved (B7-8). See Thomas P. Rausch, S.J., "The Los Angeles Catholic/Evangelical Dialogue," *Ecumenical Trends* 26, no. 6 (June 1997) 13/93-16/96, for an interesting example of confusion between a denomination and a sect.

[6] The Roman Catholics, National Council of Churches, and Southern Baptists (all U.S.A) have invested much money and personnel in the organization of contacts with other religions. Perhaps the most interesting regional effort is the Newsletter *Inter-religion*, published by the Network of Christian Organizations for Interreligious Encounter in East Asia, available from the Christian Study Centre on Chinese Religion and Culture, 6/F Kiu Kin Mansion, 566 Nathan Rd., Kowloon, Hong Kong. In Washington, D.C., there is both an ecumenical organization for Christians (The Council of Churches of Greater Washington) and an interfaith organization (Interfaith Conference of Metropolitan Washington). Both are very active; the Mormons belong only to the latter.

[7] The American Interfaith Institute/World Alliance of Interfaith Organizations (321 Chestnut St., Philadelphia, PA 19106) advertises itself as "Rethinking Relationships among Protestants, Catholics, and Jews" and publishes the journal *Explorations*, now in its eleventh volume. The Skirball Institute on American Values (635 S. Harvard Blvd., Suite 214, Los Angeles, CA 90005) has several interesting projects, such as a National Seminary Conference, to promote Christian-Jewish understanding.

[8] See also the work of The Institute of Judaeo-Christian Studies, Seton Hall University, South Orange, NJ 07079.

BIBLIOGRAPHY

Abbott, Walter M, ed. 1996. *The Documents of Vatican II*. New York: Crossroad.

Ashcraft, Richard. 1996. "Religion and Lockean Natural Rights," in *Religious Diversity and Human Rights*, edited by Irene Bloom et al. New York: Columbia University Press.

Barrett, David B. 1968. *Schism and Renewal in Africa, An Analysis of Six Thousand Contemporary Religious Movements*. Nairobi: Oxford University Press.

Bloom, Irene, and J. Paul Martin and Wayne L. Proudfoot. 1996. *Religious Diversity and Human Rights*. New York: Columbia University Press.

Brown, Robert McAfee. 1969. "Roman Catholicism and Religious Freedom," in *The Ecumenical Revolution*, revised edition, 244-95. Garden City, N.Y.: Doubleday.

Burrows, William R., ed. 1993. *Redemption and Dialogue*. Maryknoll, N.Y.: Orbis Books.

Carpe, William D. 1995. "Religious Pluralism Consultation Held," *Ecumenical Trends* 24, no. 1 (January).

Colson, Charles, and Richard Neuhaus, eds. 1995. *Evangelicals and Catholics Together*, xv-xxxiii. Dallas: Word Pub.

Cooney, Monica, S.M.S.M. 1996. "Towards Common Witness," *International Review of Missions* 85, no. 337 (April).

Donohue, John W. 1983. "Time for Edith Stein," *America* (February 26).

———. 1997. "Edith Stein, Saint," *America* (June 21, 1997).

Hargrove, Katherine T. 1997. *Seeds of Reconciliation*. N. Richard Hills, Tex.: BIBAL Press.

Human Rights Watch. 1991. "Report on Sudan, New Islamic Penal Code Violates Human Rights" (April 9).

Huntington, Samuel P. 1996. *The Clash of Civilizations and the Remaking of World Order*. New York: Simon and Schuster.

International Bulletin of Missionary Research 20, no. 1 (January 1996).

Joint Working Group (WCC). 1970. Third Official Report (May). Appendix II; available, for example, in *One in Christ* 8 (1972).

———. 1980. *The Common Witness of Christians*.

Koshy, Ninian. 1996. "The Ecumenical Understanding of Religious Liberty: The Contribution of the World Council of Churches," *Journal of Church and State* 38, no. 1 (Winter): 137-55.

Küng, Hans, et al. 1993. *Christianity and World Religions, Paths to Dialogue*. Second edition. Maryknoll, N.Y.: Orbis Books.

Martin, J. Paul. Forthcoming. *Assessing the Outcomes of Proselytization: Missionaries among Moshesh's Sotho in Nineteenth Century Southern Africa*.

McGarry, Michael B. 1977. *Christology after Auschwitz*. New York: Paulist.

McLean, George, ed. 1997. *Civil Society and Social Reconstruction*. Cultural Heritage and Contemporary Change. Series 1. Volume 16. Washington, D.C.: The Council for Research in Values and Philosophy.

Missiology 24, no. 2 (April 1996).

Motte, Mary, F.M.M., and Joseph R. Lang M.M., eds. 1982. *Mission in Dialogue*. Maryknoll, N.Y.: Orbis Books.

Nelson, J. Robert. 1995. "The Ecumenical Reception of the Dignitatis Humanae Declaration of the Second Vatican Council," *Ecumenical Trends* 24, no. 5 (May).

Neuman, Matthias. 1990. "Confessions of a Twentieth Century Christian Judaizer," *America* (November 3).

Newbigin, Lesslie. 1989. *The Gospel in a Pluralist Society*. Geneva: World Council of Churches.

Niebuhr, H. Richard. 1967. *The Social Sources of Denominationalism*. Cleveland, Ohio: World Publishing.

Peachey, Paul, George F. McLean, and John Kromkowski, eds. 1997. *Abrahamic Faiths, Ethnicity and Ethnic Conflicts*. Series 1. Culture and Values. Volume 7. Washington, D.C.: The Council for Research in Values and Philosophy.

PIME World. 1997. Volume 19, no. 6 (June).

Ryan, Patrick J. 1994. "Is Dialogue Possible with Muslims?" *America* (December 31).

The Institute for Ecumenical and Cultural Research. 1995. *Confessing Christian Faith in a Pluralistic Society*. Collegeville, Minn.

WCC [World Council of Churches]. 1982. *Mission and Evangelism* no. 17, available in *International Bulletin of Missionary Research* 7, no. 2 (April 1983).

Witte, John, and Michael Bourdeaux. 1999. *Proselytism and Orthodoxy in Russia: The New War for Souls*. Maryknoll, N.Y.: Orbis Books.

Zago, Marcello. 1987. "Day of Prayer for Peace," *Kerygma* [now *Mission*] 21, no. 48.

3.

Muslims Engaging the Other and the Humanum

———————◆———————

Farid Esack

Call unto to the path of your Lord with wisdom, and good counsel, and engage them by those means which are the finest.

—Qur'an 16:125

INTRODUCTION

How do Muslims engage the religious other in a world that increasingly defies geographical, political, religious, and ideological boundaries? This is a world where the "enemy" is often the internal self (e.g., the Saudi/Iranian/Sudanese regime, or the Shiite/Qadiani/modernists) and the asylum provider the external other (Christian relief organizations, Amnesty International/a non-Muslim neighbor, etc). How do Muslims respond when we come face to face with the humanum, the essentially human, and its manifestation in lives of a tireless quest for compassion and commitment to justice that the other may lead? How do the various forms of engagement with the other facilitate or militate against efforts to challenge unjust socioeconomic systems and create possibilities for more humane alternatives?

The first part of this essay is a broad overview of the various ways in which different tendencies among Muslims relate to the other, along with a brief comment on the ideological function of each. This relationship is discussed within a broader context of liberalism and globalization. Such a context problematizes overt religious or ideological proselytism when the object to which one is invited is often nonmaterial (faith, God, salvation, etc.) but lauds more obviously similar covert activity when the objects are clearly material in the form of market commodities. The second part of this essay advocates an alternative to the form of proselytization that regards the other as being in various states of damnation. The conclusion calls for intra-religious and extra-religious "proselytization" based on liberative praxis aimed at creating a world of socioeconomic and gender justice where all human beings are free to explore and attain their unique fullness, intended with their creation.

Despite the risk of essentializing Muslims, after locating myself within the debate on Muslims and the other, I nevertheless state the three main generalized assumptions which underpin my own understanding of Muslim responses to the question of engaging the other and the humanum.

I am a South African Muslim, belonging to a small minority community that has survived, lived, and thrived among the other for three hundred forty years. My years in Pakistan as a student of Islamic theology alerted me to the oppression of Christians in a Muslim country, and my involvement in the South African struggle for liberation alerted me to the need to value religiousness and spirituality in the other (Esack 1997). The challenges of poverty and AIDS that face Africa particularly, and those of consumerism and the ongoing ravaging of our planet and its peoples by the forces of a faceless god, the Market, in general, lead me to believe that my South African Muslim appreciation of the other serves two purposes:

- It enables others to see how some Muslims are dealing with the challenges of pluralism in a world of injustice; and
- it offers my Muslim coreligionists elsewhere a possible theological path whereby one can be true to one's faith and to the voice of one's conscience in a world where virtue is clearly not the monopoly of one's coreligionists, nor vice a monopoly of the other.

Other than my own sociohistorical context, the following assumptions about Muslims underpin my appreciation of how we relate to the other:

First, the overwhelming majority of Muslims, irrespective of the nature and extent, or even complete absence, of their religiosity, have an indomitable belief that the world would be a better place if people followed the religion of Islam. Comments such as "He's such an intelligent guy; how come he's not a Muslim?" or "Desmond Tutu is such a decent person, if only he were a Muslim" are common among Muslims.

The notion of Islam as a given, and all else as aberration, is both based on and supported by a *hadith* (tradition) of the Prophet Muhammad that "every person is born in a natural state, it is the parent which makes the child a Christian or a Jew." The fact that Christianity and Judaism are portrayed as nonnatural religions leads to the refrain that Islam is *al-din al-fitrah* (the natural—also understood as "the obvious"—religion).

Second, the notion that the "world is hungry for Islam; if only we were better examples" is widespread among Muslims. They are, therefore, genuinely surprised when encountering someone who has studied Islam and not embraced it. When, for example, they first encounter a non-Muslim person interested in Islam, they are generally patient and happy to assist. After an extended period, when they realize that such interest is not transforming the researcher into a searcher ready to discover Islam, then—for most Muslims—there is only one conceivable motive for that person's motive: "He or she is learning about us in order to undermine us." This contributes to the widespread suspicion and antagonism that lurk underneath the polite surface of interreligious and even academic forums toward the professional non-Muslim Islamicist.

Third, much of conscious religiously motivated interaction with the other is based on the assumption that there is a stable "self" or "own community" with a package of essential and unchanging values, principles, and beliefs, which stands in contrast with the other equally stable, even if invariably "lesser," other. The presentation of this package of self and community is intended to destabilize the other and, upon this instability, open the other to embrace this new package.

Muslims, of course, engage non-Muslims all the time and at different levels. In this essay I am concerned with consciously religiously based forms of engagement, where the responses to the other are on the basis of that putative or actual otherness.

THE OTHER AS ENEMY

At this level of engagement, all manifestations of non-Islam—and the definition of *Islam* being the sole prerogative of that particular group and/or its leader—are viewed as a perversion of the natural order. This order, in turn, is regarded as synonymous with the Divine order. For many, such as the al-Takfir wa'l-Hijrah group in Egypt or the Spain-based Murabitun, this evaluation of the other may include "merely nominal" or "cultural" Muslims, or those whose appreciation of Islam differs from their own. While invoking the *hadith* "al-kufr millatun wahidah" (rejection or disbelief is a single community), the latter group is usually the object of greater vilification, given their "betrayal" of the "real" Islam.

This level of engagement is usually the terrain of those described as Islamic fundamentalists, who often come from a professional background and have a more pronounced ideological thrust. These groups, which include the Jordanian Hizb al-Tahrir, the Egyptian Gama al-Islamiyyah, and the Algerian Armed Islamic Group (GIA), follow a program aimed at destroying the political structures of *kufr* (literally, "rejection," i.e., rejection of Islam) and replacing these with an Islamic state. While always welcoming converts to "true" Islam, their proselytization work is in large measure aimed at other Muslims in preparation for the eventual showdown with *kufr*. A small segment of this persuasion regards the other in general, and more particularly the ideological leadership of the other, as beyond redemption. They would, therefore, either resort to withdrawing from "*kafir* society," along the lines of al-Takfir wa'l-Hijrah, or engage in active, often armed, combat against the agents of *kufr*, such as the

GIA. In these circles, hostage-taking would be justified, as would the death of civilians in the pro-active *jihad* against *kufr*.

Much has been written on the subject of religious fundamentalism as a response to modernity (Lawrence 1989; Martin and Appleby 1991). Whatever the varying sociological circumstances in different contexts, many of these Muslims feel moved and/or sustained by their religious sensitivities to seek refuge in what they believe is the ultimate certainty: an ahistorical and reified Islam. The following are some of the factors responsible for this:

- the unfettered global hegemony of the United States of America and the many agencies such as the World Bank and International Monetary Fund—viewed as mere adjuncts of neocolonialism;
- the virtual powerlessness of Muslim states and their seeming collaboration in their own subjugation;
- the moral—particularly sexual—flexibility of modernity;
- and the intellectual/philosophical tentativeness of postmodernity.

While many of the activists at this level are familiar with the discourse and utilize instruments of modernity such as the Internet, they lack an appreciation of how inextricably interwoven the fate of humankind has really become. Thus, they still believe that one can carve out pieces of liberated territories as *dar al-Islam* (the abode of Islam) freed from foreign videos, CNN, and miniskirts. More pertinently, they are indifferent to the attempts of numerous other entities throughout the world who share their concern and disdain for why globalization is becoming synonymous with "McDonaldization," with the hypocritical and self-centered nature of USA foreign policy, and the lack of political freedom and abundance of repression in their own societies.

In this lack of recognition of shared concerns lies both their greatest weakness and their strength. As isolated entities, they are destined to remain on the margins of humankind, occasionally bursting to the fore in acts of raw terror, such as the massacre of tourists at Luxor, or of covert terror, such as the closing of medical-care facilities for women in Afghanistan under the *Taliban*. Equally, as isolated entities they can march forth undisturbed by questions of the humanness of the other, which will confront them as soon as they discover a commonness in objectives to create a more just world.

THE OTHER AS POTENTIAL SELF

The second level of conscious engagement with the other is that of active proselytism, with the stated intention of saving souls and increasing the numbers of "the believers." This level is usually the domain of those who espouse a traditionalist and putatively apolitical view of Islam. They focus on personal sin, reformation, and salvation in the hereafter. Occasionally, some form of charitable work serves as an adjunct to their proselytism. This view, conversely, lacks an awareness of socioeconomic justice and an appreciation of its structural causes. Faith is narrowly defined as verbal testimony to a set of creeds, and morality to the personal sphere with the focus on matters pertaining to sex. This group confines its activity to relatively mild forms of engaging the other. While the Tablighi Jama'ah may concentrate on knocking on the doors of the non-praying or "unrighteous" internal other, those who opt for increasing the numbers of the nominally faithful adopt a wide range of strategies. These include the following:

- coercion, such as withholding food ration cards or complicating access to them in Pakistani villages;
- the incessant anti-Christian haranguing over mosque loudspeakers in Bangladesh and Indonesia;
- the exploitation of social problems, such as lack of health and educational facilities, by combining *da'wah* (literally, "invitation") with concrete assistance in these fields by the Africa Muslim Agency in Southern Africa; and,
- the regular public debates with Christian evangelists of the world-renowned South African Muslim polemicist, Ahmed Deedat, an exception in a world where *da'wah* is rarely individualized.

The latter form of engagement is particularly meaningful to Muslims who feel disempowered through colonialism and the seeming religio-cultural hegemony of "the West." It is thus not unusual to find up to fifty video tapes of Deedat in a single Muslim home in Britain or Abu Dhabi. The compulsion appears to be "what we are losing daily in the world of economic and cultural power can be compensated for by our victories in religious slanging matches."

THE OTHER AS UNAVOIDABLE NEIGHBOR

There are numerous Muslims who are engaged in interfaith or interreligious dialogue in various parts of the world. With the exception of the Al al-Bayt Institute in Jordan, such activity rarely enjoys the support of mainstream Muslim institutions in the Arab world. Significant pockets of such initiatives are, however, found in countries such as Nigeria, Indonesia, and Malaysia and, more particularly, in those countries where Muslims are a minority. Other than the occasional high-powered and largely symbolic gatherings of an organization such as the World Conference of Religion and Peace, much of interreligious dialogue at a local level comprises one or more of the following:

- clarifying some basic guidelines for proselytization;
- promoting good neighborliness; and
- learning the basics of the other's religion.

In the case of the latter, presentations usually border on apologetics, with each side keen to show the finest side of the religion's heritage and careful to avoid reference to the actual historical or contemporary conduct of its adherents.

The number of Muslims, usually individuals rather than groups, engaged in such dialogue with the other are few and far between, and where they are participants in organized forums then these have generally been organized by

Christians. At this level there is some appreciation of the other, recognition of some worth attached to them and of the need to nurture this worth. ("These are good people; they would be even better if they were Muslim.") While there is an explicit acknowledgment of the duty of proclaiming "the good news" or "*da'wah*," the participants acknowledge the need to learn about the other for effective religious tolerance or proselytization. A number of Muslims initially enter such dialogues under the misunderstanding that their (usually) Christian counterparts are engaged in conversation because of the wavering nature of their own faith and, therefore, present fertile grounds for their own *da'wah*.

While many participants in interreligious dialogue start at this level, the often ongoing nature and the unpredictability of the outcome of any truly listening experience ensure that, for some at least, the perception of the other changes and, along with it, their objectives in the dialogue. As for those who were incapable of listening, they normally just disappear after a few meetings, dismissing the exercise as "a waste of time."

At a more scholarly level there are a number of Muslim intellectuals who form an intrinsic part of the "dialogue scene." Some of them, such as Jamal Badawi, the Toronto-based scholar, and Mahmoud Ayoub, the Lebanese scholar based in Philadelphia, believe that exposing the other to the intellectual face of Islam, represented by them, is itself an invitation to Islam. There is little awareness among them that this very intellectualizing of the face of Islam means a transformation of the product and is in effect a denial of an essentialist Islam.

Despite the seeming objective nature of this approach, it is still essentially characterized by an assumption of superiority. First, it is not atypical to find suggestions in these circles that the Christian or Jewish partner—the "noble savage"— is actually a Muslim, even if he or she is unaware of it. This notion of the "anonymous Muslim" assumes that goodness is synonymous with, even exclusive to, Islam. Many Muslims, when coming face to face with goodness, cannot relate this with integrity to the person as a person or as a Christian. Instead, they feel compelled to go through the initial act of making him or her "one of us."

While the activities of this tendency are usually characterized by political noninvolvement, it does often support moderate political action to promote "righteous causes." At other times those involved at this level may also cooperate with one another in seemingly benign activities, such as tree planting or literacy campaigns. Seldom, if ever, in the forefront of challenging unjust sociopolitical systems or practices, they often play a significant role in the agenda of national states struggling to fuse diverse cultural religious identities into a broader national one.

THE OTHER AS SELF
AND INTELLECTUAL/THEOLOGICAL SPARRING PARTNER

"In our age," says Ghrab, "the purpose of dialogue must be solely knowledge . . . of the other as the other wishes to be and not as it pleases us to imagine him, and on the basis of his texts, and his heritage and not merely on the basis of our texts" (Ghrab 1987, 107). This scholarly and "objective" approach to the other is the position of a growing number of individual Muslim intellectuals, such as Mohammed Arkoun and Ebrahim Moosa, who eschew any hint of *da'wah* (objectives), however subtle. These individuals, often working on the margins of Muslim society, nonetheless embrace a calling, "the creation of a new space of intelligibility and freedom" (Arkoun 1990, 20). Utilizing this space, they may embrace ideals of finding areas of commonality. In many ways this approach is a classic liberal one, which values individual freedom and space and the intellectual quest for their own sake.

What is often ignored at this level is that liberal ideology is not without its hegemonic interests. Leonard Binder has raised the pertinent question whether the critique of Muslim liberals has not been a "form of false consciousness, an abject submission to the hegemonic discourse of the dominant secular Western capitalist and imperialist societies, an oriental orientalism, or whether it was and is practical, rational and emancipatory" (Binder 1988, 5).

The call for "knowledge as a sphere of authority to be accepted and respected unanimously, a knowledge independent of ideologies, able to explain their formation and master their impact" (Arkoun 1988, 69) does little other than further the ideological interest within which such knowledge is located and formulated. Knowledge, like any other social tool, can be critical but is never neutral. As Segundo has argued: "Every hermeneutic entails conscious or unconscious partisanship. It is partisan in its viewpoint even when it believes itself to be neutral and tries to act that way" (Segundo 1976).

While this group of scholars makes for the most interesting partners on the dialogue circuit, I do not share the enthusiasm of those who insist on letting a million thoughts bloom for the fun of diversity and pluralism, a kind of social venture which often claims not to take sides because "this is the perfect ideology for the modern bourgeois mind. Such a pluralism makes a genial confusion in which one tries to enjoy the pleasures of difference without ever committing oneself to any particular vision of resistance, liberation and hope" (Tracy 1987, 90).

A second area of concern with dialogue at this level is that it is essentially confined to those whom Muslims regard as People of the Book, i.e., Jews and Christians. In some ways this reflects the relative Qur'anic gentleness toward the People of the Book, the current politico-economic hegemony, and the social location of these thinkers engaged in dialogue. However, I believe that this preference also betrays a more serious prejudice, a subject to which I will later revert: that people of the Fourth World, often adherents of "pagan" traditions, are of little or no consequence.

THE OTHER AS SELF AND SPIRITUAL PARTNER

For a number of Muslim scholars, such as David Chittick, Fritchoff Scoun, Martin Lings, and Sayyed Hoosein Nasr, as well as a few Muslim groups, such as the Deutsche Muslim Liga, as well as a host of loosely organized *sufi* groups in different parts of the world, *dialogue* is also an act of mutual spiritual enrichment against what is viewed as the march of modernity and postmodernity toward a world wherein God as the sacred is dethroned or confined to the margins of human life. Dealing with the negative impact of Western education, Martin Lings, for example, argues that one needs to teach "as far as possible, the whole truth, which would mean teaching many truths that were not taught in better times, for the needs of the eleventh hour are not the same as those of the sixth and seventh hour" (Lings 1988, 34). The extent of the acceptance of otherness is also reflected in Lings when he argues that a sense of the glory of God is one of the main objectives of religion: "For those who are not prepared to sacrifice that glory to human prejudices it has become abundantly clear that none of the so-called world religions can have been intended by Providence to establish itself over the whole globe" (ibid., 63-64).

THE OTHER AS SELF AND COMRADE

All of the forms of engagement cited above avoid any conscious political discourse, and some would preach and work against those who seek some political expression of their Islam although they themselves are often players within political situations. In conditions of socioeconomic or gender injustice where abstinence from overt political activity is invoked, this abstinence, willingly or unwillingly, acquires a political character. It serves a political purpose because it usually results in the accruing or maintenance of politico-economic advantages to the "abstaining party" and ruling class. These religious groups thus lose their "spiritual disinterestedness" and become an intrinsic part of the dominant political/ideological discourse. In the words of Kuzmic, "To be indifferent to the way in which social life is ordered is, in fact, to take sides—to take sides with tyranny and reaction, since these social evils feed on the indifference of ordinary folk and count on it for their continuing existence" (Kuzmic 1985, 153).

Beyond a Disengaged Pluralism

I now turn to the problem of disengaged pluralism before proposing a path of engagement with the other that not only nurtures the intellectual potential of the participants but also seeks to discover the humanity of all within the context of a broader struggle to create a more humane world.

We live in a world where individuals are less and less formed by the wealth of their traditions and their own cultures. Rather, it is one where the Market is so pervasive that all of our so-called freedom of choice is steered into particular directions—all of them ultimately serving the Market and impoverishing the human spirit. While one must guard against essentializing any community and culture, even more so against glossing over the multifarious injustices, ranging from xenophobia to homophobia, often intrinsic to these, the truth is that globalization and the celebration of individual liberty are not ideologically neutral. For me, as a Muslim theologian, this represents the single most significant ideological and spiritual difficulty. I can only truly be who I am in my unceasing transforming self within the context of personal freedom. In today's world this freedom is intrinsically connected to all the ideological baggage of the modern industrial state along with the "CocaColanization" of global consciousness through a process of relentless "McDonaldization." In other words, my freedom has been acquired within the bosom of capitalism, along with all of its hegemonic designs over my equally valued cultural and religious traditions.

While many "enlightened" Muslims find Deedat's video-cassette peddling embarrassing, or door-knocking by the Tablighi Jama'ah irritating, there is little awareness that the proselytization of the global "*Taliban*" of the Market is every millimeter as ruthless, tenacious, and dogged as its Afghanistan counterpart. Thus I am afraid of the other which, for me, is not another community or other individuals but one which has entered my consciousness, the intangible and faceless Market, my eternal companion in my back pocket in the form of my credit cards.

The dominant public Muslim discourse, of course, rather simplistically reduces this problem to Islam versus the West, or Muslims versus Christians and Jews. The underlying assumption in this defensive posturing is that the other is "the enemy." In *Qur'an, Liberation and Pluralism* I have argued that for those who struggle to survive on the margins of society, living under the yoke of oppression and struggling with those from other religions who are equally oppressed in the hope of liberation, a pluralism of splendid intellectual neutrality or gentle coexistence within unjust socioeconomic or personal relationships is not a dignified option. We need to ask what causes are being advanced by our commitment to pluralism and shared existence.

When "objective" scholars fail or refuse to recognize that all of human responses and refusals to respond are located within a sociopolitical context, then "understanding" and "living together" de facto become extensions of the dominant ideological status quo. When such a status quo is characterized by injustice and exploitation, the reduction of people to commodities and death by starvation and overconsumption, then the pursuit of understanding is itself reduced to cooption to strengthen the overall ideological framework of the powerful. I am thus arguing for a theological and concrete engagement with the other which recognizes the intrinsic human worth of each person and takes place within the context of a struggle to transform our world into a more just one.

The nature of the world wherein we live today and the potency of our weapons of destruction mean that the fate of all of humankind is irretrievably interwoven. There is no selective existence for any particular community. The cake of humankind is beyond unbaking; we cannot now separate the sugar from the flour or the water. We sink or swim together. For people committed to the noblest in their religious heritage though, the question is not merely one of the survival of our own. Today the survival of the self depends on the survival of the other, as much as the survival of the human race depends on the survival of the ecosystem. We have gone beyond "no man is an island unto himself" to "no entity is an island unto itself." A vague and sentimental sense of attachment to the clan is not going to see us through the turbulent future of a world threatened by the gradual reemergence of Nazism, environmental devastation, a triumphalist New World Order based on the economic exploitation of the Two-Thirds World, a world where women continue to just survive on the margins of dignity.

There are many ways of dying. There is, however, only one way to live: through discovering what the self and other and their ever-changing nature are really about, to understand how much of the other is really reflected in us, and to find out what it is that we have in common in the struggle to attain a world of justice and dignity for all the inhabitants of the earth. To do so requires transcending theological categories of self and other that were shaped in and intended for another era and context.

BEYOND THE PEOPLE OF THE BOOK

Early in this chapter I referred to the preference that Muslims have for either converting or conversing with the People of the Book. The tension in the religious-ideological relationship between the Muslims and the People of the Book was inevitable from the dawn of Islam. The Qur'an claimed an affinity with scriptural tradition and furthermore claimed to be its guardian. An unwelcome response was inevitable on the part of those who claimed their own scripture to be legitimate and final. Much of the Qur'an's attention to the other is, therefore, devoted to this tension.

There are several reasons for the preoccupation with this category. First, since most of the *mushrikun* (literally "associanists," i.e., the "pagans" who associated other deities with God) converted to Islam after the liberation of Mecca (A.D. 630), at the earliest stages of its history, Jews and Christians were essentially the communities that Muslims and their jurisprudence had to deal with. Second, the historical encounter over territory (both ideological and geographical) was largely between Muslims and Christians. Third, in the modern period, as Muslims are struggling to overcome the divisions of the past and to find avenues of coexisting and cooperating with those of other faiths, they find it theologically easier to focus on a category which the Qur'an seems to have some sympathy with. Fourth, the present preeminence of the Western world—itself a product of a predominantly Christian and, to a lesser extent, Jewish heritage—in the fields of technology, science, and politics requires some Muslim focus on relations with the People of the Book, even if only as one way of coming to terms with the fact of this preeminence or domination.

There are a number of problems in focusing on the People of the Book as a distinct contemporary religious group in the belief that this is the same referent as that in the Qur'an. The Qur'anic position toward the People of the Book, and even its understanding as to who constitutes the People of the Book, went through several phases. There is, however, agreement that the term has always applied to the Jews and/or Christians whom Muhammad encountered during his mission. The Qur'an naturally dealt only with the behavior and beliefs of those of the People of the Book with whom the early Muslim community were in actual social contact.

To employ the Qur'anic category of People of the Book in a generalized manner of simplistic identification of all Jews and Christians in contemporary society is to avoid the historical realities of Medinan society, as well as the theological diversity among both earlier and contemporary Christians and Jews. To avoid this unjust generalization, therefore, requires a clear idea of the sources of beliefs, as well as their many nuances, which characterized the various communities encountered by the early Muslims. Given the paucity of such extra-Qur'anic knowledge, one would either have to abandon the search for a group with corresponding dogma today or shift one's focus to an area of practice and attitudes rather than dogma.

In practice, the latter option has always been exercised. In none of the disciplines of exegesis, Islamic history, and/or legal scholarship have Muslims known anything approximating consensus about the identity of the People of the Book. There was even disagreement as to which specific groups of Christians and Jews made up the People of the Book. At various times, Hindus, Buddhists, Zoroastrians, Magians, and Sabeans were included among or excluded from the People of the Book, depending on the theological predilections of the Muslim scholars and, perhaps more important, the geopolitical context in which they lived. In all of these attempts to extend the boundaries of the Qur'anic People of the Book, Muslim scholars implicitly acknowledged the situation-boundedness of the Qur'anic categories.

A recognition of the need of solidarity of all oppressed people in an unjust and exploitative society requires going beyond the situation-bound categories of the Qur'an. I do not wish to suggest that there are no Christians who, for example, believe in the concept of a triune deity. Justice, however, requires that no one be held captive to categories which applied to a community or individuals fourteen centuries ago merely because they share a common descriptive term, a term which may even have been imposed on them by Muslims and rejected by them. "These are a people who have passed on. They have what they earned and you shall have what you have earned" (Qur'an 2:141).

There is another significant reason why the category of People of the Book should be regarded as of dubious relevance in our world today. In the context of the political and technological power exercised by the Judeo-Christian world on the one hand, and Arab monetary wealth on the other, Muslim rapprochement with that world, based on the simplistic analogy that Jews and Christians are the contemporary People of the Book, could easily, and probably correctly, be construed as an alliance of the powerful. A Qur'anic hermeneutic concerned with interreligious solidarity against injustice would seek to avoid such alliances and would rather opt for more inclusive categories which would, for example, embrace the dispossessed of the Fourth World.

This rethinking also has to extend to another category the Qur'an particularly singles out for demonization, the *mushrikun*. Initially referring to the Meccans who revered physical objects such as sculptures or heavenly bodies as religiously sacred entities worthy of obeisance, the term *mushrikun* was also employed by some Muslim jurists to refer to the People of the Book. Two factors led to an early recognition that all *mushrikun* are not the same and were not to be treated equally:

1. the Qur'anic accusation of *shirk* (unbelief) against the People of the Book (e.g., Qur'an 9:31), while simultaneously regarding them as distinct from the *mushrikun;* and

2. the subsequent wider Muslim contact with the world of non-Islam.

Later, as the *Shorter Encyclopedia of Islam* observes, in the course of the dogmatic development of Islam, the conception of *shirk* received a considerable extension "[because] the adherents of many sects had no compunction about reproaching their Muslim opponents with *shirk*, as soon as they saw in them any obscuring of monotheism, although only in some particular respect emphasized by themselves." *Shirk* has thus become no longer simply a term for unbelief prevailing outside of Islam, but a reproach hurled by one Muslim against another inside of Islam (*Shorter Encyclopedia of Islam* 1974, 542-44). As with the category of the People of the Book, here too one finds that the actual application of the neat divisions has been far more problematic than most traditional scholars are wont to admit. There is evidently a need to rethink these categories and their contemporary applicability or otherwise. It is now more apparent than ever that the religious situation of humankind and the sociopolitical ramifications thereof are far more complex than previously understood. The following are but a few indications of this complexity:

- the emergence of the new religious movements where, in some cases, people claim to be both Christians and pagans, or Buddhist and Hindu Catholics, in Japan and India respectively;

- the situation in large parts of Asia, Australia, Latin America, and Africa where people combine a commitment to Islam, Christianity, and even Judaism with other traditional "pagan" practices, such as the veneration of graves, sacred relics, and invoking deceased ancestors for spiritual blessings or material gain; and

- the systematic use of formal and institutional religion in the aforementioned areas to oppress, exploit, and even eliminate entire nations among the indigenous people; in these situations, the marginalized and oppressed have often resorted to their ancient religions as a means of asserting their human dignity.

Like *tawhid* (divine unity), *shirk* had its socioeconomic implications in Meccan society, and one needs to retain a sense of this in a contemporary consideration of the believers in *tawhid* and *mushrikun*. Referring to the early Qur'anic texts, Fazlur Rahman has argued that they can only be understood against their Meccan background, "as a reaction against Meccan pagan idol-worship and the great socioeconomic disparity between mercantile aristoc-racy of Mecca and a large body of its distressed and disenfranchised popula-tion." "Both of these aspects," he says "are so heavily emphasized in the Qur'an that they must have been organically connected with each other" (Rahman 1982, 1).

THE QUR'AN AND THE OTHER

The Qur'an presents a universal and inclusivist perspective of a divine being who responds to the sincerity and commitment of all His servants. Flowing from this, two questions arise: First, how does traditional Qur'anic interpreta-tion present a parochial image of a deity which does not differ from that pos-tulated by the Medinan Jews and Christians and denounced in the Qur'an, an image of a deity who belongs to a small group of people and who, having chosen His favorites, turns a blind eye to the sincere spiritual and social com-mitments of all others outside this circle? Second, how does the universality of the Qur'an's message relate to the exclusivism and virulent denunciation of the other, indeed, even its exhortation to wage an armed struggle against the other?

While the context of individual verses dealing with the other are often care-fully recorded by the earlier interpreters, they do not show any understanding of the overall historical context of a particular revelation. The task of shed-ding historical light on various texts has until recently been primarily the do-main of non-Muslim scholars. Muslim reluctance to deal with the question of contextualization beyond the search for an isolated occasion of revelation has led to a generalized denunciation of the other, irrespective of the sociohistorical context of the texts used in support of such rejection and damnation.

The Qur'anic position toward the other unfolded gradually in terms of var-ied responses to the message of Islam and to the prophetic presence. Any view to the contrary would invariably lead to the conclusion that the Qur'an pre-sents a confused and contradictory view of the other. The idea of the gradual and contextual development of the Qur'anic position toward the other has significant implications. First, one cannot speak of a "final Qur'anic position" toward the other, and second, it is wrong to apply texts of opprobrium in a universal manner to all those whom one chooses to define as "People of the Book," "disbelievers," etc. in an ahistorical fashion.

Beliefs and behavior are not genetic elements, such as the color of one's eyes, in supposedly homogeneous and unchanging communities. It is to guard against the injustices of such generalizations that texts of opprobrium refer-ring to other religious communities or the associationists are usually followed or preceded by exceptions (e.g., Qur'an 3:75). Furthermore, qualifying or ex-ceptive expressions such as "from among them" (Qur'an 3:75), "many among them" (Qur'an 2:109; 5:66; 22:17; 57:26), "most of them" (Qur'an 2:105; 7:102; 10:36), "some of them" (Qur'an 2:145), and "a group among them"

(Qur'an 3:78) are routinely used throughout the Qur'anic discourse on the other.

The Qur'an provides only the basis for the attitude of Muslims at any given time toward the other. The Qur'anic position, in turn, was largely shaped by the varying responses of the different components which comprised the other to the struggle for the establishment of an order based on divine unity (*tawhid*), justice, and Islam. More often than not, these responses assumed concrete political form in decisions to side with the Muslim community or against it. Much of the Qur'anic opprobrium is directed at the way doctrine was used to justify exploitative practices and tribal chauvinism. It was not as if the Qur'an avoided the discourse on power or denounced the exercise of political power; it was concerned about whom political power served and who suffered as a consequence of it.

The Qur'an, in general religious terms, refers to various groups or types of people by various expressions, of which the following are the most frequent: "mu'minun," "righteous," "muslimun," "People of the Book," "Jews," "Christians," "associanists," "kafirun/kuffar," and "munafiqun." I want to make some brief observations about the Qur'anic use of these terms before I examine the context of its attitude toward the other.

1. The terms usually used in translation are often, at best, approximations of their Arabic meanings. The Qur'an, for example, does not use the equivalent of the words *non-Muslim* or *unbeliever*; yet these are the most common English renderings of "kafirun/kuffar" in both the process of translation and internal usage within the Arabic language.

2. Some of these terms are frequently used interchangeably in the Qur'an, such as *mu'minun* (literally, "the convinced ones") and *muslimun* (literally, "submitters"), or "People of the Book" and "Christians" or "Jews." It is essential to maintain the Qur'anic distinction in their various uses in order to avoid a generalized and unjust rubbishing of the other.

3. In addition to these nouns, the Qur'an also employs descriptive phrases, such as "alladhina amanu" (literally, "those who are convinced") instead of "mu'minun," and "alladhina kaffaru" (literally, "those who deny/reject/are ungrateful") instead of "kafirun" (literally, "deniers"/ "rejecters"/"ingrates"). These descriptive phrases express specific nuances in the text and indicate a particular level of faith conviction or of denial/ rejection/ingratitude in much the same way as "one who writes poetry" has a different nuance from "poet."

4. References to these groups are occasionally to a specific community within a historical setting and, at other times, to a community in a wider sense, transcending one specific situation.

5. Besides the terms of opprobrium, such as *kafir*, *munafiq* (hypocrite), and *mushrik*, the other terms are rarely used in a negative or positive manner without exceptions. While praise or reproach is usually inherent in some of these terms, this is not without exception. Indeed, the Qur'an at times

describes the reprehensible acts committed by some of those from among the Muslim or believing community as "kufr" or "shirk" (Qur'an 39:7).

6. These terms are often used in the sense of an historico-religio-social group, but not always. The hypocrites and righteous were invariably referred to as individuals, and the term *Muslim* and its various forms, for example, are also frequently invoked to refer to the characteristic of submission in an individual, group, or even an inanimate object.

The Qur'an's general attitude toward the other, which underpins the more specific injunctions and doctrinal issues that it raises from time to time, is based on a number of fundamental principles.

First, the Qur'an relates dogma to socioeconomic exploitation and insists on connecting orthodoxy with orthopraxis. This is equally applicable to the communities and individuals, in Mecca as well as Medina, who rejected the Prophet's message of *tawhid* and social justice. The Qur'an makes it clear that it was both the rejection and ignorance of *tawhid* that led to social and economic oppression in Meccan society (e.g., Qur'an 83:1-11, 102:1-4, 104).

Chapter 90 asserts that a denial of the presence of an all-powerful God causes people to squander their wealth. "Does he think that no one has power over him? He will say: I have spent abundant wealth" (Qur'an 90:5-6). Furthermore, this chapter links faith to an active social conscience: "to free a slave," "to feed on a day of hunger," and "to exhort one another to perseverance and to mercy" (Qur'an 90:13-15). By implication, it also links *kufr* to the refusal to display mercy toward others. In this text, those who reject "the signs of Allah" are those whose actions do not correspond with the ones who have chosen to "ascend the steep path." The rejecters of "the signs of Allah" deny mercy and compassion. This linking of the rejection of Allah and *din* (Islam) to the denial of mercy and compassion is even more explicit in chapter 107.

> Have you observed the one who belies *al-din*?
>
> That is the one who is unkind to the orphan,
> and urges not the feeding of the needy.
>
> So, woe to the praying ones,
> who are unmindful of their prayer;
>
> They do good to be seen,
> and refrain from acts of kindnesses.

The texts of *opprobrium* revealed in Medina, which relate to the various Jewish and Christian communities and individuals encountered there by the Prophet and the early Muslims, reveal a similar relationship between "erroneous" beliefs and the socioeconomic exploitation of others. Equally significant is the fact that, although the Jews were closer to Muslims in creed, the Qur'an often reserves the severest denunciation for some of them. Similarly, the Sabeans were widely believed to have worshiped stars, even angels, yet they were included among the People of the Book (Razi 1990, 3, 112-13). According to the Qur'an, the Jews and Christians justified their exploitation of their own people by claiming that their scriptures permitted such practices. The Qur'an denounced this exploitation of the ignorance of ordinary illiterate people who had no "real knowledge of the Scriptures" (Qur'an 2:78) by the priests of the People of the Book. The contempt for and exploitation of the marginalized by some of the People of the Book are further seen in their justification that they had no moral obligation to be just toward the illiterate (Qur'an 3:75). This text is followed by a denunciation of those who "barter away their bond with Allah and their pledges for a trifling gain" (Qur'an 3:77), and of "a section among them who distort their Scripture with their tongues, so as to make you think that it is from the Scripture while it is not" (Qur'an 3:79). Thus we see that while their bond and their pledges were with a transcendent God, their crimes were very much about the exploitation of the people of God.

Second, the Qur'an explicitly and unequivocally denounces the narrow religious exclusivism which appears to have characterized the Jewish and Christian communities encountered by Muhammad in Hijaz. The Qur'an is relentless in its denunciation of the arrogance of Jewish religious figures and scathing of the tribal exclusivism which enabled them to treat people outside their community, especially the weak and vulnerable, with contempt. This contempt for other people, the Qur'an suggests, was very much rooted in notions of being the chosen of God. According to the Qur'an, many among the Jews and the Christians believed that they were not like any other people whom Allah had created, that their covenant with Allah had elevated their status with Him, and that they were now the "friends of Allah to the exclusion of other people" (Qur'an 62:6). The Qur'an alleges that they claimed a privileged position with Allah merely by calling themselves Jewish or Christian. In other words, it was a claim based on history, birth, and tribe rather than on praxis and morality. Thus, they claimed to be "the children of Allah and His beloved" (Qur'an 5:18) and "considered themselves pure" (Qur'an 4:48). In response to these notions of inherent "purity," the Qur'an argues, "Nay, but it is Allah who causes whomsoever He wills to grow in purity; and none shall be wronged by even a hair's breadth" (Qur'an 5:49). The same text links these notions of being Allah's favorites to their socioeconomic implications and suggests that this sense of having an exclusive share in Allah's dominion leads to greater unwillingness to share wealth with others: "Have they perchance, a share in Allah's dominion?" the Qur'an asks, and then asserts: "But [if they had] lo, they would not give to other people as much as [would fill] the groove of a date stone!" (Qur'an 4:53).

The Qur'an denounces the claims of some of the People of the Book that the afterlife was only for them and "not for any other people" (Qur'an 2:94, 111), that the fire (of hell) will only touch them "for a limited numbered days" (Qur'an 3:24), and that "clutching at the fleeting good of this world will be forgiven for us" (Qur'an 7:169). The Qur'an, furthermore, takes a rather dim view of the boasts of the Jews and the Christians that their creeds are the only ones of consequence. While the Qur'an does not accuse Christians of claiming to be free of any moral accountability in their behavior toward non-Christians, they too, according to the Qur'an, held that they were the beloved of Allah:

> And they say: "None shall enter paradise unless he be a Jew or a Christian." Those are their vain desires. Say: "Produce your proof if you are truthful." Nay, whoever submits his whole self to Allah and is a doer of good, will get his reward with his Lord; On such shall be no fear nor shall they grieve (Qur'an 5:18).

> And the Jews say the Christians have nothing [credible] to stand on and the Christians say the Jews have nothing to stand on while both recite the Book. Even thus say those who have no knowledge. So Allah will judge between them on the Day of Resurrection in that wherein they differ (Qur'an 2:111-13).

Attempts to appropriate the heritage of Abraham and to make it the property of a particular socioreligious group is also denounced: "It is not belonging to the community of Jews or Christians which leads to guidance, but the straight path of Abraham" (Qur'an 2:135), who "was neither a Jew nor a Christian but an upright person who submitted to Allah" (Qur'an 3:67).

Third, the Qur'an is explicit in its acceptance of religious pluralism. Having derided the petty attempts to appropriate Allah, it is inconceivable that the Qur'an should itself engage in this. The notion that Abraham was not a Jew or a Christian, but "one of us" (i.e., a Muslim) is at variance with the rejection of all exclusivist claims in these texts. For the Qur'anic message to be an alternative one, it had to offer the vision of a God who responds to all of humankind and who acknowledges and responds to the sincerity and righteousness of all believers. The Qur'an, thus, makes it a condition of faith to believe in the genuineness of all revealed religion (Qur'an 2:136; 2:285; 3:84).

The Qur'an acknowledges the de jure legitimacy of all revealed religion in two respects:

1. It takes into account the religious life of separate communities coexisting with Muslims, respecting their laws, social norms, and religious practices.

2. It accepts that the faithful adherents of these religions shall also attain to salvation, and that "no fear shall come upon them neither will they grieve" (Qur'an 2:62).

These two aspects of the Qur'an's attitude toward the other may be described as the cornerstones of its acceptance of religious pluralism. Given the widespread acceptance among the most conservative Muslim of respect for the laws of the other, even if only in theory, and the equally widespread rejection of their salvation, I want to focus on the latter.

The Qur'an specifically recognizes the People of the Book as legitimate socioreligious communities. This recognition was later extended by Muslim scholars to various other religious communities living within the borders of the expanding Islamic domain. The explicit details, restrictions, and application of this recognition throughout the various stages of the prophetic era, and subsequently in Islamic history, point to a significant issue at stake in dealing with the other. The socioreligious requirements of the Muslim community, such as community building and security, rather than the faith convictions, or lack thereof, in these other communities shaped the Qur'an's attitude toward them.

There are a number of indications in the Qur'an of the essential legitimacy of the other. First, the People of the Book, as recipients of divine revelation, were recognized as part of the community. Addressing all the Prophets, the Qur'an says: "And surely this, your community [ummah], is a single community" (Qur'an 23:52). Furthermore, the establishment of a single community with diverse religious expressions was explicit in the Charter of Medina. Second, in two of the most significant social areas, food and marriage, the generosity of the Qur'anic spirit is evident: the food of "those who were given the Book" was declared lawful for the Muslims, and the food of the Muslims lawful for them (Qur'an 5:5). Likewise, Muslim males were permitted to marry "the chaste women of the People of the Book" (Qur'an 5:5). If Muslims were to be allowed to coexist with others in a relationship as intimate as that of marriage, then this seems to indicate quite explicitly that enmity is not to be regarded as the norm in Muslim-other relations. Interestingly, this text mentions the believing women in the same manner as the women of the People of the Book: "[permissible in marriage] are the virtuous women of the believers and the virtuous women of those who received the Scripture before you" (Qur'an 5:5). The restriction of permission for marriage to the women of the People of the Book indicates that this ruling related to the social dynamics of early Muslim society and the need for community cohesion. The fact that most jurists, while agreeing on marriage to women of the People of the Book, who are also the People of Dhimmah, differ as to whether it is permissible if they are from states hostile to Islam, also reflects this point (Al-Tabari 1954, 212-14). Third, in the area of religious law the norms and regulations of the Jews and of the Christians were upheld (Qur'an 5:47) and even enforced by the Prophet when he was called upon to settle disputes among them (Qur'an 5:42-43). Fourth, the sanctity of the religious life of the adherents of other revealed religions is underlined by the fact that the first time permission for the armed struggle was given, it was to ensure the preservation of this sanctity: "But for the fact that God continues to repel some people by means of others, cloisters, churches, synagogues and mosques, [all places] wherein the name of God is mentioned, would be razed to the ground" (Qur'an 22:40).

The Qur'anic recognition of religious pluralism is not only evident from the acceptance of the other as legitimate socioreligious communities, but also from an acceptance of the spirituality of the other and salvation through that otherness. The preservation of the sanctity of the places of worship, alluded to above, was thus not merely in order to preserve the integrity of a multi-religious society in the manner which contemporary states may want to protect places of worship because of the role they play in the culture of a particular people. Rather, it was because it was Allah, a God who represented the ultimate for many of these religions and who is acknowledged to be above the diverse outward expressions of that service, who was being worshiped therein. That there were people in other faiths who sincerely recognized and served Allah is made even more explicit in the following text:

> Not all of them are alike; among them is a group who stand for the right and keep nights reciting the words of Allah and prostrate themselves in adoration before Him. They have faith in Allah and in the Last Day; they enjoin what is good and forbid what is wrong, and vie one with another in good deeds. And those are among the righteous (Qur'an 4:113).

If the Qur'an is to be the word of a just God, as Muslims sincerely believe, then there is no alternative to the recognition of the sincerity and righteous deeds of others and to their recompense on the Day of Requital. Thus, the Qur'an says:

> And of the People of the Book there are those who have faith in Allah and in that which has been revealed to you and in that which has been revealed to them, humbling themselves before Allah, they take not a small price for the messages of Allah. They have their reward with their Lord. Surely Allah is swift to take account (Qur'an 3:198).

> And whatever good they do, they will not be denied it. And Allah knows those who keep their duty (Qur'an 3:112-14).

THE QUR'ANIC RESPONSE TO RELIGIOUS DIVERSITY

The Qur'an regards Muhammad as one of a galaxy of Prophets, some of whom are mentioned specifically in the Qur'an while "others you do not know" (Qur'an 40:78). The same faith, the Qur'an declares, "was enjoined on Noah, Abraham, Moses and Jesus" (Qur'an 42:13): "You are but a warner," the Qur'an tells Muhammad, "and every people has had its guide" (Qur'an 13:08; see also 16:36 and 35:24). The fact that the Qur'an incorporates some of the accounts of the lives of these predecessors of Muhammad and makes it part of its own history is perhaps the most significant reflection of its emphasis on the unity of faith. These Prophets came with identical messages that they preached within the context of the various and differing situations of their people. Basically, they came to reawaken the commitment of people to *tawhid*, to remind them about the ultimate accountability to Allah, and to establish justice. "And for every *ummah* there is a messenger. So when their messenger comes the matter is decided between them with justice, and they will not be wronged" (Qur'an 10:47).

> We have revealed to you the Book with the truth, verifying that which is before it of the Book and a guardian over it. So judge between them by what Allah has revealed and follow not their desires, [turning away] from the truth that has come unto you. For every one of you we have appointed a *shir'ah* and a *minhaj*. And if Allah had pleased, He would have made you a single *ummah*. However, He desires to try you in what He gave you. So vie with one another in virtuous deeds. To Allah you will all return, so that He will inform you of that wherein you differed (Qur'an 5:48).

In a similar vein, it says: "To every community, We appointed acts of devotion, which they observe; so let them not dispute with you in the matter, and call to your Lord. Surely you are on a right guidance" (Qur'an 22:67).

Viewing the deceased adherents of supposedly abrogated *shari'ahs* as the addressees of this text, as many orthodox exegetes are wont to do, dispensed with the need for any detailed discussion on the text itself or its implications for religious pluralism. The traditional interpretations of the text present several difficulties and are evidently inconsistent with both its context and apparent meaning.

These difficulties compel me to choose an alternative inclusivist interpretation.

- The entire Qur'anic discussion, including the preceding sentences of the same verse and the subsequent verse, refers to the relationship between the Prophet as arbitrator and an actual community. The context of this text makes it plain that other religious communities coexisting with the Muslims in Medina are addressed and not an ahistorical community existing in a nonphysical world or in a different historical context.
- The text under discussion says that, upon returning to Allah, "He will inform you of that wherein you differed." If one supposes that this text referred to the pre-Muhammadan communities whose paths are acknowledged as valid, pure, and divinely ordained for a specified period—as the doctrine of supercessionism holds—then there is no question of the Muhammadan community differing from them, nor a need of information regarding the differences.
- The text asks that the response to this diversity be to compete with each other in righteous deeds. Given that any kind of meaningful competition can only be engaged in by contemporaneous communities who share similar advantages or disadvantages, one can only assume that the partners of these Muslims were to be those others who lived alongside them.

In the light of the above, the text can best be understood as follows: Looking at the context, one observes that it comes toward the end of a fairly lengthy discourse on the significance of specific scriptures for specific communities. Qur'an 5:44-45 deals with the Torah, which has "guidance and light," "should not be sold for a trivial price," and those Jews who do not judge by its injunctions are denounced as "ingrates" and "wrongdoers/oppressors." This is followed by Qur'an 5:46-47, which describes the revelations to Jesus Christ in similar terms ("light and guidance and an admonition for those who keep their duty"), and denounces the followers of Christ who do not judge by its standards as "transgressors" (see also Qur'an 7:170). It is at the end of this chronological discourse on the significance and importance of adhering to revealed scripture that the text "To each of you we have given a path and a way" appears. Given this context of recognizing the authenticity of the scriptures of the other, it follows that the text refers to the paths of the other in a similar vein.

As for its meaning, the essence of this text is located in the words *shir'ah* and *minhaj*; both relating to "a path." While paths must be clear, comfortable and scenic, and even at times a part of one's goal, they are never synonymous with it. The word *shari'ah* and its variants appear only three times in the Qur'an; the word Allah approximately three thousand times. Hassan Askari, referring to the question of religious pluralism, asks:

> How may it be that the One and Transcendent, the Creator and Almighty be equated with the form of one religious belief or practice? And if we equate thus, we make a God out of that religion, whereas we are all called upon to say: "There is no deity except God" (Askari 1986, 4).

The text thus means that God has determined a path for all people, both as individuals and as religious communities; and that one should be true to the path determined for oneself. Furthermore, should it be so covered by cobwebs that it is no longer possible for one to move along it, then one is free to choose another of the paths determined by Allah. The purpose is to vie with one another in righteousness toward Allah.

The text cited and discussed above (Qur'an 5:48) is one of two that specifically employ the metaphor of competition. Both appear in a Medinan context of the Prophet engaging the People of the Book. The second one reads as follows:

> And each one has a goal toward which he strives/direction to which he turns [*li kulli wijhah huwa muwalliha*]; so compete with one another in righteous deeds. Wherever you are, Allah will bring you all together. Surely Allah is able to do all things (Qur'an 2:148).

COMPETING IN RIGHTEOUSNESS

The metaphor of competition in righteousness is not regarded seriously in Qur'anic exegesis. The challenge to competition is immediately preceded by a statement on the diversity of religious paths: "And if God had pleased He would have made you a single *ummah*. However He desires to try you in what He gave you. So vie with one another in righteous deeds." Given that this competing in righteousness is between diverse communities, several implications follow: First, righteous deeds which are recognized and rewarded are not the monopoly of any single competitor, as the Qur'an says: "O humankind, We have created you from one male and female. We have made of you tribes and nations so that you may know one another. In the eyes of God, the noblest among you is the one who is most virtuous" (Qur'an 49:13). Second, the judge, God, has to be above the narrow interests of the participants. Third, claims of familiarity with the judge or mere identification with any particular team will not avail the participants. Fourth, the results of any just competition are never foregone conclusions.

The Qur'an makes several references to the theological difficulties of religious pluralism and of *kufr*. If God is One, and if *din* originates with God, why is it that humankind is not truly united in belief? Why do some people persist in rejection when "the truth is clearly distinguished from falsehood" (Qur'an 2:256; 23:90)? Why does God not "will" faith for everyone? These were some of the questions which appear to have vexed Muhammad and the early Muslims. In response to these, several texts urge an attitude of patience and humility; these questions are to be left to God, who will inform humankind about them on the Day of Requital. Other than the text under discussion (Qur'an 5:48), which addresses the people who have a *shir'ah* and *minhaj* saying "unto God you will return, so that he will inform you of that wherein you differed," the following text also conveys the call to patience and humility:

> God is your Lord and our Lord: Unto us our works and unto you your works; let there be no dispute between you and us. God will bring us together and to Him we shall return (Qur'an 42:15; 2:139).

As for those who persist in *kufr*, the Qur'an says:

> If your Lord had willed, all those on earth would have believed together. Would you then compel people to become believers? (Qur'an 10:99).

> If God had so wanted, He could have made them a single people. But He admits whom He wills to His grace and, for the wrongdoers there will be no protector nor helper (Qur'an 42:8).

> Revile not those unto whom they pray besides God, lest they wrongfully revile God through ignorance. Thus, unto every *ummah* have we made their deeds seem fair. Then unto their Lord is their return, and he will tell them what they used to do (Qur'an 6:108).

The Prophetic Responsibility in the Face of Religious Pluralism

If—as I have argued above—the Qur'an acknowledges the fact of religious diversity as the will of God, then a significant question which arises is that of Muhammad's responsibility to the adherents of other faiths. Rahman has correctly described the Qur'anic position regarding this relationship as "somewhat ambiguous" (Rahman 1982, 5). From the Qur'an it would appear as if the fundamental prophetic responsibility was twofold. First, with regard to those who viewed themselves as communities adhering to a divine scripture, it was to challenge them regarding their own commitment to their own traditions and to engage them regarding their deviation from it. Second, with regard to all of humankind, it was to present the Qur'an's own guidance for consideration and acceptance.

There are two ways of approaching this ambiguity:

1. to relate the first responsibility to the second one, for they are not entirely divorced from each other; and
2. to understand the context of different responsibilities and their applicability to specific components of the other at specific junctures in the relationship with the other.

The Qur'anic challenge to the exclusivist claims of the People of the Book has already been dealt with above. At other times various groups and individuals, among the People of the Book in particular, were challenged by Muhammad regarding their rejection of the signs of God (Qur'an 3:70-71; 3:98), their discouraging of others to walk the path of God (Qur'an 3:98-99), and their knowingly covering the truth with falsehood (Qur'an 3:70; 3:98-99).

As for their scriptures, Muhammad—as indicated earlier—was expected to challenge them regarding their commitment to their own scriptures (Qur'an 5:68), their deviation from them, and their distortion of them. Muslim scholarship has largely argued that, given the distortion of the scriptures, nothing in them has remained valid. In dealing with the Qur'anic references to the truth contained in these scriptures and exhortations to the People of the Book to uphold them, they have limited this obedience to the scripture to those texts which putatively predict Muhammad's prophethood. Notwithstanding this recognition of the legitimacy of the other revealed scriptures, Muhammad is still asked to proclaim: "O humankind! I am a Messenger of God unto all of you" (Qur'an 7:158). Muhammad thus had a task of proclaiming and calling in addition to that of challenging (Qur'an 16:125; 22:67).

On the face of it, these seem to be a set of contradictory responsibilities, for if a text is distorted, how can one ask for adherence to it? In the second responsibility, that of inviting, the question arises regarding the purpose of inviting to one's own path if that of the other is also authentic. First, the problem of the authenticity of the text, as against its being distorted and therefore invalid, only arises if one thinks in terms of a singularly homogeneous and unchanging entity called the People of the Book and all Qur'anic references to it divested of contextuality. It has been shown above that this is not the case. The Qur'an itself is silent about the extent and nature of this distortion and castigates "a section of the People of the Book." As indicated earlier, the uniformity of praise or blame for a particular religious group is contrary to the pattern of the Qur'an. It is thus possible that the references to the authenticity of their scriptures refer to those held by the rest. Indeed, even the Qur'anic denunciation of particular doctrinal "errors" is not uniform in tone, indicating thereby either a particular moment in the Muslim encounter with the other or different components of the other with specific nuances to those "errors."

Second, Muhammad's basic responsibility in inviting was to call to God. For some components of the other the response to this call was best fulfilled by a commitment to Islam, thus they were also invited to become Muslims; for others, the call was limited to Islam. The invitation to the delegation of Najran is one such example; after they declined to enter into Islam they were invited to "come to a word equal between us and you that we worship none but God, nor will we take from our ranks anyone as deities" (Qur'an 3:64). The Qur'an, thus, is explicit only about inviting to God and to the "path of God." In the following text, for example, the instruction to invite people to God comes after an affirmation of the diversity of religious paths. Here again one sees the imperative of inviting to God, who is above the diverse paths which emanate from Him.

CONCLUSION: THE PREEMINENCE OF PLURALISM

The basis for the recognition of the other was clearly not the acceptance of reified Islam and Muhammad's prophethood with all its implications, nor was it the absence of any principles. The fact that it was Muhammad and the Muslims who defined the basis of coexistence and who determined which form of submission was appropriate for which community clearly implies a Qur'anic insistence on an ideological leadership role for itself. This was explicit in the Qur'anic approach to relationships with other religious groups. This is a significant departure from the liberal position which equates coexistence and freedom with absolute equality for all. A fundamental question arises here: How is this Qur'anic position compatible with pluralism and justice?

The preeminence of the righteous does not mean a position of a permanently fixed socioreligious superiority for the Muslim community. It was not as if the Muslims as a social entity were superior to the other, for such a position would have placed them and their parochial God in the same category of others who were denounced in the Qur'an for the crimes of arrogance and desiring to appropriate God for a narrow community. There is no reason to suppose that the Qur'anic reprimand to other communities, that they cannot base their claims to superiority on the achievements of their forebearers, should not be applied to the post-Muhammadan Muslim community: "That is a community that is bygone; to them belongs what they earned and to you belong what you earn, and you will not be asked about what they had done" (Qur'an 2:134).

Furthermore, the Qur'an does not regard everyone and all ideas as equal but proceeds from the premise that the idea of inclusiveness is superior to that of exclusiveness. In this sense the advocates of pluralism had to be "above" those who insisted that the religious expressions of others counted for nothing, and that they are the only ones to attain salvation in the same way. The relationship between the inclusivist form of religion and the exclusivist form can be compared to that of a democratic state and fascist political parties, as Askari has cogently argued:

> If a group or party arises which does not agree to the democratic rule and works to overthrow the government of the day by violent means in order to create a fascist social order wherein there is no room for democratic expression and exercise of opinion and power, that group cannot lay claim to those rights enjoined by a democracy (Askari 1986, 328).

Inclusivity was not merely a willingness to let every idea and practice exist. Instead, it was geared toward specific objectives, such as freeing humankind from injustice and servitude to other human beings so that it may be free to worship God. As explained previously, according to the Qur'an the beliefs of non-accountability to God and *shirk* were intrinsically connected to the socio-economic practices of the Arabs. In order to ensure justice for all, it was important for Muhammad and his community to work actively against those beliefs and not accord them a position of equality.

The responsibility of calling humankind to God and to the path of God will thus remain. The task of the present-day Muslim is to discern what this means in every age and every society. Who are to be invited? Who are to be taken as allies in this calling? How does one define the path of God? These are particularly pertinent questions in a society where definitions of self and other are determined by justice and injustice, oppression and liberation, and where the test of one's integrity as a human being dignified by God is determined by the extent of one's commitment to defend that dignity.

BIBLIOGRAPHY

Al-Tabari, Abu Ja'far Muhammad Ibn Farir. 1954. "5 Jami' Al-bayan 'An Ta'wil Ay Al-qur'an," edited by Mahmud Muhammad Shakir, 212-14. Cairo: Mustafa al-Babi al-Halabi, Dar al-Kutub. n.p.

Arkoun, Mohammed. 1988. "The Concept of Authority in Islamic Thought: 'La Hukma illa li-llah,'" in *Islam, State and Society*, edited by K. Ferdinand and M. Mozaffer. London: Curzon Press.

———. 1990. "New Perspectives for a Jewish-Christian-Muslim Dialogue," in *WCRP-Informationen—Weltkonferenz der Religionen für den Frieden* 26 (June). Rundbrief von WCRP, Europa.

Askari, Hassan. 1986. "Christian Mission to Islam: A Muslim Response," *Journal of International Muslim Minority Affairs* 4.

Binder, Leonard. 1988. *Islamic Liberalism: A Critique of Development Ideologies,* 5. Chicago: University of Chicago Press.

Esack, Farid. 1997. *Qu'ran, Liberation and Pluralism.* Oxford: Oneworld.

Ghrab, Sa'ad. 1987. "Islam and Christianity: From Opposition to Dialogue," *Islamo Christiana* 99.

Kuzmic, B. J. 1985. "History and Eschatology: Evangelical Views," *Word and Deed: Evangelism and Social Responsibility* 153. Paternoster.

Lawrence, B. 1989. *The Defenders of God: The Fundamentalist Revolt against the Modern Age.* San Francisco: Harper & Row.

Lings, Martin. 1988. *The Eleventh Hour: The Spiritual Crisis of the Modern World in the Light of Tradition and Prophecy.* Lahore: Sohail Academy.

Martin, E. M., and Scor Appleby, eds. 1991. *Fundamentalism Observed.* Chicago: University of Chicago Press.

Rahman, Fazlur. 1982. "Islam's Attitude towards Judaism," *Muslim World* 1, 5.

Razi, Muhammad Fakhr al-Din al-. 1990. *Tafsir al-Fakhr Al-Razi.* 32 volumes. Mecca: Mahtab al-Tijariyyah.

Segundo, Juan Luis, S.J. 1976. *The Liberation of Theology.* Maryknoll, New York: Orbis Books.

Shorter Encyclopedia of Islam. 1974. s.v. "shirk." Edited on behalf of the Royal Netherlands Academy by H. A. R. Gibb and J. H. Kramer. Third impression. Leiden/ NewYork: E. J. Brill, 542-44.

Tracy, David. 1987. *Plurality and Ambiguity: Hermeneutics, Religion, Hope.* San Francisco: Harper & Row.

4.

CHURCH AND STATE RELATIONS

Western Norms, Muslim Practice,
and the African Experience:
A Comparative Account of Origin and Practice

———————◆———————

Lamin Sanneh

INTRODUCTION

The principle of the separation of church and state, and hence of politics and religion, on which America as a nation was founded, has advanced the struggle for human rights by allowing the separate development of these two spheres, a separation that has produced mutually reinforcing effects. Thomas Jefferson summed it up with his aphorism, "United we stand, divided we fall," by which he meant dividing the sphere of state authority from that of religion, thus setting up a wall of separation between church and state (Koch and Peden 1993). In Jefferson's scheme, uniting church and state would bring ruin to both institutions, although, we should observe, dividing them into mutually antagonistic spheres would be no less damaging. Thus Jefferson may have underestimated the fact that our well-being as human beings demands our flourishing spiritually as well as politically.

As it happens, the original sixteenth- and seventeenth-century Puritan proponents of separation (Miller and Johnson 1963) recognized the importance of religion in a liberal democratic state by conceding an autonomous domain to each of the two spheres. Religion became even more central when, under the pressure of growing pluralism and of democratic liberalism, it was cleansed of its territorial "Christendom" complex and allowed to merge into a culture of choice and moral agency. Territorial "domain" was discarded as framework for organized religion.

This principle of non-territoriality was carried to the New World and eventually enshrined in the American Constitution. However, the assertion in the

Declaration of Independence that all citizens are endowed by their Creator with certain unalienable rights, among which are life, liberty, and the pursuit of happiness, concludes where it did not begin. Life is the Creator's gift, unearned and undeserved, and liberty is of a piece with that, the unconditioned, unqualified abatement of divine omnipotence to give room for human choice and freedom. So far so good. But the pursuit of happiness, a phrase dear to Jefferson, comes as an anticlimax to the Declaration's exalted opening, and in fact falls pretty close to what de Tocqueville suggested about the useful trumping the moral (Tocqueville 1966).[1] Tocqueville is right that happiness is a byproduct rather than an object in its own right. Thus the Constitution's own theocentric logic looks to justice rather than to happiness as sharing the primacy of life and liberty.

SEPARATION NECESSARY BUT INADEQUATE

The subject of separation can be taken in its own right as representing a genuine religious insight that allows for real political innovation. Its use in the American Constitution as the removal from the state of the power to enjoin religion is accompanied by the complementary rule of religion protected from state control. By law, the democratic liberal state may not prescribe religion, but it may not proscribe it either.

However, while the state is excluded from religious exercise, it is implicated in the effects and consequences of religious practice. For example, murder is a crime, not because it threatens the public order (Mafia-style executions can enforce a certain order and deterrence), but because life is sacred. "Thou shalt not kill" as a religious commandment is founded on the divine right of personhood, the same warrant that fostered notions of human rights and minority rights. Thus separation is *necessary* in distinguishing and safeguarding the political rule in public life from the religious end in the moral life, but separation is *inadequate* in grasping the convergence of interests and values at the level of practice. In a liberal democratic state such as the United States, religion has the space to flourish, and as such has had effects, both good and bad, on national life and politics.

A liberal democratic society thus presumes the free exercise of religion as an inalienable right. As the seventeenth-century divines put it, religion that is forced upon individuals becomes an impeachment of God's honor, for a person so compelled ceases to be a fit subject for religious regeneration. Thus did the Baptist leader in the antebellum South petition the Georgia legislature to condemn slavery as a violation of God's law. Said he: "Soul-liberty is the rightful heritage of all God's moral creatures. Not over the religion of the slave has civil authority any power, nor yet has it over that of the citizen" (Raboteau 1978, 195-96). (The irony here is that it was by Federal legislative authority that slavery was ended in the United States.)

In the new ethical scheme so envisaged, freedom would be an act of faith based on spiritual commitment, rather than being just a state concession. Freedom in this notion is self-evident in the sense of being noncontestable as a source-value. Freedom thus shares with the gift of life the quality of divine warrant. Freedom is not ultimately a subject of state sanction but its controlling axiom, because freedom is grounded in the fundamental truth of our original moral freedom, though its expression and effects are practical and social, too.

The operative axiom of liberal jurisprudence that persons who are impaired to the degree that they cannot tell the difference between right and wrong are deemed incompetent to stand trial, and furthermore, that no one may be compelled to testify or to appear before the bar of judgment, as enshrined in the Fifth Amendment, is of a piece with the religious doctrine of the knowledge of good and evil. Thus government is by the consent of citizens with whom political sovereignty lies. Here, too, liberal opinion backs the free exercise of citizen rights. Yet political liberalism is not able to guarantee our freedom and our equality at the same time, because in terms of competition for political or economic goods we are not equal, some having more advantage than others, though from the point of view of the divine law we are all equal before God. Equal citizenship under the law is the application in the public sphere of that theocentric doctrine.

NATURAL-LAW THEORY

The natural-law theory of politics demands not so much our being able to prove the objective truth of its central metaphysical assumptions as our recognizing that striving for perfection invests our actions with a credible but penultimate character, with plenty of room in that striving for differences, contests, and self-restraint. It may be the case today that jurisprudence no longer seeks to deduce fundamental principles from metaphysics, as did the old jurisprudence, but rather seeks to base law and policy on social facts and social operation. Yet modern jurisprudence has not abandoned the notion of separation entirely, even when it advocates a social-activist view of the state. In this sociological view the state is not preoccupied with the individual rights and the moral independence of the believer from state control, things that Puritan doctrine promoted. For, according to the Puritans, the state is not an arbitrary power that is free of all moral constraints. Roger Williams of Rhode Island, for example, insisted that God's commandments are written on the two tablets of conscience and civil obedience, that while both are intended for our well-being, they are not identical and, therefore, should not be confused. On the divine tablet is inscribed our eternal security and on the worldly tablet our political welfare (Ferm 1983, 20-39; Miller and Johnson 1963, 214-25). Accordingly, the separate branches of church and state have a single religious root, and, by extension, a common moral source. This Puritan notion of personal rights was rejected by the new jurisprudence.

However, even though the new jurisprudence sought to overthrow this Puritan scheme of the appeal to rights, it did not jettison the principle of separation, a principle important to limiting state power. Which is the same as saying that the new jurisprudence would take from the visible hand of institutional curbs on state power what it declined from the invisible hand of what Oliver Wendell Holmes Jr. called "a brooding omnipresence in the sky" (Holmes 1938; Lerner 1989). The religious habit would thus have conditioned the state to accede to norms of self-restraint until the time came for these norms to be based on public reason. Clearly, religion had laid the foundation of a bulwark against state tyranny.

In any case, while sociological theories of the state, such as those of Louis Brandeis, Roscoe Pound (Pound 1921; 1938; 1942; Kelsen 1945), and Oliver Wendell Holmes, would wish to free the state of a higher law of nature on the grounds that that restricts the power of government, those theories would resort to other checks and balances, such as separation of powers or the balancing effects of competitive social and political interests, to limit state power. Pound and Holmes, for example, reduced Puritan effusions on rights and freedom to nothing more than a pious attempt by prudes to stop pigs from putting their feet in the trough. Yet with those natural-law safeguards removed, the state would be left unchecked in its despotic power. Holmes thus proposes sterilizing those considered socially unfit and economically burdensome, in other words, those considered politically intolerable, all this on the pretext that freedom is not absolute but relative. It is hard to see how the state itself cannot but be imperiled by this teaching.

Natural theology establishes a similar safeguard for religion, so that objective merit may accrue to human effort on the grounds of our common humanity rather than by virtue of adherence to any particular creed. Natural theology overlaps with natural-law theory in this important sense: both are designed to avoid the extremism of the right and left at the same time. Natural theology moderates the extreme Puritan notion of an unbridgeable gulf between God and humanity, so that any business with God, and with one another, is conducted ipso facto on contested, sectarian ground. The "other" is the enemy, and God will help in the hunting and containing of the enemy. It is a notion that makes you ask of any institution whether it is of God, in which case you fall down and worship it, or whether it is of "man," in which case you attack and destroy it. Natural theology softens this dialectical extremism by harmonizing the natural sphere, the sphere of public reason, with the religious, the sphere of the moral law, at least in terms of the public interest.

Yet the theological moderation of natural theology is accompanied by the radical religious posture that the whole created order stands within the comprehensive doctrine of the providence and sovereignty of God. For instance, in his reflections on Christianity in the empire, Saint Augustine answers those who claim that the teachings of Christ, being so idealistic and impractical, are inimical to civil law and custom. Turning the other cheek, going the extra mile, not repaying evil for evil, or not taking up arms, the critics charged, may be perfectly sound moral teachings, but they undercut the public interest. Augustine responds that the commonwealth is the repository of the interests of the people, interests that are common to all, including the state. In fact, he insists, the state itself is a community of people united by a bond of agreement. The conduct of public affairs requires more than the rule of efficiency: we need sanctions to restrain evil, norms to produce works of mercy, precepts to guide and direct, warrants to instill and commend virtue, and sacraments to change and transform life.

> Accordingly, let those who say that Christ's teaching is in opposition to the commonwealth give us an army made up of the kind of soldiers Christ's teaching orders them to be, let them give us citizens, husbands and wives, parents and children, masters and servants, rulers, judges, and even tax payers and tax collectors, such as Christian teaching commands them to be, and then let them say that this doctrine is in opposition to the commonwealth! Let them instead not hesitate to confess that— if it were to be obeyed—this teaching would be the salvation of the commonwealth (Saint Augustine 1992, 146).

Even in this Augustinian view, then, separating the natural sphere from revelation does not deny their connection at the level of what is prudent and expedient, or at that of the public good and in matters of personal ethics.

WAR

In few other areas are politics and religion more controversially linked than in the idea and practice of war. This is so, in part because war deals with both political method and moral end, with effects as much as with source, and thus pushes at the wall of separation between church and state, and in part also because war as such looks beyond individual freedom and rights to national commitment and personal sacrifice, which is the highest moral act. Implicated in war, then, is the ultimate conception of human life, with limited military or political objectives, for instance, begging the moral-source question about the limitless value of human life. Risking your life in devotion or obedience to the state as a contingent worldly instrument evokes a noncontingent moral question. For this reason, the political state can scarcely be indifferent to moral ends when its method in war involves so final and comprehensive a moral act as the taking of human life.

Oliver Wendell Holmes expresses the view that war is the state's weapon to discipline and rehabilitate a heedless and irresponsible modern youth, a view that ends up moralizing the state instrument, transmuting public reason into a moral imperative. The state thus accedes to an exclusive warrant to command our obligation on the questionable basis that the state, without our consent, can claim to know what is best for us. In Holmes's opinion, the state, like the universe, is a blind machine that is indifferent to the fate of men and women. Idealism and sentiment are without public merit and are politically meaningless, which indicates that in war the state may do whatever is necessary to save and protect itself. However, apart from dismissing pacifists and other conscientious objectors, Holmes has no answer for why a belligerent state, facing popular opposition, may yet retreat from war as the great discipliner, or even avoid war, suggesting there are moral constraints on state power that political prudence would come to heed. Holmes embraced the austere Darwinist principle that the struggle for state survival requires and justifies the instruments imperative to success. That comes pretty close to the Hobbesian doctrine that compacts without the sword are but mere words. All of that would transform the state into a combative superstructure and society into a battlefield. It would be a setback for freedom, justice, and pluralism.

COMMON SECURITY

State encroachment on the moral sphere thus has in certain circumstances provoked religious activism in response with the aim of capturing the state instrument to serve the truth-claims of religion. A combative secular state thus evokes its religious doublet. In the theocratic contest for state takeover there is implied not a weakening of the state but its growing supremacy, with religion seeking to anoint it for its own end. Theocracy is still statism exalted. Instead of fostering the sharing of a common security interest, a theocratic reaction to state fundamentalism reproduces on the right a perfect replica of its secular foe on the left. It comes to the same thing whether the state instrument serves religious truth-claims, or religious truth-claims serve the state. In these circumstances, the religious reaction produces results that are no better or worse than those of state encroachment on the moral sphere. Moralization of political ends comes to the same thing as the politicization of moral truth. In either case the principle of separation is destroyed. The sword of the magistrate that is supposed to rule only in the outward sphere would now acquire a twin blade to rule in the inward sphere as well. State jurisdiction would now extend over the temporal as well as the spiritual domain, with political tyranny a common fate.

The cautionary lesson here is that a left-wing secular fundamentalism begets its nemesis in a right-wing religious fundamentalism, a situation that results in the effective dismantling of separation. The alternative to such extremism and its undesirable consequences is recognizing that politics and religion do overlap, that truth-claims and political values do converge, and that such convergence need not result in the denial of the rule of functional separation. Thus qualified separation is necessary to maintaining the separate spheres of the outward and inward jurisdiction, so that political method may advance the moral end, and vice versa, without the moral and political becoming wholly identical with each other. Accordingly, rules of procedure need not become matters of substance, for we know that laws may be effective without their being necessarily just, that technically sound laws may abort the ends of honor and fair play. As was first expressed in the promulgation of Pope Gelasius I (492-96), the divine and the temporal are two interdependent ends, with church and state "each equal to the other when acting in its own sphere, and each equally dependent on the other when acting in the sphere of the other."

The way forward, then, between politics and religion lies in preserving their common security zone. It involves a fine balancing act in which the state is not so out of step with the church, neither so far ahead in terms of a messianic state, nor so far behind in terms of prescriptive atheism, that it provokes strategic intransigence as the risk in every political action, leaving the state with coercion and repression as its signature tools. By the same token, the state should not become so identical with religion that political acts assume the status of moral dogma. Moderate versions of separation, then, tailored to suit different situations, would be required to prevent all conflict and disagreement from becoming a fight to the finish, with politics and religion each other's hostage. Some such mildly prescriptive rule would need to accompany all meaningful struggle for human rights.

THE GLOBAL SCENE

In a good deal of global political and religious turmoil and unrest, the secular role of religion has remained a burning issue for religions of the left and right equally. The future of religions in a world energized by newfound freedoms and marked by growing pluralism is fundamentally bound up with the issue of freedom and choice, and that in turn is connected with separation, however we define it. Therefore, any effective understanding or any long-lasting solution to the struggle for human rights and personal dignity requires attention to the relation of politics and religion, in particular to how areas of overlap between the two centers of life do not become grounds for mutual hostility or collusion. The issue is not whether proselytization and tolerance, for example, are compatible or in conflict, but whether tolerance is meaningful at all in the absence of religion, suggesting that tolerance is a function itself of religious freedom. We may express the issue thus: religion is important and comprehensive enough for it not to overlap with politics, but it is too important and comprehensive for politics to coopt it. As Alexis de Tocqueville hinted, government by habit prefers the useful to the moral and will, if tempted, require the moral to be useful. The otherwise religiously based argument that freedom to believe in God belongs with the truth-claim of God's design for human well-being turns out to have public rationale for the democratic liberal enterprise, i.e., a free environment marked by political and moral choice.

In any event, the liberal democratic enterprise as such is constrained to promote a certain secular worldview, say, a Lockean or a Jeffersonian liberalism, as its own precondition, and demand universal acceptance. Yet to speak of universal acceptance, to speak of a general, impartial allegiance in a diverse, pluralist society, is to make an objective natural-law claim about the political community as the moral community, even if the political is not synonymous with the moral. Such a view is expressed, say, in the Miltonian doctrine of men and women having been "created in the image and resemblance of God." As Jefferson himself testified: "I have no fear but that the result of our experiment will be that men may be trusted to govern themselves without a master. Could the contrary of this be proved, I should conclude either there is no God or that he is a malevolent being" (Dewey 1989, 125). The religious premise, invoked in that statement and defended by John Dewey no less, is necessary to the liberal democratic enterprise, even if from a position of separation.

The political expression of this separation is thus important for religion, too, largely because religion is its source. The state is not its own orthodoxy, and the church exists as public safeguard of that truth. Religion thus offers a longer-range view of our interest than the goals of political organization. The liberal democratic enterprise and the religious vocation under this conception run on a parallel but unequal course, leading to church and state being independent of each other in their own spheres, but interdependent when each acts in the sphere of the other.

It turns out that this independence of church and state has in America and elsewhere been extremely fruitful for conceiving a society of diverse, plural interests and pursuits, and is at the same time well designed to elevate human rights to the center of politics where the state is constrained by the higher law, the law that says that state authority is subordinate to the general ethical norms of human rights, freedom, and justice. As such, separation could scarcely be confined to American shores, and so in time the idea, or some forms of it, was carried into other societies and cultures where it produced new currents of thought and the framework for political and religious action and reaction. Church-state separation has been an indispensable safeguard for personal freedom as well as being one of the most crucial factors behind the rise (and crisis) of national secular states in non-Western societies.

MUSLIM AFRICA:
RELIGION AND THE LIMITS OF STATE POWER

In leaving now questions of origin, we should point out that even before the rise of the modern national secular state in the West there was debate in other parts of the world about how religious masters and political leaders should respect each other's sphere of authority, and what the implication might be of practice in one sphere for the other sphere. It happens that some of this debate about practice took place in Muslim Africa long before the advent of European colonialism. Consequently, it would be useful to look at historical aspects of such debate to discover how contemporary figures in pre-colonial Africa tackled issues in church-state relations, and, indirectly, what the significance may be for issues we face today.

KINGS AND CLERICS

One example, relating to a twelfth-century incident, comes from the seventeenth-century chronicle *Ta'ríkh al-Súdán* by 'Abd al-Rahmán al-Sa'dí. The ruler of the ancient Sudanic city of Jenne, Kanbara, decided one day to embrace Islam. He summoned into his presence all the leading scholars of the city, numbering above forty-two hundred. In their midst he relinquished traditional religious worship and adopted Islam, and, almost as a bargain, promptly put three requests before them. First, that any one coming to Jenne to seek refuge might find in the city ease and abundance and might as a consequence forget his former country. Second, that foreigners might flock to Jenne as their home and their numbers outstrip the original inhabitants. Finally, that merchants traveling to the city might lose patience with conditions prevailing there and, eager to leave it, might be compelled to dispose of their merchandise at derisory prices, to the benefit of the inhabitants.

The difficulty of this threefold request might be seen not so much in its range of demands as in how the first appeal to hospitality and the last appeal for a glut could be reconciled. In any case, the congregation concluded the meeting with a recitation of the *Fátihah* as a prayer seal. The chronicler was in no doubt that the requests were granted, his own patriotic faith standing to be vindicated. Following this public conversion of the king and as a sign of his good faith his royal palace *(dár al-sultánah)*, perhaps more the locus of the imperial cult, was demolished and a community mosque raised on the site. A second edifice, most likely the residence of the new religious functionaries, was constructed adjacent to the mosque (*al-Súdán* 1964, 12-14).

The account portrays Islam as having been in long contention with traditional worship and eventually establishing its sway over well-charted religious territory. Instead of creating a fresh power base, Islam merely occupied the space and status vacated by its rival. What part internal or material factors played in the disintegration of the old religion is a matter for debate, but that Islam arrived on the scene quietly, without the drama of military confrontation and state intervention, is self-evident. Indeed, the prayer technique employed to confirm Islam in the city is a replica of the role traditional worship has played. Like the account of al-Bakrí, al-Sa'dí's story resonates with the strong commercial ethos of the town, and while it would be extreme to suggest it was produced to promote the commercial interests of the town, we would be gullible to ignore that motive altogether. Even at the minimum, commercial calculations might not be entirely absent from the motivations of the ruler, and it would be natural that he would wish his capital to become the nerve center of regional trade. Nevertheless, when it is all said and done, we must include in our explanation the stress in the account on the role of the clerics in setting the religious pace for the town, though in so doing they kept a safe distance from political authority.

Another example, still on Islamic influence on rulers, comes from ancient Mali and is given by Mahmúd al-Ka'ti in his book, the *Ta'ríkh al-Fattásh*. The local Muslim clerics founded a settlement on the Bafing River called Diakhaba, which acquired immense stature as a clerical missionary center dedicated to the spread and practice of Islam. So powerful was this clerical tradition that the ruler of Mali was banned from entering it except once a year, on the 27th Ramadan, when, as the deferential guest of the *qádí*, the chief judge and also the city's highest official, the king undertakes certain religious obligations. He arranges for meal offerings to be prepared. He places these in a large bowl, which he carries on his head. Calling together Qur'an students and little boys, he distributes the food from his head in a standing position. After consuming the food, the pupils call down blessings on the king as a concluding act. The *Ta'ríkh al-Fattásh* says that Diakhaba ('Ja'ba') remained an impregnable clerical stronghold, so that even those who were guilty of acts of hostility against the king could claim inviolable sanctuary within its borders. It continues: "They gave it the epithet, 'the city of God—*yaqál lahu balad Alláh*'" (al-Ka'ti 1964, 179). The phrase "city of God" enshrines a fundamental, explicit principle; namely, the repudiation of religion as a state construct, and of the state as a religious construct.

Although clearly possessing extraordinary authority as a religious missionary center, Diakhaba was by no means atypical. A similar arrangement existed in Gunjúr, another clerical center founded by emigrants from Diakhaba. There also power was exercised by the *qádí*, to whom the ruler, residing in a different place, paid his respects in his annual religious retreat to the center. Both places were founded by a West African clerical clan, the Jakhanke (Sanneh 1976b, 49-72), whose religious life and practice I have described in another work (Sanneh 1976a).

This account of the *Ta'ríkh al-Fattásh* introduces many novel features about clerical Islam which need not detain us here. Some obvious parallels with the preceding examples stand out: the town was an important nexus on the trading artery of the river trading system; and its organized religious hierarchy made it appropriate for the king to visit it, and on terms, too, that suited the resident clerics. Something of the peaceful reputation of the settlement assured it kingly attention, if not protection. War, or Ibn Khaldún's "power of wrathfulness," seems to play an insignificant role in all the accounts. That is to say, at the point of religious change there seems little indication of military upheaval or dramatic violent change. The role of Africans as recipients and missionary agents of Islam is similarly underlined. Finally, Islam appears as a less self-secure religion, pursuing a defensive course alongside traditional worship until it is able sufficiently to undermine it from within and eventually to replace it. That a ruler takes on the mien of a humble pilgrim and, in an unregal balancing posture, looks to the prayers of young innocents for his earthly and heavenly security smacks too much of local genius to need a theory of external intervention. The original model for this practice must be lodged deep in the bosom of the African religious environment, in particular, in its sacramental ethos of channels of grace.

Another example, also from the *Ta'ríkh al-Fattásh,* spotlights the importance of the cleric vis-à-vis the political magistrate. The present example improves on earlier ones by giving the cleric the upper hand in a confrontation with the ruler. After many attempts to assert his authority over Timbuktu, Askiya Muhammad Turé, king of Songhay, visited the city in person and summons the *qádí,* Mahmúd b. 'Umar, to an audience. In the ensuing discussion the *askiya* demanded to know why the *qádí* had resisted his orders and turned away his message-bearers. After a flurry of short questions and answers between the two of them, the *qádí* explained his conduct in these words:

> Have you forgotten, or are you feigning ignorance, how one day you came to my house and, crawling up to me, you took me by the feet and held on to my garments and said, "I have come so that you may place yourself in safety between me and the fire of damnation. Help me and hold me by the hand lest I stumble into hell fire. I entrust myself in safe-keeping to you"? It is for this reason that I have chased away your message-bearers and resisted your commands (al-Ka'ti 1964, 60-61).

A remarkable position with which the king, more remarkably still, unreservedly concurred. He declared in turn:

> By God, it is true that I have forgotten this, but you have now reminded me and you are absolutely right. By God, you deserve great reward for you have saved me from harm. May God exalt your rank and make you my security against the fire. What I have done has provoked the wrath of the All-Powerful, but I beg His forgiveness and turn in penitence to Him. In spite of what I have done I still invoke your protection and attach myself to you. Confirm me in this position under you and God will confirm you (and through you) defend me (al-Ka'ti 1964, 61).

It is just possible that the chronicler may in this passage be attempting to paint an exaggeratedly pious image of the *askiya,* but if so he is employing a device which shows his royal patron being challenged with impunity by a subordinate official. Unless the story is true, the king stands more to lose by it than to benefit from it. That such an encounter took place, perhaps in less dramatic circumstances, I think we can safely accept. It is credible in the context of the separation of religion from political authority, and it also shows, furthermore, the esteem in which religion is held by Africans, king and commoner alike. In incidents reported by the chronicles, political rulers had a hard time securing the subordination of religious functionaries, as we have already seen. A well-known case involves the king of Songhay, Askiya Da'wúd (reigned 1549-82), who appointed, as was his royal prerogative, the *qádí* of Timbuktu. The official, the revered scholar Muhammad Baghayogho, refused the appointment. The city's leading jurists subsequently interceded with him on the king's behalf, but even that failed to secure the appointment. It is said that the scholar agreed to be *qádí* only after the king threatened to offer the job to an ignoramus! That particular dispute lasted over a year, with the king forced to find a stopgap (al-Sa'dí 1964, 176). In another incident, the king is said to have felt slighted when the prestigious Sankore mosque was being built, because he was not informed. He found out only when the project was nearing completion. Undeterred, he sent a generous donation, which was not turned down as such; only it was not used for the mosque but on repairs to an adjoining cemetery. The king could not have missed the pointed symbolism, that his contribution should be a goodwill offering toward the repose of faithful souls rather than a stake in the affairs of the living lest it become political meddlesomeness.

We may place this kind of case study of local Muslim politics in the larger context of classical Muslim political thought. Thus we may turn to the scholar al-Fakhrí, a hard-nosed student of the science of politics. In his work entitled *Government and Dynasties in Islam* (composed in A.D. 1302) al-Fakhrí gives a detailed discussion of the relationship between political pragmatism and moral prescriptions. He cautions against a simplistic view of power and against facile extrapolation from one domain of human activity to another, say, from success in running a home to success in ruling a realm. A commander of the army does not necessarily make a successful commander of the faithful, and vice versa. The complex nature of politics defies a rule-of-thumb approach. As a ruler was once warned,

> The world is ups and downs. Your gains therein have come to you despite your weakness, your losses therein you could not avoid by your strength. . . . Frequently good "comes out" of evil and evil out of good. This (conception) is taken from the Word of God, "Perhaps a thing which you dislike will be better for you, and a thing you like worse for you; God knows and you know not" (al-Fakhrí 1947, 46-47).

A similar uncertainty obtains over the respective merits of the sword and the pen, of force and persuasion, and how precisely we should order their true relation: Should the sword stand in relation to the pen as a guardian and a servant? What is the right balance between them? People who urge a middle course say that "a realm is fertilized by generosity, populated by justice, secured by commonsense, protected by courage, and administered by leadership" (al-Fakhrí 1947, 47). Accordingly, one should not separate sword and pen.

Al-Fakhrí's account of politics underlines the complex and unpredictable nature of human affairs, a state of affairs that requires compromise, prudence, wisdom, and above all flexibility. In al-Fakhrí's view the nature of politics belongs with living things, growing, changing, reemerging, and adapting like a green plant exposed to the elements. Human motivation is similarly complex, more readily amenable to here-and-now sanctions than to injunctions of the hereafter. Actually, the hereafter lies beyond the competence of the ruler, though its reality may act as a brake on an all-powerful state. Al-Fakhrí gives great prominence to knowledge in his political scheme, knowledge of the elementary rules of politics, certainly, but knowledge also of fundamental moral teachings to prevent the ship of state from drifting in the eddy. Political vigilance is anchored for al-Fakhrí in God's purpose for human life, and he hints in several places at the danger of reducing that purpose to the humdrum terms of crude expedience. When he turns to the person of the ruler, however, al-Fakhrí is at his most Machiavellian, for the end of power as the success and survival of the ruler, he seems to say, justifies the means to achieve that end. Yet the ruler is so dependent on others, so deeply enmeshed in the interlocking net of divergent interests, that the competition that is natural in his realm reduces his freedom to do as he pleases. So al-Fakhrí invokes political realism to argue that the ruler narrow his options, define his goals, conserve his resources, avoid costly entanglements, reward his allies, and, above all, seek wise counsel from the repositories of knowledge. Thus scattered through al-Fakhrí's work are the seeds of that kind of political realism, of the sense that politics is framed by its own terms of reference, and that if, in the light of reality, political rules should not be made absolute and inflexible, they also should not in the light of divine injunctions be made impervious to the transcendent claims of religion.

Al-Fakhrí's extensive discussion, briefly introduced here and supplemented with the historical examples noted, points to the complex relationship between Islam and the state. Certainly this complexity abounds in both precolonial and colonial Africa, where the organized, hierarchical nature of Islam, its structures of mosque, school, prayer, the pilgrimage, and the religious calendar, rendered it appealing for cooption by the state (but not necessarily for takeover) and in turn made the state attractive to Islam. However, in the prevailing conditions of civil society, Islam and the state could not combine without threatening the moral patronage system controlled by the clerics. This clerical power strove to keep its distance from state control, doing so by stressing religious neutrality, and limitation, in secular affairs. It demanded a similar hands-off policy from the state in religious matters.

WAR AND THE ETHICS OF PEACEFUL PERSUASION: MUSLIM SOUNDINGS

In the special field of *jihád*—"holy war," narrowly construed—church and state as symbols of the moral and the expedient are necessarily interconnected, as we pointed out above. The Muslim consideration of this subject is deeply illuminating for the issues with which we are concerned, and we should briefly turn to that now. Thus, in an instructive piece of debate between two Muslim scholars on the need for a theocratic state, we find crucial issues being raised. One of the scholars in question, Muhammad al-Kánemí (d. 1838), the ruler of Kanem-Bornu in West Africa, challenged the *mujáhid* 'Uthmán dan Fodio (d. 1817), with regard to the use of the sword for religious ends. Al-Kánemí said the sword is too rough-and-ready a weapon to use in settling religious questions, especially questions between Muslims themselves, since they would attempt to resolve by force majeure what might be substantial matters of theology, or even only differences of opinion. He insisted that Muslims must either settle for tolerance and mutual acceptance or else unleash a smoldering permanent war that would exempt, in his words, not even "Egypt, Syria and all the cities of Islam . . . in which acts of immorality and disobedience without number have long been committed." "No age and country," al-Kánemí cautioned, "is free from its share of heresy and sin" (Hodgkin 1960, 198ff.), and any inflexible division of the world between *dár al-Islám* and *dár al-harb* would fly in the face of this reality and reduce to ashes all sincere but inadequate attempts at truth and obedience. We could not find revealed truth in the blinding flames of fanaticism fed by short-fused *fatwas*.

It might be appropriate here to recall the words of John Locke about religious triumphalism, for the point he makes is pertinent to the issues raised by al-Kánemí. Let us imagine, Locke argues, Christian missionaries, destitute of everything, arriving in a so-called pagan country and inserting themselves into the society by taking advantage of the kindness and hospitality of their so-called pagan hosts. The new religion then takes root in the country and spreads gradually. While Christians remain a minority they publicly espouse peace, friendship, faith, and justice for all. But at length they grow powerful and achieve substantial victory, with the magistrate of the country converting and becoming a Christian. This fact emboldens the Christians to break all previous accords with the pagans, on whom they turn, requiring them to repudiate their ancient religion and customs on pain of being dispossessed and reduced to servitude. Such a Christian religion, Locke concludes, would be merely "the pretense of religion, and of the care of souls," and would be "a cloak to covetousness, rapine, and ambition" (Locke 1990, 50).

That constructed tableau has an uncanny similarity to the condition of countless communities in Muslim Africa. To take one well-known instance of two hundred years ago, the sarki, or king, of one West African pagan state, Gobir, woke up one day to find his Muslim guests had grown in number and confidence, turned implacably militant, and were threatening his kingdom. They were in no mood for conciliation and concession. He had been too sanguine and rued the day, he said, when he gave friendly sanctuary to Muslims. He later complained to his fellow kings "that he had neglected a small fire in his country until it had spread beyond his power to control. Having failed to extinguish it, it had now burnt him. Let each beware," he lamented, "lest a like calamity befall his town also" (Bello 1957, 131; Trimingham 1962, 199). By then the flames were raging, and Locke is small comfort: the sarki's warning had come too late.

All religious systems are equally vulnerable to the temptations of power, because human instrumentality in the service of revealed truth incites its own contradiction. In that spirit, the preface to *The First Book of Common Prayer* (1549), taking somber stock of what had overtaken a religion trapped in human systems, expresses the sentiment well when it says, "There was never any thing by the wit of man so well devised, or so sure established, which in continuance of time hath not been corrupted." Herein is echoed 'Uthmán dan Fodio's own painful musing in his poem *Wallahi, Wallahi,* where he bemoaned the corruption that had riddled the theocratic reform program he had initiated with the highest public ideals (Hiskett 1971). Religious truth cannot survive this corruption, for believers surrounded by political trophies would become either cynics or Eliot's "hollow men," a social presence without moral consequence. The only reasonable answer is to separate church and state, to desacralize the political instrument while safeguarding religion's independence. It is significant that such issues were discussed in pre-colonial Muslim Africa.

THE COLONIAL LEGACY

The Western colonial encounter with Muslim Africa had a direct impact on the pre-colonial legacy of church-state relations. In general the encounter helped strengthen the Muslim religious and political impulse, either through direct provocation or through conciliation and collaboration. Thus the British invasion of north Nigeria provoked resistance among the guardians of the Muslim theocratic state founded in 1804, forcing the British to use conciliation and concessions to overcome that resistance and to legitimize their power. The British proceeded to cut a deal with Muslim leaders: there would be no undue interference in religious institutions and local customs, but instead the colonial administration would work through those religious structures to govern the people. In effect, Muslims would become partners in the colonial enterprise.

The French colonial policy was a variation of the British. In theory, the French demanded total surrender and commitment from their Muslim subjects, setting up the colonial bureaucratic state to reformulate and regulate Muslim affairs, with military muscle added for demonstrated effect. In practice, however, bureaucratic or military confrontation was too costly a way to achieve permanent subjugation, and so the French decided to invest in the Muslim rosary and the ink pot to reach the hearts of the people. As a result, pious saintly figures were courted and patronized; they were invited to state functions, sent on pilgrimage to Mecca at state expense, and otherwise treated to lavish official blandishments. For another, Muslim learning was endowed; schools supported; colonial administrators trained in Arabic language and literature and in Islamic subjects; Arabic works collected and translated; and libraries furnished with Islamic books, manuscripts, and journals. By thus identifying themselves with Islam's intellectual and educational heritage, the French hoped to earn the lasting gratitude and respect of their Muslim subjects, which in many significant places they were able to do.

Yet it became clear that this policy of colonial reinforcement was contradictory, because the justification of colonial rule as the transmitter of Western enlightenment and progress sat awkwardly with the contrasting logic of the colonial system as the propagator of political Islam. Ultimately, colonial rule would have to abdicate to the Muslim agents it had successfully raised and trained, handing over to them the fruits of power and the machinery of a modern state.

Thus both in the British and French cases the Muslim religious and political impulse was strengthened with the decision to conciliate and reward. A certain identity of interest came to exist between administrators and Muslim leaders, allowing the imperial overlords to press one of two options: either colonial rule could continue through strategic alliance with Muslim structures and institutions, or else it could cease formally through an equally strategic handing over to predisposed Muslim elites.

Insofar as Britain had an official Muslim policy, one colonial authority described it in the 1870s as follows:

> The Mohammedan question is regarded by the Government as one of the most important in the future of West and Central Africa. If Islam is properly understood, if its youth inoculated with British civilization and British ideas are utilized by British administrators and merchants, it will give England a wider and more permanent influence upon the millions of the Soudan than can possibly be wielded by any other agency (Sanneh 1997, 164).

In the particular case of north Nigeria and its large and significant Muslim population, the British targeted the Muslim political elites, the *emírs,* as indispensable to this Islamic policy. The administrators reasoned that "the placing at the disposal of the Emirs of the resources of an ordered State inevitably strengthened and developed all Moslem institutions in Northern Nigeria" (Sanneh 1997, 150).

To repeat: The Western colonial encounter with Muslim Africans strengthened their political resolve and offered them the resources and prestige of an organized modern state. Yet the mixing of religion and politics in that fashion implicates both of them, with religion becoming a tool of control and politics a cover for intolerance. Thus in post-independent states, the explosive issue of joining religion and politics has bedeviled efforts at limiting state power and promoting religious freedom and tolerance of difference.

The central question becomes whether the Muslim religious experience has undergone, or is undergoing, a change similar to the fateful revolution that occurred with Christendom, or whether Muslims in general, and Muslim Africans in particular, are engaged in a massive case of denial and defiance. Did the colonial concordat with Islam merely evade rather than resolve the question of separation? Is the phenomenon widely described as "Islamism," defined as the imposition of religious prescriptions in the sphere of state power, in the last throes of the long reaction to the West, or does it have roots in Muslim self-understanding? Whatever its source, can Islamism be spared the fate that overtook Christendom? Is separation of church and state avoidable? Can that eventuality be ultimately averted for Muslims, too?

REVOLUTION IN "CHRISTENDOM"

We should point out that separation, without precedent, was natural to Christianity because its founder, considered a public nuisance, was executed at the political altar, and because for three centuries that fate stalked Christianity as a persecuted religion. Its formative image, deeply etched in the catacombs of the empire, set it apart from the phantom of political triumphalism. The founder of the religion held no earthly political office; in fact, he rejected the earthly throne and sword as unworthy of his life and example. Though Christians later came to enjoy political recognition and even power, and to believe that this was an acceptable status quo, their roots in persecution reminded them it was not always so. If need be, they, or some of them, could break with the tradition of territorial "Christendom" to assert their moral autonomy. That is why eventually Christians turned their backs on religious "territoriality" and accepted secularism, i.e., the idea of separation, a move whose byproduct was the strengthening of the moral authority of religion, the backbone of civil society.

Yet when the time came, Christians were not at all reluctant to accede to a "territorial" view of religion. Thus, in the era of the Christian Roman Empire, the church was absorbed as an agency of imperial politics, an era when faith and territory were joined as a principle of membership in church and state. Constantine secured the freedom of Christianity, not its establishment as an exclusive state religion. He saw himself as Pontifex Maximus, the visible earthly vessel of an all-too-misty divinity whose intuitive, malleable purpose he could attach to the robust will of the state. He claimed to be the colleague of the bishops of Nicea, but only as a "bishop of external affairs" and of those things in Christianity deemed useful and convenient. The real shift came only with Charlemagne, who took Christianity out of the sacristy and established it as Christendom, weaving it into the fabric of the state. In that scheme the political ruler was seen as God's appointed agent, the herald and instrument of God's mission. Thus political affairs and religious matters were two strands of a single fabric. Church and state were united in purpose even though as institutions they represented different functions. In effect, the church had custody of the moral law, and the state was responsible for enforcing the rules of allegiance and conformity that gave practical expression to the higher spiritual law. Conformity rather than personal persuasion was the chief end of religious activity under this corporate arrangement.

Christendom identified itself with territoriality in the sense of making religion a matter of territorial allegiance. Church membership and territorial location belonged together, and territorial rule was established on, and made legitimate by, the ruler's professed religion (Barker 1951). In this scheme, Christianity was inevitable: tell me your ruler, and I will tell you your religion.

We must again stress that the tradition of separation and its painful development in the Christian West was peculiar, and necessary, to the religion, as is evident from the earliest records of civilization available to us, records that show the supreme sovereign as tending to be conceived as divine, with politics as a religious idea and religion as a political idea. This was the case in imperial Rome, where Caesar was God, and in the case of the Jews, as Josephus points out, where God is supreme ruler. In classical Muslim sources, similarly, God was supreme ruler, and the caliph God's mere deputy.[2] In remote antiquity the same practice obtained with the god-king identification that persisted into latter-day ideologies of divine anointing of worldly leaders. Invariably, the search for a political ideal has led to the divinization of political authority. Speaking of the ancient Chinese case, for example, Arthur Waley described how the craving for political unity produced the psychological need for the state to see itself as its own orthodoxy:

> To the Chinese of this period the word One (unity, singleness, etc.) had an intensely emotional connotation, reflected equally in political theory and Taoist metaphysics. And, indeed, the longing—or more accurately, the psychological need—for a fixed standard of belief was profounder, more urgent and more insistent than the longing for governmental unity. In the long run man cannot exist without an orthodoxy, without a fixed pattern of fundamental belief. It is hard for us today who live in societies, like those of France or England, which despite a surface moral anarchy, are in fact rooted upon Christian ethics, to imagine such a state of chaos as existed in China in the fourth and third centuries (Waley 1934, Introduction: 69-70; Toynbee 1987, 496).

The fundamental pattern of the political development of human society was the unique place accorded to a supreme personal monarch, usually exercising power at the behest of a divine impersonal law. The supreme personal ruler would thus attract the worship of his or her subjects as a god incarnate, the terrestrial likeness of a heavenly potentate whose will was then translated into action in the manner of an irresistible impersonal law of nature. Dissent or resistance in that scheme became unthinkable. It was the ultimate rebellion. The subjects of such a ruler would ascribe to their sovereign not only credit for their material well-being but for personal qualities like joy and sorrow, good and evil, blessing and curse, success and failure. Conversely, the supreme personal ruler received religious anointing as moral sanction of the political ideal, as is illustrated in the famous remark of Henry IV that "Paris is worth a Mass."

In either case, whether in the instance of a supreme personal ruler or in that of a supreme impersonal law of nature, at the level of society the outcome was the same: the unity of the universe was deemed synonymous with the unity of rulership, and vice versa. Perception of political authority was recast into a conception of divine authority, with ethnic or racial ideals sublimated into a moral mandate. It was the seed from which religious territoriality emerged, with religious faith being a matter primarily of membership in a society where rulership was fused with territorial identity and given a transcendent value. The traits of birth, soil, and authority culminated eventually in religion as a national and racial rite. It would be instructive to examine aspects of this Christendom theme in the early stages of the colonial and missionary movements in West Africa.

CHRISTENDOM AND AFRICA: MISSION AND COLONIALISM AS A COMMON CAUSE

The principle of religious non-territoriality that the New World of Jefferson had embraced with such zeal would in time expand to Africa, especially under the impetus of the antislavery movement and its support of new forms of society freed of slave-ridden chiefly castes and the social stigma of captivity.[3] As such, the movement led to the founding of free Christian colonies along the African coastline. Eventually, under the terms of the Act of 1807 abolishing the slave trade, a Vice-Admiralty Court was established in Freetown to ensure the effective implementation of the Act. The Royal Navy would set up a patrol along the West African coast, and the slaves it captured on the high seas would be brought to Freetown, and their status as slaves established in law before they would be set free. The procedure was called being "condemned," for it allowed the authorities to invoke the right to seize enslaved Africans as forfeitures to the Crown, their captors receiving as compensation a bounty for each slave. It was hoped that the experience gained from dealing with the original African American settlers, called "Nova Scotians" because of their Canadian transit point, would assist in resettling the recaptured Africans. With that Nova Scotian experience, a valuable precedent was established and a viable colony now took root on African soil, vindicating the official hope expressed at the time of the arrival of the African Americans in 1792. The example of these Nova Scotians, it was believed, would "produce many important consequences, and give, in some measure, a new character to the whole undertaking" (*Report of the Sierra Leone Company* 1794, 7; Kuczynski 1948-53). These recaptured Africans would be brought to Freetown and rehabilitated in that favorable milieu. Such was the confidence of the officials that Freetown would transform this new batch of dislocated Africans from mere exposure and general influence of the Nova Scotians that no concrete steps were taken to see to their welfare. Thus these recaptured Africans were simply let loose on society and left to find their own way. Most, if not all of them, offered now a second chance, had no clue where to begin, for the idea of a second chance for those bearing the stigma of captivity was unprecedented.

The lack of an official plan for what proved a veritable flood of recaptives represented a failure of administrative policy. The slave ships that plied the sea lanes between the West African coast and the Western hemisphere had cargo drawn from all over the continent, with the result that the recaptured Africans who were landed in Freetown came from a very mixed background. Now they had in common only their plight as refugees on their own continent, recently snatched from the jaws of calamity. They would be resettled under the aegis of the religious and humanitarian supervision extended to them. In 1807 the population of Freetown colony was 1,871, including 95 military. In the census of April 1811, the population was around 3,500, with most of that increase coming from the landing of recaptured Africans. In July 1814, it was 5,520. In a report drawn on 31 December 1818, the number of recaptured Africans was put at 6,406. Between 1819 and 1820, 943 recaptured Africans were landed in Freetown. The census of 1 January 1822 put the total civilian population of the colony at 15,081, of which 1,590 had landed from the slave ships in the previous year (Kuczynski 1948-53).

It was Governor Sir Charles MacCarthy's bold administrative plan, known as the Parish Scheme, that took on such human shambles and eventually created order out of chaos by parceling out the recaptives among supervised village-type "parishes," most of them under an appropriate patron saint, with government and mission collaborating in the work of resettlement and rehabilitation. Thus Catholic institutional forms would provide the structures of Protestant colonial rule, structures aimed at reforming character and promoting a sense of identity among the rehabilitated Africans.

MacCarthy wrote a memorandum in which he offered an assessment of the political development of Sierra Leone, saying the colony had changed significantly from 1808 when it became a crown possession, with only a single settlement of not more than two thousand, to 1816, when there were twenty settlements of about 17,300. Progress could be noted among the inhabitants, he contended, "who are rapidly advancing towards English manners and ideas, and are accumulating considerable permanent property." This new circumstance made the original charter for the colony inadequate and of little use. MacCarthy recommended revoking the existing charter and granting him as governor authority to establish commissions. He also recommended establishing a Supreme Court and reorganizing the administration of justice. The regulation of marriage belonged to such reorganization.[4]

MacCarthy's understanding of "English manners and ideas" extended to matters of ecclesiastical jurisdiction. Accordingly, presented with a chance to place state resources at the service of church and society, MacCarthy set up to conscript Christianity for the cause. The real qualification, he felt, for being a Christian was assimilation into the cultural customs of Europe. Thus, as soon as Africans were able to prove that they had learned enough of Europe's customs, they should be admitted into the church. When presented with contrary evidence—when reminded, for example, that European traders kept their distance from mission, and, in spite of their being European, opposed mission bitterly in centers of Christian impact—MacCarthy would not see the point, so convinced was he that European culture and administration were the requisite means for producing the polished natives of Christian profession. Christianity remained for him the king's religion, and the Bible the king's book. Worship must reflect this national character and inscribe it into the simple native habit. Rather than look to the heart for proof of moral regeneration, as he was urged, MacCarthy looked to cultural habits for marks of civilization. This view of religion as cultural necessity was the vital impulse of the old Christendom, and it had primacy and priority over the theological necessity of salvation. The method of cultural apprenticeship, of instructing Africans in the arts of civilization and impressing on their tribal herd instinct the duties and responsibilities pertaining to civilization, was the prescription for sound religion. Christian conversion for MacCarthy meant instituting establishment rules in obedience to benevolent authority.

William Davies, a Welsh Methodist missionary recently arrived in the colony, was something of a kindred spirit with the governor, with regard to whom he testified: "We meet with every encouragement from his Excellency the Governor, Col. Macarthy [sic]."[5] Davies gives the following account of MacCarthy's view of things:

> I have often heard him observing, after coming into my house, "Davies, such and such a man, that lives in such a house, is one of your members, is he not?" "How does your Excellency know?" "Why, he has whitewashed his house, his fence around the premises is good, his garden is clean and productive." "Your Excellency is right—he is a member, and Christianity alone can civilize: for godliness is profitable for all things, and when they get religion they will be industrious" (Walls 1975, 296 n.10).

MacCarthy often described himself as a worldly man, with no pretensions to religious piety. It was enough, he felt, that he acted in accordance with the dignity of his office, an agent and representative of enlightened rule. He saw no reason why such an establishment view of Christianity should not be promoted in Africa, so that Africans who thus received the blessings of civilization would reckon themselves fortunate to count the church as their ally. On one level, MacCarthy looked for a unified structure of church and state, a pair of complementary functions vested in a single authority, as in classical Christendom. However, on another level he understood only one way of going about this; that is, an orthodox Christian state into which would be subsumed the functions of the church. Christianity could spread only if it followed the lineaments of political establishment, so that the religion would become the expression of the ruler's will and mission.

The field of Christian mission in this scheme was defined by the territorial scope of the ruler's authority. Thus MacCarthy battled gallantly with the Church Missionary Society in London against establishing a mission base outside the Freetown colony where Britain's suzerainty had not yet been established. He campaigned for that reason, for example, for the closure of the Susu mission. He did not speak of divine rulership, but his reasoning that only rulership such as he knew it could act validly in the religious domain, that the territorial sphere was the proper boundary for the religious sphere, and that the will of God was properly expressed in the wishes and pleasure of the earthly prince, propelled him toward that conclusion, or at least toward the view that the establishment order was the best and most reliable representation of God's will for society. Thus, for MacCarthy, the goodwill of Great Britain became the designated channel of the blessings of Providence for the people of Africa. It was an elaboration of the doctrine of *cuius regio eius religio*, the tell-me-your-ruler-and-I-will-tell-you-the-religion philosophy.

As a faithful servant of Britain, MacCarthy could contemplate with supreme equanimity a group of happy, well-ordered villagers offering a successful alternative to the ramshackle sprawl of settlements into which hapless recaptives were herded. At the heart of the arrangement would be a village superintendent who would be judge, magistrate, adjudicator, confidante, town planner, master-builder, storekeeper, bookkeeper, intermediary, moral instructor, and consul. He would "see to the making of bricks and the erection of woodwork" (Walls 1975, 299). He would also keep school and evangelize the flock. In a memo on 15 June 1816 MacCarthy elaborated on his vision thus:

> I have explained . . . my views as to the means most likely to forward the Civilization of Africa, more particularly of the Colony and of the numerous classes of captured Negroes who under the Blessing of Providence are indebted for their emancipation from a cruel slavery to Great Britain only.
>
> I conceive that the first effectual step towards the establishment of Christianity will be found in the Division of this peninsula into Parishes, appointing to each a Clergyman to instruct their flock in Christianity, enlightening their minds to the various duties and advantages inherent to [sic] civilization—thus making Sierra Leone the base from whence future exertions may be extended, step by step to the very interior of Africa (Walls 1975, 296).

The model community of MacCarthy's design equated Christian orthodoxy with cultural quarantine, a holy domain protected by rule and sacrament, yet one that was as such tone deaf to settler and recaptive piety. The precise nature of what Africa needed existed in its full measure elsewhere, not in pious dreams of life in another realm, but in the tried and proven world of baptized Europe. MacCarthy was a Euro-evangelist for "Europeandom," and to that end he was prepared, indeed keen, to secure the collaboration of mission. As a consequence, he embarked on an ambitious scheme to import from Britain the material symbols of civilization, expecting missions to follow him into quarantine.

> Bells, clocks and weathercocks were ordered from England for church towers, forges for village blacksmiths, scales and weights to village markets. Quill-pens and copy-books, prayer books and arithmetic books were ordered for schools, with tin cases for the children to carry them in, lamps to read them by. Hats were ordered for the men, bonnets for the women, shoes for all; gowns and petticoats, trousers and braces—buttons, too, with needles, thread and thimbles, soap and smoothing-irons, even clothes-brushes, nothing was forgotten (Fyfe 1962, 130-31).

It was efforts such as these that inspired MacCarthy's chief justice, Robert Hogan, to write:

> Of this I am certain—that religion and civilization, which, as the necessary consequence of religion is but the name for it, must effect here, what they have uniformly wrought in every other part of the world, a concomitant improvement in arts and sciences, and a correspondent elevation of the human character and race. This great work is in progress: the finger of providence appears to have traced out the line to be pursued for its grand consummation.[6]

The great shortcoming in all this was that missions could not provide on so lavish a scale and at such distance, nor, for that matter, could government, and so the plan was abandoned. Yet the fact that it was conceived at all, and pursued with such purpose and energy, indicates that the phantom of a nostalgic and triumphalist Christendom still cast a spell on many in high places.

It could be argued that what ultimately saved MacCarthy from a particularly severe case of religious territorial recidivism was the opposition of settlers and recaptives themselves, and of their missionary allies. The point was made with some eloquence by MacCarthy's encounter with the colonial chaplain, W. A. B. Johnson, a German of Hanoverian background who came out to Sierra Leone in 1816 after serving a church in London.[7] MacCarthy had complained that Davies was unwilling to extend baptism to those Africans who had demonstrated enough acquaintance with European manners and customs until such Africans had shown marks of real spiritual regeneration, and he hoped Johnson would be more sensible and see matters differently. MacCarthy was simply at a loss to understand why being *civilized* was not an adequate and sufficient ground for taking the Christian name, and he told Johnson so. If missions were not in the business of producing "Black Europeans," then what, in heaven's name, were they in Africa for? Johnson kept a record of their meeting.

His Excellency the Governor came here today. He had led the conversation while we were in the garden to baptism. He wished I would baptize more people. I told him that I could not, unless God first baptised their hearts. He said the reason so many were baptised on the Day of Pentecost was that the Apostles despised none. I replied that they were pricked in the heart, and that I was willing to baptise all that were thus pricked in the heart. He thought baptism an act of civilization, and that it was our duty to make them all Christians. He spoke in great warmth about these things, and I endeavoured to show him through Scripture passages the contrary. He gave it up at last; calling me and the society a set of fanatics (Walls 1975, 301).

The establishment stakes were high enough for MacCarthy to think that it was worth the effort to make a second attempt at changing Johnson's mind, and while at it, to throw in a little spice of religious rivalry, too.

The Governor said a great deal about baptising all the people, which I refused. He said much about its necessity, but I kept to the word of God. He said that the Apostles, on Pentecost day, baptised 3000 at once. I replied that they were pricked in their hearts, and *as many as believed* were baptized. . . . He could not answer this, but said that he would write to the Archbishop of Canterbury concerning the matter . . . and would send those refused to Mr. Davies, for he thought Mr. Davies' baptism as good as ours (Walls 1975, 301).

One can imagine MacCarthy's utter consternation when Johnson refused to endorse singing "God Save the King"[8] because it was customarily sung over a beer mug, though he would mollify the disconsolate governor with his willingness to endorse saying "Honour the King" because, he claimed, that had apostolic warrant for it. Under the greenhouse imperatives of Christendom, Johnson's attitude would be inexcusable; though, without them MacCarthy's views would be inconceivable, too. However, a transplant Christendom in the new Africa could only mutate, or else wither, from its protective official custody. Thus the structures MacCarthy was busy setting up were being altered into radical strains of antislavery and antistructure. Or, as Johnson put it in language weighty with New Light meaning, society would yield to those who had been pricked in the heart or were so predisposed.

The answer of officials, both earlier ones and later, if they could not get the ear of individual missionaries, was to fix on the chaplaincy to preside over the religious life of the settlement. The settlers were congregating, often twice a day, morning and evening, to pray, testify, and witness. A passing sea captain noted in his diary in 1794 that the Nova Scotians "appear very Religious attending Services by 3 o'clock in the Morning and till Eleven at night, four, or five, times per week" (Kup 1958, 163). Officials considered this unsound religious practice and chose to smother it with restrictive measures, and to replace it with an alternative sedate Sunday worship. The Nova Scotians took that as a signal to leave the Chaplaincy Church, sending out a message to others that sanctions would be taken against those who stayed. The response in the Methodist camp was immediate, with most of them withdrawing

> from the Church entirely, and their attendance would have exposed them to ex-communication. As it was important to remove this obstacle to their improvement, the Rev. Mr. [John] Clarke [the chaplain] obtained leave to preach among them. He first called on Moses Wilkinson who gave him a long account of a revival of religion, which he said had taken place, last autumn, when it was usual for numbers of his hearers, especially children, to be struck down by the powers of his preaching, and to roar out in agony (*Report of the Sierra Leone Company* 1798, 47-48; Kirk-Greene 1960, 117-18).

This was the background to William Davies's implausible project to implant correct notions of religion, to see that the colony produced what the New Light religious enthusiasts had elsewhere derided as a breed of blow-dried citizens. Davies was thus emboldened by having in MacCarthy an ally in the cause of king, country, and God, but had, however, miscalculated the depth of settler feeling on the matter. For one thing, he came under fire from the settlers and recaptives for having become a salaried agent of the state.

For his part, we need to understand Davies's position. As a Welsh Methodist he was very keen to prove his loyalty to government and thereby remove any odious hint of Nonconformist stigma. He was aware that in 1811 a bill had been introduced in Parliament intended to impose severe penalties on Nonconformists. The law was later relaxed with the passage of the Trinity Act of 1813, which removed the stigma of illegality from Nonconformist religion. Nevertheless, the effect of the 1811 measure was to put Protestant dissenters on notice that they were only a tolerated collection of sects under law. They continued to be subject to loyalty tests until 1828, when the Test and Corporation Acts breached the Anglican constitution to give Nonconformist worship the recognition of the law. Until then Nonconformists carried with them a sense of questionable loyalty, and, thus, among Welsh Methodists and Baptists it produced the sentiment of a "Little England beyond Wales" (Halévy 1961, 476-85).[9]

Davies was smarting from such official discrimination, and it says something for the political atmosphere of the time that he felt his attitude needed little justification beyond claiming that he was a loyal subject of the king. When he set out the grounds of his differences with the settlers and recaptives, he turned the charge of disloyalty against them. He was confident his audience would recall how the American colonies recently revolted against the Crown, and how America concluded a second war with Britain in 1812. Men and women, we know, can only speak the language of their age and generation, but, because of his personal history, Davies's voice had singular resonance with his time and place. Furthermore, he had a personal incentive to being an official oracle. American republican spirit was public enemy number one, he felt, and that was what he was up against. He seemed shamed by his Nonconformist heritage and grateful not to be blamed for it. And so, implausibly, he set out to place religion on a favorable political footing in order to reclaim it for king and country. He was proud that government had taken notice of him, proud that it had paid his salary, appointed him to public positions, decorated him, and proud, too, beyond words, that the administration continued to consult him regularly. He would gladly let it be known that he had the governor's ear, a social climber who found himself in elevated company. Only the refusal of blacks duly to conform stood in his way to becoming a complete Establishment man.

The explanation for black intransigence, in Davies's view, lay in their having embraced unsound religious doctrine. That was the source of their erroneous notion of the political community as one without a king, an error that produced a culture of political ingratitude. In his own words, Davies nailed his colors to the mast of the Christendom on which America, for one, had disreputably turned its back. The irony was lost on him that under the terms establishing Christendom, his own Nonconformist tradition had been stigmatized. Yet in his forlorn plea for a transfer from Freetown he admitted in so many words that he was the wrong man in the wrong place at the wrong time. He deserved to be put out of his misery.

In January 1817 he wrote saying that he realized he could do no more useful work in the colony, chiefly because he was receiving a salary from the state. He omitted to say he had also all but repudiated the Nonconformist cause. So he pleaded to be sent to the West Indies instead.

> The Leaders of the Society in Free Town have declared against me and have refused me the pulpit, I am too *plain* for them, and truly I have found them a proud and stiff necked generation. I understand they are going to accuse me of lording it over them, of being too proud for a Methodist Preacher, and of paying too much attention to Government, the truth in this respect is, when we arrived here we found Methodism very low indeed, in the esteem of Government and the European Gentlemen in the Colony, My dear Departed Jane's and my own conduct some how or other pleased the most respectable part of the community, in consequence thereof some got jealous, Most of our Leaders as far as I can judge are of the American republic spirit and are strongly averse to Government, I am a Loyal subject to my King I wish to do the little I can for the support of that Government especially in a foreign part were [sic] there are not so many able advocates as at home. . . . I am now the Senior Alderman in Free Town and a justice of the Peace. I objected as much as I could to both without absolutely giving offence to the Governor which it was not my duty to do, for His Excellency has been and continues to be a father to me, and I feel it my duty to obey him as far as

I can consistent with religion, which teaches me to fear God and Honour the King.[10]

Davies was subsequently employed by the government as a superintendent of one of the recaptive villages, receiving £150 annual salary.[11] Still, his troubles with the settlers were far from over. "We were sorry to find Mr. Davies and the Leaders and Trustees not united," confessed a fellow missionary despondently. "I have used my influence to have Mr. Davies back to his work and office in the Town but all to no purpose," he concluded (loc. cit.).

There was nothing new in this situation where the settlers and other blacks wished to have no official interference in their religious and civil affairs, though the officials were slow to appreciate that. Thus, for example, did Zachary Macaulay proceed in July 1796 to enact measures to regulate marriage among the settlers, who mobilized a petition drive asking to rescind the promulgation. One hundred and twenty-eight signatories were appended to the petition, which was duly delivered to Macaulay in the name of "The Independent Methodist Church of Freetown." Among other things, the petition declared:

We consider this new law as an encroachment on our religious rights. . . . We are Dissenters, and as such consider ourselves a perfect Church, having no need of the assistance of any worldly power to appoint or perform religious ceremonies for us. If persons in holy orders are allowed to marry, we see no reason why our Ministers should not do it. Our meeting-house we count as fit for any religious purpose as the house you call the church. We cannot persuade ourselves that politics and religion have any connection, and therefore think it not right for a Governor of the one to be meddling with the other (Walls 1975, 27; Gordon 1992, 139-41).[12]

Such official views about religion represented a significant gulf between the authorities and the settlers and recaptives. MacCarthy's Christendom policies showed how slow officials were to grasp the force of the sentiment for church-state separation. Nevertheless, confronted with the Christendom formula of religion as political orthodoxy, the Sierra Leone settlers and recaptives, in spite of their varied backgrounds, were convinced Europe had settled on the political path to circumvent religion.

This policy of political assimilation as religious prerequisite (or substitute) was widespread in other parts of Africa, too, where it produced comparable responses. Here, for example, is the trenchant statement of one Christian African who was born in Mozambique and became a missionary in Nyasaland, now Tanzania. The irregular English medium still managed to preserve the poignancy of the native idiom.

Poor Resident, he thinks too much of his skin and not of his heart. What is the difference between a white man and a black man? Are we not of the same blood and all from Adam? This startles me much—is Europe still Christian or Heathen? . . . The three combined bodies, Missionaries, Government and Companies, or gainers of money—do form the same rule to look upon the native with mockery eyes. It sometimes startles us to see that the three combined bodies are from Europe, and along with them there is a title "christendom." And to compare or make a comparison between the MASTER of the title and his servants it pushes any African away from believing the Master of the title. If we had power enough to communicate ourselves to Europe we would advise them not to call themselves "Christendom" but "Europeandom" (Shepperson and Rice 1958, 163).

HISTORICAL DISCREPANCY

The attempts at introducing territorial Christendom revealed the great historical gap between European feudal instincts and Africa's social diversity and ethnic reality. Yet modern Christianity, too, though not necessarily with all forms of it, had come to reject territorial Christendom as incompatible with the new historical experience. Thus it was that Christendom's iron chain of identity was broken, and broken with fateful consequences for Western history. When the time was ripe, Christians broke decisively with what had until then been a universal practice by abandoning the view of religion as a construct of earthly power, and its converse of the state as a religious construct. Christian communities took the idea of Divine Personality and fixed it in the Man of Sorrows who was bruised for our iniquity, a radical departure from Divine Personality fixed in political fiat and force and in a holy territorial space, the Divine Agent, that is, as ethnic or racial world conqueror. The idea of the divine thus became for Christians the divine rule and interest in the general human project, instead of a particular human attribute hardening into a universal territorial principle. By setting themselves apart from this enslaving ideology of religion as a territorial construct and the territorial construct as revealed law, Christians shattered the chain that fettered humanity from time immemorial. With that truth secured, the way was open for undreamed of possibilities for history and human community. There simply was no possibility of going back on those gains, not if we wished to advance the global drive for human rights.

All these diverse examples and considerations prompt the following thought: Separation of church and state need not deny the connection of ethics and politics, of church and society, of principle and precedent, or of faith and the public order, a connection well described by Max Stackhouse of Princeton Theological Seminary as a "buffer zone" between church and state, between piety and power (Stackhouse 1987, 109). For example, religious ethics may provide for the maintenance and security of the public order in such matters as family life, the socialization of children, interpersonal trust, philanthropy, compassion, and humility without the public order being excluded from shared responsibility, though in that partnership public agents might be tempted to sequester religion as expedient leverage only, taking short-term advantage of revealed injunctions which are the source and spring of ethical life.

In view of the evidence we have considered here, liberal arguments for distinguishing between public and private spheres would be hard to sustain on purely free-speech grounds, as Locke has cogently shown, for, however we define them, the private and public spheres are affected by identical rules of order, freedom, and responsibility. State institutions would be expected to observe standards of freedom, justice, honesty, truth, and decency no less than persons in community. As it stands, the state in its nature does distinguish between right and wrong, does punish wrongful acts and reward right conduct. The state is not morally neutral. Thus while separation respects the distinction between the public and private domains, it does not exclude the large area of partnership and overlap that turns out to be extremely fruitful of a morally attuned society. There would be room in that partnership and overlap for absorbing Muslim ethical and moral teachings, and thus for helping advance the cause of human rights cross-culturally.

CONCLUSION

The historical, cross-cultural and interfaith perspectives we have brought to bear on the origin and practice of separation suggest a broad common interest in the subject. Besides, the subject has extensive ramifications for the nature of modern political institutions, and is as such an important basis of fundamental human rights, the operative norm in international relations, as well as being the fault line in new religious movements around the world. As we saw with pre-colonial Muslim Africa and the Christian colony of Freetown, the seeds of separation were sown in the vigorous debates concerning the proper jurisdiction of state authority and the timeless truths of religion. The Muslim and settler Christian leaders concerned felt that religion had a crucial role to play in setting the temporal limits of state power, a position that is still relevant to the unresolved tension between religion and politics in much of the present-day ferment around the world. As it happens, the insistence in classical Muslim sources that "church and state" are interdependent finds echoes in MacCarthy's views on church-state unity, though today such views conflict with the Western secular practice of strict separation. In spite of the historical discrepancy between Christendom and an Africa conceived in antislavery, MacCarthy's instincts still resonate with the theocentric impulse of Muslim leaders. The issue is how to disentangle that from the warrant for a theocratic state. Balancing such Muslim theocratic claims and Western secularism represents one of the great challenges of contemporary statesmanship.

NOTES

[1] Tocqueville was thinking of governments and their relation to the fine arts, but his ideas apply equally well to a non-utilitarian view of virtue.

[2] Bernard Lewis writes in this connection: "Secularism in the modern political meaning—the idea that religion and political authority, church and state are different, and can or should be separated—is, in a profound sense, Christian." He examines the instances of Christianity, Judaism, Islam, and the modern West ("Secularism," Yale Inter-Faculty Seminar on Church and State, unpublished paper).

[3] This section is based on my forthcoming book, *Abolitionists Abroad: American Blacks and the Making of Modern West Africa* (Cambridge: Harvard University Press, 1999).

[4] MacCarthy's memorandum can be found in the Public Record Office, London, reference CO 267/42, June 15, 1816.

[5] William Davies, Letter, 10 August 1815, Methodist Missionary Society Archives, School of Oriental and African Studies, University of London, Box no. 279.

[6] Robert Hogan, Letter, 25 May 1816, Public Record Office, London, CO 267/43.

[7] MacCarthy informed the Earl of Bathurst in a letter dated 1 April 1817 that he was recommending the appointment of Johnson as Colonial Chaplain at a salary of £150 per annum (Public Record Office, London, CO 267/45).

[8] In a letter to Edward Bickersteth at the CMS, MacCarthy expressed dismay at the public snub that the missionaries of the CMS—Collier, Nylander, and Johnson—delivered when they pointedly walked out on the school assembly as the children started singing "God Save the King." MacCarthy himself had heard the children sing it a few days before in a rehearsal and given his official approval (Letter no. 97, February 1819, CMS Archives CA1/E6-E7).

[9] The evangelical movement in England was a factor in helping to liberalize religious laws, one consequence of seeking to free the church of state control. Thus in 1797 Wilberforce supported opening the militia to Catholics after an Act of 1793 limited their admission to the army to a rank below that of colonel. In 1812 and 1813 Wilberforce again supported the admission of Catholics to Parliament, a very un-Tory thing to do. However, the commingling of Catholic emancipation with the Irish question complicated Wilberforce's logic of tolerance.

[10] William Davies, Extracts of Letter, 13 June 1817, Methodist Missionary Society Archives, School of Oriental and African Studies, University of London, Box no. 279.

[11] Samuel Brown, Letter, 14 February 1817, no. 28, Methodist Missionary Society Archives, School of Oriental and African Studies, University of London,

[12] Macaulay continued to be criticized for attempting to join church and state.

BIBLIOGRAPHY

al-Fakhrí. 1947. *Government and Dynasties in Islam*. Translated by C. E. J. Whitting. London: Luzac & Co.

al-Ka'ti, Mahmúd. 1964. *Ta'ríkh al -Fattásh*. Translated and edited by M. Delafosse and O. Houdas. Paris. Originally published 1913-14.

al-Sa'dí, 'Abd al-Rahmán. 1964. *Ta'ríkh al-Súdán*. Translated and edited by O. Houdas. Paris: Librairie d'Amerique et d'Orient, Adrien-Maisonneuve.

al-Súdán, Ta'ríkh. 1964. Originally published 1913-14. Translated and edited by Octave Houdas. Paris.

Augustine. 1992. *Letters of Saint Augustine.* Edited and translated by John Leinen-weber. Liguori, Mo.: Triumph Books.

Barker, Sir Ernest. 1951. *Principles of Social and Political Theory.* Oxford: Clarendon Press.

Bello, Muhammad. 1957. *Infáq al-Maysúr.* Edited by C. E. J. Whitting. London: Luzac & Co.

Dewey, John. 1989. *Freedom and Culture.* Buffalo: Prometheus Books.

Ferm, Robert L., ed. 1983. *Issues in American Protestantism: A Documentary History from the Puritans to the Present.* Gloucester, Mass.: Peter Smith.

Fyfe. 1962. *A History of Sierra Leone.* London: Oxford University Press.

Gordon, Grant. 1992. *From Slavery to Freedom: The Life of David George.* Hantsport, N.S.: Lancelot Press for Acadia Divinity College.

Halévy, Élie. 1961. *A History of the English People in the Nineteenth Century.* Vol. 1, *England in 1815.* London: Ernest Benn; New York: Barnes and Noble.

Hiskett, Mervyn. 1971. "'The Song of the Shehu's Miracles': A Hausa Hagiography from Sokoto," *African Language Studies* 12.

Hodgkin, Thomas, ed. 1960. *Nigerian Perspectives: An Historical Anthology.* London: Oxford University Press.

Holmes, Oliver Wendell, Jr. 1938. *The Common Law.* Boston: Little, Brown.

Kelsen, Hans. 1945. *General Theory of Law and State.* Cambridge, Mass.: Harvard University Press.

Kirk-Greene, Anthony. 1960. "David George: The Nova Scotian Experience," *Sierra Leone Studies,* no. 14. New Series. (December)

Koch, Adrienne, and William Peden, eds. 1993. *The Life and Selected Writings of Thomas Jefferson.* New York: The Modern Library.

Kuczynski, R. R. 1948-53. *Demographic Survey of the British Colonial Empire.* 3 vols. Vol. 1, *West Africa.* London: Oxford University Press. Reprinted. Fairfield, N.J.: Augustus M. Kelley Publishers, The Harvester Press, 1977.

Kup, A. P. 1958. "Freetown in 1794," *Sierra Leone Studies,* New Series.

Lerner, Max, ed. 1989. *The Mind and Faith of Justice Holmes.* Boston: Little, Brown.

Locke, John. 1990. *A Letter Concerning Toleration.* Buffalo, N.Y.: Prometheus Books.

Miller, Perry, and Thomas H. Johnson, eds. 1963. *The Puritans: A Sourcebook of Their Writings.* Vol. 1, *The Theory of the State and of Society: This World and the Next.* New York: Harper Torchbooks.

Pound, Roscoe. 1921. *The Spirit of the Common Law.* Boston: Marshall Jones.

———. 1938. *The Formative Era of American Law.* Boston: Little, Brown.

———. 1940. *Contemporary Juristic Theory.* Claremont: Claremont Colleges.

———. 1942. *Social Control through Law.* New Haven, Conn.: Yale University Press.

Raboteau, Albert J. 1978. *Slave Religion: The 'Invisible Institution' in the Antebellum South.* New York: Oxford University Press.

Report of the Sierra Leone Company. 1794/1798. On microfiche.

Sanneh, Lamin, 1976a. *The Jakhanke Muslim Clerics: A Religious and Historical Study of Islam in Senegambia.* Lanham, Md.: University Press of America.

———. 1976b. "The Origins of Clericalism in West African Islam," *Journal of African History* 17, no. 1.

———. 1997. *The Crown and the Turban: Muslims and West African Pluralism.* Denver: Westview Press.

Shepperson, George, and T. Rice. 1958. *Independent African: John Chilembwe and the Origins, Setting and Significance of the Nyasaland Native Rising of 1915*. Edinburgh: Edinburgh University Press.

Stackhouse, Max. 1987. *Public Theology and Political Economy*. Grand Rapids: Eerdmans.

Tocqueville, Alexis de. 1966. *Democracy in America*. Translated by George Lawrence. Edited by J. P. Mayer. New York: Harper Torchbooks. Reprinted 1988.

Toynbee, Arnold J. 1987. *A Study of History, Abridgement*. Vols. 1-6. Oxford: Oxford University Press.

Trimingham, J. Spencer. 1962. *A History of Islam in West Africa*. London: Oxford University Press.

Waley, Arthur. 1934. *The Way and Its Power*. London: Allen & Unwin.

Walls, Andrew F. 1959. "The Nova Scotians and Their Religion," *The Sierra Leone Bulletin of Religion*, no. 1 (June).

————. 1975. "A Colonial Concordat: Two Views of Christianity and Civilization," in *Church, Society and Politics*, Studies in Church History, vol. 12, edited by Derek Baker. Oxford: Blackwell.

————. 1992. "Nova Scotians." Also Grant Gordon. *From Slavery to Freedom: The Life of David George*.

5.

Religious Freedom
in African Constitutions

———————◆———————

J. D. van der Vyver

The constitution of a country does not accurately reflect the state of religious freedom in that country. Many issues pertinent to religious freedom may be regulated in other statutory enactments, and implementation of constitutional principles through extra-constitutional instruments may take a turn, or involve detail, not reflected clearly in the constitution itself. A survey of constitutional provisions dealing with aspects of religious freedom is nevertheless useful because the constitution of a country provides a certain guarantee of the norms enunciated therein. Although the same legal protection afforded to an aspect of religious freedom by the constitution of a particular state may also be found in legislation other than the constitution of another state, having afforded constitutional protection to that aspect would indicate the special significance attached to religious freedom in the first-mentioned state.

It is important to note that almost all the states in Africa have included in their constitutions a bill of rights, and that religious freedom in one form or another features prominently in all of those constitutions. The Constitution of Eritrea and the one of Western Sahara—the youngest African countries to receive the status of statehood—were not available for purposes of this survey. Although Swaziland had an impressive Bill of Rights in its Constitution, that chapter in the Constitution was suspended before it even entered into force on the day of the country's independence (in 1968), and the entire Swazi Constitution was indeed repealed by King Sobhuza II in April of 1973.

THE IDEOLOGICAL DIVIDE

From the perspective of religious orientation, the countries of Africa can be divided into the categories of Muslim, socialist, and secular states. These categories do not, however, represent watertight compartments, because there are many overlaps. For example, Libya and the Somali Democratic Republic represent efforts to combine their Muslim commitments with socialism, and many states professing to be secular nevertheless in one way or another pay tribute to religion. Given these constraints, I shall in any event use the above classification as my point of departure under the present heading.

Muslim States

The following African countries testify in their respective constitutions to being Muslim states and/or proclaim Islam to be the religion of the state: Algeria (art. 2), the Comoros (Preamble), Egypt (art. 2), Libya (art. 2), Mauritania (art. 5),[1] Morocco (art. 6),[2] Somalia (art. 3.1.), and Tunisia (art. 1).[3] Sudan revealed its commitment to Islam by proclaiming its constitution in the name of "Allah, the Compassionate and merciful" (Preamble).

In some instances, Muslim countries add substance to their commitment to Islam by sanctioning, as part of the administrative state structure, certain religious institutions and/or expressly requiring high-ranking state officials to be Muslims. In the Comoros (art. 63) and Morocco (art. 21), a Council of Ulemas (religious leaders) has been entrusted with jurisdiction in certain executive matters. In Mauritania (art. 23) and Tunisia (arts. 38 and 40), the president must, as a matter of constitutional compulsion, be a Muslim, and Morocco, again, requires the King, "Commander of the faithful," to ensure "the observance of Islam" (art. 19).

Almost all Muslim countries in Africa guarantee religious freedom in one form or another, but in most instances that freedom is subjected to often sweeping conditions. The Constitution of Algeria thus proclaims "freedom of conscience and the freedom of opinion" to be inviolable (art. 35), but at the same time forbids "practices contrary to Islamic morals and the values of November" (art. 9). In the Comoros, freedom of thought and conscience are limited as far as "those required to respect morality and the public order" are concerned (Preamble). The Constitution of Egypt seemingly contains an unqualified guarantee of "the freedom of belief and the freedom of practice of religious rites" (art. 46) (thereby, incidentally, also emphasizing the free exercise of religious freedom, which is not common in Muslim countries[4]), but at the same time states that Islamic jurisprudence shall be "the principal source of legislation" (art. 2); and—as we shall see later on—Islamic jurisprudence places radical restrictions on the free exercise of religion, or at least the spread of religion, by non-Muslims in Islamic countries. By instructing the legislature to found its enactments on Islamic jurisprudence, the Constitution mandates state intervention to curb proselytizing efforts by proponents of non-Muslim religions. Freedom of belief and the right to practice religious rites must in Sudan be exercised within the limits of morality, public order, and health "as may be required by law" (art. 18).

Freedom of religion is not expressly mentioned in the constitutions of Mauritania or Tunisia. The Constitution of Mauritania does make provision for the freedom of opinion and of thought (that may be limited by law) (art. 10), and the one of Tunisia speaks of "[t]he liberties of opinion" (to be exercised "in the conditions defined by law") (art. 8). Freedom of opinion and/or thought may, of course, be taken to include religious opinion or thought, but the sanctioning of legislative intervention to curtail those freedoms clearly leaves the door open for the legislature to subject the constitutional freedom and the free exercise guarantee (respectively) to restrictions that could be quite radical. In Morocco, freedom of opinion has also been made subject to restrictions that may be imposed by law (art. 9), but there the section proclaiming Islam to be the religion of the State goes on to guarantee to "all," in unqualified language, "freedom of worship" (art. 6).

There is a similar unqualified guarantee in the Constitution of Somalia of an entitlement, given to "[e]very person," "to profess any religion or creed" (art. 31). Though still rare in African Muslim countries, such concessions are indeed indicative of increasing tolerance in the Muslim world toward non-Islamic religions. It is worth noting that several Muslim states in Africa, notably the Comoros (art. 3), Egypt (art. 40), and Somalia (art. 6), included in their constitutions equal protection clauses "without regard to religion or belief" (or similarly defined) and without further qualification.[5]

The trend toward religious tolerance may be exemplified by developments in Libya. Following a period of Islamization in Libya after Colonel Qadhdhafi came to power in 1969, there seems to be an increasing divide between law and religion in the country. Initially, only the law of inheritance was governed by *Shari'a* (art. 8), but in 1976, the Holy Qur'an was elevated to the level of Constitution of the Socialist People's Libyan Arab Jamahiriya (art. 2 of the Declaration on the Establishment of the Authority of the People, 1976). More recently, in 1991, the General People's Congress ordained that "religion is a direct relationship with the Creator, without an intermediary. It is prohibited to claim monopoly over religion or to exploit it for any purpose" (art. 5 of the General People's Congress Law 20 of 1991 on the Consolidation of Freedom).

Libya and Somalia exemplify a faction within the family of African Muslim states which attempted to combine the basic political tenets of Islam with a socialist form of government.[6] The unconditional proclamation in Somalia of the freedom "to profess any religion or creed" (art. 31) and of the "equal rights and duties before the law" of all citizens "regardless of sex, religion, origin and language" (art. 6), and the 1991 law of Libya, which seemingly leans toward a separation of state and religion (art. 5 of the General People's Congress Law 20 of 1991 on the Consolidation of Freedom), may reflect a growing awareness in the Muslim world of current human rights jurisprudence pertaining to freedom of religion, but could also possibly be explained with a view to the lukewarm attitudes in regard to religion which, through Soviet influence, have come to be associated with political socialism.

Be that as it might, it is fair to say that Muslim fundamentalism of the kind commonly associated with Saudi Arabia and Iran is not current in African Muslim communities—with the possible exception of Sudan. Sudan is perhaps unique because of the presence of a substantial non-Muslim—mostly Christian—population in the southern regions of the country. The religious commitment of a government becomes precarious when the tenets of the preferred religious ideology are forced upon citizens with other religious persuasions. Political polarization and conflict become almost inevitable in circumstances—like those prevailing in Sudan—where the minority religious group constitutes a substantial percentage of the population and its members are concentrated in a particular region of the country. The process of Islamization under the repressive régime of Major-General Jaafer Mohammed al-Nemery (1969-85) set religious conflict in motion in Sudan, the end of which is not yet in sight.

The Sudanese Transitional Constitution of 1985 did hold out the promise of the freedom of belief and the right to practice religious rites, but only "within the limits of morality, public order and health as may be required by law" (art. 18). However, the Transitional Constitution also proclaimed "Islamic *Shari'a* and custom" to be "the main source of legislation" (art. 4). The same article in the Transitional Constitution also provided that "personal matters" of non-Muslims shall be governed by their personal law, but, in view of the fact that *Shari'a* regulates many more legal relationships than merely those of the law of persons,[7] this concession proved to be cold comfort to the Christian South.

Missionary activity in the interest of non-Muslim religions is generally frowned upon by Islam, whereas missionary efforts to convert non-Muslims to Islam are encouraged (Mayer 1987, 149; Sahlieh 1985, 642). It becomes particularly precarious in countries where *Shari'a* has been afforded the status of the main or principal source of legislation—as is the case in Egypt (art. 2) and Sudan (art. 4). Here, the protection of human rights inevitably translates into de facto discrimination and repression. This is evidenced, in general, by the status afforded to non-Muslim religions in the concerned countries. As pointed out by Abdullahi An-Na'im, the status of non-Muslims under *Shari'a* is inferior (An-Na'im 1987, 10 and 1993, 147), and constitutions which proclaim *Shari'a* to be a source of law therefore in effect sanction discrimination against religious minorities (An-Na'im 1987, 1; and see, in general, id., at 10-14).

In his treatise on *Religious Minorities under Islamic Law*, Professor An-Na'im therefore speaks of "Islamic cultural impediments to the full and effective safeguards of the rights of religious minorities" (An-Na'im 1987, 9). Ann Mayer, again, compared the status in Islamic countries of non-Muslims who have not accepted the official state ideology with that of a non-communist [in bygone days] in a communist country (Mayer 1987, 179). Flagrant violations of the rights of religious minorities were particularly evident in countries that embarked on a program of systematic Islamization of the community and constitutional structures (Mayer 1987, 129-30, 135-37, 152-61 and 178-83; and

1990, 140-43); that is, the process of "reinstating Islamic norms and values" in those societies (Mayer 1987, 129): as far as Africa is concerned, Libya after Colonel Qadhdhafi came to power in 1969, and Sudan through the repressive régime of Major-General Jaafer Mohammed al-Nemery in the period from 1969 to 1985. Religious repression under the banner of Islamization was especially aimed at groups regarded as apostates from Islam, such as the "Republican Brothers" in Sudan (Mayer 1987, 180-82).[8] Persecution of the Islamic Republican Brothers in Sudan exemplifies yet another feature of Islamic prejudice: Muslim states are tolerant in regard to "religions of the Book" but strongly condemn those judged to be apostates from Islam. The Sudanese Constitution thus indeed protects Christians and members of "heavenly religions," but not apostates from Islam (art. 16).

Islamic fundamentalists would not readily concede any contradiction between Islamic teaching and practices on the one hand and human rights norms on the other. Like all other major religions, Islam too—in the words of Louis Henkin—"proudly lays claim to fathering" human rights (Henkin 1978, xii). The Universal Islamic Declaration of Human Rights of 1981 thus proclaimed in its Preamble that "Islam gave to mankind an ideal code of human rights fourteen centuries ago." An Islamic politician from Pakistan explained: "When Muslims speak about human rights in Islam, they mean rights bestowed by Allah the exalted in the Holy Koran; rights that are divine, eternal, universal, and absolute; rights that are guaranteed and protected through the shariah" (Khan 1989, 37).

SOCIALIST STATES

Radical socialism, as everyone knows, has become an endangered species in the world and, as far as mainstream protagonists of communism are concerned, is currently kept alive by the People's Republic of China only. In Africa, though, liberation from colonialism was attended by the emergence in the sub-Saharan continent of several parasite states of the former Soviet Union, China, and/or Cuba. However, those African prototypes were seemingly more interested in imitating the entrenchment of a one-party system than in the typical economic arrangements of Marxist-Leninist communism. Angola, Mozambique, and Tanzania may serve as examples of African socialism.

The Constitutional Law of the People's Republic of Angola thus proclaimed the MPLA-Workers' Party, being a "Marxist-Leninist party," to be responsible for the political, economic, and social leadership of the State in its efforts to construct a socialist society (art. 2). The Constitution of the People's Republic of Mozambique similarly placed its trust in the dominant liberation movement—in this instance FRELIMO—as "the legitimate representative of the Mozambican people" (Preamble). Drafters of the Tanzanian Constitution described the body politic as "a democratic and socialist nation with one political party," with the Revolutionary Party as the chosen one (art. 3(1)).[9]

Socialist states are known to be areligious, if not altogether antireligious. One would almost invariably find constitutional guarantees of religious freedom in the fundamental laws of those countries—subjected, though, to often sweeping limitations. Angola, for example, expressly sanctioned the "complete separation" of the State and religious institutions (art. 7). It promised respect for religion and protection of churches and places and objects of worship, but subject to state laws, the substance of which remained undefined in the Constitution itself (ibid.). It likewise proclaimed freedom of conscience and belief to be inviolable, and "recognise[s] equality and guarantee[s] the practice of all forms of worship," but only insofar as such equality and practice are "compatible with public order and the national interest" (art. 25). The Constitution more generously guarantees equality before the law, and further provides that all citizens shall be subject to the same duties without any distinction based on, inter alia, religion (art. 18). The limitation provisions of the religion clauses in the Constitution of Angola provided ample backing for the persecution of pacifist religious groups, such as the Jehovah's Witnesses, who refused to participate in military activity during the Angolan civil war that erupted after independence in 1975.

Mozambique in similar fashion proclaimed the unqualified freedom of "all citizens" to practice or not to practice a religion (art. 78.1), but subjected the right of all citizens to disseminate their opinion "by all legal means" to the requirement of that right having to be "regulated by law based on the necessary respect for the Constitution, for the dignity of the human person, and for the mandates of foreign policy and national defence" (art. 74.4). The Mozambican Constitution also addressed a problem of special significance for religious freedom, namely, the autonomy of religious institutions to mind their own internal affairs. It provides that religious denominations shall have the right to freely pursue their respective religious aims and to own and acquire assets for the purpose of achieving those aims (art. 78.2). It should be noted that the People's Republic of Mozambique succeeded the pre-1975 Portuguese colonial era where Roman Catholicism predominated among the mainstream religions in the country, and the attentive observer will recognize in this provision the remnants of the Catholic doctrine of subsidiarity, according to which religious (and other social) entities derive their legal status and competencies from the state. In a unique free exercise clause, the Constitution speaks of freedom to practice or not to practice a religion (art. 78.1). Mozambique also sided with a number of Francophone African states, such as Gabon, Niger, and Senegal (to be discussed later on), which in their constitutions rendered religious discrimination punishable—with the added rider in the case of Mozambique that such discrimination shall be punished "according to law" (art. 69).

The Constitution of Tanzania touches upon many of the same themes. It defines the government's task of "encouraging" equal protection regardless of, inter alia, religion or creed (art. 9(1)(g); and see also art. 13(1), read with art. 13(5) [the equal protection and non-discrimination clause]). It proclaims that the administration of religion will be outside the jurisdiction of the State, but this is conditioned by a proviso: "[w]ithout jeopardising the laws applicable in the Union Republic" (art. 19(2)). And here we find the first provision thus far addressing the question of proselytization in express terms: Promotion of religion, worship, and evangelization will be free and matters of personal voluntary choice, Tanzania proclaims, but "[w]ithout jeopardising the laws applicable in the Union Republic" (art. 19(2); and as to limitations, see also the sweeping provisions of arts. 30 and 31). The laws that may not be jeopardized are not bound to any substantive human rights criteria, and the right to promote one's religion through worship and evangelization is furthermore subordinated to additional general directives outlined elsewhere in the Constitution: Those rights may not be exercised in any way that will result in interference with, or curtailment of, the rights and freedoms of others, or with the public interests (art. 30(1)). The constitutional rights and freedoms, including the one under consideration, will not trump any statutory provision or executive act ("legal action") enacted or performed with a view to a long list of objectives:

- to ensure that justice and freedom of others, or interests of the public, are not violated by misuse of a freedom or individual right;
- to ensure that security, safety of the society, peace, community health, development programs in cities and villages, the production and utilization of minerals, the development and promotion of resources, or any other interests aimed at development of the well-being of the public will not be prejudiced;
- to ensure the implementation of judgments, decisions or court orders in civil or criminal matters;
- to maintain the reputation, justice and freedom of the majority of people, or the individual life of people involved in court decisions, to prevent conveyance of secret information, and to maintain respect for, and the authority and freedom of, the courts;
- to impose restrictions on, and administer and guard against, the establishment, operation and matters of unions and private organizations in the country; or
- to allow any other activity to take place which will help develop and preserve the interests of the nation in general (art. 30(2)).

And that is not all. Special sanction is afforded to laws in a state of emergency; and "in case of ordinary times," action may lawfully be taken that violates, as a matter of "acts of war," the right to exist, or which impinges on "the right to be free and to live as a free person," of persons "believed to be" engaged in action that endangers or harms the security of the nation (art. 31(1), read with art. 31(3)). We shall see later on that the right to spread one's religion is a recurring theme in the constitutions of many Anglophone countries.

Tanzania finds itself in a situation of transition at the present time. Although not officially a Muslim state, the government of Tanzania is dominated by Muslims. This disposition has been the cause of profound conflict in the country, and there are already signs that the struggle between the Muslim government of Sudan and the Christian minority in the South of that country is spilling over the southern borders of Sudan into (Uganda and) Tanzania.

The MPLA Draft Constitution of the Republic of Angola (1990)—seeking to create conditions that would facilitate a compromise with the UNITA leadership with a view to putting an end to the civil war—also promises to introduce more liberal innovations in the law of religious freedom in the country. The Draft guarantees the right of all persons to freedom of thought, conscience, and belief (art. XXVIII(1)(b)), and freedom to practice any religion of one's own choice, and to manifest such practice (art. XXVIII(1)(c)). It makes provision for the right to enjoy, practice, profess, maintain, and promote any religion, subject only to the terms of the Constitution and the rights and freedoms of others (art. XXV). It promises to adhere to the Universal Declaration of Human Rights (1948) "as an inalienable standard of human rights for all mankind" (art. III), and in fact incorporates into the municipal law of Angola the provisions of the Universal Declaration, provided only that any of the dictates of the constitutional Bill of Rights is not thereby removed or reduced (art. XXXI). The implications of these provisions will appear from the exposition later on in this survey of the thematic components of religious freedom.

OTHER IDEOLOGICAL STATEMENTS

Colonialism facilitated the coming of an impressive variety of Christian religions to sub-Saharan Africa. While Roman Catholicism seemed to predominate in countries formerly colonized by France, Portugal, and Belgium, Lutheranism enjoyed majority support in Namibia (due to its pre-1919 German colonial past). Other Protestant religions became prominent in Anglophone countries, with a particularly strong presence of Calvinism in South Africa (kept alive by descendants of the early Dutch settlers at the Cape of Good Hope).

Several African countries make reference to God in their constitutions. For example, Ghana proclaimed its Constitution "in the name of Almighty God" (Preamble). Liberia testified to its "gratitude to God" and recognized "His Divine Guidance for our survival as a nation" (Preamble). The National Council for Development of Rwanda, responsible for establishing and adopting the Constitution, in doing so testified to "[t]rusting in God Almighty" (Preamble). The people of Seychelles confessed their gratitude to Almighty God "that we inhabit one of the most beautiful countries in the world" and expressed their conscious pride for having learned as descendants of different races to live together as one Nation under God (Preamble). Although said to be a secular state (art. 1), the Constitution of the Democratic Republic of Madagascar bears testimony of the Malagasy People's "belief in God the Creator" (Preamble). The Republic of Congo, while likewise professing to be a secular state (art. 1), acknowledged its "responsibility before God" (Preamble).

There is a clear tendency in Africa, if not in the world, for non-Muslim states to move away from such religiously based constitutional testimonies.

Proclaiming a state to be "Christian" still enjoys some appeal in many (non-African) countries where Roman Catholicism predominates, but even there, one finds the tendency to do away with the established status of the church (van der Vyver 1996, xl). Except in the context of an established church, ideological statements in a constitution of non-Muslim states have very little juridical relevance, if any relevance at all.

The tendency to discard confessions of faith in constitutional instruments may be illustrated with reference to recent developments in the Republic of South Africa. The South African governments of yesteryear had always claimed that the country represents a Christian state and sought to testify to its religious commitment with all kinds of quite nonsensical provisions, such as the one which proclaimed that "[t]he people of the Republic of South Africa acknowledge the sovereignty and guidance of Allmighty God" (sec. 2 of Act 110 of 1983). The "Allmighty God" referred to in this provision was intended to denote a kind of "potpourri god" that could be interpreted by all and sundry to suit their own conception of the deity (van der Vyver 1986, 175)—which, ironically, should be unacceptable to Christians who believe that one ought not to pay homage to any god other than the Trinity testified to in the Holy Bible. South Africa proclaimed its 1993 (interim) Constitution "[i]n humble submission to God" (Preamble). This phrase has altogether been omitted from the 1996 Constitution, which in its Preamble only appeals to God—in the words of the national anthem—to "protect our people."

Zambia recently reversed the trend of eliminating a special state commitment to Christianity. In an amendment of the Constitution that entered into force on May 1, 1996, it included a preambular clause declaring "the Republic a Christian nation while upholding the right of every person to enjoy that person's freedom of conscience or religion." President Frederick Chiluba of Zambia and his vice-president, General Miyanda, the driving forces behind this constitutional amendment, are both born-again Christians.

It is to be expected that, in spite of this development in Zambia, more and more countries will follow the example of those who avoided constitutional confessions of faith. Burundi, perhaps, has set the example of religiously neutral ideological statements in constitutional instruments. Its Constitution simply charges citizens to "contribute to the establishment of a morally healthy society" (art. 46). The type of political community that South Africa currently seeks to establish is depicted in the 1996 Constitution as "an open and democratic society based on human dignity, equality, and freedom" (sec. 36(1) and 39(1); see also sec. 7(1)).

SECULAR STATES

An increasing number of African states, including some already referred to which nevertheless retained religious confessions of faith in their respective constitutional instruments (see art. 1 of the Constitution of the Democratic Republic of Madagascar (1992) and art. 1 of the Constitution of the Republic of Congo (1990)), expressly proclaim the secularity of the state: Bénin (art. 2), Burkino Faso (art. 31), Burundi (art. 1), Cameroon (Preamble), Chad (art. 1), Congo (art. 1), the Republic of Congo (art. 1), Guinea (art. 1), Guinea-Bissau (art. 1), Ivory Coast (art. 2), Madagascar (art. 1), Mali (Preamble), Mozambique (art. 9.1), Namibia (sec. 1(1)), São Tomé and Principes (art. 1(6)), Senegal (art. 1), and Togo (art. 1).

Ethiopia (art. 27.5; see also art. 11.3.) and the Republic of Niger (art. 9) proclaimed the independence of government from religion, while Ethiopia (art. 11.3) and Libya (art. 5) decreed the independence of religion from government. Several African countries—Djibouti (art. 1), Ivory Coast (art. 6), Liberia (art. 14), Niger (art. 9), Senegal (art. 1), and Togo (art. 2)—promised to respect all religious beliefs.

RELIGION-STATE RELATIONS

Except in Muslim countries, the notion of an established religion no longer finds favor in African states. The Republic of Congo (art. 12), Ethiopia (art. 11.2), Liberia (art. 14), Nigeria (art. 10), and the Seychelles (art. 21(6)) expressly stated that they will not adopt any religion as a state religion. The separation of state and religion, or of law and religion, has been made part of the constitutional systems of Angola (art. 7; see also art. XXVII of the Draft Constitution of the Republic of Angola), Cape Verde (arts. 2(2) and 48(3)), Ethiopia (art. 11.1), and Guinea-Bissau (art. 6.1).

Several countries, in particular the Republic of Congo (art. 12), Liberia (art. 14), and the Seychelles (art. 21(5)), included promises in their constitutions not to require any religious test as a qualification for public office. The opposite holds true in Nigeria. It is there provided that the nondiscrimination provisions of the Constitution do not apply to any law which imposes restrictions based on religion with respect to the appointment of any person to any office under the State, or as a member of the armed forces or the police force, or in the service of a body corporate established directly by any law in force in Nigeria (art. 39(3)). This provision stands in stark contrast to those proclaiming the need to promote national integration in Nigeria (art. 15). In some countries, political parties are constitutionally prohibited from identifying themselves with any religious organization or denomination. This is the case in Djibouti (art. 6), Equatorial Guinea (art. 9), Guinea-Bissau (art. 4.5), the Republic of Niger (art. 9), and Senegal (art. 3).

In the context of state-religion relations, the autonomy of religious institutions—their competence to regulate their internal affairs without state intervention—seems evident but has remained a scarce commodity in African countries. The Second Republic of Guinea endorsed that competence in clear and unambiguous terms: "Religious institutions and communities freely create and administer themselves. They shall not be subject to the tutelage of the state" (art. 14). The Constitution of Senegal states this principle as follows: "Religious institutions and communities shall have the right to develop without hindrance. They shall not be subject to direct supervision by the state. They shall regulate and administer their affairs autonomously" (art. 19). Other Francophone constitutions with similar provisions include those of Bénin (art. 23) and Cape Verde (art. 48(3)). Ethiopia simply decreed that "[g]overnment shall not interfere in the conduct and practice of any religion"—adding that religion shall also not interfere in the affairs of government (art. 11.3).

Constitutional guarantees of the autonomy of religious institutions are not always granted on unconditional terms. In Tanzania, for example, the administration of religion must be conducted "[w]ithout jeopardising the laws applicable in the Union Republic" (art. 19(2)); and in Togo, the right to create religious organizations and to conduct organizational activities must likewise occur "within the framework of the law" (art. 25). Mozambique requires the activities of religious institutions to be conducted subject to the law (art. 9.2), and the Republic of Congo demands that religious sects be constituted under conditions established by law (art. 17).

Subjecting the internal autonomy of religious institutions to constraints imposed by law is in itself not necessarily reprehensible. Many countries of the world have introduced a system of registration of religious institutions in order simply to administer tax concessions and similar privileges applying to such institutions. Statutory constraints of this nature can, however, be abused— for example, if the political authorities should prescribe minimum membership requirements for registration, or under the law introduce other subtle means of control and religious repression.

In Liberia, state-imposed restrictions apply to foreign (noncitizen) missionary institutions: the Constitution grants such institutions the right to own property, but they are instructed to use the property only for the purpose for which it was acquired; and properties no longer used will be forfeited to the State (art. 22(c)). In Guinea-Bissau, the State promised to "respect and protect" religious sects, but this applies to "legally recognised" sects only, and the activities of such sects and the exercise of religious worship must be executed "subject to law" (art. 6.2).

Perhaps the most elaborate constitutional regulation of the internal autonomy of religious institutions is to be found in Gabon. The competence of religious communities to conduct and administer their own affairs "in an independent manner" is there subject to the following constraints: The right to form religious communities is made subject to "conditions fixed by law"; their internal autonomy must be exercised "under reserve of respect of the principles of national sovereignty, public order and the preservation of the moral and mental integrity of the individual"; and religious communities whose activities are "contrary to law" may be prohibited "according to the terms of the law" (art. 13).

In Egypt, fairly general restrictions apply to all non-state social entities, including (non-Muslim) religious institutions. The creation of "syndicates and unions" is indeed encouraged, but "should have a moral basis." The law regulates syndicates and unions, and they are under a constitutional responsibility "for questioning their members about their behaviour in exercising their activities according to certain codes of morals" (art. 56). Nigeria, in its constitutional circumscription of freedom of thought, conscience, and religion, prohibits the formation of, and participation in, secret societies. Formerly, religious bodies were excluded from the definition of "secret society," but this concession has been omitted from the most recent Constitution, and the proscription pertaining to secret societies therefore now also applies to religious institutions (art. 37(4)).

EQUAL PROTECTION AND NONDISCRIMINATION

Almost all African constitutions contain provisions that guarantee equality before the law irrespective of religious affiliation and promises not to discriminate against any person because of opinions held, conscientious persuasions, and/or religious belief. Equal protection provisions are often defined in absolute terms, for example, in the constitutions of Bénin (art. 26), Burundi (art. 15), the Central African Republic (art. 5), the Republic of Congo (art. 12), Djibouti (art. 1), Ethiopia (Preamble), Guinea (art. 8), Guinea-Bissau (art. 23), the Ivory Coast (art. 6), Mozambique (art. 66), Niger (art. 9), Senegal (art. 1), Tanzania (art. 13(1), read with art. 13(5) and (6)), and Togo (art. 2). The wording of the Constitution of the Second Republic of Guinea may be cited as a prototype of equal-protection decrees falling in this category: "All human beings shall be equal before the law. Men and women have the same rights. No one shall be favored or disadvantaged by reason of his birth, his race, his ethnicity, his language, his political, philosophical or religious beliefs and opinions" (Preamble).

In some instances, equality of treatment is guaranteed in respect of the constitutionally protected rights only. Ghana (art. 12(2)), Mauritius (art. 3), Namibia (Preamble), Sierra Leone (art. 15), and Zimbabwe (art. 11) may be cited as examples of this approach. The Constitution of Ghana thus provides: "Every person in Ghana, whatever his race, place of origin, political opinion, colour, religion, creed or gender shall be entitled to the fundamental human rights and freedoms of the individual contained in this Chapter but subject to respect for the rights and freedoms of others and for the public interest" (art. 12(2)). The Seychelles more cautiously proclaimed a general equal-protection clause, which includes the rights and freedoms set out in the Bill of Rights (art. 27(1)).

The Ghanaian provision cited above exemplifies yet another trend in equal protection arrangements of African constitutions: their subjection to all kinds of limitations—in that instance, the rights and freedoms of others and the public interest. In Congo, equal protection of the laws applies only insofar as it falls within limitations dictated by the public order and good mores (art. 11). Nondiscrimination provisions are also at times couched in unqualified terms, but less frequently than the equal protection of the law. Burkino Faso (art. 1), Cape Verde (art. 48(2)), and Togo (art. 11) may be cited as instances where the proscription of discrimination based on, inter alia, religion has been proclaimed in sweeping terms. Among the specific limitations worth mentioning are those that make allowance for affirmative-action programs. Ghana (art. 17(3)), the Seychelles (art. 27(1) and (2)), South Africa (sec. 9(2)), and Uganda (art. 21(4)) may serve as examples in this regard.

Malawi, on the other hand, exemplifies African countries that have subjected guarantees of the Bill of Rights, including the nondiscrimination provisions, to general limitations. In Malawi, the nondiscrimination clause (art. 20(1)) may be subjected to restrictions prescribed by law and which are reasonable, are recognized by international human rights standards, and are considered necessary in an open and democratic society (art. 44(2) and (3)). In South Africa, limitation of constitutionally protected rights, including the nondiscrimination guarantees, must be sanctioned by a law of general application, be reasonable, and be justifiable in an open and democratic society based on human dignity, equality and freedom (sec. 36(1)). Uganda adds to the affirmative-action provision already referred to (art. 21(4)), that a limitation of equal-protection and nondiscrimination decrees may be sanctioned by legislation authorized by the Constitution, or providing for matters acceptable and demonstrably justifiable in a democratic society (ibid.). In Ghana, the nondiscrimination provision may be subjected to limitations, prescribed by law, which are reasonably necessary to provide for the implementation of policies and programs aimed at redressing social, economic, or educational imbalances in the society, for matters relating to adoption, marriage, divorce, burial, devolution of property on death, or other matters of personal law; for placing restrictions on non-citizens in respect of the acquisition of land and on political or economic activities of aliens, within the spirit of the Constitution; or for differentiating between communities (art. 17(3)).

In many countries, guarantees of nondiscrimination based on religion (and several other grounds) are specifically applied to particular branches of public life. Several countries thus make special provision for nondiscrimination in the work place. Here we might cite the examples of Chad (art. 21), Congo (art. 31), the Republic of Congo (art. 27), Gabon (art. 7), Liberia (art. 18), Madagascar (art. 28), Rwanda (art. 16), and Sudan (art. 17(2)).

Also worth noting are those constitutions that not only prohibit religious discrimination but render punishable acts of discrimination based on, inter alia, religion. Gabon (art. 13), the Ivory Coast (art. 6), Mozambique (art. 69),[10] Niger (art. 9), and Senegal (art. 4) are cases in point. Nigeria in general terms prohibits discrimination on grounds of religion (art. 15(1)), while the Central African Republic more specifically forbids "any form of religious integration and intolerance" (art. 8). Guinea is more concerned with the national interest than with religious values as such. It renders punishable religious discrimination "which could have a grave effect on national unity, the security of the State, the territorial integrity of the Republic or the democratic functioning of its institutions" (art. 4). It does, however, promise asylum to any person persecuted by reason of his or her political, philosophical or religious opinion (art. 11). In certain other countries, further legislative intervention is anticipated that would render religious discrimination unlawful. Madagascar (art. 8) and Malawi (art. 20(2)) thus charged the state with an obligation to prohibit discrimination based on, inter alia, religion or opinion. Directive Principles of State Policy in the Constitution of Ghana burdened the State with the responsibility to "actively . . . prohibit discrimination and prejudice on the grounds of . . . religion, creed or other belief" (art. 35(5)).

The important question as to the *Drittwirkung* of nondiscrimination provisions in the constitution of a country has been expressly addressed by drafters of the South African Bill of Rights. In terms of the 1993 interim Constitution, unfair discrimination (sec. 8(2) of Act 200 of 1993) based on, inter alia, religion was outlawed if such discrimination was sanctioned by any law (public or private, statutory law or the common law, or even through customary law) (sec. 33(2)), or emerged from decisions taken or acts performed by any organ of state, belonging to either the legislative or executive branch of government, and acting on any of the levels of government (sec. 7(1)). Provision was made for civil-rights legislation that could outlaw, if and when the need might arise, unfair discrimination by persons other than organs of state (sec. 33(4)). The 1996 Constitution subsequently outlawed unfair discrimination based on religion by the State (sec. 9(3)) as well as any other person (sec. 9(4)), and went on to instruct the legislature to enact national legislation "to prevent or prohibit unfair discrimination" (ibid.).

The blank prohibition of discrimination by persons and institutions other than the state in the 1996 Constitution of South Africa is most unfortunate. Discrimination within the private enclave of a person's day-to-day life (the decision to reject Ann because she is Hindu and to marry Mary because she is Dutch Reformed), or within the internal sphere of a religious institution (the resolve of the Roman Catholic Church not to ordain women as priests) is thereby regulated by state-imposed constraints and again converted the liberated South Africa into a totalitarian régime. The civil-rights option of the 1993 interim Constitution was preferable in this regard: It permitted the state legislature to intervene on an ad hoc basis if and when unfair discrimination in the private sphere were to become a public menace warranting state intervention. In this way, unfair discrimination by persons and institutions other than the State could be responsibly addressed without falling into the overall trap of totalitarianism.

FREEDOM OF RELIGION

Freedom of religion, conscience, thought, opinion, and the like, circumscribed in a variety of ways, is guaranteed by almost all African constitutions—but seldom without reservations. Perhaps the most sweeping protection afforded to religious freedom is to be found in the Constitution of Malawi. Having proclaimed the right of every person to "freedom of conscience, religion, belief and thought, and to academic freedom" (art. 33), the Malawian Constitution goes on to assert that there shall be no derogation, restriction, or limitation with regard to this right (art. 44(1)(h)). The Republic of Guinea does not expressly exclude derogations, restrictions, or limitations of religious freedom, but nevertheless defines that freedom in unconditional terms: "He [human being] shall be free to believe, to think and to profess his religious faith, his political or philosophical opinions. He shall be free to express, to manifest and to diffuse his ideas and opinions by speech, by writing and by image. He shall be free to instruct and inform himself from sources available to all" (art. 7). The constitutional systems of Mali (art. 2) and Uganda (art. 29(1)(b) and (c)) may also be cited as instances where freedom of religion seemingly enjoys unqualified protection. Although the Constitution of Cape Verde in one of its articles seemingly protects religious freedom in absolute terms (art. 27(2)), there is a further provision in the Constitution which, while reiterating the inviolability of freedom of religion, conscience, and worship, subjects the right to spread a particular doctrine or conviction to the obligation of not jeopardizing the rights of others or the common good (art. 48(1)).

I shall not dwell upon the many contingencies foreseen by different African constitutions that may be relied upon for the limitation, and perhaps even the suspension, of religious freedom. In this context, constitutional policies may be classified into three distinct categories:

1. those that leave it up to the legislature to define such limitations or conditions of suspension;
2. those that specify the particular bases of limitations and/or suspension in respect of religious freedom; and
3. those that seemingly protect religious freedom in absolute terms, but in actual fact subject that freedom to general principles of limitation (and/or suspension) that apply to all constitutionally protected rights and freedoms.

The Constitution of Guinea-Bissau belongs to the first category: Freedom of expression, of thought, as well as the "freedom of choice of religion" (among others) is guaranteed "according to conditions provided by law" (art. 44). Other African countries with similar arrangements include the Central African Republic (art. 8), Chad (art. 23), Djibouti (art. 11), Equatorial Guinea (art. 13(f)), and the Islamic Republic of Mauritania (art. 10). Egypt (art. 47) and Morocco (art. 9) subjected freedom of opinion—which may be taken to include freedom of religion—to restrictions imposed by law.

Leaving it up to the legislature to define the limitations of freedom of religion may be seen as a concession to the principle of majoritarian democracy. A bill of rights, founded on the notion of constitutionality (a system where the constitution constitutes the supreme law of the land) does not necessarily reflect the will of the majority. Based on the assumption that the legislature represents the political majority, one could argue that the power given to a majoritarian legislature to flesh out certain general constitutional directives does justice to the democratic premise of majority rule. However, in countries where "majority rule" derives from manipulation of popular demands, or where an existing régime maintains power through undemocratic interventions or political repression—which is often the case in Africa—the argument would lose its essential supposition. It is furthermore always risky to provide a law-maker with legislative powers without feasible substantive constraints imbedded in the basic notions of human rights protection.

In certain jurisdictions, confining religious freedom to standards established by law (and regulation) is indeed combined with other specific limitation criteria, such as the public order. One finds this in the constitutions of, for example, Burundi (art. 25) and Togo (art. 25). The Constitution of Liberia emphatically defined the objectives for which freedom of thought, conscience, and religion may be limited by law: The law must be designed "to protect public safety, order, health, or morals, or the fundamental rights and freedoms of others" (art. 14).

The second category mentioned above may be illustrated with reference to the Constitution of Burkino Faso: There, freedom of belief, of non-belief, of conscience, of religious and philosophical opinion, and of religious exercise (among others) is guaranteed subject to respect for the law, for the public order, for good morals, and for the human person (art. 7). The public order features prominently in the limitation provisions of Francophone countries, such as Bénin (art. 23),[11] Burundi (art. 25), Cameroon (Preamble), Congo (art. 26),[12] Gabon (art. 2), Madagascar (art. 10), Niger (art. 24), Senegal (art. 19), and Togo (art. 25). Bénin (art. 23), Burundi (art. 25), and Togo (art. 25) imposed the further special requirement of the free exercise of religion having to comply with respect for the principle of secularity of the State. The Republic of Niger, again, combined the public-order requirement with the further need to secure social tranquility and national unity (art. 24). In Cameroon, respect for the public order constitutes the confines of the right not to be harassed because of one's opinion or belief in religious, philosophical, or political matters (Preamble).

Other eventualities that feature prominently in the limitation provisions of African constitutions are the national interest (The Gambia (art. 13), Ghana (art. 12(2)), Kenya (art. 70), Namibia (art. 19)); good morals (Congo (art. 26), Liberia (art. 14)); the common good (Cape Verde (art. 48(1))); the terms of the Constitution itself (Ghana (art. 26(1)), Liberia (art. 11(a) and (b)), Namibia (art. 19)); and the rights and freedoms of other persons (The Gambia (art. 13), Ghana (art. 12(2)), Kenya (art. 70), Liberia (art. 14), Madagascar (art. 10), Namibia (art. 19), Togo (art. 25)).

The Constitution of Liberia contains an interesting variation on the latter theme: The protection of the Constitution is there promised to those persons "who, in the practice of religion, conduct themselves peaceably, not obstructing others and conforming to the standards therein" (art. 14).

Sierra Leone (art. 15) and Zambia (art. 11) in a similar fashion combined most of the above bases for the limitation of religious freedom[13]: Freedom of conscience (among other constitutional rights) was made subject to the rights and freedoms of others and the public interest, and further subject to such limitations as are contained in the provisions of the Bill of Rights, being limitations designed to ensure that the enjoyment of the concerned rights and freedoms by any individual does not prejudice the rights and freedoms of others, or the public interest. Mauritius followed the same trend in the formulation of limitation criteria, but added the further rider that the limitation must in any event (and in every case) be provided for in the section of the Constitution dealing with the particular right or freedom in question (art. 3)—and I might add that Mauritius does subject freedom of conscience to fairly sweeping limitations (art. 11(5)).

The Rwandan Constitution makes it abundantly clear that criminal conduct committed under pretenses of religious freedom will not be tolerated. It stipulates that liberty of religion and of conscience shall not preclude "punishment of infractions committed during the exercise thereof" (art. 18).

The third option mentioned above seems to be popular in Anglophone African countries. Perhaps the most far-reaching general conditions for the limitation of constitutional rights and freedoms have been proclaimed in Ghana. Freedom of thought, conscience, and belief (art. 21(1)(b)), and freedom to practice any religion and to manifest such practice (art 21(1)(c)), have been subjected to limitations "under authority of a law" that makes provision for, inter alia, the imposition of restrictions that are reasonably required in the interest of defense, public safety, public health, or the running of essential services, on the movement or residence in the country of any particular person or class of persons, for restricting the entry into Ghana or the movement in Ghana of non-citizens, or "that is reasonably required for the purpose of safeguarding the people of Ghana against the teaching or propagation of a doctrine which exhibits or encourages disrespect for the nationhood of Ghana, the national symbols and emblems, or incites hatred against other members of the community"—which restraints must however remain within the confines of "the spirit of this Constitution" (art. 21(4)).

Other general limitation provisions include those of Namibia. Freedom of thought, conscience, and belief (art. 21(1)(b)), and freedom to practice any religion and to manifest such practice (art. 21(1)(c)), are subject to "the law of Namibia, in so far as such law imposes reasonable restrictions on the exercise of the rights and freedoms conferred, . . . which are necessary in a democratic society and are required in the interest of the sovereignty and integrity of Namibia, national security, public order, decency or morality, or in relation to contempt of court, defamation or incitement to an offence" (art. 21(2)).

The Constitution of Congo speaks of limitations "established by law with a view to assure the recognition and the respect of the rights and liberties of others and the goal of satisfying just exigencies of morale, public order and the general well-being in a democratic society" (art. 56). In Ethiopia, freedom to express and manifest one's religion or belief may be subjected only to "such limitations as are prescribed by law and are necessary to protect public safety, order, health, education, morals and the fundamental rights and freedoms of others, and in order to guarantee the independence of the government from religion" (art. 27.5).

Mention may finally be made of the general limitation provisions in the Constitution of South Africa. Freedom of conscience, religion, thought, belief, and opinion (sec. 15(1)), as well as the nondiscrimination provisions (sec. 9(3) and (4)), may be limited, provided:

- the limitation is contained in a law with general application;
- is reasonable; and
- is justifiable in an open and democratic society based on human dignity, equality, and freedom;

and taking into account the nature of the right, the importance and purpose of the limitation, the nature and extent of the limitation, the relation between the limitation and its purpose, and less restrictive means to achieve the purpose (sec. 36(1)).

THE QUESTION OF PROSELYTIZATION

If constitutional regulation in Africa is anything to go by, the question of proselytization has several critical components: (a) the free exercise of religion; (b) the right to spread one's faith; (c) freedom to choose and to change one's religion or belief. Within these broad contours, several more specific themes emerged from time to time in the constitutional dictates pertaining to religion, including: (d) religion in education; (e) the spread of religion through communications media; (f) religion in marriage and family life; (g) religious considerations pertaining to the rights of the child; (h) protection of religious feelings; (i) protection of places of worship and religious symbols; (j) religious comfort in hospitals, prisons, and the armed forces; and (k) conscientious objections. I will now address each of these headings:

THE FREE EXERCISE OF RELIGION

There is a difference, I suppose, between the right to entertain a certain belief and the right to practice one's faith. It is often said that the first is absolute, while the second is subject to state-imposed constraints. This is seemingly not necessarily the case. For example, the Republic of Guinea is quite generous in proclaiming, without qualification, that "[t]he free exercise of religious sects shall be guaranteed" (art. 14), and Uganda only requires that belonging to, and participating in, the practices of any religious body or organization—which it proclaims to be a component of the freedom to practice any religion and manifest such practice—must occur "in a manner consistent with this Constitution" (art. 29(1)(c)).[14]

Such generosity is not common, however, when executing one's religion through word and deed is at stake. In fact, the limitation provisions dealt with above in the context of religious freedom by and large apply to the exercise of, rather than the mere commitment to, a particular religion. The distinction based on absoluteness of the right to believe is, in my opinion, the only possible basis for differentiating between that right and its counterpart, the free exercise of religion. The exercise of religion presupposes the freedom to believe; and freedom to believe without the right to convert one's religion into action would be an empty shell. The South African Constitution ranks among those that do not make special mention of the free exercise of religion (sec. 15(1)), but it is difficult to conceive "the right to freedom of conscience, religion, thought, belief and opinion" without its concomitant implementation component.

As we have established earlier, freedom to believe may be taken to be axiomatic in probably all African constitutional systems. It is perhaps worth noting that the Constitution of Burkino Faso also expressly mentions the freedom of non-belief (art. 7); and the Constitution of Mozambique speaks of the freedom to practice or not to practice a religion (art. 78.1). It is submitted that freedom of religion in any event essentially includes the right not to entertain any particular religious belief.

The free exercise of religion is proclaimed in most African constitutions. In the Ethiopian Charter it is succinctly defined as "the freedom, either individually or in fellowship with others, in public and private, to religious worship, observance and teaching" (art. 27.1). The Mozambican Constitution refers to the right of religious denominations "to pursue their religious aims freely" (art. 78.2).

Returning next to the question of limitation of the free exercise of religion, a few country-specific examples, selected here at random, will suffice to illustrate the general nature—and great variety—of limitation contingencies. In Namibia, the free exercise of religion must be practiced subject to the terms of the Constitution, and with due regard to the rights and freedoms of others and the national interest (sec. 19). In terms of another section of the Constitution, the "freedom to practice any religion and to manifest such practice" (sec. 21(1)(c)) must be exercised subject to the law of Namibia, insofar as such law imposed reasonable restrictions necessary in a democratic society and as required in the interests of the sovereignty and integrity of the country, national security, public order, decency or morality, or in relation to contempt of court, defamation, or incitement to commit an offence (sec. 21(2)). Senegal, on the other hand, simply subjects the free exercise of religion to the demands of the public order (art. 19). Niger added to the requirement of public order, considerations of social tranquility and national unity (art. 24), and the Constitution of the Republic of Congo subjected the free exercise of religion to the public order and morality (art. 17). Rwanda afforded a blank check for the free exercise of religion, except in cases where punishment is imposed for infractions committed in the public exercise of that freedom (art. 18). Sudan is set on upholding standards of morality, public order, and health "as required by law" in preference to the free exercise of religion (art. 18). Togo requires the practice of religious beliefs to be conducted with respect for the liberties of others, maintenance of public order, standards established by laws and regulations, and respect for the secularity of the State (art. 25).

Many Anglophone countries in Africa include in the constitutional protection of freedom of conscience a free-exercise guarantee taken from the European Convention for the Protection of Human Rights and Fundamental Freedoms (213 U.N.T.S. 222), which provides: "Everyone has the right to freedom of thought, conscience and religion; this right includes freedom to change his religion or belief and *freedom, either alone or in community with others and in public or private, to manifest his religion or belief, in worship, teaching, practice and observance*" (art. 9.1, emphasis added). Variations on this theme are to be found in the constitutions of Botswana (art. 11(1)), The Gambia (art. 21(1)), Kenya (art. 78(1)), Lesotho (art. 13(1)), Mauritius (art. 11), Nigeria (art. 37(1)), the Seychelles (art. 23(1)), Sierra Leone (art. 24(1)), Zambia (art. 19(1)), and Zimbabwe (art. 19(1)). These constitutions[15] also follow closely the limitation criteria stipulated in the European Convention: "Freedom to manifest one's religion or belief shall be subject only to such limitations as are prescribed by law and are necessary in a democratic society in the interest of public safety, for the protection of public order, health or morals, or for the protection of the rights and freedoms of others" (art. 9.2).

Standard requirements for confining the free exercise of religion in the above group of countries are that the limitation of the concerned freedom must be sanctioned by legislation reasonably required (i) in the interest of defense, public safety, public order, public morality, or public health; or (ii) for the purpose of protecting the rights and freedoms of other persons, including the right to observe and practice any religion [or belief] without the unsolicited intervention of members of any other religion [or belief], and provided the limitation is justifiable in a democratic society.[16]

THE RIGHT TO SPREAD ONE'S FAITH

The right to engage in missionary activity is perhaps the most controversial component of religious freedom. Muslim countries encourage the conversion of people to Islam, but in general render punishable efforts to convert Muslims to any non-Islamic religion. Several religions do not engage in missionary activity at all, except perhaps in the sense of "internal proselytizing": that is, efforts to persuade existing members of the group to become better or more faithful adherents to the concerned religion. Judaism and Hinduism fall within this category. Christianity, on the other hand, is essentially a missionary religion: it mandates its followers to actively engage in efforts to convert non-believers to the Christian faith.

These intricacies are not accurately reflected in the constitutions of Africa. At best one might note the absence of missionary rights in the constitutions of self-professed Muslim states. Several African states, however, have included in their circumscription of religious freedom express references to the right to spread one's faith. The Constitution of Uganda, for example, guarantees "the right to enjoy, practice, profess, maintain, and *promote* any creed or religion" (art. 37, emphasis added). Here, too, the proof of genuine guarantees is in the constitutional confines attending the right to spread one's religion. The nature of those confines will next be considered.

The Constitution of Cape Verde guarantees the right of every denomination "to spread its doctrine or conviction," but this must be done without jeopardizing the rights of others or the common good (art. 48(1)). In the Republic of Congo, the right to exercise religion or convictions by services, education, practices, rites, and religious life was made subject to "public order and morals" (art. 17). In Namibia, the right to enjoy, practice, profess, maintain, and promote any religion must be exercised within the terms of the Constitution and subject to the further condition that the right does not impinge on the rights of others or the national interest (art. 19).

Perhaps the most sweeping limitations of missionary activities are to be found in the Constitution of Tanzania. The Constitution indeed asserts that the promotion of religion, worship, and evangelization shall be free and matters of personal voluntary choice, but then goes on to proclaim that such activities must be conducted "[w]ithout jeopardising the laws applicable in the Union Republic" (art. 19(2)). As we have established earlier, the laws envisaged in this regard are not substantively defined; and Tanzania, furthermore, subjected the exercise of religious rights (among others) to sweeping limitations that could be applied so as to render the constitutional protection of those rights practically meaningless (arts. 30 and 31).

The Anglophone countries, mentioned earlier, which followed the religious freedom directives of the European Convention, also embodied in their respective constitutions the right to manifest and propagate any particular religion or belief in worship, teaching, practice, and observance; and this component of religious freedom in the concerned countries is evidently subject to the limitations of the European Convention stipulated above in the context of free-exercise considerations.

Within the confines stipulated for the limitation of the right to promote a particular religion one would probably find ample constitutional backing for action taken in many African countries, such as Angola and Malawi, against particularly the Jehovah's Witnesses. Refusal to serve in the armed forces may be taken to violate the national interest; and the methods used by the Jehovah's Witnesses for spreading their religion could be seen as violating the rights and freedoms of others, such as their right to privacy.

In the present context, mention should finally be made of instances where special restrictions apply to foreign missionary activities in a particular country. In Malawi, for example, noncitizen missionary institutions may indeed own property, but, as a matter of constitutional imperative, their properties may only be used for the purposes for which they were acquired; and the property of foreign missionaries no longer used shall encheat to the State (art.

22(c)). In Ghana, there are also sweeping limitations applying to, or which can be made applicable to, noncitizens that might restrain their freedom to practice a religion in the country (art. 21(4)).

FREEDOM TO CHOOSE AND TO CHANGE ONE'S RELIGION OR BELIEF

There evidently is an intimate relationship between the freedom to adopt a religion or belief of one's own choice and the right to exchange one religion for another. The right freely to choose a religion or belief is specifically guaranteed in Ethiopia (arts. 27.1 and 27.3) and Guinea-Bissau (art. 44). The Anglophone countries that in their religious-freedom provisions imitated the European Convention—Botswana (art. 11(1)), The Gambia (art. 21(1)), Kenya (art. 78(1)), Lesotho (art. 13(1)), Mauritius (art. 11), Nigeria (art. 37(1)), the Seychelles (art. 23(1)), Sierra Leone (art. 24(1)), Zambia (art. 19(1)), and Zimbabwe (art. 19(1))—included in their definition of that freedom the right of a person to change his religion or belief[17]; and that freedom was made subject to the same limitations, mentioned earlier, that apply in general to religious freedom and the free exercise of religion.[18] The Seychelles, however, differ in the present regard from the other countries in this group. On those islands, freedom to manifest and propagate a religion or belief, but not the freedom to change one's religion or belief, may be subjected to limitations (i) prescribed by law; (ii) which are necessary in a democratic society; (iii) in the interests of defense, public safety, public order, public morality, or public health, or for the purpose of protecting the rights or freedoms of others (art. 21(2)). The freedom to change one's religion or belief may therefore be taken to apply without reservation in the Seychelles.

It should be noted that African constitutional provisions dealing with the different components of religious freedom cannot in all instances be evaluated without reference to international law standards. The Constitution of Togo, for example, renders the Universal Declaration of Human Rights (1948) (G.A. Res. 217 A(III), U.N. Doc. A/810 at 71 (1948)), and ratified international instruments relating to human rights, self-executing in the country (art. 50). In terms of the Universal Declaration, freedom of thought, conscience, and religion includes "freedom to change . . . [one's] religion or belief" and "freedom, either alone or in community with others and in public or private, to manifest . . . [one's] religion or belief in teaching . . . " (art. 18). The self-executing clause thus incorporated these provisions of the Universal Declaration into the municipal law of Togo.

The Ethiopian Constitution in similar vein proclaimed all ratified treaties to be "an integral part of the laws of the country" (art. 9.4). The Constitution furthermore provides that the fundamental rights and liberties in the Constitution must be interpreted in conformity with the Universal Declaration of Human Rights, international human rights covenants, humanitarian conventions, and with the principles of other relevant international instruments which Ethiopia has accepted and ratified (art. 13.2). Since Ethiopia has ratified the

International Covenant on Civil and Political Rights (G.A. Res. 2200A (XXI), 21 U.N. GAOR Supp. (No. 16) at 52, U.N. Doc. A/6316 (1966)), the definition of freedom of thought, conscience, and religion contained in that instrument is law in Ethiopia; and that definition includes "freedom . . . to adopt a religion or belief of . . . [one's] choice, and freedom, either individually or in community with others and in public or private, to manifest . . . [one's] religion or belief in . . . " teaching (art. 18.1). The Covenant goes on to provide: "No person shall be subject to coercion which would impair his freedom to have or to adopt a religion or belief of his choice" (art. 18.2).

This component of the concerned freedom applies without reservation. The second component of the cited portion of the definition of religious freedom—the right to manifest one's religion or belief through, inter alia, teaching—may, however, be made subject to "only such limitations as are prescribed by law and are necessary to protect public safety, order, health, or morals, or the fundamental rights and freedoms of others" (art. 18.3).

The South African Constitution did not incorporate international human rights standards into its municipal law, but instructed courts to consider international law when interpreting the provisions of the Bill of Rights (sec. 39(1)). Although the Constitution does not specify the substance of freedom of religion (sec.15(1)), it is reasonable to assume that the courts will interpret that freedom, in view of the international law directive, to include free exercise, the right to spread one's religion, and freedom to choose and to change one's religion.

The Constitution of Malawi also includes a directive instructing courts of law to confine the limitation provisions of the Constitution to those "recognized by international human rights law" (art. 44(2)). For purposes of religious freedom, this provision is neither here nor there, since the protection of freedom of conscience, belief, thought, and religion applies in that country without any derogation, restriction, or limitation (art. 44(1)(h)). The right to spread one's religion or belief, and freedom to choose or to change one's religion or belief, are not expressly included in the constitutional definition of religious freedom. Nor can the clause subjecting limitation provisions to international law standards per se be relied upon to read proselytizing rights into the constitutional guarantee of religious freedom. However, Malawi also included in its Constitution "principles of national policy," which are merely "directory" but which courts are entitled to consider when interpreting and applying any of the provisions of the Constitution or of any other law, or when adjudicating on the validity of executive decisions; and those principles include a commitment "[t]o govern in accordance with the law of nations and the rule of law" (art. 13(k)). This provision may indeed inform courts to include the right to spread one's religion, and freedom to choose or change one's religion, in the definition of religious freedom of that country. Everything seems to indicate, in a word, that profound persecution of Jehovah's Witnesses in Malawi—for which the Banda régime was notorious—was unconstitutional.

Several other African countries, including Bénin, Burundi, Mali, and Niger, included in the Preamble to their respective constitutions a commitment—

short of self-executing incorporation—to the human rights principles of the Universal Declaration of Human Rights, and also to the African Charter on Human and People's Rights of 1981 (OAU Doc. CAB/LEG/67/3 rev. 5, 21 I.L.M. 58 (1982)). In Bénin, the African Charter was actually adopted by the people in a referendum of December 2, 1990, and incorporated into the Constitution, as an "integral part" thereof, by means of an annexure. The African Charter guarantees, as a component of the freedom of conscience, the profession and free practice of religion—subject though to the demands of law and order (art. 8). It seemingly does not go beyond the protection of free exercise (subject to law and order).

RELIGION IN EDUCATION

Education may be utilized as a powerful medium for the promotion, propagation, and spread of religion. Many African constitutions address this question, taking diverse positions. Islam and Calvinism share the common belief that there is no such thing as objective knowledge or neutral education. South Africa and Malawi represented perhaps the last African outposts of a régime professing to be Christian with a strong commitment to Calvinism. With the transition of South Africa to a democracy in 1994, and the defeat of the Banda régime in Malawi in 1993, that commitment no longer obtains in Africa. There still are several Muslim states, though, on the continent; and—as indicated above—Zambia recently opted for proclaiming itself to be a Christian state (Act 18 of 1996).

Only one Muslim state deals in its constitution with religion in education, however. In Egypt, the society is said to have committed itself to "the high standards of religious education" (art. 12). Religious education is furthermore proclaimed to be "a principal subject in the courses of general education" in that country (art. 19). Several non-Muslim states could also find peace with religious education, and tuition in religion, in state-sponsored educational institutions. In Bénin, special provision is made for religious institutions and communities to cooperate equally in the education of the youth (art. 14). In Togo, the State recognized private, religious and secular education (art. 30).

The Republic of Congo perhaps represents the opposite extreme. It outlaws in its Constitution any law or executive act amounting to discrimination in education based on religion (art. 12). Cape Verde, likewise, provided in its Constitution that "[p]ublic education shall not be religious" (art. 49(5)). The State is emphatically forbidden to program education and culture to follow any philosophical, aesthetic, political, or religious directives (art. 49(4)). The Constitution does, however, contain guarantees of "freedom of religious instruction" (art. 48(4)), and allowance is made for private schools and educational establishments, "as provided by law" (art. 49(6)), which presumably may be parochial. It is further provided that families may educate their children according to "the ethical and social principles resulting from their philosophical, religious, ideological, aesthetic, political, or other convictions" (art. 49(3)). In Ethiopia, a similar provision obtains: "Parents and guardians, on the basis of their beliefs, have the right to provide religious and moral education to their children" (art. 27.4).

State neutrality in matters of religious education is demanded by several other African constitutions. Gabon proclaimed the "religious neutrality" of public education, but authorized religious instruction of children in public educational institutions "upon demands of their parents, under conditions determined by regulation" (art. 19). South Africa is of much the same mind. Religious observances may be conducted at state or state-aided institutions under rules established by an appropriate authority for that purpose, and provided that religious observances are conducted on an equitable basis and attendance at them is free and voluntary (sec. 15(2)). Several countries—including Botswana (art. 11(3)), The Gambia (art. 21(2)), Kenya (art. 78(3)), Lesotho (sec. 13(3)), Mauritius (art. 11(2)), Nigeria (art. 35(2)), Sierra Leone (art. 24(2)), Zambia (art. 19(2)), and Zimbabwe (sec. 19(2))—provided that students may not, without their consent (or in the case of minors, the consent of their guardians), be required to receive religious instruction or to take part in religious ceremonies or observances based on a religion other than their own. The other partner in this Anglophone consortium, the Seychelles, formulated the same principle somewhat differently. No one may be compelled to impart or receive (any) religious instruction or to take part in or attend any religious ceremony or observance in a place of education (art. 21(3)). Religious communities or denominations are there (art. 21(7))—and also in Sierra Leone (art 24(3))—permitted to provide religious instruction to persons of that community or denomination in the course of education provided by that community or denomination.

In certain Francophone countries, such as Bénin (art. 14) and Gabon (art. 19), provision is made for private schools, secular or parochial, with the authorization and control of the State and with state subsidies under conditions determined by law. In Ethiopia, a similar arrangement has been sanctioned (art. 27.2), but this arrangement was made subject to another, which provides: "Education, public and private, shall be provided in a manner that is free from any political partisanship, religious influence or cultural prejudice" (art. 90.2).

Zambia may perhaps also be cited as a country where privately established parochial schools are entitled to state subsidies. The right of religious communities to establish and maintain places of education, and to provide religious instruction, is there authorized without any mention of the financing of such places (art. 19(3)); and since this right is constitutionally guaranteed, it is reasonable to assume that religious communities exercising that right will be entitled to state-sponsored financial support. The Zambian Constitution also sanctioned the right of religious communities to provide social services for persons of the religious community or denomination concerned (ibid.).

In Zimbabwe, religious communities are likewise entitled to provide religious instruction, but such instruction—the Constitution provides—may only be given by persons lawfully in the country, and that irrespective of whether or not the religious community receives state subsidies (art. 19(3)). State laws may prescribe the standards to be maintained, and the qualifications required for, private education, "including any instruction, not being religious instruction" (art. 19(5)(c)). The right of religious communities to establish and maintain places of education, and to provide religious instruction in such institutions, is also authorized in several other countries, but here clearly without any claim to state subsidy ("at its own expense"): Botswana (art. 11(2)), The Gambia (art. 21(3)), Kenya (art. 78(2)), Lesotho (sec. 13(2)), Mauritius (art. 14(1)), and Nigeria (art. 35(3)), are cases in point.

In the case of Mauritius, the right to establish parochial schools is made subject to legislative restrictions enacted (i) in the interests of defense, public safety, public order, public morality, or public health; (ii) for regulating such schools in the interest of persons receiving instruction in them; and provided (iii) the limitation is shown to be reasonably justifiable in a democratic society (art. 14(2)). Parochial schools must be open to every person wishing to send his or her child to the school, even though the school was not established by government (art 11(3)). The Constitution further provides: "No religious community or denomination shall be prevented from making provision for the giving, by persons lawfully in Mauritius, of religious instruction to persons of that community or denomination in the course of any education provided by that community or denomination" (art. 14(3)).

The South African Constitution makes provision for the establishment of independent educational institutions, provided only that there shall be no discrimination based on race, that such institutions are registered with the State, and that they maintain standards not inferior to those of comparable public educational institutions (sec. 29(3)). The independent educational institutions are to be established and maintained by their founders "at their own expense" (ibid.). The State may, however, at its own discretion subsidize independent educational institutions (sec. 29(4)). Nothing is expressly stated in the Constitution about the establishment of religious educational institutions, but it is submitted that the independent educational institutions contemplated in the Constitution may be parochial. Religious observances may furthermore be conducted at state and state-aided educational institutions, on condition only that the religious observances follow rules made by the appropriate authorities, are conducted on an equitable basis, and attendance thereof is free and voluntary (sec. 15(2)).

The MPLA Draft Constitution of the Republic of Angola also permits the establishment of private schools at the expense of its founders (art. XXVI(4)). The Angolan Constitution—like its South African counterpart—prohibits racism in the admission policies of private schools (art. XXVI(4)(d)); but, in the case of Angola, the creed of potential appointees to such institutions may be taken into account (art. XXVI(4)(e)).

The Spread of Religion through Communications Media

Cape Verde is one of the few African countries which expressly deals with the question of utilizing the state-sponsored mass media for purposes of religious services and missionary activity. The message there is short and sweet: "Churches shall have the right to use the communication media to accomplish their activities and purposes, as provided by law" (art. 48(6)).

The South African Interim Constitution of 1993 dealt indirectly with the same question. It simply provided that all media financed by or under the control of the State must be regulated in a manner which ensures impartiality and the expression of a diversity of opinion (sec. 15(2)). In consequence of this provision, the radio and television authorities in the country allocated broadcasting times to different religious denominations on basis of equality (proportional to the numerical support of each one of the denominations competing for the available time slots). The question thereupon arose whether a particular denomination could buy extra broadcasting time. The broadcasting authorities decided against it, since disproportionate broadcasting time for those who could afford it would violate the egalitarian base of the South African Constitution. The provision referred to above has been omitted from the 1996 (final) Constitution. It is submitted, however, that the principle of that provision is implied in the equal-protection clause and will therefore remain part of the South African constitutional system.

Religion in Marriage and Family Life

In certain Muslim countries, such as Egypt (art. 9) and Libya (art. 3), the family is held to be "the basis of society founded on religion, morality and patriotism." In Bénin, the State is instructed to protect the family, and particularly the mother and child (art. 26). The Constitution of Burkino Faso provides: "Every discrimination founded on . . . religion . . . shall be forbidden in the matter of marriage" (art. 23). In Namibia, the right to marry and to found a family belongs to "[m]en and women of full age," without any limitation due to religion or creed (sec. 14(1)).

The problem addressed in the Namibian Constitution stems from a rule of the Roman-Dutch law—the common law system of South Africa, Lesotho, Botswana, Swaziland, Namibia, and Zimbabwe—which denies the status of marriage to all potentially polygamous unions. In South Africa, the problem was initially raised by a Muslim delegation while the transition to democracy was being negotiated at Kempton Park in 1993. In consequence of the delegation's representations, a clause was added to the interim Constitution which authorized legislation that would afford legal recognition to a system of personal and family law adhered to by persons professing a particular religion, and the validity of marriages concluded under a system of religious law subject to specified procedures (sec. 14(3)). Since this provision was evidently intended to sanction legislation that would afford legality to polygamous Muslim marriages, feminists were up in arms, since polygamy is generally regarded as an affront to the equal treatment of, and as constituting discrimination against, women.

Two problems attending the South African provision came to light in the ensuing debate. Since the legislation contemplated in the concerned section of the Constitution was authorized notwithstanding any other provision in the Chapter on Fundamental Rights (ibid.), the constitutionality of the legislation would remain unaffected by considerations of equal protection and nondiscrimination. Second, because the Constitution only afforded sanction to legislation that would legalize personal and family law, and marriages, founded on a particular religion or religious law (such as those that obtain in the Muslim community), African polygamous marriages (referred to in South African legal jargon as "customary unions") could not be legalized under auspices of the provision in question, since "customary unions" are not founded on any particular religious scruples.

The 1996 Constitution remedied both of these concerns. It now authorizes legislation recognizing marriages concluded under a system of religious, personal, or family law, or under *any tradition*[19]; and whereas the original provision was preceded by the phrase: "Nothing in this Chapter shall preclude legislation . . . ," it is now provided that recognition of marriages and of systems of personal and family law in terms of the constitutional provision under consideration must be consistent with other provisions of the Constitution (sec. 15(3)).

In Nigeria, the State is charged with the rather peculiar responsibility of encouraging intermarriage among persons of different religions with a view to promoting national integration (art. 16(3)(c)). This provision constitutes part of several strategies contemplated in the Constitution to counteract tribalism. The State must, for example, also promote or encourage the formation of associations that cut across religious barriers (art. 16(3)(d)); and, in order that "national integration shall severely be encouraged," the Constitution prohibits discrimination based on "place of origin, sex, religion, status, ethnic or linguistic association or ties" (art. 16(2)).

Other African countries striving toward national unity and seeking to create constitutional directives to that end include Uganda and Sierra Leone. Uganda does not deny the salience of diversity in the community. Its Constitution provides that every effort is to be made to integrate all the peoples of the country while at the same time recognizing their ethnic, religious, ideological, political, and cultural diversity (art. III(ii)). Everything must be done to promote a culture of cooperation, understanding, appreciation, tolerance, and respect for each other's customs, traditions and beliefs (art. III(iii)). In Sierra Leone, the State must, with a view to promoting national integration and unity, "discourage" discrimination based, inter alia, on religion (art. 6(2)).

RELIGIOUS CONSIDERATIONS PERTAINING TO THE RIGHTS OF THE CHILD

Congo stands alone in Africa in proclaiming the principle of nondiscrimination based on religion in regard to measures of protection to be afforded to children by the family, society, and the State and which measures of protection stem from the conditions of the child as a minor (art. 42). The South African Constitution contains an impressive inventory of children's rights (sec. 28), including the right to education (sec. 29). As already noted elsewhere, educational institutions based on a common religion are currently not taboo in the country. The 1996 Constitution includes in the section on children's rights a proscription of child labor that, among others, places at risk the child's "spiritual, moral, or social development" (sec. 28(1)(f)(ii)).

It is also important to note that all African countries, except Somalia, have ratified the Convention on the Rights of the Child of 1981 (G.A. Res. 44/25 (annex), 44 U.N. GAOR Supp. (No. 49) at 167, U.N. Doc. A/44/49 (1989)). In most instances ratification was unconditional, but certain Muslim states, including Algeria, Egypt, and Morocco, did enter reservations which in one way or another testified to the subordination of their responsibilities under the Convention to the dictates of *Shari'a*.[20] Djibouti, where Islam happens to be the dominant religion but which in its Constitution professes a certain neutrality in regard to religion (arts. 1 and 6), nevertheless—somewhat mysteriously—subjected its accession to the Convention to norms dictated by "its religion and its traditional values." In countries such as Ethiopia and Togo, where international treaties have been rendered self-executing (arts. 9.4 and 50, respectively), the provisions of the Convention constitute part of the law of the land.

PROTECTION OF RELIGIOUS FEELINGS

In Sierra Leone, every citizen is under an obligation to "respect the dignity and religion of other individuals" (art. 13(e)). The Constitution of Cape Verde prohibits the imitation or mockery of religious symbols or ceremonies (art. 48(7)). While affirming its "attachment to the fundamental freedoms embodied in the Universal Declaration of Human Rights and the United Nations Charter," the Constitution of Cameroon proclaimed a preambular commitment to various human rights principles, including one that proclaims that no one shall be harassed because of his or her beliefs in religious matters, "subject to respect for public order" (Preamble). In the present context one is again reminded of those constitutions, alluded to earlier, which criminalized acts of discrimination based on religion, including Gabon (art. 13), the Ivory Coast (art. 6), Mozambique (art. 69), Niger (art. 9), and Senegal (art. 4).

PROTECTION OF PLACES OF WORSHIP AND RELIGIOUS SYMBOLS

The Constitution of Cape Verde protects places of worship, as well as religious symbols, emblems, and ceremonies (art. 48(7)). The Constitution of Angola likewise promises protection of churches and of places and objects of worship, subject though to state laws (art. 7).

Religious Comfort in Hospitals, Prisons, and the Armed Forces

Cape Verde has again taken the lead in providing constitutional guarantees to secure "religious presence" in hospitals, prisons and the armed forces (art. 48(5)).

Conscientious Objection

In Congo, "religious opinion" may not be relied upon to relieve one from the duty of "fulfilling a civic duty" (art. 26). Cape Verde, on the other hand, guarantees the right to conscientious objection, "as provided by law" (art. 48(8)). It is common in Anglophone countries—at least those that took their lead from the European Convention for the Protection of Human Rights and Fundamental Freedoms—to maintain the principle of religious freedom when regulating the taking of an oath.[21] In Botswana it is stated thus: "No person shall be compelled to take any oath which is contrary to his religion or belief or to take any oath in a manner which is contrary to his religion or belief" (art. 11(4)).

ENFORCEMENT OF RELIGION CLAUSES

In conclusion of this survey, a few remarks need to be offered on the question of implementation. It has often been said that constitutional protection of human rights in many African countries is not worth the paper it is written on. That, perhaps, is a gross overstatement. It is true, though, that democracy is not always apparent in Africa. One-party states, repression of political opposition by the powers that be, and the advent of coups d'états are fairly common occurrences on the continent. Several kinds of constitutional arrangements place the de facto implementation of constitutional decrees for the protection of human rights under stress in Africa. Tanzania may be singled out as a country where lofty protection provisions are rendered ineffective by sweeping limitation and suspension mechanisms (see arts. 30 and 31). The Constitution of Tanzania furthermore excludes the jurisdiction of courts of law "to offer any judgment on a course of action or lack of action on an issue against a person or any Authority, if the law or any judgment is in compliance with the conditions in this Section of this Chapter" (art. 6(2)).

Several African constitutions contain human rights provisions enacted as (nonenforceable) directive principles of state policy. Those principles mostly apply to economic and social rights—as is the case in Namibia (Ch. 11 (secs. 95-101))[22]—but in Ghana, directive principles of state policy include a commitment of the State to "actively promote the integration of the peoples of Ghana and prohibit discrimination and prejudice on grounds of . . . religion, creed or other belief" (art. 35(5)).

Perhaps the most unfortunate aspect of human rights protection in Africa is the ease with which, and the relative frequency in which, constitutional bills of rights are suspended. In The Gambia, for example, the Constitution was suspended in 1994 ((Suspension and Modification) Decree No. 1 of 1994). The Constitution was indeed subsequently reinstated, except for particular provisions, which left the Bill of Rights unaffected by the emergency that prompted the suspension (art. 3 of the Suspension and Modification Decree).

There is the further tendency in certain African countries, including Zimbabwe and Zambia, to render obsolete, by means of constitutional amendments, judgments of the courts interpreting or applying bill of rights provisions in a manner disapproved of by persons in political command.

CONCLUSION

There is more to human rights protection than simply constitutional guarantees. Besides effective enforcement mechanisms, including a courageous judiciary willing and able to stand up to the powers that be, human rights protection is also to a large extent dependent upon a certain consciousness—a public morality founded on respect for human rights and fundamental freedoms—that manifests itself in a belief on the part of the government and the subjects of state authority that implementation of the values embodied in the doctrine of human rights makes for better living conditions within the body politic. That consciousness has not come to fruition in most African communities.

Absence of the will—or the ability—to uphold the constitutional ethos of human rights protection appears, inter alia, from the repression of political opposition in many African countries, and from interference by a régime in the due process of law to nullify the enforcement of bill of rights provisions that do not find favor with the government of the day. In Zimbabwe, for example, the Constitution was amended to exclude the jurisdiction of the Supreme Court to find that corporal punishment (sec. 5(3) of the Constitution of Zimbabwe Amendment (No. 11) Act 1990), and execution of condemned criminals by means of hanging (id., sec. 5(4)), constituted cruel and inhuman punishments within the meaning of Section 15(1) of the Constitution. These amendments of the Constitution were enacted to stifle a judgment of the Court as to the constitutionality of executions by hanging,[23] and following a judgment of the Supreme Court that corporal punishment (flogging) was indeed unconstitutional.[24] In a subsequent matter, Chief Justice Gubbay of Zimbabwe held that unreasonable delays in executing persons sentenced to death (fifty-two and seventy-two months after the appellants in the case had received the death sentence) rendered capital punishment a cruel and inhuman punishment.[25] The Constitution was again amended to undo this judgment (sec. 2 of The Constitution of Zimbabwe Amendment (No. 13) Act 1993). New subsections added to Section 15 of the Constitution now provide that it shall not be within the province of a court of law to find that delays in execution of a sentence of death contravene the constitutional proscription of cruel and inhuman punishments (sec. 15(5)); and if a sentence was constitutional at the time of its being imposed but subsequent eventualities rendered that sentence cruel and inhuman, the convicted person would nevertheless not be entitled to a stay, alteration, or remission of that sentence (sec. 15(6)).

The latter provision was afforded retroactive effect so as to apply to sentences imposed after and before its entering into force. In the case of *Nkomo v. Attorney-General, Zimbabwe* (1994 (3) SA 34 (25)), the appellants sought a remission of sentence on the grounds that their lengthy detention in death row converted the death sentence in their case to a cruel and inhuman punishment. The Court found that at the time when the Amendment Act denying the appellants that line of argument entered into force, the appeals had already been noted and their right to a reprieve of sentence had already accrued to them. In spite, therefore, of the retroactive implementation of the Amendment Act, their vested right to a remission of sentence remained unaffected. The sentence of death was consequently set aside and substituted by one of life imprisonment.[26]

Religious freedom in Africa is finally rendered dubious by the many instances of political repression of religious leaders. This kind of religious repression is particularly current—and difficult to expose as instances of religiously motivated intolerance—in cases where religious differences serve as a criterion of political divides. In 1994, for example, the Kenyan government stripped Khalid Balala, leader of the Islamic Party of Kenya, of his citizenship. Earlier that year, a book written by Kennith Matiba, entitled *Kenya: Return to Reason*, was banned. Matiba was the leader of the Asili faction of the Forum for the Restoration of Democracy, and his book was particularly critical of the Kenyan president, Daniel arap Moi.

It would seem, therefore, that the constitutional protection of religious freedom in many African countries provided cold comfort to religious groups disapproved of by the political authorities. Repression of and intolerance toward certain religious sects are commonplace on the African continent. It is perhaps worth noting that the relatively peaceful transition in South Africa from a racist régime to a democratic dispensation was in part attributable to the fact that political divides in the country cut across racial and religious barriers, and that at least the mainstream religions[27] include members of different racial and political groups. In the elections of 1994, a few participating parties did represent sectional interests. The Freedom Front, which opted for an "Afrikaner homeland" and represented right-wing "white" interests, received only 2.2 percent of the votes.[28] The African Christian Democratic Party, which had little to do with Christianity, attracted 0.5 percent of the votes. The African Muslim Party was one of twelve smaller parties which together could not muster more than 0.9 percent support.

Separation of political interests from religious conviction or affiliation is perhaps the best guarantee of de facto religious freedom.

NOTES

[1] (" . . . of the people and of the State"). In the constitutional Preamble, Mauritania confesses the "omnipotence of ALLAH" and depicts the Mauritanian nation as "a Muslim, African and Arab people." In art. 1 of the Constitution, Mauritania is described as "an indivisible, democratic and social Islamic Republic."

[2] See also the Preamble to the Constitution (proclaiming the country to be "a Muslim . . . State").

[3] See also the constitutional Preamble (proclaiming the Constitution "[i]n the name of God, the Clement and the Merciful" and further testifying to a commitment "to remain faithful to the teachings of Islam [and] to the unity of the Greater Maghreb").

[4] But see also art. 18 of the Constitution of Sudan; and also art. 6 of the Constitution of Morocco (protecting "freedom of worship"), and art. 31 of the Constitution of Somalia (referring to freedom "to profess any religion or creed").

[5] See also art. 28 of the Constitution of Algeria (affording to all citizens equality before the law "without any possible discrimination on the basis of . . . opinion").

[6] See art. 3 of the Constitution of Libya (professing that "[s]ocial solidarity constitutes the foundation of national unity"); art. 1.1. of the Constitution of Somalia (proclaiming Somalia to be "a socialist state led by the working class").

[7] Islamic criminal law is, for example, far-reaching in its identification and definition of offenses, and particularly vicious in its designations of punishment for transgressions of the law, such as theft, adultery and the use of alcohol.

[8] See also, in general, An-Na'im 1993, 145-48. Mahmoud Mohammed Taha, founder of the Islamic Republican Brothers, was executed in June 1985 on charges of heresy and anti-government conduct.

[9] See also art. 3(3), identifying the Revolutionary Party as that party, and art. 9(1), reiterating the resolve "to develop as a nation of equal and independent people, who enjoy freedom, justice, brotherhood and peace by following the policies of socialism and self-reliance, which require the implementation of the philosophy of socialism by taking into account the existing conditions in Tanzania."

[10] Providing that discrimination "shall be punished according to law."

[11] Referring in this regard to "the public order established by law and regulations."

[12] Subjecting the free exercise of religion to "limits compatible with public order and good mores."

[13] Art. 3 of the Constitution of the Kingdom of Swaziland (1968) contained similar provisions, but as stated in the introductory paragraph, those provisions were suspended on the day they were intended to enter into force, and the entire Swazi Constitution was subsequently discarded by the king.

[14] See also art. 37 (proclaiming the right to practice and promote any creed or religion in absolute terms).

[15] The Constitution of the Kingdom of Swaziland also fell into this category, but see note 13. It is worth noting that in the case of Swaziland—which never professed to be a democracy—there was no reference to the limitation of a constitutionally protected right having to be justifiable in a democratic society (see sec. 11(5) of the Swazi Constitution).

[16] Art. 11(5) of the Constitution of Botswana; art. 21(5) of the Constitution of The Gambia; art. 78(5) of the Constitution of Kenya; art. 13(5) and (6) of the

Constitution of Lesotho; art. 11(5) of the Constitution of Mauritius; art. 43(1) of the Constitution of Nigeria (omitting the proviso "including the right to observe and practice"); art. 21(2) of the Constitution of Seychelles; art. 24(5) of the Constitution of Sierra Leone; art. 19(5) of the Constitution of Zambia; art. 19(5) of the Constitution of Zimbabwe.

[17] It is worth noting that in the case of Swaziland—which never professed to be a democracy—there was no reference to the limitation of a constitutionally protected right having to be justifiable in a democratic society (see sec. 11(5) of the Swazi Constitution).

[18] Supra note 16.

[19] The Recognition of Customary Marriages Act 120 of 1998 was enacted pursuant to this constitutional provision to afford recognition to all existing and future (African) marriages, irrespective of such marriages being polygamous or not.

[20] See U.N. Doc. CRC/C/2/Rev. 5 of July 30, 1996.

[21] Art. 11(4) of the Constitution of Botswana; art. 21(4) of the Constitution of The Gambia; art. 78(4) of the Constitution of Kenya; art. 13(4) of the Constitution of Lesotho; art. 11(4) of the Constitution of Mauritius; art. 21(4) of the Constitution of Seychelles; art. 24(4) of the Constitution of Sierra Leone; art. 19(4) of the Constitution of Zambia; art. 19(4) of the Constitution of Zimbabwe.

[22] Progressive implementation provisions in the Constitution of the Republic of South Africa include those dealing with access to land (sec. 25(5)), housing (sec. 26(2)), and health care (sec. 27(2)).

[23] While appeals were pending against the sentences in certain death-penalty cases, the appellants were granted amnesty under pretenses of amnesty regulations that attended the independence of Zimbabwe, but for which they clearly did not qualify. The amnesty was evidently given to prevent a judgment of the Court on the question of executions by hanging (a major ground of the appeals) and so as to give the legislature time to put in place the constitutional amendment under consideration.

[24] See S v. A JUVENILE, 1990 (4) SA 151 (ZSC); see also S v. NCUBE; S v. TSHUMA; S v. NDHLOVO, 1988 (2) SA 702 (ZSC) (holding that corporal punishment of an adult person constitutes a cruel and inhuman punishment).

[25] See Catholic Commission for Justice and Peace, Zimbabwe, Attorney-General, Zimbabwe, 1993 (4) SA 239 (ZSC).

[26] Limitation of the jurisdiction of courts of law in Zimbabwe was also extended to the implementation of the Land Acquisition Act, 1992, which authorized the compulsory acquisition (taking) of rural (mainly agricultural) land for population resettlement purposes. An administrative body was created to determine just compensation to be paid to landowners whose property was to be expropriated, and an amendment of the Constitution, enacted in 1993, excluded the jurisdiction of courts of law to determine questions of compensation payable in terms of the Act. See sec. 3 of the Constitution of Zimbabwe Amendment (No. 13) Act, 1993, amending sec. 16 of the Constitution.

[27] The so-called independent churches, of which there are approximately six thousand varieties in the country, are almost exclusively confined to the African community. However, those African independent churches tend to be apolitical.

[28] The Interim Constitution of 1993 actually made provision for the feasibility of an Afrikaner homeland to be considered at a later date (see Constitutional Principle XXXIV in Schedule 4 of Act 200 of 1993) but—as everyone knows—there simply is no part of South Africa which is exclusively occupied by (white) Afrikaners.

BIBLIOGRAPHY

An-Na'im, Abdullahi A. 1987. "Religious Minorities under Islamic Law and the Limits of Cultural Relativism," *Human Rights Quarterly* 1.

———. 1993. "Cross-cultural Support for Equitable Participation in Subsaharan Africa," in *Human Rights in the Twenty-first Century: A Global Challenge*, edited by Kathleen E. Mahoney and Paul Mahoney. Dordrecht/Boston/London: Martinus Nijhoff.

Flanz, Gisbert H. 1999. *Constitutions of the Countries of the World*. Dobbs Ferry, N.Y.: Oceana Publications.

Henkin, Louis. 1978. *The Rights of Man Today*. Boulder, Colo.: Westview Press.

Heyns, Christof H. 1996. *Human Rights Law in Africa*. The Hague/Boston: Kluwer Law International.

Khan, Khan Bahadur. 1989. "The World of Islam," *Proceedings of the Third World Congress on Religious Liberty*. IRLA.

Mayer, Elizabeth Ann. 1987. "Law and Religion in the Muslim Middle East, *American Journal of Comparative Law* 127.

———. 1990. "Current Muslim Thinking on Human Rights," in *Human Rights in Africa*, edited by Abdullahi Ahmed An-Na'im and Frances M. Deng. Washington, D.C.: The Brookings Institution.

Sahlieh, Aldeeb Abu. 1985. "Les Droits de l'Homme et l'Islam," *Revue Generale de Droit International Public* 626.

Universal Islamic Declaration of Human Rights. 1981. London: Islamic Council.

van der Vyver, J. D. 1986. "Religion," in *The Law of South Africa*, vol. 23, edited by W. J. Joubert and T. J. Scott. Durban/Pretoria: Butterworths.

———. 1996. "Introduction: Legal Dimensions of Religious Human Rights: Constitutional Texts," in *Religious Human Rights in Global Perspective: Legal Perspectives* xi, edited by Johan D. van der Vyver and John Witte Jr. The Hague/Boston/London: Martinus Nijhoff.

6.

POSTCOLONIAL STATE STRATEGIES, SACRALIZATION OF POWER AND POPULAR PROSELYTIZATION IN CONGO-ZAIRE, 1960-1995

———————◆———————

Tshikala K. Biaya

Zaire (now the Democratic Republic of Congo) is notorious among African countries for its poor human rights record (Amnesty International 1990, Human Rights, 1992). Yet, this country subscribes to international conventions on this matter. The Universal Declaration of Human Rights always features in the preamble of the national Constitution. This acceptance shows the good intentions of this State to promote a democratic postcolonial society. All national constitutions recognize religious freedom; the challenge lies in its application. Religious freedom becomes an issue when its exercise questions political interests, particularly the politics of national integration (Nsangi 1981, Ngindu 1974, 209-30). Moreover, religious freedom can become the core issue and raise the level of conflict between the State and the different churches. These institutions, through their public workings, can transform themselves into effective or probable counter-powers to the regime that intends to mobilize its people. In this "church-state" conflict, the local established church pushes this paradox by reconverting the church and its evangelistic mission toward its followers. Only the Catholic Church expressed this new theological position and its orthopraxis in pastoral actions. Even though this new stance has been perceived as valid for all ecclesiastical institutions, it created a conflictual tension between the temporal and the spiritual powers. Yet only the Roman Catholic Church went to war with the regime that claimed an exclusive right to provide and control the citizens' freedom through a progressive secularization of the state and the subordination of the spiritual to the temporal power. This chapter sets out to clarify the hidden agenda of the religious policy of Mobutu's regime that took place over more than three decades. Another face of proselytizing as a process of converting the other to one's religion or beliefs arose with the second awakening of the local pentecostal movement. It provoked a variety of reactions on the part of the state and the established churches. These will also be examined here.

This chapter has four parts. The first concerns the history of Zairean nationalism and the secularization of the postcolonial state, 1960-95. The second part analyzes the relationships, conflicts, tension, and alliances between the state and the churches and Islam. The third part studies the reaction of the state and churches toward popular pentecostalism, followed by a brief analysis of popular proselytization. The conclusion describes the proselytizing of the Zairean State as a failure to sacralize itself. This political mechanism stimulated negative or diverse reactions that it tried to control or administer without success.

THE SACRALIZATION OF A STATE:
NATIONALIST IDEOLOGY AND THE POLICY
OF BUILDING A NATION-STATE

In 1960, when Zaire became an independent State, its motto was "Unified Congo, strong country." The state founders promoted a militant nationalism and unitarism in a multiethnic nation. The Zairean State has a bicameral national parliament and provincial parliament, together with central and provincial governments. It underwent a political crisis and civil war for the first five years of its existence. These micronationalistic conflicts (1959-63), called secessions and ethnic conflicts, were followed by the revolutionary wars led by Lumumbists and Marxists who felt they were excluded from power (1963-67). These actions targeted the central government, which was accused of neo-colonialism, being a predator of local resources, etc. Zaire then experienced a period of peace thanks to the intervention of UN troops, the aid of the U.S. government, and the Belgian-American military cooperation—all of which were backed by the Constitutional amendments of 1964 and 1967.

The question of national integration (social, administrative, ethno-political, and cultural) became the overriding political concern. In the context of the Cold War and hegemonic rivalry, the construction of a dictatorial, secular, and unitary State would stop the progression of Communism in central Africa. The "Strong Man" policy, sustained by the United States, relied on the control of the people by means of a single party which would ensure the diffusion of the regime's ideology. Mobutu was well aware of this when he seized power in 1965. He proclaimed himself and his revolution as deriving from Lumumba's ideology, whereby he won all the nationalists to his cause. Then he revised the Constitution and imposed a centralized administration, creating a single national party two years later. The following year he unified all the trade unions in the national one, UNTZA. In 1971, he institutionalized the party and succeeded in erasing all the sources of possible opposition.

This project of an ideological integration of the State coincided with the process of nationalization taking place in the established churches (Catholic, Protestant, and Kimbanguist) and in the Islamic community. The alignment of these religious institutions with the single-party regime reached a peak with the "Pax Mobutu," in which they actively participated from 1965 to 1968. In return, the State endorsed the movement toward Africanization within the Protestant churches, which led to the creation of their representative council, the "Eglise du Christ au Zaire" (Church of Christ or ECZ), in 1969, and supported the emergence of the Islamic Community of Zaire in 1972.

Between 1970 and 1985, Mobutu's dictatorship became stronger and more focused. At the end of 1971 he launched the ideology of Authenticity, whose roots went back to the theory of the Africanization of the church proposed by J. Malula, the archbishop of Kinshasa (Malula 1958) and to the philosophy of mental disalienation. His own doctrine was Mobutism (Biaya 1993b, 3-16). This new politics disguised the establishment of a new state bourgeoisie and its hegemony. The Catholic Church, which had been part of the ruling class from 1960, was expelled. Mobutu launched a strict nationalism by secularizing the state, and forced the churches to relinquish any control over the youth. Between 1971 and 1975 the political bureau banned all the religious youth and student movements and organizations. All the youth were enrolled in the Youth League of the single party, the JMPR. The former replaced even the UGEC and AGE—the students' unions. The excuse was found in the student riots of 1969 when the army charged and killed many students on campus in Kinshasa. They were accused of communist activities and ties with China because they contested the revisionist orientation of the Zairean government since 1968. By these two actions, the regime suppressed all opposition from the church and the students' unions. The revised constitution of 1974 confirmed this new option: the MPR was the "organized Zairean nation." The Political Bureau was "the guarantor and orthodox organ of Mobutism." This doctrine is defined as "thoughts, actions, and teachings of the Guide." Authenticity became the central ideology of the Constitution from 1974 onward.

In the meantime, Mobutu launched a new law, the law of 31 December 1971, regulating public worship and the conditions to fulfil in order to be recognized as a legal religious institution in Zaire. This law broke down the historic monopoly of the Catholic Church as a partner of the state according to the agreement between King Leopold II and Rome, from 1906 (Eglise catholique au Zaïre 1981, 302-3). This new law granted legal status to the three established churches, ignoring the Islamic community. It imposed a payment of 200,000 zaires (of which 100,000 was to be deposited into a bank) to gain a license and the right to have a legal representative. A three-month grace period was allowed for the remaining churches, sects, and cults to legalize their own status. The refusal to comply with the law was sanctioned by a ban on religious activities. This law granted the state the power and the monopoly of recognition of religious institutions, of control over public worship, and the power to suspend or ban any church when this institution troubled the security or the established order. Since then, the state has conducted regular censuses. In 1985, the Department of Justice reported 542 churches and sects in Zaire. Three years later, G. Buakasa acknowledged more than 1,000. In 1995, Kinshasa alone had 464 churches legally established and operating.

One can see that this law was embedded in the national policy of integration and its unitary ideology that justified the successive revision of the Zairean Constitution. It also justified the various agreements that the state made with the churches as a way of settling the differences between these two institutions. On the other hand, this law provided them with a juridical framework where all religious institutions, small and large, national and international, Christian and Islamic, would henceforth function according to the secular state. Any departure from or lack of respect for this law of Mobutism led to conflict with the regime's ideology.

In 1973, this "national saga" took on an international dimension. Mobutu accused the local Catholic Church of being under the control of foreigners while other church leaders were more nationalist, such as Bokeleale of ECZ and Diangienda of the Kimbanguist Church. The same year, when Mobutu broke diplomatic ties with Israel at the UN General Assembly, Islam became a means of attracting investments from Arab banks and countries. In return, the Zairean State gave its support to Islamic proselytizing that the colonizers had repressed under unfair rules since 1893 (Young 1967, 14-31). In 1975, Mobutu nationalized the educational system and replaced religious courses with civic studies and Mobutism.

Two years later, Zaire found itself in the midst of a social and political crisis. In spite of the support from the IMF and the World Bank, the democratization process and the consecutive economic measures all failed. The "kleptocratic" state refused to break from its source of enrichment that was the state itself. To the contrary, the regime radicalized its ideology, and strengthened the Head of State and party powers by creating a central committee in 1980. The suffering of the people and the suppression and violation of human rights were inversely proportional to the growing repression and the greed of the ruling class in plundering national resources.

The regime became more oppressive drawing on the policy of Authenticity and a false historic past to bolster its own legitimacy. Its contention was that African democracy is not Western and does not accept any opposition in the Western way. However, this led internal opposition groups to become more visible—denouncing the regime's failure to develop the country. They were to create a clandestine political party, the UDPS. In 1990, the growth of social and political movements forced the regime to admit the democratic transition process. But the ailing regime continued to resort to violence. It used new strategies of resistance like the killing of Christians during their demonstration in February 1992, the inciting of hatred and ethnic conflicts, the massacre of the bishop of Bukavu, etc. Under its policy of national integration, the violation of human rights was the state's way of controlling social groups and individuals including religious institutions and their followers.

STATE AND ESTABLISHED RELIGIOUS INSTITUTIONS, 1960-1995

A retrospective analysis of the relations between the state and the various religious institutions in Zaire shows that a power game and its exercise for the control of the population had been set in motion at the dawn of independence, in 1960. It reached its climax with the politics and philosophy of Authenticity, which originated from the local Roman Catholic Church. This nascent local church detached itself from the "colonial Trinity" (administration, capital and missionary Catholic Church) when it claimed its nationalization. It Africanized sooner than the postcolonial state and other Protestant churches. It had its first black bishops in 1959 and its Cardinal, J. Malula, in 1969. Its University Lovanium opened its doors in 1954, followed by the first African Faculty of Theology in 1956. It followed in the footsteps of its future cardinal by laying out the foundations of an African theology in 1959. This Christian nationalism, which began in 1956 with the "Manifesto of African Conscience," and which flourished into the Africanization of the church, was wrongly perceived as an alliance between Cardinal Malula and the Mobutu regime. This perception was based on the fact that Malula's ideal in the late 1950s was to "build a Congolese church within a Congolese nation" and to search for autonomy vis-à-vis Rome and the Belgian Mission (Malula 1958). This nationalistic and theological-philosophical project, launched in 1958, was publicly announced the day of his consecration as bishop in 1959. It also both stimulated and enriched Kalanda's *La remise en question* (1965) as a way to decolonize one's own mind, as well as the policy of Authenticity (Mobutu 1971). Mobutu, in launching his movement, acknowledged Malula's action in the church as the precursor of this philosophy that he intended to extend to the wider philosophical, social, political, and cultural notion of Authenticity.

In this context of ideological integration, three main themes constituted the core of the relations between the state and religious institutions: (1) the secularization of the state, (2) the administration of the youth, and (3) the struggle for democracy. These are the subject of the next three sections.

THE SECULARIZATION OF THE STATE OR A GREAT IDEOLOGICAL PLOY

This secularization of the state posed a problem in that it took place jointly with the implementation of the dictatorship and the brutal exclusion of the Roman Catholic Church from the rising national group. The process is well expressed in the celebrated "church-state struggle." From 1960, Pierre Mulele expressed the main concern of his party—the PSA—about a secular postcolonial state and its program of nationalizing the educational system, of which 80 percent at the time was administered by the missionary churches. Some months later, Lumumba appointed him minister of education. He explained this policy to Msgr. Gilon, then chancellor of the Catholic Lovanium University. In 1967, Mobutu appropriated the concept of a secular state from the Lumumbists and combined it with his national integration and foreign policies. Meanwhile, he had already succeeded in using the churches as a catalyst for establishing his credibility as a nationalist and unitarist leader. Of course, the churches contributed a lot to his "Opération Pacification" or Pax Mobutu, which attempted to heal the country of its civil wars. The Catholic Church involved the clergy and personnel, youth associations, and its infrastructure in this enterprise.[1] The Protestant churches organized a national campaign called "Christ for All," which Pastor P. Shaumba supervised in 1967-68. They invited H. Jones and R. Bell, two African-American preachers from the renowned Billy Graham team. This campaign aimed to bring a "message of peace and hope" to the Zairean population devastated by the rebellion. This double cooperation allowed the regime to reconcile Zairean political nationalism with the nationalization of the church set in motion by Malula and the progressive faction of the Protestant Church of Zaire.

In return, the regime, which used to consult the church and the student unions (UGEC and AGE) in regard to political decisions, changed its mind. Instead of allowing them opposition status, Mobutu decided to disempower them. In 1968, the ruling class's monolithic vision of and quest for power compelled it to force the unification of the Protestant Churches into one single organization, namely the ECZ, and similarly for the Muslim communities, the COMIZA. Both committees were led by strong men attached to Mobutu. His main political objective was to keep religious institutions out of the political sphere. They were to be responsible for only conversion, social welfare, public health, and education.

The conflict between the state and the Catholic Church began early in 1966, when Mobutu suppressed the office of prime minister and turned the government into a presidential one without changing the Constitution. As a matter of fact, there was no Constitution. Msgr. Bakole, the auxiliary bishop of Kananga and vice-chancellor of the Catholic University, protested against this rising dictatorship. He received a strident reply: clergy must stay in their churches and look after their flocks.[2] The affairs of state pertain to politicians alone. This was the first confrontation. The regime expressed its intention to cut all ties with the Catholic Church even further in 1969 when Mobutu refused the call from Msgr. Malula for distributive justice and for an end to the illegal enrichment of politicians. Mobutu turned this accusation into a political argument. He justified the nascent bourgeoisie by the existence of social stratification in every human community whether socialist, communist, or capitalist. In 1971, after Mobutu nationalized the Catholic and Protestant universities of Kinshasa and Kisangani, he warned the church that one day a non-Christian might rule the country. Paradoxically, he built a Catholic church in Mangobo, claiming that it was a gift to the city that supported Lumumba by rioting against the colonizers. The truth was that Mobutu could no longer tolerate Msgr. Fataki, the archbishop of Kisangani, who urged social justice in the face of the growing suffering of the people. The next year, J. Malula criticized the ambiguity of Authenticity. According to him, this philosophy was another way of alienating the people by a blind return to the past when what was needed was an intelligent use of the past in modern times. This was the last straw that brought state-church conflict into the public sphere.

It was in this context of ideological hegemony, and of defining church-state relationships, that the rapid process of fostering the ECZ and the COMIZA can be fully understood. The state could not succeed in reducing the power of the Catholic Church without obtaining the submission or the alliance of its two contender institutions, on the one hand. On the other hand, it had to separate this church from its followers. This double Machiavellian action took place in two stages: the secularization of the state and the imposition of state control over national youth organizations, as stated earlier.

From the time of independence, the nationalization and the unification of the Protestant Churches were issues at stake. From 1964, two opposed tendencies existed. The conservative one was pro-mission and its continuity in the decolonized Zaire. The progressive tendency was more nationalistic and led by young African theologians. They disagreed about the necessity and the form of the nationalization and the unity of the local Protestant Church. The latter went as far as invoking even state intervention in case of failure to obtain this reform through negotiation because it associated its decolonizing position with the end of missionary churches in Zaire. In 1969 the ECZ was created. In 1972, the Executive Committee defined clearly its position in the church-state conflict:

> For us as Protestants, the resorting to Authenticity is a movement for liberation and restoration of humanity. And because every fight for human liberation and disalienation incarnates the divine mission of Christ on earth, the ECZ will make this its noble national option (CEN 1972, 2).

At the Zaire Symposium on human rights in Washington D.C. in 1983, Msgr. Bokeleale minimized the seriousness of violation of human rights in Zaire and insisted on Mobutu's generosity toward the ECZ and the Kimbanguists. He situated this action in the direct line of the unitarist and hegemonic ideology of Mobutism and its attempts to sever the colonial state policy that privileged the Catholic Church to the detriment of other religious institutions. Thanks to the new privileges they obtained from the postcolonial state, he stated, "all of us, Protestants, Catholics, Kimbanguists, we are all on the same footing" (Bokeleale 1983, 42). This alliance between the regime and the ECZ constituted, in part, a revenge that the Protestants took against the Catholics. Indeed, in 1962, the former requested without success the secularization of the Congolese State that would lead to the renunciation of its

Catholicism. They protested against the arrival of the apostolic nuncio in Kinshasa from Rome (Kabongo-Mbaya 1992, 144-55). This disturbing and anticolonialist discourse from Protestants, even if unrealistic, took on meaning in the context of Bokeleale's action. On the other hand, the COMIZA did escape the state's ideological process. It gained its legal status in March 1972, only a few days before the deadline. Its diverse communities were subjected to the same state pressure as the Protestants. We shall return to this later.

This strong emerging nationalism of January 1972 was supported by a symbolic legitimization (through political actions) and the production of Mobutu's image as Father of the Nation. This double process was conducted in perfect ambiguity. Mobutu deployed a symbolization of state power, fostering unity and impartiality—a power beyond the churches. Mobutu attended the fiftieth anniversary of the arrest of Simon Kimbangu. Some months later, he participated in a Kimbanguist service in Matete in honor of the seventh anniversary of his regime. He maintained his position as the State President and as a Christian, while distancing himself from the Catholics. Later, he built a private chapel in Gbadolite, his private city. He always recalled the colonial past of the Catholic Church and its propaganda against the Arabs and Islam to justify his support for the Zairean Islamic community. Finally, he reminded his people that Msgr. Malula, Msgr. Bokeleale, H. E. Diangienda, and the Cheikh Amrani Juma, before being religious leaders, were first of all citizens of a country and militants of the MPR before the secular state and himself, the Head of State. As he affirmed, "This submission cannot be a matter of faith, nor a benevolent engagement; it is a constitutional duty." This discourse of submission on the part of religious organizations to the state and the party served to disconnect the local Catholic hierarchy from its followers, who were declared first and foremost citizens and members of the MPR. These apparently isolated facts reveal the hegemonic strategy that came to dominate Authenticity and Mobutism throughout the eighteen years of dictatorship.

The politics of Authenticity, as political ideology and philosophy, legitimized a new interpretation of state power and built up a new hierarchy of national institutions leading to dictatorship and "kleptocracy." Its doctrine, Mobutism, gained support from the ECZ, the Kimbanguist Church, and Islamic community leaders. In the heat of this cultural revolution, Mobutu was identified with the Messiah and Mobutism with Christianity, the state party with the church, and the party's house with the temple. These provocative metaphors, even when Mobutu denied his messianic status, were confirmed in the 1974 Constitution that institutionalized the MPR as "an organized Zairean nation." This Constitution proclaimed a secular state with a clause restricting public religious worship. The Catholic Church was not able to claim any power over the nation's citizens. They were enrolled in the party and its different social and political bodies. They abandoned their Christian identity by renouncing their Christian names as the law requested them to do. This operation confirmed them as party members by birth or enrollment. This law defined their citizenship: "Olinga olinga te ozali kaka na MPR" (willingly or not you are member of MPR). Even newborns did not escape this new identity marker, as it was inscribed in the baptismal book and the identity card.

All these political measures also aimed at secularizing the public sphere. The changes to the national calendar expressed the effort to reorganize a new life cycle that controlled everyday life according to the party's activities or events. Religious activities were reduced to the private sphere. Officials were no more entitled to represent the state at religious events; religious TV and radio programs and newspapers were forbidden; religious holidays and those recalling colonial victories, i.e., the First and Second World Wars, were suspended. Even Christmas was threatened. Religious icons which were numerous in the public sphere, were displaced and replaced by images of Mobutu and the party.

This secularization of national life continued unabashedly through the process of administering the youth under the auspices of the single party. At the diplomatic level, the apostolic nuncio, who used to be the chief representative of the diplomatic body, was dismissed and replaced by the senior diplomat in Zaire, much to the satisfaction of the ECZ. This phase of the state-Catholic Church conflict was directed at Msgr. Malula. The Political Bureau forbade followers to pray for their archbishop; otherwise they were labeled reactionaries through a media campaign and exposed to the party's sanctions. Mobutu presented Malula as having a "subversive" colonial past and as playing on his Luba ethnicity for political purposes. Mobutu presented Malula's return from exile in Rome in 1975 as an acknowledgment of the secularized state and the policy of Authenticity.

The Promoting of Islamic Proselytizing

Mobutu's regime had another agenda for the Islamic community in Zaire. Since the colonial period, Islam had not been able to expand freely. Administrative measures had constrained its followers causing them to miss out on social, intellectual, and cultural developments (Bibeau 1976, 179-238). Islamic communities were subject to frequent control and experienced annoying administrative measures (indirect rule, no visas for pilgrims to go to Mecca, employment discrimination, no freedom of association, etc.) Muslim cities resembled refugee camps because they were isolated from other African cities. Muslims were forbidden to participate in regional or international pan-Islamic conferences. This policy allowed the growth of Islamic centers in Bujumbura and Kigali to the detriment of the Zairean ones, and these centers played an intermediary role in linking Zairean Muslims to Udjidji, Mogadiscio, and Mecca.

After independence in 1960 the Muslim community, composed of many brotherhoods and national groups, tried to reorganize itself and to broaden its sphere of activity though proselytizing. From 1966, personal action and pressure were to be effective in this process after a visit of the delegation of the International Muslim League. This delegation aimed "to reconcile Muslims [different brotherhoods], to empower Muslim activities by offering tuition, grants, new Imams and Walimu [teachers], financing the building of new mosques and schools etc." (Nicolas 1985, 312). One can trace the state pressure for the unification of Muslim communities and brotherhoods into COMIZA in the bill granting them a legal status and their own founding texts. In return, they gave their support and enrolled into the single party and subscribed to its ideals (Statuts 1979).

Islamic proselytizing differed from Christian techniques in that Muslims did not use rallies, religious campaigns, prophecy, or divine healing. In contrast to the churches that proselytized through the clergy, "the Muslim carries in himself the spirit of proselytizing" (Nicolas 1985, 365). Muslims carry this precious burden through dress, faith, drink, and food. They resort to the *ijtihad* to interpret and explain the Qur'an to the unfaithful. This activity of contemporary conversion began in Eastern Zaire in 1900. There were three stages. The first was conducted by Tanzanians coming from Udjidji; they created the center of Wamaza at Kasongo between 1910 and 1928. The second, the Mulidi Brotherhood, arrived in 1930. And the third was a mix of Muslims from West Africa and Asia (India, Pakistan, and Lebanon). They arrived around 1945. From 1975, the opening of Kisangani's mosque along with others in different cities marked a golden age for Islam in Zaire when different brotherhoods and communities united into a single Islamic community, COMIZA. Three factors stimulated the expansion of Islam at this time. Paradoxically, Islamic proselytizing benefited from the colonial repression that forced many non-Muslims to take refuge in the Muslim cities where state control (tax, labor control, pass to settle in town, etc.) was less evident than elsewhere because these cities were ruled by their own leaders. Second, people advanced the fact that the Muslims were traders and very multiethnic. Third, healing practices and the marabouts or Mwalimu's function helped to Africanize this religion by integrating African traditional beliefs and practices into popular Islam. These three factors still account for the attraction of many Zaireans to Islam. In 1963, for example, on the single day of the Great Feast, two hundred conversions occurred in Kivu province, including eight professors and a civil servant.

From 1972, as soon as Islam was raised to the rank of national religion, ten Arab embassies in Kinshasa provided financial, material, and personnel support to COMIZA to help it with conversion and greater visibility in the public sphere. COMIZA built mosques, provided student scholarships, etc. It became a solid partner of the regime by supporting Authenticity politics. The kleptocratic regime took advantage of this official recognition of COMIZA as a way to get investments from the Arab countries. In 1973, Mobutu broke relations with Israel. From 1973 to 1982, he obtained funds for petroleum and investments up to 4,444 million dollars from Arab banks and countries. When Zaire changed its policy toward Israel in 1982, the state had already manifested its worries about the rapidly growing Islamic presence. It restricted the movement or travel of the Arab embassies' members out of Kinshasa. It forbade Zairean officials to participate in Islamic events in small cities where Islam was growing quickly. As soon as Zaire resumed diplomatic relations with Israel, it severed its support for Islam. This did not affect the expansion of Islam, which has continued until today.

CONTROLLING THE YOUTH: A CULTURAL REVOLUTION

The second step of the golden age of Zairean nationalism began with the historic decisions of the Political Bureau on December 30, 1974 (*Bureau politique 1974*). This cultural revolution started with the ban on all youth movements and associations. They were replaced by the party's youth movement called "la Jeunesse du Mouvement populaire de la révolution" (JMPR). Young people were divided into three categories. The youth pioneers—"la jeunesse pionière"— were the pupils and students from elementary to high school. The student youths—"la jeunesse estudiantine"—contained all the students from colleges and universities. The labor youths—"la jeunesse ouvrière"—represented all the workers, the MPR youth brigades and members of political and cultural animation groups.

Since its creation in 1967, the party's youth movement never elaborated an alternative ideology to attract the youth or stimulate any enthusiastic commitment to the party. This cultural revolution never succeeded in being integrated into the schools or university settings where it had replaced the student associations five years before. To the contrary, Christian associations and the Scouts were the only youth movements that stood out in the nation. This political decision caused shock and panic in the Catholic Church, which considered it a threat to the fundamental rights of the youth and to the freedom of association linked to the religious freedom contained in the Constitution. The measure was unequal because it never applied to the other churches or to the Islamic community—maybe because they did not have such visible youth movements as the Catholic Church. However, Catholic movements such as MIEC, Pax Romana, JOC, the Scouts, JOCF, and others disappeared and were replaced by the single party's youth movement, the JMPR.

The next year, the Political Bureau reinforced its measures by recommending the implanting of the party's youth structures in the seminaries, the nationalization of the educational system, and the replacement of religion courses by civic studies. It decreed the suppression within the National University of Zaire (UNAZA) of the faculties of theology—Catholic, Protestant, and Kimbanguist. But these faculties were to be independent and organized by the religious institution in question without state support. The Political Bureau imposed a compulsory "ideological week" in universities and colleges for professors and students to discuss the party's future and duties. The Catholic Church lost its control over 80 percent of the schools in Zaire. Then the party imposed, on top of civic studies, a further secularization of the educational system through the teaching of Mobutism and the N'Sele manifesto. Every weekday, school activities started with cultural and political animation: students sang, performed revolutionary dances, saluted the flag, and sang the national anthem. These measures were aimed at bringing the local Catholic Church to its knees when it was already engaged in negotiations with the state. In this negotiation process, the church bargained and obtained at least that a Zairean priest could control the party's youth cells in the seminaries. This radicalization of the revolution aimed to:

1. reinforce and intensify the program of political and ideological education for the youth to strengthen their unconditional devotion to the Guide;
2. assure youth participation in the ambitious program of economic and social development proposed by the President-Founder [of the Nation];
3. intensify activities of youth vigilance in the struggle against the consequences of mental alienation;
4. succeed in implementing the pioneering movement and to reenforce student participation in the JMPR (*Bureau politique* 1974, 13-14).

For two years, from 1974 to 1976, the state controlled the educational system before returning it to the religious institutions. Thanks to the scholarly convention of 1978 they were able to benefit again from financial support for elementary and high school education.

The control of the youth was an important issue for the state because the party considered this social category as the spearhead of its cultural revolution. Unfortunately, this cultural revolution (Bokonga 1978) ended up in immorality, corruption, urban hedonism, the inversion of values, and a drop in the educational level in less than two years. The Political Bureau's criticism that launched this cultural revolution had addressed the "10 plagues" that undermined Zairean society (*Bureau politique* 1974). Ironically this revolution increased them. For the nationalist ideology and the political doctrine of Authenticity did not inculcate any valuable and worthy ethos into the youth. The failure occurred mainly because the regime's enemy, which had been the Catholic Church, avoided any open conflict with the state about the secularizing process and did not oppose any resistance to the implementation of the dictatorship (Documentation catholique 1976, 58-59). The second reason was because the party did not have any serious plans for the youth, nor for the nation itself, except to plunder national resources.

The Catholic Church recognized the sovereignty of the state and its new law on religious freedom of 1972. This apparent submission hid a secret weapon. The church launched a more aggressive pastoral action to counter the state action. However, one could witness the unfairness of state decisions toward the Catholics. The state party never applied the severe measures to the youth organizations of the Kimbanguist or the Protestant Churches. It aimed to keep apart and under its own control the Zairean cultural revolution as in the Chinese case in 1949 and 1966. Using strong nationalism to fight Christian missionary alienation was just another form of local alienation that served to marginalize national youth. It imposed a kind of African fascism, whose ideology, even if a nebulous one, led to the instituting of structural violence in the country. The youth in uniform, without any ideals or jobs, turned into organized bands of delinquents. They used the political and state structures to exercise their power over the masses, and to harass and extract money from citizens (Biaya 1997). Sometimes the state used them to disband public religious services.

DEMOCRACY AND RELIGIOUS FREEDOM

The educational system and youth organizations were vital activities for the Catholic Church, which administered 83.7 percent of the Zairean youth and its elite. These two groups helped this institution to reproduce itself and maintain its vitality without having to resort to an active proselytization. Through its "Bureau de l'Enseignement catholique" (BEC, the Board of Education), the International Organization of Catholic Students (MIEC) and the national Scout movement, the church capitalized its colonial conversion into a wealthy establishment financed by the same state. It was this system that the state wanted to dismantle. In this conflict, the Catholic Church reinterpreted the Gospel and redefined itself as "a people's servant and not a rival power to the temporal power." It produced a "discourse of liberation for the Zairean people." Henceforth, this pastoral discourse included human rights, the search for social justice, and a new pastoral orientation according to this new perspective of the church, that dissociated itself from the theoretical practice of African theology. Active ecclesial communities rose up (Mandefu 1990). Pastoral letters—from bishops and the Episcopal Council Office—launched this new discourse affirming openly their new role as pastors. A new kind of proselytization began in the country.

In 1976, Msgr. Kabanga published *Je suis un homme* (I Am a Man), where he warned the people and the state about violent social movements if rich people and politicians did not convert. This conversion would be sharing and welcoming the poor because of the growth of human misery. Workers' strikes, the Shaba wars (1977, 1978), and the struggle for democracy shook the country. The Catholic Church took the lead and protested openly against corruption, self-seeking urban culture and its immorality, the underdevelopment caused by the administration, the cult of militancy that led to lack of competency (Déclaration des Evêques 1977, 1978) and human rights abuses (Bakole 1983). In December 1996, this pastoral activity spearheaded by Christian youth had reached 1,444 million young people from diverse parochial organizations (Biaya 1997).

Since 1976, political opposition to the state party became more visible and resulted in the creation of the UDPS (Union pour la démocratie et le progrès social) (Union for Democracy and Social Progress) in 1982. The democratization process took off eight years later, after a popular consultation where all institutions, including the Catholic Church, contributed with a memorandum (Gbabendu and Gobassu 1991). The church's memorandum, even though it provoked President Mobutu's anger, was less forceful in denouncing the regime's ethnic policy, patrimonialism, and dictatorship than the one from the Department of Foreign Affairs. Still it followed along the lines of the Episcopal Council of 1972. To the contrary, the ECZ—Church of Christ of Zaire—and the Kimbanguist Church attempted meekly to adjust their old discourse of collaboration to the popular movement of democratization.

Two major events should be mentioned in regard to the ambiguity of the church leaders during this period of strong Christian popular activism. This contestation movement went beyond the secular division and quarrels between churches and led to the production of a political violence that priests/pastors and followers administrated instead of the bishops or the ecclesial hierarchy. Whereas the church leaders were divided and hesitating over camps in this democratization process, their followers joined the Amos Group, created by Abbé Mpundu.[3] This group, with its significant name, led a march in Kinshasa in February 1992. The army disbanded the protest, killing about seventy Christian protesters and wounding even more. This Amos Group combined conversion, religious freedom and political struggle as a path to national development. Its ideology was centered on the respect of human rights and a conviction that the church was part of the nation in construction. This Christian pacifist demonstration or protest of 16 February 1992 was banned in Kinshasa by Cardinal Etsou, bishop of Kinshasa (de Dordolot 1994). While in Kivu Province, the bishop was on the front line of the protesters. He removed the weapons from the first member of the armed forces and the march went ahead.

The second event was the stoning of the corpse of His Eminence S. E. Diangienda, of the Kimbanguist Church, when it was brought back from Switzerland. When the church announced the death and the return of the body of its leader, people shouted for joy that the owl had passed away and threw stones at the funeral cortège. The qualifier "owl"—*hibou*—designated in popular political discourse someone who opposed the democratization process and was a collaborator of Mobutu and his despised regime.

On a political level, these two events—the killing of Christians from all churches protesting against dictatorship, and the stoning of a church leader—showed the paradoxes and limitations of the dictatorship and the strength of the new definition of the pastoral ideology that now characterized the church as the servant of the nation. This ideology also redefined this Christian institution as a citizens' society where religious freedom is guaranteed. Secondly, these events, led by the people for the people, under a Christian banner, denounced the hesitations and compliances of their ecclesiastical leaders and showed the strength of new ways of proselytization in their struggle against Authenticity politics and the Mobutu regime.

PENTECOSTALISM, A THREAT TO THE STATE AND ESTABLISHED CHURCHES

THE SECOND AWAKENING OF PENTECOSTALISM

The awakening of pentecostalism in Zaire, as in many other African nations, is independent from the revival movement that appeared at the beginning of this century in the United States. It rose and spread quickly in Zaire in the years 1967-68. It was not imported from the West, even though the Roman Catholic Church attempted to codify its practices a decade later (Malula 1983). This movement with fundamentalist tendencies took as its source the meeting of Christianity and local African religions in the context of colonial exploitation and oppression. In 1915, Maria N'Koyi launched the first pentecostal movement in the Equateur province. She was arrested and deported with her husband and family to Haut-Zaire. In 1921, Simon Kimbangu healed people in the name of Jesus and the Holy Spirit. He resuscitated a baby at Nkamba. Crowds left Kinshasa, deserting the Sunday mass, to obtain his blessings. Following Kimbangu's arrest and sentencing to death, the Belgian king reduced his penalty to a life sentence. Kimbangu died in 1951, in the Lubumbashi prison. His followers, estimated at twelve thousand, were also deported until 1959, the eve of independence. In 1931, the sect "Satana," founded by the prophetess Kaki, led the Pende Rebellion. The Pende, under her leadership, fought the colonial administration for six months. In 1950, the Apostolic Church of J. Maranke, the so-called Bapostolo, entered and became active in the industrial cities of Southeastern Zaire. This pentecostal movement followed the path traced by its predecessor, the Kitawala (from the Watch Tower Movement) founded by Mwana Lessa, that entered the country during the Second World War. The Bapostolo and their church spread quickly all over the Kasai province before independence and, since then, in the rest of Zaire. After independence, Protestantism became the main resource where this spirit rose freely as "the Holy Spirit began to speak to Africans themselves." New prophets declared that "missionaries did not tell us the truth of the Gospel. Now the Holy Spirit is living in us, we have the true Gospel." This outline of local pentecostalism has never been documented, but it shows us that the origin and the growth of the context and spirit of local pentecostalism are rooted deeply in the dual cultural transfer that occurred with the meeting of Christianity and African religions.

The second awakening of pentecostalism came in 1967. It was occasioned by the national campaign "Christ for All"—*Christ pour tous*—organized by the Council of Protestant Churches:

> In mid-1967, Pastor Makanzu gave the first balance-sheet of this national campaign: 5000 converted in Kinshasa; 1160 at Thysville; 3000 new converted in Bukavu; 3000 to 5000 people participated in the Kasai Campaign. 123 prayer cells were counted at Thysville; 3000 in the Kasai province. In the city of Kinshasa, the Pentecostal Church started a series of public services where evangelization and healing prayers were both connected. The French Pastor Jacques Giraud came also to that pentecostal campaign. They edited a journal with an eloquent title: *Viens et Vois* [Come and Witness] (Kabongo-Mbaya 1992, 180).

This campaign aimed to bring "a message of peace and hope" to the Zairean people who had just experienced civil wars on the axis Kisangani-Bukavu-

Kasai-Bandundu. The campaign, organized with state support, took place in a soccer stadium. Thousands of followers attended the celebrations, which lasted almost two years.

The outcome of the campaign was the breakthrough and proliferation of local pentecostal churches and movements. This inexorable growth of pentecostalism forced the established churches to produce new strategies and tactics to retain their followers. On the political level, the ruling class discovered the power of the popular meeting and its impact on the masses. Since 1977, the pentecostal movement became a serious threat when it was boosted by the negative social effects of economic crisis and structural politics. On the other hand, this indigenous pentecostal movement received help from the foreign pentecostal churches newly implanted in the country, and some of them succeeded in incorporating some of the local ones. Pentecostal conventions painted a picture of a unified pentecostal church, where local and international churches congregated. National and international pentecostal rallies and their evangelization process strengthened the implantation of related local churches, whose founders came mostly from Protestant churches. This complex religious movement of conversion, conducted through the broadcasting and print media, forced the state to quickly release new measures to control religious organizations according to its objective of national political and ideological integration as stated in the 31 December 1971 law on religious freedom.

The second wave of the pentecostal campaign (1967-80) put an end to the monopoly of conversion held by the established churches since the colonial period. New churches threatened mostly the Roman Catholic Church, which considered the priesthood as being the core of religious (rituals, mass, sacramentalism, liturgy, etc.) and conversion practices. The Catholic Church reacted in instituting charismatic prayer groups. While the Protestant Churches appeared unaffected by this phenomenon, they cast triumphant glances at their "secular" rival. For the new churches reproduced the Protestant model of evangelization and its liturgical practices: reading and interpretation of the Bible, religious practices limited to a minimum, etc. However, pentecostalism, because of its fundamentalist reading of the Bible, and practice of free prayers and healing, opened the door to religious spontaneity. It moved close to African religion and spirituality. The second wave effected a fundamental rupture with the colonial era that political independence or the decolonization process had begun twenty years previously. It also manifested the existence of a quest for religious freedom and the will to build a real African church in Zaire— something not tolerated by the colonialists. The war against Maria N'Koyi, Kimbanguism, Kitawala, and J. Maranke's Bapostolo, as evidenced by the numerous deaths, imprisonments and deportations of their believers, was proof enough for ordinary people of the intolerance and the refusal of the colonial churches to see black people having their own black prophets and desiring to build their black churches (Chomé 1960, 54-90). However, the mission churches lost their own credibility because of their strong links with colonialism. Thanks to the complexity of these factors, pentecostalism expanded widely and quickly in the country.

RELATIONS BETWEEN THE STATE AND NEW CHURCHES

From 1971, the main objective of the Authenticity politics was to enroll all the citizens into one single party and ensure that they would not escape the ideology of national integration. In this context, the church and through it, religious freedom, appeared as a site of counter-power, a possible location of popular resistance to the regime. The state expressed its willingness to control this social body by launching the 31 December Law on Public Worship, followed by the Ministerial Decree of January 1972. This law recognized "the freedom of thought, of conscience and religion" (art. 10) and proclaimed that "there is no State religion in Zaire." It defined the conditions necessary for the various churches to acquire a civic status which it granted only to the Catholic Church, those Protestant Churches which were members of the ECZ, and the Kimbanguist Church. The remaining national churches, movements, and the Islamic community had to apply for this legal status within a three-month period. According to this law, only the churches with legal status were allowed to function, the rest were suspended from all activities. This law threatened the existence of several new churches and movements by imposing a tax payment of 200,000 zaires. This amount covered the license and a security deposit in a bank to cover their religious activities. It was beyond the reach of many religious organizations. The law also forced these churches to create a position of a legal representative who would deal with the regime. By doing so, the regime created the possibility of political control over the Church and its members.

In contrast to the existing relations of tension between the state and the established churches, the majority of the new churches were docile and submissive to the state, which controlled them through regular censuses. In 1973, the presidential law (ordonnance-loi) of 14 February suspended forty-five local pentecostal churches. But this administrative act was not easily enforced. Many examples existed showing the churches' resistance to this law even if they were suspended as a result. The Apostolic Church of J. Maranke, or the Bapostolo, which never had a hierarchy or a building, was the first target. This church attracted many members from the Luba ethnic group that constituted the core of political opposition to the regime (Biaya 1985b). Known as the Luba church, it organized its worship services at the margins of the city, in the mountains or near a river. The Bapostolo survived colonial oppression and set themselves up as independent workers and traders. They obeyed a number of strict purificatory norms (such as a ban on the use of medicines, recourse to prayers and absolutions, mountain retreats, etc.) They resorted to divine gifts (speaking in tongues, healing, etc.) to control their congregation and to reproduce according to divine will. The church had many rich members (traders, diamond smugglers, independent entrepreneurs, etc.). However, under state pressure the Bapostolo chose a legal representative who negotiated with the state from 1978 onward. Before this date, the church was banned and its public worship forbidden.

In 1973, the Jehovah's Witnesses were banned because they did not pay respect to the national flag and anthem; they objected to wearing the state party badge; and they refused to participate in political meetings or rallies. They claimed that acting this way was a form of idolatry of the state, including the party and its leader, Mobutu. In their opinion, these political practices violated their religious conscience and their freedom of thought. In 1976, the youth brigade of the MPR, the state party, disbanded their assembly and any meeting they organized. Ten years later, a presidential decree banned their activities as contrary to public order. Many of their members were arrested and put in prison without being charged or judged. The creation of the Département des Droits et Libertés du Citoyen (the Department of Citizen's Rights and Freedom) did not change the situation even though Amnesty International denounced it (Amnesty International 1990, 11-12). This doctrinal position of the Jehovah's Witnesses was contrary to the single-party ideology and Zairean nationalism. This conflict ended in 1989. For the same reasons, the state party oppressed the Seventh-day Adventists in Kananga and Lubumbashi which up until 1988 had many rallies and Saturday meetings disbanded. They had to agree with the Party to fulfil the national duty—*salongo,* public work—before organizing their meeting. The church postponed its meeting from 9 A.M. to 4 P.M.

The second face of the application of the ideology of political integration appeared in the 1980s, when political opposition became more overt. The regime attacked openly the new churches whose leaders were politically active. This violence was apparently directed at pentecostal churches. In 1980, the army killed no fewer than three hundred members of the Kasongo church in Idofa. Kasongo, the prophet from Lumumba's ethnic group, the Otetela, was identified as an agitator. In 1989, Iyesi, well known as Ebale Mbonge, was a former ambassador to Israel. His church became successful in Kinshasa and attracted even members of the ruling class. These people were in Mobutu's palace in the morning, and in the evening they kneeled before Ebale Mbongo and received his "protective blessings" against the evil powers and national witchcraft of the President Mobutu and his sect, Prima Curia. This practice was commonly known in high places as "recharging batteries." The meaning of the prophet's and the church's name—"river stream that conveys everything"—was quite meaningful at this time of political opposition against the regime and of the pentecostal awakening. His prophecies announced Mobutu's defeat and the triumph of the opposition; he also denounced the occult political practices of the state. The military security service—SARM—and General Mahele killed him in cold blood in his residence. D. Sakombi and W. M. Bofosa continued this prophetic movement which arose among the ruling class and the political bourgeoisie (Ndaywel 1993). However, these two prophets, perceived as madmen by the regime, benefited from the freedom and credentials accorded to mad people in oral societies.

The state's control over new churches was part of its strategy to administer any social organization or body despite the violation of human rights. The state limited when necessary the respect of fundamental human rights even when constitutionally recognized. The creation of the Département des droits et libertés du Citoyen, in 1986, did not put an end to the disregard of rights. The regime banned this department in 1990, when the democratization process started. But the law of 1971 on religious worship had never been revoked. Only the presidential speech of 24 April 1990 introducing the transitional process was perceived as a warranty for religious freedom. The Full Gospel Church of Zaire resorted to this speech as a law covering its activities at a convention in Bukavu in August 1991.

The Counter-Offensive of the Established Churches against the New Churches

In 1970, the Catholic Church launched the first reaction of the established churches to the growth of the pentecostal movement (Malula 1970). The reaction, based on theological and pastoral positions, seemed ambivalent and undecided. On one side, the church organized a pastoral offensive by organizing the basic Christian cells—les communautés ecclésiales vivantes-CEV—in 1970 and a lay ministry five years later. These groups were concerned about the pentecostal practices that spread quickly as prayer groups or charismatic groups.

The theological offensive began with R. de Haes, a Jesuit, who warned the national Catholic community against the pentecostal movement. Later on, in a more conciliatory fashion, he stated that "sects wanted to meet a living God, a God with legs, arms, love and mercy. They are looking for a religion that gives more place to imagination and spontaneity." In 1986, Rome sent extensive documentation to the national committee, whose report summed up this movement as a pastoral challenge that could be countered only by education and information. It published guidelines for charismatic groups (Secrétariat pour l'Unité des Chrétiens 1986). It also denounced "the danger that can ruin the integrity and the specificity of the Christian Faith" through "this unleashing of Satan, who has multiplied his messianic diversions" (Nguezi 1993, 139-40). This theological interpretation constituted a firm response to healing practices that Zairean priests such as Abbé Kasongo in Lubumbashi, Abbé Tshinayama from Kananga, and Abbé Kibwila of Kinshasa had resorted to, since 1975, to help their parishioners. After a short period of failed adaptation (1975-82), when the church devoted itself to the formation and implementation of a lay ministry, it established a structure of controlling and administering charismatic movements. Only lay ministers ran these groups and by fulfilling followers' needs stopped them from leaving the established church.

The ECZ that had stimulated this second pentecostal awakening by its campaign "Christ for All" in 1967 was less indifferent to this movement than it appeared to be. Its counter-strategy was quite simple. It turned to the history of Christianity and its heresies and atheist ideologies to face the current situation. It proposed its secular remedy: "A solid and adequate formation of its servants," the pastors, will come to end with this pentecostal whirlwind (CEN 1972). Some pastors considered this movement as a schism occurring in Protestant churches due to personal ambitions for leadership. These ambitions were brought about by the Africanization of the church which was still under control of the missionaries' conservative wing.

The Kimbanguist Church had a softer attitude toward the newer churches. It certainly saw reflections of itself therein. The necessity and obligations imposed by its quest to obtain membership in the ecumenical movement and the defense of its status as established church forced this church to displace its own pentecostal practices and structures to the periphery. Only His Eminence K. Diangienda inherited from S. Kimbangu the powers of blessing, healing, and communicating with the divine as a gift of the Holy Spirit.[4] He practiced them at his private residence. In the hinterland parishes, pastors imposed hands on believers and sick persons. They invoked the power of Jesus and healing power from S. Kimbangu's spirit to heal or chase a bad spirit that possessed the person. Pastors conducted these pentecostal rituals at the temple, after Sunday worship. Only family members participated in the ceremony.

The counter-offensive conducted by the Catholic Church and the ECZ against local or indigenous pentecostalism was well formulated in the qualifier these churches utilized to designate the movement, "emanating from the devil." This expression encompassed African prophetic churches, the so-called messianic, syncretic, or indigenous churches. It expressed their ideological confusion in the face of this rising religious wave and their fear of the real threat to their raison d'etre as their members left the ranks. They were drawn to the new indigenous churches, where their aspirations and need for spontaneous religious expression were fulfilled. The first balance-sheet of the 1967 "Christ for All" campaign exhibited these same characteristics as had obtained, years before, with the birth of Kimbanguism (circa 1921-30)(cf. Bazola 1968; Munayi 1974). This pentecostal awakening indicated that a new phase of the African church was taking place on the continent. But the questions, then as now, are whether the church can stop being mission-related and transform itself into a local and evangelistic one without renouncing its foundation. Can it reject the anthropology of conversion that distinguished between the Same and the Other? Can this rupture occur smoothly along with a respect for religious freedom for everybody?

POPULAR PROSELYTIZATION

The theological rationality that guides established churches and their pastoral orientations never goes beyond ecclesiastical cells and parishes. Beyond this, popular religious practices give rise to popular forms of proselytization. Popular proselytization encompasses a set of religious actions and practices of conversion sustained by the different churches. These practices never rely on the intellectual aspects of the evangelistic process. To the contrary, they are out of reach or control of theology as scientific discipline since they pertain to the realm of orality and its creative dynamism. Popular proselytization conveys a discourse about challenge and competition among the different churches and their followers. It is popular since it builds its niche in the structures and genres of oral performances that function as social praxis in the society (Drewal 1992).

Popular proselytization—a common practice in colonial times—did not disappear with independence. To the contrary, every day it takes on new forms, enriching the oral literature with sententious idioms, proverbs and folk songs that leaders and members of rival churches address to each other within the context of conversion. This production creates a kind of dynamic oral dialogue that filters into the wider society, conveying the churches' points of view on different issues. Church members spread and vulgarize them, using them to convert and attract new members. Even though there is no open conflict between leaders of different churches, there exists a palpable tension surrounding the issue of conversion at the heart of this oral religious literature. I have chosen four examples to illustrate the situation.

Mishonyi ke mutoka
ikaleyi mutoka washile mwa Kalonda.

The Protestant missionary is not a White
If he were he would not have built his stations at Kalonda [far from big cities].

Mumpele wetu mwimpe
mwedu ununka fier
muzabi mutwa panshi
Mishonyi nkantu kayi
kapusu kuditenge
kenda kanyenya mayi.

Our priest is great and good
his beard reflects his majesty
his robe sweeps the ground.
Who is a Protestant missionary?
the one who has a tail [of the devil].

Tunzambinzambi twashila mu mfwanda

New churches are devoted to bush spirits and they were built in the bush in conjunction with witches [since they used to pray in the bush or the mountains and are possessed by the Holy Spirit].

Postolo mandevu ya kuchoma
anaiba kabobo.

Do not tell me about the Apostolic Church of J. Maranke,
their devotees have these long beards that deserve to be burnt.
When out of our sight, they act hypocritically eating catfish [and all other forbidden foods according to their faith].

In the national oral literature, this tension is rendered in the Catholic irony that tries to impeach or to deny to Protestant missions the right to convert. Catholic believers, when they manipulated these negative anthropological images of the savage, identified Protestant pastors with the primitive, the barbarian, and the damned *non-white* or the *anti-Western* subject. They denied them the power to convert and accused them of being the embodiment of the devil and the assassin of Jesus Christ. As argued by Michel de Certeau in connection with the Amerindians, the colonial geography of missions was also employed to create the metaphor of the dominated colonial and/or primitive figure. Protestants became identified with this metaphor, because Protestant missions or stations were located in the hinterland or "bush," while Catholic ones were located in cities and operated in collaboration with the colonial administration. In the social construct of urbanity, the city—*la ville*—was the antithetical space to the bush—*la brousse*—and was perceived as the space of colonial power and civilization; it was where the white man stood as capitalist (trader, entrepreneur, etc.), colonial agent, or Catholic bishop.

This rhetoric of the "meaningless mission"—*la mission insignifiante*—still continues to nurture popular proselytization. It operates as a significant image, strong enough to express all kind of religious competition in the public sphere. In his Easter sermon of 1985, Msgr. M. Bakole, the archbishop of Kananga, openly (counter)attacked the prophet Kadima wa Nzambi, of the Sacrificial Church—"Christ de la parousie." His speech gave birth to an abundant oral literature alluding to the use of magic, black birds, the dead dove, the powerful cane, etc. I pick up on two formulae most representative of this process in the third and fourth examples above.

The above syntagmata depict conflictual relations between new and established churches. Their origin can be traced as well in the sermons and dialogical answers of church leaders. In the course of this oral religious performance they reformulate visions, dreams, divine messages, and pastoral positions that can lead to social praxis and religious conflicts. This dialogical production, whose producer is forgotten, has generated a recent literature on popular proselytization. This production is still an unexplored field.

FINAL ISSUES: THE SECULAR STATE EXPERIENCE AND PROSELYTIZATION IN A CONTEXT OF NATIONAL INTEGRATION

This study on religious freedom in the Congo-Zaire region raises three main issues: the sacralization of the state, popular proselytization, and the eruption of the politics of representation from the religious realm into the public sphere. The process of ideological integration that Mobutu's regime stimulated led to the sacralization of the state instead of all the metaphors and ideological and political procedures the regime used to impose itself. Mobutu, through his appropriation of the symbol of a secular state and his conflict with the Catholic

Church, succeeded only in creating a monster that bites itself. All his struggle to institutionalize new churches and to control the devotees was conducted with the aim of codifying their political behavior. For the politics of Authenticity, which was to facilitate the national integration process, functioned as a process of cultural homogenization by implementing the anthropology of the "Father of the Nation" and a sacred Nation. This process ended in the sacralization of the power and of the individual in power. This disciplinary mechanism did not lead as A. Mbembe concluded in the epitomization of the "épistémè of commandment," but to a sort of reproduction of the colonial Léopoldian State in reverse, for it lacked a real power of control over the society, as F. Eboussi-Boulaga noted.

Popular proselytization opens a series of questions not only about this massive movement of conversion but also about the popular spirituality observed these last years in Congo-Zaire. Many urban and male prophets are former members of the ruling class. They contributed to the collapse of the state and were involved in the embezzlement and the ruin of the state. One can see in their spirituality a way of exorcising the state and justifying its misconduct toward the people. This can work as a strategy for them to threaten or to blackmail their chief who had kept them away from the state power and its kleptocracy. So their "mystical fable" became a way of begging a return into the political sphere. Other people thought that the recent spiritual wave which originated from the ruling class is part of the true conversion that is rooted in the continuing process of the cultural transfer that occurred with the encountering of African religions and Christianity. It should be placed in the realm of the Afro-Christianity in process based on the assumption that "God begins to speak again" through the prophet's mouth. And the prophet must be defined as "the mouth-piece of God," according to E. Evans Pritchard.

The last issue is political, notably the politics of Mobutu's representation. Sacralization of the state is the opposite of what the ruling class expected: the production of a secular state. The failure to produce a secular state can be looked at in the contradiction that brings about the use of religious symbolic rhetoric and the paradox of the secular state in the Weberian conceptualization. The secular modern state is born from the cadaver of the religious state; it carries always the individualization and procedures of control over citizens inherited from the Christianity of the Middle Ages. Though, when the secular state comes into question in postcolonial society, one never analyzes the nature of the African State experience itself from 1885 onward and the role played by Christian missions in implementing it. In the Congo-Zairean case, established churches worked strongly with colonization and the first republic. They marginalized new churches by resorting to colonial proselytization with the help of the state. Now, when the ruling class tries to secularize the state, it reopens the space for new counter-powers and sites of popular resistance. New churches in their search for religious freedom produced representations of political contestation which flowed into the public sphere, questioning the state and its experience.

NOTES

[1] The majority of the national elite and ruling class attended Catholic schools and universities. They worked hard to build up these Christian youth and student associations.

[2] The reply appeared in *La tribune africaine*, which became in 1972 *Elima* under the politics of Authenticity. This daily newspaper, financed by the regime, was perceived as the regime's voice.

[3] Abbé Mpundu created Le Groupe Amos in 1989. This lay organization aimed to boost the democratization process in Zaire by working with human rights associations to mobilize and raise the consciousness of the people (Dorlodot 1994, 4).

[4] In his last sermon of 1992, he told his followers that he had received a divine message with three numbers—3, 5, and 15. These numbers were the key to deciphering what was going on with the national conference.

SELECT BIBLIOGRAPHY

Amnesty International. 1990. *La République du Zaïre. En Marge de la loi, les forces de sécurité répriment les opposants au gouvernement (1988-1990)*. AFR 62/10/90.

Bakole wa I. 1983. *L'Eglise et les droits de l'homme*, Editions de l'Archidiocèse, Kananga.

Bazola, E. 1968. "Le Kimbanguisme," *Cahiers des religions africaines*, vol. 2:121-52.

Biaya, T. K. 1985a. "L'Eglisé catholiqué, la Foi et les peuples du Kasai colonial, 1885-1959." Thesis, Institut Supérecur Pédagogique de Kananga.

———. 1985b. "La «cuistrerie» de Mbujimayi (Zaïre). Organisation, fonctionnement et idéologie d'une bourgeoisie africaine," in *Genève-Afrique*, vol. 23,1:61-83.

———. 1993a. "Femmes, Possession et Christianisme au Zaïre. Analyse diachronique des productions et pratiques de la spiritualité chrétienne africaine." Doctoral thesis, University of Laval, Quebec.

———. 1993b. "Ethnicity: The Root of Nationalist Ideology," in *Zaïre: What Destiny?*, edited by M. Kankwenda, 3-16. Dakar: CODESRIA.

———. 1997. *Youth, Street Culture and Urban Violence in Kinshasa, Zaire*. Ibadan: Institut Français de recherche en Afrique.

Bibeau, G. 1976. "La communauté musulmane de Kisangani," in *Kisangani 1876-1976. Histoire d'une ville*, t.1. *La population*, edited by B. Verhaegen, 179-238. Kinshasa: Presses Universitaires du Zaïre.

Bokeleale, Msgr. 1983. "The ECZ and the State," in "Africa Committee 1983 Zaire. A Symposium," November 2-3, 1983, Africa Committee, National Council of the Churches of Christ in the USA, Washington, D.C.

Bokonga, I. 1978. *La politique culturelle en République du Zaïre*. Paris: UNESCO.

Bureau Politique. 1974. Décisions historiques du Bureau Politique (du 30 novembre 1974). Une révolution dans la révolution. Kinshasa: Editions AZAP.

CEN. 1972. "Rapport de la réunion du Comite Exécutif National de l'ECZ," Kinshasa: ECZ.

Chomé, J. 1960. *La passion de Simon Kimbangu*. Bruxelles: Les amis de Preésence africaine.

de Haes, R. 1980. "Les sectes: une interpellation," in *Zaïre-Afrique*, 142:89-96.

Documentation catholique. 1976. "L'Eglise catholique et l'Etat au Zaïre," DIA:58-59.

Dorlodot, P. de. 1994. *"Marche d'espoir" Kinshasa 16 février 1992. Non violence pour la démocratie au Zaïre.* Paris: Groupe Amos-L'Harmattan.

Drewal, M. T. 1992. *Yoruba Rituals: Performers, Play, Agency.* Bloomington: Indiana University Press.

Eglise catholique au Zaïre. 1981. *Un siècle de croissance (1880-1980).* Kinshasa: Éditions du Secrétariat Général de l'Épiscopat.

Gbabendu, E., and E. Gobassu. 1991. *Volonté de changement au Zaïre* 2t. Paris: L'Harmattan.

Kabongo-Mbaya, P. 1992. *L'Église de Christ au Zaïre.* Paris: Karthala.

———. 1994. "Les églises et la lutte pour la démocratie au Zaïre," in *Belgique/Zaïre: Une histoire en quête d'avenir,* series editor G. de Villers, 157-83. Brussels: CEDAF-Institut africain.

Malula, J. 1958. *L'âme bantoue face á l'Évangile in Vivante Afrique,* 198.

———. 1970. *Mission de l'Église à Kinshasa. Options pastorales.* Kinshasa: Saint Paul Edition; Rome: Pontificia Facultas Theologica Teresianum.

———. 1983. "Allocution d'ouverture," in *L'Afrique et ses formes de spiritualité,* in *Cahiers des religions africaines,* 17:33-34.

Mandefu, B. 1990. *L'impact d'un discours anthropo-théocentrique sur communautés ecclésiales vivantes. L'enjeu d'une nouvelle maniére d'être église.* Rome: Pontificia Facultas Theologica Teresianum.

Manifesto of the Popular Revolutionary Movement. 1967. N'Sele Domain, May 17.

Mobutu. 1971. "Le retour à l'authenticité," Présidence de la République, Kinshasa.

Munayi, M. M. 1974. "Le mouvement kimbanguiste dans le Haut Kasaï, 1921-1959," 2 volumes. Thèse de doctorat de 3è cycle, Université de Provence.

Ndaywel, I. 1993. *La société zaïroise dans le miroir de son discours religieux (1990-1993).* Brussels: CEDAF-Institut africain.

Ngindu, M. 1974. "A propos du recours à l'authenticité et le christianisme au Zaïre," *Cahiers des religions africaines* 8(14).

Nguezi, H. 1993. *Jésus-Christ peut-il être Africain?* Marquain: Hovine Edition.

Nicolas, B. 1985. "L'islam au Zaïre." Thèse de doctorat de 3è cycle, University of Paris.

Nsangi, E. 1981. *La saine collaboration entre l'Église et l'État Zaïrois, qui est Laïc, en référence au Concile Vatican II.* Rome: Pontificia Universitas Urbaniana.

———. 1991. *Une révolution dans la révolution.* Kinshasa: AZAP edition.

Secrétariat pour l'Unité des Chrétiens. 1986. *Le phénomène des sectes ou nouveaux mouvements religieux: défi pastoral.* Interim report.

Statuts = COMIZA. 1979. "Statuts de la Communauté islamique du Zaïre." Kinshasa.

Young, C. 1967. "L'islam au Congo," *Etudes congolaises* [Congolese Studies] 10, no. 5:14-31.

7.

RETURNING TO MY ROOTS

African "Religions" and the State

———————◆———————

Makau Mutua

INTRODUCTION

Four decades after physical decolonization, the African state is today mired in crises of identity (Zartman 1995a; Mutua 1995b; Nyong'o 1992; Jackson and Rosberg 1982; Schatzberg 1988; Cohen, et al. 1993; Irele 1992, 296-302).[1] Multidimensional and complexly dynamic, these crises primarily feed from the traditional troughs of culture and religion, ethnicity and race, history and mythology, and politics and economics[2] (see also Mutua 1995b, 505; Richardson 1996, 1, 11; Zolberg 1992, 303-11). In the quicksand known as the modern African state, this potent and volatile alchemical mix has all too frequently either been cataclysmic or fostered political dysfunction (Zartman 1995b, 1-11; Human Rights Watch 1995, 39-48; French 1997, 9).[3] The realm of religion, together with its essential linkage to philosophy and culture, has been one of the pivotal variables in the construction of the identity of the modern African state (Munro 1975, 147-48; Mbiti 1970, 300-317).[4] Religion has been one of the critical seams of social and political rupture in several African states (Pobee 1996, 402-6).[5]

Due to the centrality of religion in the construction of social reality, this critical examination of the treatment of African religions within the African state will necessarily probe the intersection of Islam, African religion, and

---

I qualify African religions in the subtitle of the chapter because I do not think that the term captures—if it ever could—the phenomenon under discussion. *Religion,* as a word, was unknown to many African languages; hence the difficulty of unpacking the African cosmology, segregating the "religious" aspects of it, and translating that universe in a Western idiom.

169

Christianity—the three dominant religious traditions in Africa—and the role of the state in the establishment or disestablishment of one or other tradition (Mazrui 1986).[6] Thus, the favor or prejudice of the state toward these traditions lies at the heart of this inquiry. Within the crucible of the African state, this chapter primarily argues that the modern African state, right from its inception, has relentlessly engaged in a campaign of the marginalization, at best, or eradication, at worst, of African religion (Barrow 1900; see generally Mbiti 1970).[7] Further, it argues that the destruction and delegitimation of African religion have been actively effected at the urging, or with the collusion and for the benefit of, either or both Islam and Christianity, the two dominant messianic traditions.

It is the contention of the chapter that the conscious, willful, and planned displacement of African religion goes beyond any legitimate bounds of religious advocacy and violates the religious human rights of Africans. This orchestrated process of the vilification and demonization of African religion represents more than an attack on the religious freedom of Africans; it is in fact a repudiation, on the one hand, of the humanity of African culture and, on the other, a denial of the essence of the humanity of the African people themselves (Mbiti 1970, 8-13).[8] In other words, at the core of the attempts to subjugate Africans to the messianic traditions is a belief not only in the superiority of the missionary and his or her messianic dogma but also in the sub-humanity of the missionary's subjects and their cosmology. Finally, the chapter explores, through the case of The Republic of Benin, the raison d'etre, pressures, and tensions that attend the state-directed attempt at protecting and returning to the African past.

This inquiry does not rigidly draw an "us" and "them" dichotomy because cross-cultural penetration and counterpenetration will occur regardless of the insular impulses of cultural guardians. In fact, contact with "otherness" can be a spur for positive social change and progressive development. Societies that prevent the entry of "foreign" values or the export of their values into other cultures deny themselves the benefits of cross-fertilization. Closing off avenues for intercultural exchanges may preserve negative aspects of tradition to the detriment of the group. "Insiders" or those who map the margins of culture need to continually interrogate themselves about the effects of intercourse with "outsiders" and whether, how, or at what pace the exchange should occur. But the strategies employed in creating or managing that contact, as well as its form and content, require constant vigilance to avoid, as much as possible, dehumanizing, degrading, or destroying the "other." Culture should not be essentialized because people, time, and place conspire to construct it. But it represents the accumulation of a people's wisdom and thus their identity; it is real and without it a people is without a name, rudderless, and torn from its moorings.

It is not the argument of this chapter, therefore, that there is a purity to African religion. The genesis of ideas and cultures is always difficult to establish. What a culture has borrowed and the extent to which dynamics internal to it are the engines of change must largely remain fluid questions. At least one respected scholar has argued that even Islam and Christianity can be seen as indigenous African religions (King 1971, 1-35).[9] This point is only interesting because even Mbiti distinguishes Islam and Christianity from African religion.[10] Each religious tradition has its own signature, a religious DNA or "genetic" fingerprint, so to speak. Semitic religions, such as Islam, Judaism, and Christianity, share certain core characteristics such as belief in the afterlife and conceptions of heaven and hell (Marty and Greenspahn 1988, ix).[11] Thus, one can identify, as Mbiti does, the distinguishing characteristics of African religions, although some scholars have questioned the normative framework he has employed to construct African religions (see generally, Mbiti 1970, 19-20; Mutua 1996, 417, 431; Shaw 1990, 339; Hackett 1990, 303, 305; Hackett 1996, 9-10).[12] The important point here is the recognition of the existence of an African religious universe, a spiritual space, separate and distinct from either Islam or Christianity, and the role of the state in contracting or eradicating that sphere and promoting the messianic faiths in its stead. This chapter is therefore an attempt to unmask the perverted role of the state and to argue for its reorientation in addressing African religions. This chapter does not pretend to be what it is not. Its scope is very narrow in that it only seeks to underline the denigration of African religions in the context of modernity. In addition to pleading for the better understanding of African religions, it asks that political space be created to allow the expression of that cosmology.

CIVILIZATIONAL CLASH: IDENTITY RECONSTRUCTION

No African country has officially allocated a national holiday in honor of the gods of indigenous religions. All African countries, on the other hand, have a national holiday that either favors Christian festivals (especially Christmas), Muslim festivals (such as Idd el Fitr), or both categories of imported festivals. The Semitic religions (Christianity and Islam) are nationally honored in much of Africa; the indigenous religions are at best ethnic rather than national occasions (Mazrui 1991, 69-70).

The official suppression of African religions from public visibility throughout Africa, with the recent exception of The Republic of Benin, speaks volumes about identity reconstruction in Africa (*Chicago Tribune* 1996, 8).[13] Indeed, the status of indigenous religions within African states cannot be understood without resort to the nature and purposes of the colonial state. More specifically, the relationship between religion and the state has hinged on the ideological, cultural, and philosophical outlooks of the African intellectual, political, and civil service classes germinated during colonial rule.

There is no doubt that colonization was primarily motivated by economic reasons (Young 1991, 19).[14] As a process, colonization deployed racist dogma, religious penetration, military force, and commerce to subject Africa to Europe (Davidson 1991a; Davidson 1991b). The role of mission Christianity, with its near exclusive delivery of services in formal Western education and health, was central in coercing conversion from African religions (Munro 1975, 148).[15] Missionaries saw themselves as agents for Westernization, and made little distinction between the church and the colonial state. According to one European author whose mission was in Africa, the entire colonial project had to involve all those responsible for the "development of a primitive people" (Shropshire 1938, xiii). He used the term *primitive* to define "all peoples who, in the main, are in the barbaric and pre-literary stage of sociological and cultural development" (*id.*). He likened the Bantu child (the name given to most African peoples inhabiting eastern, central, and southern Africa) to a marsupial cub, the species of "lowly" mammals like the kangaroo (*id.*, 67).[16]

These racist misconceptions and attitudes toward Africans and their religions found fertile ground in the interpretations, dogma, and philosophy of Christianity and other Semitic religions. The view, held by many adherents of these traditions, that monotheism is the critical difference "between advanced (Western) religion and primitive paganism" has long been a basis for the treatment of other beliefs as satanic or devilish (Marty and Greenspahn 1988, ix). Monotheistic religions thus sit at the top of the hierarchy while *polytheism* and *animism,* the terms used to describe African religions, dwell at the bottom of the evolutionary process (Mbiti 1970, 9-12). This theory of religious evolution, which asserts the upward, single-directional track of development from so-called animism to monotheism allows the missionary to believe in the superiority of his or her faith (*id.*, 8-9).[17] These exclusive claims of a final, inflexible truth provide the foundation for proselytization and spur zealotry and missionary activity.

In contrast, African religions are communal and non-universalist; unlike Christianity or Islam, they do not seek to convert or remake the "other" in their image (Mazrui 1991, 77). The notion of converting the "other" is alien because the religion of the people is their identity and being; as one author has put it, it is redundant and tautological to talk of the religion of the Yoruba, for instance, because their identity is their religion, their way of life (Long 1988, 3-4). Mbiti has written that in traditional society there was no dichotomy between the secular and the religious, no distinction between the religious and the irreligious, and no separation between the material and the spiritual (Mbiti 1970, 2). He writes, further, that

> Wherever the African is, there is his religion: he carries it to the fields where he is sowing seeds or harvesting new crop; he takes it with him to the beer party or to attend a funeral ceremony; and if he is educated [formal Western education], he takes religion with him to the examination room at school or in the university; if he is a politician he takes it to the house of parliament. *Although many African languages do not have a word for religion as such, it nevertheless accompanies the individual from long before his birth to long after his physical death* (*id.*, 2-3, emphasis added).

That is why the degradation of African religions should be seen as the negation of the humanity of the African people. In the internationally acclaimed novel *Things Fall Apart,* Nigerian writer Chinua Achebe tells the story of this civilizational clash, and the simultaneous deconstruction and reconstruction of the African identity by mission Christianity and the agency of the colonial state (Achebe 1959). This meeting of cultures is captured through the tragic life of Okonkwo, a pre-colonial Igbo man whose world literally disintegrates before his eyes. A man of status and a guardian of Igbo culture and religion, Okonkwo and other Igbo resist the new faith and the authority of the colonial state; but when the resistance is almost certainly crushed, Okonkwo kills a meddling local collaborator of the colonial regime and then hangs himself rather than accept physical and spiritual surrender to the church and the colonial state (*id.,* 207).

Okonkwo had watched with bitterness as the missionaries mocked the Igbo religion (*id.,* 146),[18] converted some of his people, including his son, to Christianity, and then used them against Igbos opposed to the new dispensation (*id.,* 148-67). In one telling moment, an Igbo who had become a missionary himself congratulates Okonkwo's son for running away to study at a mission school. The missionary tells him: "Blessed is he who forsakes his mother and father for my sake" (*id.,* 152). When Okonkwo and his Igbo resisters burn down a church, they are arrested and physically beaten on orders of the local colonial administrator (*id.,* 189-97). Here, the church fuses with the state. According to an elder, the white man "has put a knife on the things that held us together and we have fallen apart" (*id.,* 176). In *Things Fall Apart,* the colonial administrator decides to write *The Pacification of the Primitive Tribes of the Lower Niger,* a book based on Okonkwo's life and death, which he sees as symbolic of Europe's victory over the Igbo (*id.,* 208-9).

In history, Achebe's fiction was played out repeatedly throughout Africa. The encounter between Christianity and the Igbo religion has been characterized as a four-part process: the establishment of a mission; recruitment of converts, usually from among the social "rejects"; attack or "persecution" of the mission by elders and guardians of Igbo religion; and the imposition of colonial rule, and its protection and promotion of the mission (Isichei 1970, 209, 212). As put clearly by Isichei:

> Towns [African] felt an urgent need for allies and advocates in the face of the violence with which it [colonial rule] was established. They had to learn the language of the invader, to communicate with their new rulers. Large numbers of employment opportunities existed, and there was an obvious benefit to be gained from education (*id.,* 212).

Education in missionary schools was perhaps the most decisive weapon in the reconstruction of African identity. The mission usually preyed on the youth, capturing them and tearing them from their cultural moorings. The colonial state financially supported the mission schools, thus enhancing the capacity to transform social reality (Shropshire 1938, 431).[19] Isichei writes, again:

> The missionaries succeeded in maintaining their virtual monopoly of education, and obtained adherents, not through dialogue with adults, but by cutting children off from their traditional culture and placing them in the artificially unanimous environment of the school. Today most Igbo have been baptized, and traditional religion is the preserve of a small aging minority (Isichei 1970, 212; see also Debrunner 1967, 103; Beidelman 1982, 198).[20]

Without regard to which agency was the first to penetrate an African community, both the colonial state and the church worked hand in glove in the civilizing mission. In Ghana, for example, the colonial state paternalized African rulers for their "good relations" with missionaries but attacked what it called "fetishism" and "fetish priests" (Debrunner 1967, 175). The colonial government's disapproval and attack on African religions and customs further encouraged new converts to reject the ways of their forebears (*id.*, 189).[21] For instance, female circumcision, which Christians denounced as satanic, was one such custom (Kenyatta 1965; Lewis 1995).[22] Most significantly, the colonial state passed laws and implemented policies designed to purge the continent of African religions (see, for example, Fasuyi 1973). In Nigeria, for instance, African religions, dances, education, and art were banned (*id.*, 21).

> The early missionaries came to introduce a new religion; all the former religious rites and manifestations (including the dance and music) were banned, and new converts were encouraged to dispose of any art works which had been used in religious rites (*id.*; see also Young 1991, 31).[23]

The processes of social transformation and identity reconstruction set in motion by the invasion of Africa by both Christianity and Islam, and particularly the former, dislocated and distorted the African worldview almost in its entirety. The colonial state buttressed that process through the delegitimation of African religious beliefs, and the legitimation, at the political and social levels, of the spiritual and religious cosmologies of the invaders. In the span of several decades, the peoples of Africa were largely reconstructed, never to be the same again.

Postcolonialism and the Culture of Silence

In most of Africa, the current states do not predate colonialism, but were created by European imperial powers. The governing classes in Africa—both intellectual and political—are the products of the colonial state or its uncritical successor, the postcolonial state (Hansen 1993, 160-62). Though formally independent, the postcolonial state is conceptually much like its predecessor. According to Hansen:

> African leaders have adopted and continued to use political forms and precedents that grew from, and were organically related to, the European experience. Formal declarations of independence from direct European rule do not mean actual independence from European conceptual dominance (*id.*, 161).

The uncritical acceptance by many African leaders of the postcolonial state is not surprising considering the conceptual aspirations of the African elite. Many of the new rulers were forged in the mission and colonial schools, a process that almost certainly entailed the ideological renunciation of African religions, traditions, and beliefs, on the one hand, and the embrace of Christianity and the traditions of the Europeans, on the other. Even as the new converts straddled the fence, as many inevitably did, and mixed the "old" with the "new," there was little doubt that the new was expected, as a matter of course, to overcome the old. The new religious, cultural, and educational structures were designed to create local servants of colonialism.

> The West European educational system was introduced, replacing the informal traditional system; it was geared to the needs of the colonial administration. This objective was stated in a 1921 speech by the first [British] Governor of Nigeria: "The chief function of Government Primary and Secondary Schools . . . is to train the more promising boys from the village schools as teachers for those schools, as clerks for the native courts, and as interpreters" (Fasuyi 1973, 21; Nduka 1965).

The new curriculum was usually conceived in the metropole, either in England or France, and required the study of political, cultural, and literary forms which were alien to Africa. The British Empire, its language, and the English themselves were presented as the agents of civilization, replacing African worldviews (Fasuyi 1973, 21).[24] It was these "products" who would lead their countries to formal independence and become its rulers. In Ghana, Kwame Nkrumah, who led the country into formal independence from Britain, invoked his Christian and Western educational background when he proclaimed, "Seek ye first the political kingdom and all other things shall be added to you" (Isichei 1995, 339). Little wonder that Ghana was one of the earliest conquests of the church on the continent (Debrunner 1967).[25]

Elsewhere on the African continent, mission-educated men took power as Africa emerged from direct European colonial rule. The list is long. Leopold Senghor, the first president of Senegal, now a member of the *Académie Francaise* (Vaillant 1990),[26] is a former seminarian and a leading Catholic intellectual (Isichei 1995, 339). The late Felix Houphouet-Boigny, the Ivorian president who constructed the world's largest Catholic basilica in the country's interior, was obviously another devout Catholic (*id.*, 339-40).[27] Others share similar backgrounds: Julius Nyerere of Tanzania was a Catholic; Kenneth Kaunda of Zambia was Presbyterian; and General Ignatius Acheampong of Ghana had been born into a Catholic family (*id.*, 338-40). With the possible exception of the king of Swaziland, the head of one of the few African states that predates colonialism, to my knowledge there is no African leader who openly professes African traditional religions. Note, however, that 77 percent of the population of Swaziland is Christian but only 20.9 percent adheres to African religions (*1996 Britannica Book of the Year* 1996, 721). Virtually all African heads of state or government are Christian or Muslim. The religious affiliation of the leadership greatly influenced the character of the nascent black-governed African state, and provided a smooth conceptual continuum between itself and its predecessor, the colonial state.

There is little doubt that over the last century Christianity has expanded enormously in Africa. It is estimated that the number of African Christians will have risen from 10 million in 1910 to 393 million in 2000, making one in every five Christians an African (Isichei 1995, 1; Moreno 1996, 13).[28] Although European colonial powers saw Islam as a threat to their cultural hegemony, many writers now agree that Islam prospered during the colonial period (Hiskett 1984; King 1971). Once colonial conquest was established, the British, for example, instituted indirect rule, using or inventing local rulers to act as the agents of the new state. A good example of indirect rule was the governance of the northern Nigerian emirates for the British by the emirs (Hiskett 1984, 276-301). Both the French and the British supported Koranic schools throughout most of Africa, and used them to train civil servants and teachers to serve the colonial state (Oliver 1991, 202). Needless to say, Islam was favored over African religions.

> In situations where Muslim towns supplied the local government services for a countryside that was still in practice pagan [African religions], colonial support for the Islamic authorities helped greatly to consolidate Muslim observance among the country people (*ibid.*).

While both messianic religions grew, there was a corresponding decline in African religions (Isichei 1995, 324). The position of African religions and cultures has not differed, either substantially or qualitatively, under the postcolonial state. The combination of colonial norms and structures—which were deliberately conceived as hostile to African heritage—survived intact into the independent, African-ruled states and continued to be the conceptual basis for those new states. In essence, the new elites took over the civilizing mission of the departing colonial power and have generally sought the re-creation of Africa in the image of Europe, even in those states which were ruled by Islamic elites. The constitutional and legal norms adopted on the eve of independence, as well as subsequent laws and policies, continued to suppress African cultures and religions, in spite of demagogic overtures by some rulers to the contrary (Mutua and Rosenblum 1990).[29]

African constitutions and laws are generally either openly hostile to African religions and culture or they pretend that such religions do not exist. Such pretense is a tacit hope that African religions have either been eliminated or marginalized and so fundamentally delegitimized that they warrant no attention. The independence constitutions, which were largely written by Europeans for Africans on the eve of independence, sought to transplant a formal liberal state to the continent, an entity whose continued survival would be guaranteed by the metropolitan power and would therefore be subservient to it (Nkrumah 1965; Jackson 1992). None of the independence constitutions, as far as this author knows, make any mention of indigenous African religions (Mutua 1996, 434). Instead, they offer liberal generic protection of religious freedoms. The language used strongly suggests that "received" and not indigenous religions are the target for such protection.

A survey of several independence constitutions will suffice. Kenya's 1963 independence constitution, for example, guaranteed to each person freedom of religion, including the "freedom to change his religion or belief, and freedom, either alone or in community with others, and both in public and private, to manifest and propagate his religion or belief in worship, teaching, practice and observance" (section 22(1), Constitution of Kenya 1963). It defined religion as inclusive of a "religious denomination, and cognate expressions" (section 22(6)). Further, it limited religious freedom to the interests of public morality and health, and guaranteed individuals the right to observe and practice any religion without the "unsolicited intervention of members of any other religion" (section 22(5)).

The limitations placed on religion for reasons of "public morality" and "public health" were most likely aimed at elements of indigenous African religions which many colonial states regarded as abominable (Shropshire 1938). Significantly, these provisions protect the right to proselytize, a feature common to Christianity and Islam. The constitutions of Malawi (section 19, Constitution of Malawi, 1964), Nigeria (section 24, Constitution of Nigeria, 1963), Zambia (section 24, Constitution of Zambia, 1964), and Congo (Leopoldville) (article 25, Constitution of Congo (Leopoldville) [Zaire], 1964) offer similar, if not identical, rights and protections to those granted by the Constitution of Kenya. None attempts to protect or reclaim African religions. Interestingly, the constitution of Guinea (article 41, The Constitution of the Republic of Guinea, 1958) tersely and barely protects religious freedom while the Ivory Coast (article 6, Constitution of the Ivory Coast, 1960) and Mali (article 1, Constitution of the Republic of Mali, 1960) only mention religion with reference to the nondiscrimination clause.

In the three decades since independence, African constitutions have not assumed a different posture toward African religions. The constitutional silence and the absolute refusal to acknowledge the existence of African religions or cultures has continued to this day. For instance, no changes have been made to the religious clause of the Constitution of Kenya (section 78, The Constitution of Kenya, 1988).[30] Similarly, no substantial changes have been made to the constitutions of Nigeria (section 37, Constitution of the Federal Republic of Nigeria (Promulgation) Decree, 1989),[31] Zaire (now the Democratic Republic of Congo) (article 17, Constitution of the Republic of Zaire, 1990),[32] and Zambia (section 20, Constitution of Zambia, 1991).[33] They do not even make vague references to African religions or cultures. This silence has, additionally, been given negative meaning by government policies and laws in a number of states.

The current regime in Sudan is perhaps one of the clearest examples of the active use of the state and its resources to destroy non-Islamic religions, including African religion (see generally, Lawyers Committee for Human Rights 1996; *1996 Britannica Book of the Year* 1996, 719).[34] Attempts by the state to impose Islam on Christians and adherents of African religions in the south of the country have escalated the civil war, leading to the killing of an estimated 1.3 million southern, non-Islamic civilians. There have been widespread reports of enslavement and forced conversions of black African southerners and their indoctrination to Islam (Hentoff 1995, A17; Moreno 1996, 36-37). A report by a right-wing Christian group terms the process "cultural cleansing" which "seeks to eliminate a cultural group by forcibly stripping these children [adherents of Christianity and African religions] of their names, language, freedom, families, and religion" (Moreno 1996, 36).

There are numerous examples of other African states that favor or promote the Semitic religions. President Frederick Chiluba declared Zambia a Christian nation, although there are substantial numbers of believers in African religions, Hinduism, and Islam (US Department of State 1994, 330; *1996 Britannica Book of the Year* 1996, 754; Mwalimu 1991, 233).[35] In Zaire (now the Democratic Republic of Congo) a state decree in 1971 declared the Catholic church, some Protestants, and the Kimbanguists (an independent Zairian church) the only legally recognized churches (Moreno 1996, 41). Elsewhere, African postcolonial states have banned elements of African religions (Munro 1975, 106; Kenyatta 1965, 261). The colonial state and church, and later the postcolonial state, banned important elements of African culture and religion. Among the Akamba of Kenya, for example, the colonial rulers abolished the recognition of Kamba shrines, the consultation of medicine men, work on Sundays, beer and tobacco consumption, dancing, polygamy, bridewealth, and use of the oath. A number of African states, including Algeria (article 2, Constitution of Algeria, 1989), the Comoros (Preamble, Constitution of the Federal Islamic Republic of the Comoros, 1992), Egypt (article 2, Constitution of the Arab Republic of Egypt, 1971),[36] Libya (article 2, Constitutional Proclamation of the Socialist People's Libyan Arab Jamahiriya, 1969), Mauritania (article 5, Constitution of the Islamic Republic of Mauritania, 1991), Morocco (article 6, Constitution of the Kingdom of Morocco, 1992), and Tunisia (article 1, Constitution of the Tunisian Republic, 1959) are either constitutionally Islamic or proclaim Islam to be the religion of the state. Other states substantiate their commitment to Islam by providing for certain religious institutions or requiring that senior officials be Muslims (article 21, Constitution of the Kingdom of Morocco, 1992; article 23, Constitution of the Islamic Republic of Mauritania, 1991; articles 38, 40, Constitution of the Tunisian Republic, 1959; van der Vyver 1997, 1-2).[37] But in an unusual turn, the 1996 South African Constitution expressly recognized the "institution, status, and role of traditional leadership, according to customary law" subject to the Constitution (1996 South African Constitution), chapter 12, sections 211-12). While there is no explicit mention of African religions, this provision openly recognizes African values in the governance of the state. What most of these examples point to, however, is the delegitimation of African religions, and that spiritual universe, through the implementation by the state of norms and policies in education and other arenas of public life that are based on European, American, or Arab conceptions of society or modernization.

THE MYTH AND REALITY OF COUNTERPENETRATION

There can be no doubt that over the last century Africa has undergone one of the most dramatic and fundamental transformations ever witnessed in human history. Crawford Young has written that the indelible imprint of Europe on Africa is unique among world regions (Young 1991, 20).[38] The fact of the displacement, transformation, and reorientation of African norms by European values has been documented and is not a source of much controversy. What is contested is the qualitative effect of those processes on the African universe. At the extremes, some cast the encounter as completely detrimental to Africa, while other apologists of colonial rule see it as the unquestioned redemption of the "dark" continent. In the middle there is a multiplicity of "moderate" characterizations of the encounter, a kind of a sliding judgmental scale which sees the benefits as well as the costs of the culture clash. This section explores these dichotomous views and probes the claim of counterpenetration.

Although the delegitimation of African cultures and religions has proceeded apace over the last century, there are still substantial numbers of Africans who adhere to them or use some of their conceptions to construct new identities. The process of incorporating European normative frameworks in addressing the changing reality started at the outset of the encounter with the West. Among the Akamba of Kenya, for example, politico-religious movements which have been termed a worldwide phenomenon at the revitalization and reorganization of indigenous societies arose in the wake of colonial expansion (Munro 1975, 110). Many of the movements utilized African religious thought although they combined it with elements of Islamic and Christian theology (*id.*).

In the early years of colonial penetration, resistance was widespread. For example, Syokimau, the Kamba priestess, prophesied the detrimental effects of the culture clash (*id.*, 11). Others in Kamba society, such as Siotune Kathuke and Kiamba Mutuavio in 1911 used Kamba religious conceptions to mobilize resistance to the missions and colonial rule, actions for which they were deported to distant parts of the country by the colonial authorities (*id.*, 114-17). But frustration with colonial rule among the Akamba was heightened because of the economic pressures of taxation, forcible conscription into the colonial armed forces, and the imposition of new justice and religious orders (*id.*).

Once the earlier, more indigenous protest movements were crushed, others arose in their stead, this time identifying themselves more explicitly with Christian theology. In 1921, Ndonye Kauti led one such movement, with the promise of delivering the Akamba to a Golden Age after expelling the missions and the "evil" Europeans (*id.*, 118-21). Like his predecessors, Kauti was arrested and deported (*id.*, 120). The successful establishment of colonial rule vanquished these protest movements but left space for more "benign" and less "political" African Christian sects. Among the Agikuyu of Kenya, for example, Watu wa Mngu [Kiswahili for People of God] arose as a response to the opposition of clitoridectomy by Christian missions (Kenyatta 1965, 263). Christianity, which was now the establishment religion, selectively allowed the incorporation into its liturgy and ritual only those African conceptions which legitimized the church within Africa. The Zaire Rite, which "Africanized" worship in the Zairian Catholic church, and the use of African names for African Christians where previously missionaries insisted on European names, are some examples of the "Africanization" of the church (Isichei 1995, 2-3). However, this model of counterpenetration is superficial and symbolic; it does not exert meaningful normative or conceptual African influence on the church.

Between 1880 and 1920, more serious attempts to "Africanize" Christianity took place in the movement called Ethiopianism (Idowu 1975, 206). Although based largely on Christian theology, these churches born of Ethiopianism have been described as utilizing more conceptions of African traditional religions. According to Idowu, the Nigerian scholar of African religions, elements of Ethiopianism sought to recover Africa's "enslaved soul" (*id.*). He writes:

> "Ethiopianism" has taken various forms, ranging from attempts at the indigenization of the Christian Church, the founding of churches by charismatic, Christian African leaders, and the establishment of splinters from European-dominated churches as separatist churches which are completely free from any form of foreign interference (*id.*).

Idowu regards some aspects of the "Ethiopian" churches as "positive repudiations of Christianity" because they only used the "scaffolding of the Christian church to erect new structures for the self-expression of the traditional religion" (*id.*). But another scholar downplays the "Africanity" of such churches; she notes that although the new religious organizations were established by Africans, they "differed only in detail from the mission churches from which they had separated themselves" (Isichei 1995, 3).[39] Whatever the case, there has been a complex process of innovation and interaction between African churches—both European and African separatist churches—and forms and conceptions of African religions (see generally, Olupona 1991). Many of the "Ethiopian" churches appear to have been more interested in political and financial autonomy, with lesser degrees of conceptual independence from Christian theology and philosophy. This is not to say that the Christian church in Africa has not been concerned with the vexing questions of inculturation and identity. These are important issues because of the European origin of the church and the inherent white racism within it (Isichei 1995, 3). Even the most devout African Christians or Muslims at best remain either as "insider-outsiders" or "outsider-insiders," because the religions they profess are anchored and mediated through other cultures, in this case either European or Arab. Africans remain the bearers of a suspended and distorted identity, because the adopted religions cannot fully express their history, culture, and being.

In any event, it is the contention of this chapter that whatever "spin" is given to Christian penetration and its conquest or delegitimation of the African spiritual world, the process of Christianization cannot be isolated from Westernization and the consequent devaluation of the cultural identity of Africans and their humanity. It is not possible, as Sanneh contends, to legitimately consider the Christian penetration of Africa as not being part of the imperial cultural package of the West, and its ideological and conceptual repudiation of Africa (Sanneh 1993, 15-17). Sanneh asks for the transcendence of the view that

[c]onverts [African] have capitulated to Western cultural imperialism, and that their sins have been visited on their children who are condemned to an ambiguous identity, being born, as it were, with a foreign foot in their native mouth. Converts may, for that reason, be considered cultural orphans and traitors at the same time (*id.*, 16).

Sanneh further contends that there was a "vital compatibility" between African cultures and Christianity, although he admits to the distortion of that relationship (*id.*). Moreover, he emphasizes the "assimilation" of Christianity into local idioms and cultures, and suggests a "benign" encounter with the West (*id.*). This characterization of the meeting of the two cultures decontextualizes Christianity from the entire colonial project and the violence with which it was accomplished. Such violence was not always physical; it was also the psychological, emotional, and cultural denigration of African peoples and cultural norms.

The fact that Christianity emerged victorious in this cultural contest, and has been "embraced" by the majority of Africans today, does not make the process less violent or more humane. Others say that Christianity has been "translated" through African languages and cultures, as if to suggest that such a process authenticates or humanizes the encounter. It is clear that conversion, for example, was one-dimensional: the African converted to either Christianity or Islam, never the reverse. I need not abstract my views about the encounter with the West; I witnessed the schism between my parents and my grandparents as the encounter played itself out in their lives. On the one hand, my parents converted, thereby forsaking their identity and cutting themselves off from my grandparents. My parents presented their "choice" as "enlightened" and "progressive." To them, my grandparents represented a past without a future in the new society. But that "choice" had a lot to do with managing the new colonial dispensation. Based partially on my family history, I have concluded that the peoples of Africa have been spiritually enslaved, as it has become impossible for them to carry their cultures forward in the new global normative order. Later in life, my parents could not articulate to my inquiring mind why they had forsaken the past so completely. In my view, the programmatic agenda of the African postcolonial state demands an immersion into Eurocentric norms and forms of culture and society.

BENIN: A RETURN TO THE ROOTS?

On January 10, 1996, The Republic of Benin became the first African state to officially recognize a traditional religion when it declared a National Voodoo Day (*Chicago Tribune* 1996; *Africa News* 1996). Unlike many Africans in other states, the majority of Béninois are open adherents of the African religion known as voodoo, a fact which made it easier for the government to recognize the religion (*1996 Britannica Book of the Year* 1996, 565). Sixty-two percent of Béninois practice voodoo as opposed to only 23 percent and 12 percent who profess Christianity and Islam respectively (*id.*). These numbers, together with the history and politics of Benin, were instrumental in the state's official recognition of voodoo.

The territory now constituting The Republic of Benin, also known at other times as the Kingdom of Dahomey, was a firmly established state five centuries ago, before the advent of colonialism (Elias 1988, 11).[40] Benin was conquered and declared a French colony in the late nineteenth century (*Constitutions of Nations* 1965, 1:149). One of the country's earlier independence constitutions made no mention of voodoo although it protected religious beliefs in its non-discrimination clause (article 13, Constitution of Dahomey, 1964).[41] In a departure from earlier constitutional jurisprudence, the 1990 constitution of The Republic of Benin creates a secular state but protects the "right to culture," and puts the duty on the state to "safeguard and promote the national values of civilization, as much material as spiritual, as well as the cultural traditions" (article 10, Constitution of The Republic of Benin, Law No. 90-32, 1990).[42] Elsewhere, the constitution allows religious institutions to operate parochial schools (article 14, *id.*) and protects the freedom of religion (article 23, *id.*). The 1990 Constitution, the most democratic in the country's history, resulted from the popular defeat of the repressive Marxist regime of Mathieu Kérékou, the dictator who had ruled The Republic of Benin since the 1972 coup d'etat (US Department of State 1992).

Benin has been viewed by many as the birthplace of voodoo although until recently the religion was suppressed by the state (Cowell 1993, 11). The colonial state equated voodoo with witchcraft and banned it (*Africa News* 1996, 108). The first indication that the state would rehabilitate voodoo and remove the stigma associated with it came in 1993 when the first festival of voodoo culture and arts was held in Ouidah, only forty-five miles outside Cotonou, Benin's capital (*id.*). At the festival, also attended by invitees from Haiti, Trinidad and Tobago, and other west African states, President Nicephore Soglo, the former World Bank economist and the first democratically elected leader in two decades, underscored the importance of voodoo to the majority of Béninois and to descendants of Africans in the diaspora sold to captivity in the Americas (*id.*). Critics called Soglo's recognition of voodoo a ploy to pander to the electorate in the 1996 presidential elections, which he lost to Kérékou, the former dictator (*Phoenix Gazette* 1996, A2; Aplogan 1996).

There is little significance to whatever political motivations lay behind the official recognition of voodoo in Benin. What is important is the acknowledgment by the state of the religion of the overwhelming majority of its citizens. The Republic of Benin recognized facts on the ground and started the process of restoring dignity to the identity and humanity of voodoo, and of the human beings who practice it. Benin's example should be emulated elsewhere in Africa to end the culture of silence and repression of the identity of millions of Africans.

At the continental level, African states took an important step in reclaiming part of the past when in 1981 they adopted the African Charter on Human and Peoples' Rights, the basis for the regional human rights system (The African Charter on Human and Peoples' Rights, 1981; Mutua 1995a, 339).[43] Although critics have pointed out numerous problems with the African Charter (Shivji 1989; Okoth-Ogendo 1993; Mutua 1995a; Flinterman and Ankumah 1992, 159), the instrument claims to be inspired by the "virtues" of African "historical tradition" and the "values of African civilization" (African Charter, 1981, Preamble). It prohibits discrimination based on religion (*id.*, article 2) and guarantees the freedom of religion (*id.*, article 8). Most significantly, it burdens the state with the "promotion and protection of morals and traditional values recognized by the community" (*id.*, article 17). It also requires the state to assist the "family which is the custodian of morals and traditional values" (*id.*, article 18(2)) and enlists the state in popular struggles against foreign cultural domination (*id.*, article 20(3)). Although these provisions raise questions about the states' understanding of tradition and culture, the African Charter makes a radical statement: African traditions, civilization, and cultural values must be part of the fabric of a human rights corpus for the region.

The African Charter officially rehabilitates African philosophy and norms and may very well contribute to the reclamation of Africa's spiritual universe. This could be an essential part of the solution to the crises of identity wracking Africans and the states they claim as theirs. A return, a recognition, and a coming to terms with the African past—both cultural and religious—would help heal the spirit and lead to the creation of more stable and humane societies. I believe that this is one of the essential means through which the humanity stolen from Africa by the imperial religions can be restored.

NOTES

[1] For the analyses and descriptions of the crises which threaten the survival of the postcolonial African state and have occupied scholars and academics since decolonization, see those listed.

[2] Although these traditional sources of friction beset virtually all states, their centripetal and centrifugal forces have tended to lay bare the high vulnerability of the African state, and on occasion, to cause its implosion. See generally, *Collapsed States*, edited by I. William Zartman (identifying and analyzing the reasons for, and process of, the collapse of a number of African states, including Chad, Uganda, Ghana, Somalia, Liberia, Mozambique, and Ethiopia).

[3] While over the last decade a number of African states have failed, many of them have been reconstructed. The collapse of the Rwandan state in 1994 has been the most dramatic to date. The latest casualty has been the Zairian state (now renamed the Democratic Republic of the Congo) of Mobutu Sese Seko, which in May 1997 unraveled under military pressure from forces loyal to Laurent Kabila, now the head of state.

[4] The modern African state (started as the colonial enterprise known as the colonial state), the proselytization of Christianity, and the imposition of European social, economic, and political values and structures were interwoven in a continuum of cultural divestiture and alienation from pre-colonial African values. The church, the flag, and formal European education were all closely intertwined.

[5] Two African states, Nigeria and Sudan, have particularly been ravaged by religious conflict between Muslims and Christians in the contexts of the struggles for group autonomy and the control of the political state.

[6] Africa's domination by Islam, Christianity, and African religions has been seductively termed its *triple heritage,* terminology which may suggest peaceful coexistence and mutual enrichment.

[7] Although I recognize the plurality of African religious expressions, I will often use the singular terminology of *African religion* to emphasize the near-total uniformity of assault and denigration of African religions by messianic faiths. In addition, the term also points to the similarities in cosmology and philosophy among different African religions.

[8] Discussing early missionary attitudes toward Africans and their religions, and concluding that most missionaries regarded African religions as primitive and savage, Mbiti notes further that

African religions and philosophy have been subjected to a great deal of misinterpretation, misrepresentation and misunderstanding. They have been despised, mocked and dismissed as primitive and underdeveloped. One needs only to look at earlier titles and accounts to see the derogatory language used, prejudiced descriptions given and false judgments passed upon these religions. In missionary circles they have been condemned as superstition, satanic, devilish and hellish (Mbiti 1970, 13).

[9] Mbiti has noted that "Christianity in Africa is so old that it can rightly be described as an indigenous, traditional and African religion" (Mbiti 1970, 300). But

Mbiti here distinguishes between early Christianity in north Africa, Egypt, and Sudan (which he dubs indigenous) and mission Christianity beginning in the fifteenth century but particularly toward the end of the eighteenth century (according to him, this latter version is not indigenous) (*id.*, 300-303). Mbiti notes that Islam, too, is traditional, indigenous, and African in northern Africa, the Horn of the continent, and southward along the east coast (*id.*, 317). See King 1971 (describing the entry of both Christianity and Islam into Africa in pre-modern times).

[10] According to Mbiti, Africans have their own religious ontology, which he groups into four categories: god as the supreme being responsible for humans and all things; spirits, the superhuman beings of the dead; human beings, the living as well as the unborn; and objects and phenomena without biological life (Mbiti 1970, 20).

[11] Semitic religions often distinguish themselves from other beliefs by the emphasis they place on monotheism.

[12] More particularly, Mbiti paints the following picture of African religions:

For Africans, the whole of existence is a religious phenomenon; man is deeply a religious being living in a religious universe. Failure to recognize and appreciate this starting point has led missionaries, anthropologists, colonial administrators and other foreign writers on African religions to misunderstand not only the religions as such but the peoples of Africa.

Elsewhere, I have defined *indigenous* as all African religious expressions whose cores predate Islamization and Christianization. Such religions denote the beliefs of native, non-settler peoples and exclude Islam and Christianity.

Several scholars have charged Mbiti and other African writers with employing Judeo-Christian templates to translate African religions into a Western idiom. Some have argued that his and similar works, which they see as perpetuating a hegemonic version of African religions, are inspired by "theological" cultural nationalism. This prevalence of Western Christian discourse has remained normative within African religious studies, resulting in distortions of that universe.

[13] On January 10, 1996, the government of The Republic of Benin inaugurated National Voodoo Day, officially recognizing for the first time in post-independent Africa the importance of indigenous religion.

[14] Describing pre-colonial Africa on the dawn of colonialism as a "ripe melon" with "sweet, succulent flesh" awaiting carving by European imperial powers.

[15] Munro notes the use of education to "attract" converts in the Machakos district of Kenya. He writes, further, that

Christian missionaries gained an edge over their rival proselytizers. Islam, which seemed less appropriate than Christianity as a religion for those seeking to use a colonial system controlled by European Christians, made few new converts in the 1920s and the Haji [Muslim community] remained peripheral on the Kamba [Akamba, the indigenous people of Machakos district] scene (Munro 1975, 148).

[16] Shropshire asserts that like marsupial cubs, the children of the Bantu are more dependent on their mothers than children of "civilized" [European] parents (Shropshire 1938, 67).

[17] According to Mbiti, *animism* was coined by Europeans to describe the beliefs of "primitive" peoples who consider all objects to have a soul, hence the presence in their cosmology of countless spirits.

[18] In one particular incident, a missionary tells a crowd of Igbos:

All the gods you have named [Igbo gods] are not gods at all. They are gods of deceit who tell you to kill your fellows and destroy your children. There is only one true God and He has the Earth, the sky, you and me and all of us.

[19] Shropshire writes: "The education of the Bantu is largely in the hands of the missionaries whom the Government support with special grants."

[20] This view was captured by another Christian imperialist who wrote: "Let the Missionaries and the schoolmasters, the plough and the spade, go together. It is the Bible and the plough that must regenerate Africa." In Tanzania, mission schools were recognized as the "most important means by which the mission attracts converts and promotes its message."

[21] Emboldened by the government's rejection of African customs, Christian school-girls, for example, refused to undergo the "dipo" custom, which culminated in initiation into womanhood.

[22] For a description and analysis of female circumcision or *irua*, and its role in the construction of an individual's social identity within the Agikuyu, one of the African nations in modern-day Kenya, see generally Kenyatta 1965. For a thoughtful exploration of feminist debates on the practice, see Lewis 1995.

[23] Young has written:

African culture was for the most part regarded as having little value, and its religious aspect—outside the zones in which Islam was well implanted—was subject to uprooting through intensive Christian evangelical efforts, which were often state-supported. European languages supplanted indigenous ones for most state purposes; for the colonial subject, social mobility required mastering the idiom of the colonizer. In innumerable ways, colonial subjugation in Africa brought not only political oppression and economic exploitation but also profound psychological humiliation.

[24] One writer notes:

Students [African] had to learn things which had little bearing on their own way of life, e.g., the geography and the political, social and economic history of Britain and the British Empire. Foreign literature was studied. English became the official language, in which all transactions were affected. Indigenous languages were neglected; oral poetry gave way to Shakespeare and English literature. Those who managed to study abroad frequently came back alienated from their own society.

[25] Christianity was brought to Ghana as early as the fifteenth century.

[26] The *Académie Francaise*, the pinnacle of French culture, has forty "immortals," persons whose contribution to French culture and statecraft is unparalleled. Senghor was the first African to achieve the honor.

[27] Pope John Paul II opened the basilica in person, even though it was attacked as unconscionable and wasteful spending in the midst of human poverty and suffering in a country that is only 10 percent Catholic (Isichei 1995, 339-40).

[28] According to another count, in 1993 Africa was 57.3 percent Christian, 26.7 percent Muslim, and 15.4 percent African religions. For more comprehensive statistics on religious affiliations by country, see *1996 Britannica Book of the Year*, 783-85.

[29] An example of such cynicism and manipulation of African culture as a veil for a despotic regime is that of Mobutu Sese Seko, the former Zairian president, and his "authenticity" campaign through which he forbade the use of European names and

dress while running one of the most corrupt and abusive regimes with the support of France, Belgium, and the United States.

[30] Albert P. Blaustein and Gisbert H. Flanz, eds., *Constitutions of the Countries of the World,* Binder X (1988).

[31] Ibid., Binder XIV (1990).

[32] Ibid., Supplement Binder (1991).

[33] Ibid. (1992).

[34] The National Islamic Front (NIF) government in Sudan came to power in 1989 following the overthrow of the democratically elected government of Saddiq Al-Mahdi. The NIF has sought to impose an extreme version of *shari'a* or Islamic law on all citizens, including non-Muslims. It is estimated that Sudanese are 74.7 percent Islamic, 17.1 percent African religions, and 8.2 percent Christian.

[35] Zambia is 72 percent Christian, 27 percent African religions, and 0.3 percent Muslim.

[36] As amended in 1980.

[37] In Morocco, for instance, a council of religious leaders has responsibility over certain executive functions. In both Mauritania and Tunisia, the president must constitutionally be a Muslim.

[38] Crawford Young notes:

The cultural and linguistic impact [of Europe on Africa] was pervasive, especially in sub-Saharan Africa. Embedded in the institutions of the new states was the deep imprint of the mentalities and routines of their colonial predecessors. Overall, colonial legacy cast its shadow over the emergent African state system to a degree unique among major world regions.

[39] Isichei notes that in any event such churches are in a "state of relative, and sometimes absolute, decline, overtaken by the immense proliferation of 'prophetic' or Zionist churches" (Isichei 1995, 3).

[40] For example, the Oba [king] of Benin sent envoys to Portugal in 1514 to procure arms.

[41] *Constitutions of Nations* 1965, 1:151.

[42] Blaustein and Flanz, *Constitutions of the Countries of the World,* Binder II (1993).

[43] OAU Doc. CAB/LEG/67/3/Rev.5 (1981). Reprinted in 21 I.L.M. 59 (1982). The African Charter came into force in 1986.

REFERENCES

1996 Britannica Book of the Year.

Achebe, Chinua. 1959. *Things Fall Apart.* Anchor Books, 1994 edition.

Africa News. 1996. "Benin Voodoo Receives Official Nod" (January). Available in LEXIS, News Library, CURNWS File.

The African Charter on Human and Peoples' Rights. 1981. OAU Doc. CAB/LEG/67/3/Rev.5 (June 27). Reprinted in 21 I.L.M. 59 (1982).

Aplogan, Jean-Luc. 1996. "Benin's President's Camp Acknowledges Poll Defeat" (April 2), *Reuters.* Available in LEXIS, News Library, CURNWS File.

Barrow, A. H. 1900. *Fifty Years in Western Africa.* Reprinted in 1969.

Beidelman, T. O. 1982. *Colonial Evangelism.* Bloomington: Indiana University Press.

Chicago Tribune. 1996. "In Benin, Government Gives Voodoo New Respect" (February 15).

Cohen, Ronald, et al., eds. 1993. *Human Rights and Governance in Africa*. Gainesville: University Press of Florida.

Constitutions of Nations. 1965. Volume 1, *Africa*. Edited by Amos J. Peaslee. The Hague: M. Nijhoff.

Constitutions of the Countries of the World. 1993. Edited by Albert P. Blaustein and Gisbert H. Flanz. Dobbs Ferry, N.Y.: Oceana Publications.

Cowell, Alan. 1993. "Pope Meets Rivals in the 'Cradle of Voodoo,'" *New York Times* (February 5).

Davidson, Basil. 1991a. *Africa in History*. New York: Collier Books.

———. 1991b. *African Civilization Revisited*. Trenton, N.J.: Africa World Press.

Debrunner, Hans W. 1967. *A History of Christianity in Ghana*. Accra: Waterville Publishing House. *The Memoirs of Sir T. F. Buxton* are quoted therein.

Elias, T. O. 1988, *Africa and the Development of International Law* 11. Dordrecht and Boston: M. Nijhoff.

Fasuyi, T. A. 1973. *Cultural Policy in Nigeria*. Paris: UNESCO.

Flinterman, Cees, and Evelyn Ankumah. 1992. "The African Charter on Human and Peoples' Rights," in *Guide to International Human Rights Practice*. Philadelphia: University of Philadelphia Press.

French, Howard. 1997. "In Congo, Many Chafe under Rule of Kabila," *New York Times* (July 13).

Hackett, Rosalind I. J. 1990. "African Religions and I-Glasses," *Religion* 20.

———. 1996. *Art and Religion in Africa*. London and New York: Cassell.

Harbeson, John W., and Donald Rothchild, eds. 1991. *World Politics*. Boulder, Colo.: Westview Press.

Hansen, Art. 1993. "African Refugees: Defining and Defending Their Human Rights," in Cohen 1993.

Hentoff, Nat. 1995. "Slavery and the Million Man March," *Washington Post* (November 28).

Hiskett, Mervyn. 1984. *The Development of Islam in West Africa*. New York: Longman.

Human Rights Watch. 1995. "Genocide in Rwanda: April-May 1994," *World Report 1995*, 39-48.

Idowu, E. Bolaji. 1975. *African Traditional Religion*. Maryknoll, N.Y.: Orbis Books.

Irele, Abiola. 1992. "The Crisis of Legitimacy in Africa," *Dissent* (Summer).

Isichei, Elizabeth. 1970. "Seven Varieties of Ambiguity: Some Patterns of Igbo Response to Christian Missions," *Journal of Religion in Africa* 3.

———. 1995. *A History of Christianity in Africa*. Africa World Press.

Jackson, Robert H. 1992. "Juridical Statehood in Sub-Saharan Africa," *Journal of International Affairs* 46.

Jackson, Robert H., and Carl C. Rosberg. 1982. *Personal Rule in Black Africa*. Berkeley and Los Angeles: University of California Press.

Kenyatta, Jomo. 1965. *Facing Mt. Kenya*. New York: Vintage Books.

King, Noel Q. 1971. *Christian and Muslim in Africa*. New York: Harper & Row.

Lawyers Committee for Human Rights. 1996. *Best by Contradictions: Islamization, Legal Reform and Human Rights in Sudan*.

Lewis, Hope. 1995. "Between 'Irua' and 'Female Genital Mutilation': Feminist Human Rights Discourse and the Cultural Divide," *Harvard Human Rights Journal* 8.

Long, Charles H. 1988. "Religions, Worlds, and Order: The Search for Utopian Unities," in Marty and Greenspahn 1988.

Marty, Martin E., and Frederick E. Greenspahn, eds. 1988. *Pushing the Faith: Proselytism and Civility in a Pluralistic World*. New York: Crossroad.

Mazrui, Ali A. 1986. *The Africans: A Triple Heritage*. Boston: Little, Brown.

———. 1991. "Africa and Other Civilizations: Conquest and Counterconquest," in Harbeson and Rothchild 1991.

Mbiti, John S. 1970. *African Religions and Philosophy*. New York: Praeger.

Moreno, Pedro C., ed. 1996. *Handbook on Religious Liberty around the World*.

Munro, F. 1975. *Colonial Rule among the Kamba: Social Change in the Kenya Highlands 1889-1939*. Oxford: Clarendon Press.

Mutua, Makau wa. 1995a. "The Banjul Charter and the African Cultural Fingerprint: An Evaluation of the Language of Duties," *Virginia Journal of International Law* 35.

———. 1995b. "Why Redraw the Map of Africa: A Moral and Legal Inquiry," *Michigan Journal of International Law* 16.

———. 1995c. "Putting Humpty Dumpty Back Together Again: The Dilemmas of the Post-Colonial African State," *Brooklyn Journal of International Law* 21 (book review).

———. 1996. "Limitations on Religious Rights: Problematizing Religious Freedom in the African Context," in *Religious Human Rights in Global Perspective: Legal Perspectives*, edited by Johan D. van der Vyver and John Witte Jr. Boston: M. Nijhoff.

Mutua, Makau, and Peter Rosenblum. 1990. *Zaire: Repression as Policy* (Lawyers Committee for Human Rights).

Mwalimu, Charles. 1991. "Police, State Security Forces and Constitutionalism of Human Rights in Zambia," *Georgia Journal of International and Comparative Law* 21.

Nduka, Otinki. 1965. *Western Education and the Nigerian Cultural Background*.

Nkrumah, Kwame. 1965. *Neo-colonialism: The Last Stage of Imperialism*. New York: International Publishers.

Nyong'o, Peter Anyang', ed. 1992. *Thirty Years of Independence in Africa: The Lost Decades*. Nairobi, Kenya: African Association of Political Science.

Okoth-Ogendo, H.W.O. 1993. "Human and Peoples' Rights: What Point Is Africa Trying to Make?," in Cohen 1993.

Oliver, Roland. 1991. *The African Experience*. London: Weidenfeld & Nicolson.

Olupona, Jacob K., ed. 1991. *African Traditional Religion in Contemporary Society*. New York: International Religious Foundation.

Phoenix Gazette. 1996. "Voodoo Day Called Play to Get Votes" (January 11).

Pobee, John S. 1996. "Africa's Search for Religious Human Rights through Returning to the Wells of Living Water," in *Religious Human Rights in Global Perspective: Legal Perspectives*, edited by Johan D. van der Vyver and John Witte Jr. Boston: M. Nijhoff.

Richardson, Henry J. 1996. "'Failed States,' Self-determination, and Preventive Diplomacy: Colonialist Nostalgia and Democratic Expectations," *Temple Int'l & Comp. L. J.* 10.

Sanneh, Lamin O. 1993. *Encountering the West*. Maryknoll, N.Y.: Orbis Books.

Schatzberg, Michael G. 1988. *The Dialectics of Oppression in Zaire*. Bloomington: Indiana University Press.

Shaw, Rosalind. 1990. "The Invention of 'African Traditional Religion,'" *Religion* 20.

Shivji, Issa. 1989. *The Concept of Human Rights in Africa*. London: CODESRIA Book Series.

Shropshire, Denys. 1938. *The Church and Primitive Peoples*. London: Society for Promoting Christian Knowledge; New York: The Macmillan Company.

US Department of State. 1992. *Country Reports on Human Rights Practices for 1991*.

US Department of State. 1994. *Country Reports on Human Rights Practices for 1993*.

Vaillant, Janet G. 1990. *Black, French, and African: A Life of Leopold Sedar Senghor*. Cambridge, Mass.: Harvard University Press.

van der Vyver, Johan D. 1997. "Religious Freedom in African Constitutions." Forthcoming. Maryknoll, N.Y.: Orbis Books.

Young, Crawford. 1991. "The Heritage of Colonialism," in Harbeson and Rothchild 1991.

Zartman, I. William. 1995a. "Introduction: Posing the Problem of State Collapse," in Zartman 1995b.

Zartman, I. William, ed. 1995b. *Collapsed States: The Disintegration and Restoration of Legitimate Authority*. Boulder, Colo.: L. Rienner Publishers.

Zolberg, Aristide R. 1992. "The Specter of Anarchy: African States Verging on Dissolution," *Dissent* (Summer).

8.

Scramble for Souls

Religious Intervention among the Dinka in Sudan

———————◆———————

Francis M. Deng

Melville Herskovits, the father of African studies in the United States, observed: "Whenever peoples having different customs come together, they modify their ways by taking something from those with whom they newly meet. They may take over much or little, according to the nature or the intensity of the contact, or the degree to which the two cultures have elements in common, or differ in basic orientations. But they never take over or ignore all; some change is inevitable" (Herskovits 1962, 6). The experience of the Dinka with Islamic and Christian missionary work bears out this observation. The incoming religions interacted with the indigenous religious beliefs and practices and influenced one another, giving and taking. The degree of acceptance depended largely on the extent to which the elements involved were compatible or antagonistic, enriching or degrading. The impact was, however, not uniform in the society, but varied according to the specific sector of the community involved and its objectives in a particular context.

MODES OF RELIGIOUS INTERVENTION IN SUDAN

Since religion is a vital element of peoples' identities, both as individuals and as members of communities, proselytization, aimed at converting people to another religion as it is, constitutes a fundamental challenge to their identity and sense of worth. Depending on how it is carried out, the rewards it promises, the deprivations it imposes, and the extent to which the respective values involved are mutually reinforcing or conflictual, proselytization may be accepted or resisted, and may succeed or fail.

Several models or modes of religious intervention can be identified in Sudan's history since the advent of Islam in the seventh century and its final victory over Christianity at the beginning of the sixteenth century. The first model is that of an informal, relatively persuasive process of Islamization, carried out within the framework of Islamic hegemony, primarily in the Northern part of the country, but with limited ripple effects extending southwards. The second is the more organized Christian missionary work in the South that was encouraged and even supported by the colonial government, but softened by the separation of religion and state. The third model is the postcolonial program of Islamization and Arabization, which successive governments in Khartoum have pursued as a means of fostering national unity through uniformity.

While persuasion and coercion are the qualitatively distinguishing factors in these modes of proselytization, there was an element of each in all of them, but in significantly varying degrees. As a general formula, the nature of the response has been correlative to the method of conversion used, with persuasive approaches meeting with more positive responses than coercive methods, which, while sometimes forcing subjugated people to submit, on the whole met with resistance. Beyond these pragmatic considerations, the methods used in conversion need to be evaluated by the degree to which they conform with or deviate from international human rights standards.

HUMAN RIGHTS FRAMEWORK

Although all religions presumably preach peace, love, and respect for the inherent dignity of the human being, "disregard and infringement of . . . the right to freedom of . . . religion or whatever belief," in the language of a preambular paragraph of the U.N. Declaration on the Elimination of All Forms of Intolerance and of Discrimination Based on Religion or Belief, "have brought, directly or indirectly, wars and great suffering to mankind." The preambular paragraph goes on to emphasize that this is especially the case "where they serve as a means of foreign interference in the internal affairs of other States and amount to kindling hatred between peoples and nations." Conversely, "freedom of religion and belief," according to the Declaration, "should also contribute to the attainment of the goals of world peace, social justice and friendship among peoples and to the elimination of ideologies or practices of colonialism and racial discrimination." The Declaration resolves "to adopt all necessary measures for the speedy elimination of such intolerance in all its forms and manipulations and to prevent and combat discrimination on the ground of religion or belief."[1]

The Declaration defines religious intolerance and discrimination based on religion or belief to mean "any distinction, exclusion, restriction or preference based on religion or belief and having as its purpose or as its effect nullification or impairment of the recognition, enjoyment or exercise of human rights and fundamental freedoms or an equal basis."

An issue that arises in dealing with the problem of religious intolerance relates to the linkage between religion and such other factors of identity as race, ethnicity, language, or culture. Although a case can be made for separating religion from those factors, there is a close interconnection that makes such separation often untenable. As David Little, who directs the U.S. Institute of Peace project on religious intolerance, has cogently argued:

> If religion is all that incidental a factor, why does ethnic conflict and the struggle over national identity in so many places—in Sudan, Sri Lanka, Tibet and China, Israel, India, Nigeria, Lebanon, Northern Ireland and so on—have such a conspicuous and enduring religious component? Even if religion is used or manipulated for ulterior purposes, why, exactly, is it *religion* that repeatedly gets used for ethnic and nationalist purposes? To put it another way, why does the assertion of ethnic and national identity so frequently involve, as it obviously does, intolerance and discrimination in regard to religious and other forms of fundamental belief? Why, for example, are nationalists so readily inclined to favor a "repressive ideology demanding strict adherence to the authority of the official embodiments of national tradition," and thereby to try to compel and control not only behavior but also belief? In short, what, precisely, is the connection between belief, ethnicity and nationalism? (Little 1995, 284-301).

Once the link between religion and other factors in conflictual identities is established, religious tolerance should by implication improve relations between the groups involved. "It follows that in those societies in which there is wide compliance with the norms of tolerance in a number of different areas—in religion, race, gender, language—there will be a higher degree of social tranquility and nonviolent communication. In societies like Sri Lanka and Sudan, religion, race, and language become intermingled, and the reduction of tension in one of the areas will presumably mean reduction of tension in the other areas as well" (Little 1996, 38).

The freedom of choice provided for in all human rights instruments relating to religious freedom, including the freedom to change one's religion or belief, means that religious conversion without coercion is an exercise of that right. Persuasive proselytization is the other side of that equation. On the other hand, the point made in the preambular paragraph of the Declaration, that disregard and infringement of the freedom of religion have brought wars and great suffering to humankind, "especially where they serve as a means of foreign interference in the internal affairs of other States and amount to kindling hatred between peoples and nations," can be construed to apply internally to groups with differentiated identities, of which religion is a distinctive factor. Granting such groups the right of self-determination becomes both a human rights principle and a means of conflict resolution.

Self-determination is by definition about the right of a people to self-governance through their freely elected agents and legally appointed officials who are accountable for the effective and equitable performance of their obligations to the totality of the population, without any discrimination on grounds of race, ethnicity, religion, gender or language (An-Na'im and Deng 1996, 199-223). It is now widely accepted that the non-Muslim, non-Arab populations of the Southern Sudan are entitled to the right of self-determination, including the option of secession. Indeed, Sudan is often mentioned as a country whose viability is threatened by the seeming incompatibility of the two visions for the nation represented by the Arabized Muslim North and the racially, culturally, and religiously more African south, whose educated elite is predominantly Christian. This dualism is the culmination of a long history of evolution of identities in which the hegemonic processes of Arabization and Islamization in the North, and their relatively successful resistance by the South, have been the dominant features.

SPREAD OF HEGEMONIC ISLAM

The origins of Arabization and Islamization can be traced to several thousand years before Christ, when the Egyptians and the Arabs began to expand southward, looking for slaves, gold, ivory, and revenue from taxation. Christianity entered the scene in the sixth century and was able to establish kingdoms that survived for a thousand years. But the intervention of Islam in the seventh century set in motion a process of gradual decline for Christianity. This decline culminated in the eventual overthrow of the Christian kingdoms in 1504 by an alliance of the Arabs and the Islamized kingdom of the Funj, whose origin remains obscure, but is known to have been "Black," as its Arabic name, *El Saltana El-Zerga*, "The Blue (meaning Black) Sultanate" reflects.[2] In due course, Islamization and Arabization gained hold in the North and eventually overshadowed the preexisting indigenous and Christian elements.

Although the process of Arabization and Islamization in Northern Sudan was not coercive, it should be noted that it was carried out in a context of a racially stratified society that deemed the Arab people and their culture superior and the African Blacks and their belief systems inferior. The Arabs were propped up by military conquest, supported by material wealth, and elevated in status by the universal image of Islam and Arab civilization. In contrast, the Black African was considered a real or potential slave, the downtrodden of the earth. Many Black Africans in the North converted to Islam because, by simply uttering the formula "There is no god, but the (One) God, and Mohammed is His Prophet," they suddenly became freemen and respectable members of the community. For many, the motivation to do so was irresistible. To the new members of the Muslim community, which was associated with the Arabic language and culture, the sense that they had been promoted into a superior class was more than religious or cultural; it developed into a gift of birth and descent, assumed and sometimes fabricated, ultimately a belonging to the Arab race. Over the centuries, these elements evolved eclectically, embracing indigenous races, customs, and practices, but retaining the emphasis on the Arab-Islamic umbrella as the uniting feature of the community and ultimately of the emerging nation-state. The stratification and the discrimination remained, however, and would continue to demean the non-Arabs and non-Muslims.

It has been argued that there was a coercive factor in the process of Islamization and Arabization and that "the earlier Sudanese identification with [Islam and] Arabism was nothing but a survival tactic by an overwhelmed people" (Binagi 1984, 15). The result was that Arabization and Islamization led to the evolution of descent groups in the North bearing the names of their original Arab founders and sometimes associating themselves with the tribes of the dominant lineages in Arabia (Owen 1937, 147-208).[3] These genealogies have been known to be traced with many jumps or lacunae back to Arabia, and in cases where the Sudanese lineage is politically or religiously prominent, back to the Prophet Muhammad, his tribe, the Quraysh, his relatives, and close associates.[4]

Arabism and Islam in the North have been consistently reinforced by all successive regimes, from the Turko-Egyptian administration that invaded the country in 1821, to the Mahdist Islamic revolution that overthrew it in 1885, to the Anglo-Egyptian Condominium that reconquered the country and ruled until independence in 1956. This reinforcement was persuasive in that it signified recognition and respect for the Arab-Islamic identity that already existed. However, in the case of the Mahdist state, which represented a most violent, fundamentalist revolution, it can be said to have been inherently coercive. Nonetheless, it was predicated on the assumption that the Islamic identity and values of the country had been violated by colonial rule and that the establishment of an Islamic state was an exercise of self-determination.

In contrast to the North, the identity of the African South has been primarily one of resistance to the pressures for Arabization and Islamization from the North. The significant aspect of the southern confrontation with the Arabs, whether before or after the advent of Islam, is that while the Arabs persistently invaded the South for slaves, they never penetrated deeply and did not attempt to settle. Swamps, flies, tropical humidity, and the fierce resistance of the peoples kept the contact marginal, even as it was devastatingly violent. Furthermore, since the Arab Muslim was interested in the material value of the Black African as a slave, he did not desire to interact and integrate with him in the same manner as he did in the North. If the Negroes of the South had been converted to Islam, the Arabs could not have justified slave raids on them.

Although the Turko-Egyptians and the Mahdists invaded the South to extend their control, and might therefore be distinguished from the ordinary commercial slave traders, their raids also involved slavery and were in fact indistinguishable from those of ordinary slave hunters. Indeed, local Southern memory conceptually fuses them and associates them with the total destruction of the world as they knew it. Indeed, it was not until the Turko-Egyptian government opened the Bahr al-Ghazal and Equatoria provinces in the 1820s and established more security for the outside invaders that the slave trade became well established and assumed large proportions. For that reason, local sentiment associates British intervention with the redemption of the South from the slave raids by the Arabs from the North. Efforts to spread Islam southwards through traders, soldiers, and civil servants were confined to the urban centers and were significantly frustrated by the separatist policies of the British.

CHRISTIAN MISSION UNDER COLONIAL RULE

In contrast to the hostile interaction with the Muslims, Christian missionaries came to the South as peaceful messengers of the universal word of God. The earlier phase of the Christian mission was purely private and spiritual, without the benefit of government encouragement and support (Kurdi 1986, 89-92).[5] With the reconquest of Sudan in 1898 and the establishment of the Condominium Administration, Christian missionaries were encouraged to proceed to Southern Sudan to survey future areas of activity. The Roman Catholics were the first to pioneer the Christian mission in the South in Shillukland in 1900. In 1902, the American Presbyterians began missionary work at Sobat. The Church Missionary Society came to the South in 1906. From that date on, Christian missionaries continued to multiply.

To facilitate their work and to avoid conflictual sectarian competition among various missions, the administration allotted spheres of religious influence and operations. Early Christian missionary activity was more directed toward saving souls than toward enhancing the material well-being and welfare of the people. As a result, and applying the worldly orientation of traditional African religion, it was not perceived as particularly relevant, since the people did not doubt their own spirituality. Later orientations, which associated the Christian mission with education, health services, and the overarching goal of "progress" or development, provided concrete incentives for potential converts.

Notwithstanding British favoritism toward the Christian missions in the South, the government pursued a policy of separation between religion and state in a manner that appeared, even to Christians, too neutral on the issue of the potential Arabization and Islamization of the South. Indeed, the rather passive manner in which the government encouraged Christian proselytization in the South disturbed the missionaries. Reverend Wilson Cash observed: "The Government is scrupulously fair to Moslems and pagans, and in religious matters adopts a strictly neutral attitude. The task of evangelization is no part of the Government's work and it falls to the mission alone to decide whether these Southern pagan tribes shall be left to be captured for Islam or whether they shall be won for Jesus Christ" (Cash 1930, 54).[6] Thus, while the government felt that strict separation of religion and the state was not acceptable to the Muslim population in the North, it introduced state neutrality or impartiality on religious matters in the South.

As Christianity came to the South through peaceful means and with the support of the colonial administration and was associated with modern benefits in education and medical services, it was favorably received in due course. Christianity also benefited from the belief of the Southerners that the Europeans, far from being slavers themselves, had come to rescue them from Arab slavery. The role of the Europeans in the global slave trade was not visible locally, since it was the middlemen, Egyptians and the Northern Sudanese, who were perceived as the slavers. On the spiritual front, while converts were substantially transformed in their belief system, the society as a whole remained traditional in its religious orientation and treated the conversion of the educated class as a spiritual anomaly that was integral to development, a new concept to the traditional Dinka.

STATE POLICIES OF ARABIZATION AND ISLAMIZATION

With independence, the Arab-Muslim-dominated governments sought to reverse the separatist policies of the British through Arabization and Islamization, believing that homogenizing the country would facilitate national unity. These policies were closely associated with political domination, oppression, and coercion. While some Southerners converted out of conviction or for opportunistic reasons, most resisted. Indeed, the civil war in the South that began in 1955, was halted for a decade through the 1972 Addis Ababa Agreement that granted the South regional autonomy, but was resumed in 1983 under the leadership of the Sudan People's Liberation Movement and its military wing, the Sudan People's Liberation Army (SPLM/SPLA), representing Southern Sudanese resistance to Northern domination and threat of assimilation.

Since the resumption of hostilities, the crisis of national identity has intensified. The relationship between religion and the state, in particular the role of *shari'a*—Islamic Law—as the law of the land, has emerged as the central factor in the conflict. The full significance of this factor can be appreciated only if religion is seen as a starting point into the complex political, economic, social, and cultural life of the country. Religion becomes pivotal in defining the identity and status of individuals and groups, determining who gets what from the system, especially as Islam in the Sudan is closely connected with Arabism as a racial, ethnic, and cultural phenomenon.

Although the issue of an Islamic constitution has been debated since independence, President Jaafar Mohamed Nimeiri's imposition of *shari'a* on the country by presidential decree in September 1983 placed the issue on the public agenda. After Nimeiri's overthrow in 1985, the Muslim Brotherhood (*Ikhwan al Muslimeen*), a radical group from the religious right, reorganized itself into a broader-based political party, the National Islamic Front (NIF). In the parliamentary elections of 1986, the NIF won the third largest number of seats. The group's Islamic national agenda was endorsed and significantly reinforced by General Bashir, who, in alliance with the NIF, seized power on June 30, 1989, in the name of the Revolution for National Salvation.

Since then, Southern reaction to Islamization and Arabization appears to be working in favor of Christianity. Southerners now see their identity as welding together indigenous cultures with received Christianity and the English language as modern tools for combating Islam and Arabism.

A Northern Islamist scholar, Abdelwahab El-Affendi, addressing the progress of Islam and Arabism among the Northerners in the face of the increasingly self-assertive Africanism among the Southerners, articulated the dilemmas for the country when he wrote, "The close association between Islam and Northern Sudanese nationalism would certainly rob Islam of an advantage . . . [as] it remains beset by problems similar to those that limited the appeal of the SPLA's Africanism" (El-Affendi 1990, 371). Likewise

> Northern Sudanese, who identify strongly with their Arab heritage, are in no danger of being seduced by Africanism. Far from being inclined to sing with Cesaire "Hurrah for those who never conquered anything," their poets have long boasted about "our many exploits in Spain which showed the Franks who they really were." But, equally, Islamic ideology is by definition, unacceptable to non-Muslims. Its association with Arab Northern self-assertion makes it even more unpalatable to Southerners (ibid).

DINKA MORAL AND SPIRITUAL VALUES

Foreign penetration of Southern Sudan has largely been motivated by the assumption that there is no coherent Southern culture or system of spiritual and moral values worth recognition and respect. The earlier invaders from the Arab-Muslim North justified their raids for slaves with this belief. For the Christian missionaries and the post-independence efforts at Islamization and Arabization, the competitive objective was to fill this assumed vacuum. The only issue was which of the competing models should capture the field. Much of this attitude on the part of both the Muslim North and the Christian West has been the result of ignorance of the cultures and values of the South. Even today, despite the volumes that have been written about various Southern peoples, the North remains almost entirely ignorant of Southern cultural values, religious beliefs, and moral outlooks.

Nilotic beliefs and practices follow a segmentary lineage system, structured along autonomous territorial and descent-oriented units. This provides for autonomous and personal linkages with God through the ancestral spirits. This gives continuity in intergenerational succession with deep emotional ties to the legacy of the ancestors, adapted to changing conditions. Chief Arol Kachwol of the Gok Dinka, in his late seventies when he articulated these values, said:

It is God who changes the world by giving successive generations their turns. Our ancestors, who have now disappeared . . . held the horns of their life. Then God changed things . . . until they reached us; and they will continue to change. When God comes to change your world, it will be through you and your wife. You will sleep together and bear a child. When that happens, you should know that God has passed to your children born by your wife, the things [by] which you lived your life" (Deng 1978, 50; and Deng 1980, 51-52).

Godfrey Lienhardt, the British anthropologist who specialized on the Dinka, highlighted the Nilotic value of permanent identity and influence when he wrote, "Dinka greatly fear to die without issue, in whom the survival of their names—the only kind of immortality they know—will be assured" (Lienhardt 1961, 26).[7] A man who dies without issue to carry on his name is said to perish, *riar*, and become truly mortal. Even then, members of his family are under a moral obligation to marry a woman for him, to live with a relative and beget children to his name, according to what anthropologists call "ghost marriage." Equally, a man who dies leaving behind a widow of childbearing age devolves a moral obligation to his kinsmen to have one of them cohabit with the widow to continue bearing children to his name in accordance with the custom of levirate. The amount of cattle paid as compensation for homicide is approximately equivalent to the average amount of bride price paid in marriage and is, in fact, used to procure a wife to beget children to the name of the dead man. Sharon Hutchinson observed of the Nuer, "The social identity of every woman is fundamentally rooted in her procreative powers and the children they create" (Hutchinson 1980, 375).[8]

The ultimate objective of Nilotic religious devotion is not so much to ensure salvation in a life hereafter as it is the physical and spiritual well-being of life in this world. Well-being among the Dinka is expressed in the word *wei*, which as a verb means "to breathe" and as a noun means "breath," but unlike the English equivalent, *wei* as a noun is conceived of as a plural continuum. This is because by *wei*, the Dinka do not mean a single act of breathing, but the continuing chain that constitutes life. Nor is *wei* as an objective confined to the condition of breathing or being alive. As a goal, *wei* requires physical and moral well-being at its best. But as long as there are *wei*, however weakened, one is said to be "alive," *apir*. Death is the absence of *wei* in the body, although, as in English, the dead person is said to have "passed away," *aci wer wei*.[9] Of course, the dead person in his or her full integrity, body and *wei*, is believed to be then transformed into a different kind of existence in the world of the dead. That continued existence, especially whenever it comes back to the living in the form of dreams or afflictions, is expressed in the intangible term of *atiep*, literally "the shadow" of the dead. The Dinka, of course, know that the body without *wei* lies decomposing in the grave, so that it is the memory of the dead person, conceptualized in the form of *atiep*, that reconstitutes the dead person as a whole being, with body and *wei*.

The Dinka solve the paradox of their preoccupation with life as the objective of their religious practice and their recognition that death is inevitable by viewing the ultimate goal not as the preservation of life, but rather as the regeneration and continuation of life through genetic and social reproduction by successive generations in the agnatic lineage or the clan. Dinka notions of immortality and the unknown world of the dead and the spirits explain their beliefs in a hierarchy of deities and their potential power to generate, weaken, and eliminate *wei* or the breath of life. Religious prejudice and intolerance against traditional beliefs, reflected in such words as *animism* and *polytheism,* are based on the assumption that they do not embody any notions of One God. In fact, the Dinka believe in a supreme being they call Nhialic, connoting abiding in the sky, whose attributes are similar, if not identical, to those of the Judaic, Christian, or Muslim God. To the Dinka, there is only one Nhialic, the creator of the human race and all things in this world. Godfrey Lienhardt wrote that the Dinka "assert with a uniformity which makes the assertion almost a dogma that 'Divinity [God] is one.' They cannot conceive of Divinity as a plurality and, did they know what it meant, would deeply resent being described as polytheistic" (Lienhardt 1961, 156). The Dinka often state positively, "Nhialic *ato thin*" ("God exists"), which implies that he is watching human behavior and will sooner or later uphold and sanction the principles of the moral order of his authority. To say that God exists is therefore a way of expressing confidence in God's ultimate justice in rewarding virtue and punishing evil.

Because of the centrality of religion in their culture, the Dinka believe that their value system is ordained and ultimately sanctioned by God and the ancestral spirits. The principles of their moral order are embodied in a complex concept known as *cieng*—"order, custom, behavior." At the core of *cieng* is living together in mutual understanding and cooperation. *Cieng* not only advocates unity and harmony through attuning individual interests to those of others; it requires positive assistance to one's fellow human beings. Consistent with the deferential ideals of human relationships, *cieng* favors persuasion against violence or other means of coercion. This is revealed particularly well in Dinka concepts of leadership and education. The leader is seen as a peacemaker who makes adjustments to correct whatever might have gone wrong in communal relations and then maintains the continuity and stability of the corrected situation. Similarly, knowledge is a normative concept, expressed not so much in accumulating objective facts or truths, as a process of knowing the moral code, *nginy e wel*, "knowing the words [of wisdom]." A person learns to know through counseling and advice, obtaining moral knowledge rather than just technical skills.

Within this moral order, great emphasis is placed on the attributes of *dheng*—personal pride, honor, dignity, and social courtesy (Deng 1971, 24-25, 209; see also Deng 1972[1984], 14-24). A remarkable feature of Dinka culture is that traditionally it gave virtually everybody some avenue to dignity, honor, and pride. The degree varied, and the means were diverse: there were the sensuous means concerned mostly with appearance, bearing, and sex appeal; there were the qualities of virtue in one's relations to others; and there were the ascribed or achieved values, material or spiritual, which help determine one's social standing. These ways were interrelated and could not really be separated, but only by seeing them as alternatives and by realizing that all ways led to the same ends can we fully understand why every Dinka had some share in the values of self-esteem, inner pride, and human dignity.

From a religious perspective, the most important and pervasive implication of the Dinka value-system is that it gives the eternal issues of religion—the origin and the destiny of life—a worldly orientation that makes the people intensely religious, ethical, and moral, constantly preoccupied with the word of God, fearful of committing wrong, by commission, omission, or inadvertence. According to the Seligmans, "The Dinka, and their kindred the Nuer, are by far the most religious peoples in the Sudan" (Seligman and Seligman 1932, 178). As Lienhardt observed, "Divinity [God] is held ultimately to reveal truth and falsehood, and in doing so provides a sanction for justice between men. Cruelty, lying, cheating, and all other forms of injustice are hated by Divinity, and the Dinka suppose that, in some way, if concealed by men, they will be revealed by him. . . . The Dinka have no problem of the prospering sinner for they are sure that Divinity will ultimately bring justice" (Lienhardt 1961, 46).

THE ADVENT OF ISLAM

The adverse conditions of slave raids under which Islam was initially introduced to the South and the constraints of the Islamic mission under British rule have already been alluded to as accounting for the limitations Islam faced among the Southern peoples. However, despite Southern resistance to religious and cultural incursions from the North, centuries of contact, albeit marginal, have left their mark on the South. Indeed, the history of hostility between the North and the South often blinds the Sudanese to the legacy of interaction and mutual influences that have existed in the Nile Valley for centuries and maybe thousands of years.

Evidence from interviews which I conducted with Dinka chiefs and elders in the early 1960s into their past, present, and projected future dramatizes the theme of dichotomy and diversity, but it also provides a wealth of information that throws considerable light on aspects of South-North relations that have been overshadowed by a negative disposition and preoccupation. For instance, the myths of the Dinka about God, creation, original leadership, and early migration strikingly confirm the observations of anthropologists about the close resemblance between the traditional religions of the Nilotics and those of the Holy Books. These myths indicate that early contacts between Nilotics and the outside world might have been more substantial than has been supposed. While the Dinka themselves do not consciously make the religious link, and their conception of the people encountered during their early migration is

that of "spirits" or "powers," they provide detailed descriptions of the characteristics of these entities and mention geographical areas that leave little doubt
that their conception is a mythologization of the real world and, for that matter, the world to the North. Although it has been argued that these myths
reflect recent Christian or Muslim influences, the possibility of more distant
origins cannot be discounted (Johnson 1988, 170-82). Many of the chiefs and
elders who furnished the information are men in their seventies, eighties, and
even nineties, and they all claimed to have heard from their fathers and grand-
fathers, who would surely predate the advent of modern Christianity into the
area. Also noteworthy is the consistency with which these stories are told
throughout Dinkaland, thereby showing the depth and uniformity of the cultural roots.

If the theory of South-North mutual isolation prior to the nineteenth-century hostilities is dispelled, it goes without saying that Islam, Christianity, and
Judaism have been features of Sudanese civilization from earliest times. Therefore, evidence of these classic religions among the Nilotics should not be surprising.

The spread of Islam in the South, limited and confined to towns as it was,
extends into more recent times and is associated with the nineteenth-century
incursions from the North. Although the overall climate of interaction with
the North was hostile, Islamization was conducted through the relatively persuasive influences of traders, military officers, and civil servants. This was
most intense under the Turko-Egyptian and the Mahdist periods, but it also
extended into the first two decades of the Condominium period. While the
administration was interested in promoting Christianity and discouraging Islam in the South, so successful were Islamization and Arabization in the urban
centers that Christian missionaries and the British administrators became openly
concerned. It has indeed been argued that Islam had qualities that made it
more appealing to the Southern Sudanese than Christianity. According to a
Northern Sudanese scholar of the subject, "Among these qualities were the
Arabic language, the equal status practiced among Muslims, the ease with
which the Islamic creed was understood, the comprehensive determination by
Islam of all the aspects of personal, social, and religious life, the similarities
between Islam and African traditional religions, and Islam's orientation of its
converts towards Islamization in Southern Sudan" (Kurdi 1986, 183).

It must be emphasized that while Islam spread in urban centers through
relatively peaceful means, the Nilotics, in particular the Dinka and the Nuer,
who were almost entirely rural, were hardly affected by these modern processes of Islamization and Arabization. Indeed, their rural environment provided the hunting ground for slaves and therefore part of *dar el harb*, the war
zone of Islam. Even under these conditions, the Dinka adopted elements from
the Muslims with whom they came in contact, but selectively, and assimilated
them into their own religious mold.

The response of the Dinka to the Mahdi is a good example of the selective
manner in which they have tended to adopt and to assimilate Arab-Islamic

elements into their own cultural context. The Dinka were spiritually inspired by the holy message of the Mahdi, whom they believed had appeared to free all the peoples of the country from foreign oppression. The Mahdi was believed to be a manifestation of the Spirit of Dengdit, their deity associated with rain and lightning, reflections of God's might. Mahdi, as a symbol of spiritual power and righteousness, became known as the Son of Dengdit, while the Mahdists themselves came to be viewed as Arab aggressors. The Dinka even used the very hymn they had composed in praise of the Mahdi as a prayer for the help of their assimilated spirit, Maadi, Son of Dengdit, in fighting the Mahdist aggressors.

When the British reconquered the Sudan jointly with Egypt, there were already considerable Arab-Muslim influences in Southern towns, but the Dinka, the largest group in the country, remained isolated, except for hunting invasions, culturally self-contained, proudly resistant to change, and on the whole, scornful of foreigners, whom they mostly associated with slave hunters from the North.

CHRISTIAN MISSION IN THE COLONIAL CONTEXT

Dinka reaction to British rule, viewed in the context of what had preceded it, in particular the ravishing raids for slaves from the Arab-Muslim North, was ambivalent, although the balance sheet favored the British and by derivation Christian missionaries, whose presence was associated with European rule. Initial resistance against British conquest was replaced by admiration as the Sudanese saw that the system of indirect rule permitted them to lead their traditional life. Southerners even identified the British with their own moral values more than they did the Arabs, despite the distance between them in race, culture, and place of origin. In retrospect, Southerners appreciate the separatist policies of the British, which they see as having saved them from assimilation into the Arab-Muslim identity. The disparity in development and the contrasting levels of respect that the British maintained between the North and the South became significant only when the two were thrust together in an unqualified unitary system in an independent Sudan without constitutional protection for the disadvantaged communities.

The irony is that the Christian mission was itself founded on racial and religious assumptions that relegated indigenous populations and cultures to an inferior status. The premise was that prior to Christian education, the Dinka were immersed in the abyss of intellectual, moral, and spiritual darkness or emptiness. Christian teachings promised to provide the remedy and the path to salvation. The main objective of Christian mission, as the Dinka understood it, was seen in traditional terms as the pursuit of *wei*. Dinka notions of *wei*, which focused on individual and collective well-being in this world, were molded to embody a new concept that welded the traditional Dinka view of health with the Christian doctrine of redemption in a spiritual sense. As Godfrey

Lienhardt explains: "Missionaries, using *Wei*, breath and life, as the best approximation to translate 'soul,' have presumably successfully reshaped the Dinka word for their converts into a unitary term for a moralized and spiritualized self-consciousness of each separate individual in relation to a personalized God" (Lienhardt 1980, 75).

One of the most effective ways in which the Christian message was articulated and promoted among the Dinka was through the songs of schoolchildren, composed by older boys or Dinka teachers and sung by the pupils collectively with all the aesthetic values normally associated with singing and dancing as features of aesthetic dignity, *dheng*. Schoolchildren viewed themselves in traditional terms as an age-set of warriors with a pen for the spear. Competing along ethnic lines in much the same way their traditional counterparts did, they glorified themselves in singing displays in which they exalted their newly acquired wisdom and status with an exhibitionist self-esteem, alternately referring to themselves as "I" or "we," all characteristic of warrior age-sets in traditional Dinka society.[10] It is through them that we see the expression of new Christian ideas in traditional language.

Initially, the Dinka were reluctant to send their children to school, not only through fear of cultural alienation, symbolized by the fact that schoolchildren became known as "the children of the missionaries," *mith abun*, but also because of fear of moral corruption (Lienhardt 1982, 87). The so-called *mith abun* were looked down upon by their illiterate age-mates as having lost the dignity of tradition. There was an ambivalence about learning, which was often shared by the students themselves. At the root of this ambivalence lay not only a conflict between moral values but scepticism about the skills the school taught. Slowly, the significance of the school began to make itself felt.

The implication was a revolution in knowledge and the power accruing from it, even though the educated youth—unlike their traditional counterparts, who prided themselves on their physical courage and obstreperousness as warriors—saw their dignity in obedience and orderliness. This was indeed a reversal of roles, for in traditional society knowledge was presumed to accumulate with age and proximity to the ancestors. Now, according to the new code of learning, the Dinka as a culture group not only had a lot to learn, but should indeed be ashamed of where they stood in the newly postulated scale of progress. This had direct implications on religious notions of well-being.

Dinka schoolchildren began to express in their own songs contempt for the illiterate "pagan priests" of their own society (Deng 1973a, 251-52). Paradoxically, although Dinka traditional religion was condemned as a source of evil from which Christian education was the saving grace, missionaries recognized and made use of the chiefs not only for the pragmatic purpose of reaching their people, but also because of the colonial policy of devolution. A number of prominent chiefs from Bahr el-Ghazal Province were flown to Rome to meet the pope and, at least according to this song, seek his blessing:

The chiefs were asked, "What do you want?"
"Father, it is *wei*."
"What do you have to say?"
"Father, it is *wei*."
It is *wei* that we, [the Dinka] of Ajang, are seeking.

(ibid., 258)

The Dinka have a relativist view of religion that recognizes the significance of race, ethnicity, culture, lineage, or language in the human relationship to the divine order, but they also believe that humankind as a totality is subject to the One Supreme Power of God, who creates and destroys all human beings, irrespective of race or religion. Because of the combination of their religious devotion with the universality of their conception of God's relationship to humanity, what matters most to the Dinka is not so much what religion one adheres to, as how religious one is. A holy person of whatever race, religion, or language who appears to reflect unusual spiritual powers and divine will is revered as a man of God, capable of rewarding good and punishing evil. Christian missionaries had the distinct advantage of being seen as people who were there for the sole purpose of spreading the word of God. But the inspiration behind the moral and religious exaltation of the missionaries was directed not so much toward a new spiritual order or the worship of God as toward the new notions of "going ahead," or "progress" associated with modern education. As Godfrey Lienhardt pointed out, by the 1940s many Dinka had come to appreciate "that lacking in education their people were lacking in some of the essential skills for political survival in the modern Sudan." Insofar as they were at a disadvantage in the modern world, they were also "backward." This idea was suggested to them by missionaries and administrators alike, and education began to be perceived as a way to protect Dinka autonomy through producing enough Dinka "capable of thinking in foreign ways, of meeting foreigners on their own ground while remaining Dinka in their loyalties" (Lienhardt 1982, 83, 86).

While the messages of literacy and scientific enlightenment, with their attendant value to well-being, were a major theme of schoolboys' songs, an equally preoccupying, even obsessive concern was with the supposedly inherent evils and dangers of non-Christian life and social conditions. The supposedly "evil spirits" of traditional religion and even "Mohammedism," which was morally equated with paganism, were seen as posing a serious threat to *wei*, and Christianity was extolled as the only tool of redemption. Missionaries introduced a new concept of sin which intensified Dinka moral indignation and apprehensions about wrongdoing as a provocation against God. Of course, the Dinka traditionally believe in the original wrong that offended God and brought about God's withdrawal from human beings, and they also recognize that many forms of wrongs are offensive to God and could result in spiritual contamination that might cause illness and maybe death. But they do not have a particular term comparable to the word *sin* for those wrongs. The word *adumom*, which the Dinka converts now apply to sin, is a Christian invention which connotes "darkness," a contrast to the "whiteness" with which spiritual purity is conceived. Although the dangers of sin were seen in relation to *wei* in this life, the fear of the hell to follow death was also deeply ingrained in the young converts. Conversely, the dream of the heaven to come was also inculcated as a supreme compensation for the suffering in this world.

Viewed now in hindsight, Dinka responses to the Christian mission were part of a complex process in which cross-cultural accommodation went side by side with contradictions and unwitting disregard, if not disrespect, of each other's values and institutions. The Christian missionaries took the inferiority of traditional religious beliefs and practices for granted, while the Dinka pragmatically and selectively benefited from Christian educational and medical services, which they at first resisted but eventually learned to appreciate. Although the converted youth embraced Christianity with a religious fervor, their elders accepted the conversion of their children as a tolerable component of the more significant benefits that were accruing through missionary work in the area. From the viewpoint of traditional elders, what was threatening and became increasingly disturbing was the more blatant disregard for traditional knowledge and the superior wisdom of the elders. They began to feel as if they were being pushed aside by the "educated youth."[11]

It would be wrong to conclude that the Christian missionaries were insensitive to the Dinka cultural context. Indeed, it could be argued that they used Dinka culture, perhaps even exploited it, quite effectively, especially insofar as they related the benefits of education and modern medicine to the enhancement of well-being in the physical, spiritual, and moral sense of *wei*. The last sacrament was often administered by priests not so much to save the soul after death, but as a manifest effort to save the life of a supposedly dying man, and when occasionally that objective was achieved, the Christian message benefited from the miracle in a dramatic way. But it would also be too complacent to say that both sides understood one another in a profound way and sought to reinforce each other's values and institutions through a process of equitable cross-cultural fertilization. What seems to have occurred is that because of Dinka conservatism and ethnocentric pride, their values were so deeply rooted and resilient that they persisted against the onslaught of missionary intervention.

SOUTHERN RESISTANCE TO POLITICAL ISLAM

To appreciate the motivation behind the policies of Arabization and Islamization by which successive governments tried to undermine the influence of Christianity and Western culture, it should be understood that as far as the North was concerned, the South was the legitimate domain of Arab-Islamic influence, which the missionaries in alliance with British colonial rulers had wrongly usurped. But the North was also convinced that the roots of the Christian Western influence were shallow and could easily be replaced with Islam and Arab culture. A Southern Sudanese has written of the Northern attitude toward the South at independence:

> Many northern Sudanese had the notion that there were but a bunch of uncivilised tribes in the South and very condescendingly Northerners regarded themselves as guardians of these, their backward brethren. Finding themselves in charge of the government of an independent Sudan, Northern Sudanese politicians and administrators sought to replace the colonial regime in the South with their own. Arabic was naturally to replace English and what better religion than Islam could replace Christianity? (Malwal 1981, 17).

The Southern viewpoint was in sharp contrast and can only be understood in the context of a long history of animosity between North and South, rekindled by the oppressive policies of the postcolonial era and the related strategies of Islamization and Arabization. Indeed, one of the major postcolonial fallacies is that Northerners mostly dwell on the separatist policies of the British and especially the encouragement of a Southern identity based on traditional systems with the modern influence of Christianity and Western culture. Their remedy has been to try to undo this history through Arabization and Islamization, to remove the Christian Western influence, and to integrate the country along the lines of the Northern model. What they do not realize is that traditional identity and Christian Western influence have combined to consolidate and strengthen a modern Southern identity of resistance against Islamization and Arabization.

Only a year after independence, the government nationalized all missionary schools in the South while allowing private schools in the North, including Christian missionary schools, to continue. In February 1960, the council of ministers resolved that Friday instead of Sunday should be the official day of rest in the South. In protest against this action all Southern schools went on strike. The government retaliated strongly. In one case a native priest, Poulino Dogali, was sentenced to twelve years' imprisonment under the 1958 Defense of the Sudan Act for having printed and distributed a leaflet critical of the government's decision. Two secondary-school students who were accused of the same offense received ten years each.[12]

The fear of the South that the government was waging war against Christianity and promoting Islam was soon reinforced by the enactment of the Missionary Societies Act of 1962, which regulated missionary activities. Section 3 of the act provided that no missionary society or any member thereof should do any missionary work in the Sudan except in accordance with the terms of a license granted by the council of ministers. Such license was to be in the prescribed form and should specify the religion, sect, or belief of the missionary society, and the regions or places in which it might operate. In addition, the license might impose whatever conditions the council of ministers might think fit, either generally or in any specific case.

According to the provisions of section 6, the council of ministers might refuse to grant or renew, or might even revoke, a license at its discretion. Section 7 imposed spatial limitations and prohibited a missionary society from doing "any missionary act towards any person or persons professing any religion or sect or belief thereof other than that specified in its license." Missionaries were not allowed to "practice any social activities except within the limits and in the manner laid down from time to time by regulations." Section 8 provides: "No missionary society shall bring up in any religion or admit to any religious order, any person under the age of eighteen years without the consent of his lawful guardian. Such consent shall be reduced to writing before a person appointed for that purpose by the Province Authority." Section 9 stated: "No missionary society shall adopt, protect, or maintain an abandoned child without the consent of the Province Authority." Under section 10, formation of clubs, the establishment of societies, organization or social activities, collection of money, famine and flood relief, the holding of land, and the publication and distribution of papers, pamphlets, or books were subject to ministerial regulations.[13]

In March 1964 the Sudan government took the final step of expelling all foreign missionaries from the Southern Sudan. "Foreign Missionary organizations have gone beyond the limits of their sacred mission," the government stated. "They . . . exploited the name of religion to impart hatred and implant fear and animosity in the minds of the southerners against their fellow countrymen in the North with the clear object of encouraging the setting up of a separate political status for the southern provinces thus endangering the integrity and unity of the country" (quoted in Deng 1973b, 40).

While these measures were aimed at cultural integration as a means of attaining the goal of national unity, their effect was to antagonize the South and to widen the cleavage between the two parts of the country. Southern opposition, both inside the country and from the exile community, aggravated the political instability that brought General Ibrahim Abboud to power in 1958. The repressions of Abboud's government drove domestic Southern opposition underground, and many Southerners fled to neighboring African countries, where they organized themselves politically and militarily to liberate the South.

Since Islam is seen as part and parcel of a composite Northern identity, Southern resistance was not only religious but against the racial and cultural identity of the North. In interviews for a book on Dinka oral history which I conducted after the Addis Ababa Agreement of 1972, I asked Dinka chiefs and elders how they saw the prospects of national integration. The responses were striking.[14] Chief Biong Mijak saw the differences between the Arabs of the North and the Africans in the South as inherent and sacrosanct: "Those people are brown and we are black. God did not create man at random. He created each people with their own kind. He created . . . some people brown and some black. We cannot say we want to destroy what God created; all this is in God's hands. Even God would get angry if we spoiled his work" (Deng 1980, 279).

Bulabek Malith recalled the suffering that the Arabs had inflicted on the "black man" as having created an insurmountable obstacle to Arab-African unity and integration:

> The things the Arab has done in our country, including things which we have been told about by our elders, are many. A man called Kergaak Piyin, an elder, . . . used to tell us the stories of our country's destruction. He said, "Children, as I sit here, I wish that any future destruction of the country does not find me alive. Arabs are bad" (ibid., 277).

Like Biong Mijak, Bulabek Malith regards these objectionable traits in the Arabs as ingrained in their racial and cultural make-up, and he therefore rules out any basis for genuine unity.

> If they were a people who could abandon their vile manners, they would have abandoned them a long time ago. But these are a people whom God created in their own way. . . . Even if people become really equal and the South gets educated and has full freedom, the way elders like us see it in their hearts, it seems they will one day separate. The Northerner is a person you cannot say will one day mix with the Southerner to the point where the blood of the Southerner and the blood of the Arab will become one (ibid., 276).

Most respondents, building on the bitter history of the past, saw the peace that had been achieved in 1972 as an interlude to be watched and monitored carefully. Chief Thon Wai, following that line of thought, also considered it difficult to predict unity and preferred a wait-and-see attitude: "So, we and our brothers, the time when we will unite and live together is known to God alone. We will not say it ourselves. Why won't we say it? It is because we have had some experience" (ibid., 170). Thon Wai goes on to express his view that the South and North are so different that they must maintain a certain distance to remain at peace. "Our life with the North is like that of a cold egg and a hot egg. The sun is hot . . . and the moon is cold. They keep their distance from one another. . . . They act as though they are about to meet but they miss one another" (ibid., 171). According to Chief Albino Akot, even though the future is difficult to determine, there is too much cultural diversity for integration between the South and the North to be effectively realized. "For the North and South to mix, so that they become one people, a people with one language and one religion, this is a very difficult question. . . . They cannot be one people. Why? Because there are no common ways between them, no social contacts . . . and no common culture between them" (ibid., 242.) Chief Giir Thiik concurred: "That you will intermarry and mix to be one people, I cannot see. . . . You will live together, but there will be South and North. Even living together is only possible if you people handle the situation well. There are many people who appear to be one, but inside them they remain two. I think that is how you will live. A man has one head and one neck, but he has two legs to stand on" (ibid., 44).

THE DIVISIVE ROLE OF THE STATE

Although Northerners and Southerners share mutual prejudices, what gives the attitude of the North greater poignancy from a public policy perspective is that it is reinforced by the state. The experience of neighboring communities along the North-South border shows that in an autonomous context, Northern and Southern peoples managed to establish a normative framework for coexisting in a relatively cooperative manner. Of course, conflicts occurred, but the communities also developed ways of managing and resolving them. With the state penetrating down to the local level and taking sides on the basis of racially, ethnically, religiously, and culturally determined identities, the local balance of power that had sustained cooperation became tilted in favor of the Arab-Muslim communities. Indeed, the fact that the country is identified as Arab and Islamic itself gives Northern Arab-Muslim communities an advantage over the non-Arab and largely non-Muslim South.

This shift is dramatically illustrated by the experience of the Ngok Dinka of Southern Kordofan in the North. Even prior to colonial intervention, the Ngok and their Arab neighbors to the North, the Homr, coexisted with relative harmony. Their harmonious coexistence was largely the result of the ties of friendship, indeed kinship, which were established by their respective leaders, Arob Biong of the Dinka and Azoza of the Homr, in the nineteenth century.

Because of the importance associated with blood as a symbol of lineage-oriented ethnic identity and kinship, the two leaders conducted a ritual of blood fusion to consolidate their relationship. As Ibrahim al-Hussein, a descendant of Azoza, recounted, "Arob, the son of Biong, spilt his blood and my grandfather licked it; and Azoza spilt his blood and Arob licked it. They became relatives. Drums were beaten to celebrate the occasion" (ibid). With the advent of the Mahdiya, the Arabs themselves were divided between those who supported it and those who resisted. Famine also intervened, forcing some of the Arabs to flee for both safety and relief into Ngokland. Chief Arob welcomed them and gave them land on which to settle and cultivate (Henderson 1930, 49-79). This was indeed one of the outcomes of the friendship pact between him and Azoza.

The response of the Ngok Dinka to the Mahdiya was cross-culturally and interracially pragmatic. Naturally, the Mahdi, being a Muslim and an Arab, was viewed as closer to the Homr Arabs than to the Ngok Dinka. And since the Homr leaders had become relatives of the Ngok leaders, they became intermediaries between the Mahdists and the Dinka when cooperative, and part of the Muslim-Arab camp when hostile. Arob's "relatives" brokered a contact between him and the Mahdi. According to the Arab elder Ibrahim al-Hussein, "Our ancestors took Arob to the Mahdi. He went to declare his allegiance [to the Mahdi]. . . . The Mahdi said, 'From this day your name will be Abdel Ra'uf, instead of Arob.' He initiated him with prayers and gave him a sword. Arob then returned home" (Deng 1995, 260). Here, we clearly see the emergence of religious intolerance. To be accepted and respected, Arob had to be converted to Islam and have his name changed, something his Arab-Muslim neighbors had not expected or asked of him in their previous interaction and relationship.

Arob's alleged conversion to Islam is hardly ever mentioned in the oral history of the Dinka, except for the assertion that he had gone to *Jenna*, the Arabic word for heaven or paradise. Certainly, his supposed adoption of the Islamic name Abdel Ra'uf is totally unheard of among the Dinka. That they prayed with the Mahdi is acknowledged, but with qualifications that indicate pragmatism and even cynicism. As their heads were bent to the ground in prayer, Arob's companion, Chief Allor Ajing, whispered to him, "Arob, son of Biong, do you see God?" Arob whispered back, "No, Allor, I do not see God, but let us leave matters as they are" (ibid., 261).

Arob's objective in visiting the Mahdi was to complain against ongoing slave raids by Arab factions that remained hostile to the Dinka. The Mahdi assured him that from then on Arab-Muslims would no longer raid Arob's people for slaves. He then gave Arob insignia of his sacred mission and power, including a spear and a sword, and implored him to govern in accordance with the ideals of Islam, such as the rich assuming responsibility for the poor, values that were in full harmony with Dinka culture and practice.

With the advent of colonial rule, Chief Kwol, who succeeded his father, Arob, sought protection for his people from the central government to the North by affiliating his tribe into Kordofan, thereby following the path his father, Chief Arob Biong, had pioneered. By virtue of their early contact and agreement with the government in the North, Ngok leadership was viewed by the Southern Dinka as providing a protective shield in their adversarial relations with the Arabs, mostly through diplomatic representation and management or resolution of conflicts on their highly explosive borders with the Arabs.

Later the administration changed its position and decided in favor of the Ngok joining the South. The government encouraged, indeed instigated, the Southern chiefs to persuade Chief Kwol Arob (whose father, Arob, had concluded the friendship pact with the Arabs) to join the South. Chief Giirdit (of the Rek Dinka in the South) later recalled the discussion between them and Chief Kwol: "We talked—[Kwol] was brought by the Government—the Great Kwol, son of Arob; and [the Government] said, 'You, Kwol, you are among the Arabs, but you are a Dinka. I would like you to unite with the other Dinka and become the District of Gogrial'" (Deng 1980, 39; Deng 1986, 49). Chief Makuei Bilkuei, another Dinka chief from the South, also recalled: "I talked to Kwol and said, 'These people will disgrace us later on. So why are you after [them]?'" (Deng 1980, 74-75).

Kwol Arob chose to remain in the North for calculated reasons. After a public announcement of his refusal to join the South, he pulled Giirdit aside and spoke to him: "Son of my father, what you tell me it is not that I do not know it. The Arab is a thief. Even though I am with him, I know he is a thief. If I were to pull away from him, he would destroy my things. . . . Even this land which is mine, he might say, 'It is my land'" (Deng 1980, 39-40; Deng 1986, 50).

Despite the important historic role played by successive Ngok leaders on the South-North borders, and especially by Arob Biong and his son, Kwol Arob, there is a general consensus that Deng Kwol, known as Deng Majok, was the most pivotal in consolidating the authority of the Ngok chief and the position of Abyei area in Kordofan. He and his Homr counterpart, Chief Babo Nimir, extended the traditional friendship between the ruling families to even greater heights. Interestingly enough, according to Chief Babo Nimir of the Homr Arabs, he and Deng Majok entered into a brotherhood pact that was reminiscent of what their forefathers had done: "Between [Deng Majok] and me, there was a bond of brotherhood by oath; we swore to be brothers" (Deng 1982, 53). Apparently, the agreement was motivated by Deng Majok's need for the support of Babo (who was influential with the British) in the bid for succession to his father in competition with his half-brother, Deng Abot, whom their father favored as the firstborn of the first wife, a premise which Deng Majok contested, building on the controversial circumstances of their mothers' marriages to their father.[15] According to Babo Nimir, "The circulating rumors kept saying, 'Deng Abot, Deng Abot.' He wanted to win me to his side. So, we concluded the pact of brotherhood" (ibid). And through that brotherhood, Babo Nimir and Deng Majok reconciled the Arabs and the Dinka.

As a Dinka and therefore racially or ethnically a Southerner, Deng Majok's identification with the Arabs and therefore the North was pivotal in the relationship. With a more developed view of national unity than his predecessors, Deng Majok metaphorically considered himself "the needle and the thread" that mended the two parts of the Sudan into one whole. Ngok area became a national crossroads and a microcosm of the Sudan, in much the same way that the Sudan is a microcosm of Africa.[16]

Although Deng Majok never changed his religion, dress, social habits, or even ritual practices, he adopted many Arab-Islamic ways that endeared him to his Arab neighbors. His belief system and practices as well as the response of his Muslim neighbors to his ways represented a culture of religious tolerance and eclectic cross-cultural assimilation that was reflective of the unique version of Islam practiced at the local level. However, the politicization of Islam—which first peaked under the Mahdist revolution, was contained but reaffirmed by the British, and reintensified after independence—has introduced a less tolerant version of Islam to the country. With the broader racial or ethnic concept of identity associated with Islam, this has made religion the pillar of the polarization associated with the crisis of national identity.

The implication of this for communities that had previously lived together, despite differences of race and religion, is starkly evident in the Ngok Dinka–

Homr Arab relations. With independence, the Homr became more identified with the government than the Ngok Dinka, especially as they were among the staunch supporters of the Mahdist dynasty that ruled the country. The situation was aggravated by the civil war in the South, in which the Ngok became increasingly identified with their fellow Dinkas in the Southern part of the country. Although Chief Deng Majok himself consistently asserted his loyalty to Kordofan, his educated youth developed a nationalist alliance with the South, and many joined the Southern rebel movements and called for Ngok secession from Kordofan and annexation to the South. In the Addis Ababa talks of 1971, the status of the Ngok was strongly contested and it was eventually resolved that the issue of whether the Ngok would remain in the North or join the South would be determined by the people themselves through a referendum. That referendum was never held, and the Ngok increasingly resorted to a local rebellion that contributed significantly to the resumption of North-South hostilities in 1983. Since then, successive governments in Khartoum have recruited the Homr Arabs, trained them, armed them, and deployed them as militias, supposedly against the Southern rebel movement, but in fact unleashing them against their Dinka neighbors, killing at random, looting their cattle, razing their villages to the ground, and even capturing their children and women as slaves.[17] Minyiel Row, a noted Ngok Dinka poet-singer, commemorated the events with a song pleading for ultimate justice from God, since their quest for justice from the government went unheeded,

> Fire continued to blaze [as houses burned],
> And our cattle were driven away;
> But we had no one to hear our case.
> We called and called,
> But no one asked what we were calling about;
> We cried and cried,
> But no one asked why we were crying.
> We talked and talked,
> But no one asked what we were saying.
> God, it was you who gave the Dinka the cow,
> And you gave the Arabs their wealth in money,
> The Arabs have consumed their wealth,
> And they have gone to capture our herds,
> And there is no one to whom we can take our case,
> Our cattle have been captured,
> Our children have been captured,
> And our villages have been burnt down;
> We are now clustering under trees like birds.
> (Deng 1995, 329)

In a private conversation, a leading member of the Mahdi family intimated to me that they had received inquiries from their Homr Arab followers, asking whether it was ordained or forbidden by Islam to kill a Dinka. That was indeed symbolic of the shift from traditional coexistence and cooperation between these two groups to the intensification of armed confrontation and religious intolerance which the state intervention and the politicization of Islam have added and have had the effect of fueling the identity crisis of the nation.

SPIRITUAL QUEST FOR REDEMPTION

Even as the Dinka reveal a determination to resist external domination, whether reflected in blatant political terms or disguised in cultural and religious forms, they are beginning to show signs of succumbing to the assumptions of racial and cultural stratification that underlie their relegation to an inferior status in the multiracial and multicultural context of the modern Sudan. And yet, paradoxically, their well-known ethnic and cultural pride, as well as their religious devotion, are injecting into their liberation struggle an almost divinely inspired quest for salvation.

A body of oral literature has begun to emerge among the Dinka in which they are beginning to rationalize their inferior status in modern Sudan. This newly emerging attitude is beginning to result in a novel reinterpretation of myths of ancient origin. One myth, initially the reason for their proud acquisition of cattle as the most noble symbol of wealth, is now being seen more as an explanation of their fateful devotion to cattle, attributed to their original choice of the cow in preference to the thing called "what," which God offered them and recommended as a better alternative, but which they dismissed without even seeing. This circumstance is explained by understanding that the Dinka word for "what"—"ngo"—may be used as a statement when a person hands something to another person; the donor does not specify what the thing is, and the recipient does not know unless he or she can see the thing as it is handed over. Used in this sense then, *ngo* implies, "Have this," without saying what "this" is. Both as a question and as a statement, *ngo* signifies something unknown, but about which curiosity is assumed. According to the Dinka myth, "ngo" was later given to Europeans and the Arabs and presumably became the source of their inquisitiveness and scientific invention, the source of their material superiority and power.

Another myth explains that the black man was relegated to a status inferior to his white and brown brothers because his mother favored him, forcing their father to plead with God to help take care of the disadvantaged children. The myth recalls the paradoxical tension between the subordination of women and their pivotal influence. Bulabek Malith and Loth Adija recount the story with only small variations. According to Bulabek,

> What our grandfathers used to say . . . is that . . . man was created . . . as twins. One was a brown child and one was a black child. The woman

would keep the black child to herself, away from the father. Whenever the father came to see the children, she would present the brown child and keep the black child because she loved the black child very much.

The man said, "This child whom you keep away from me, in the future, when [the children] grow up, I will not show him my secrets." That has remained a curse on us. Our father did not show us the ways of our ancestors fully. . . . It was the woman who kept her black child away from his father. Otherwise, we would have known more things than we know (in Deng 1980, 269).

Loth's version of the myth speaks of triplets and includes a white child, who apparently was the most disadvantaged of the three, suckled last and least.

As he was prevented from sucking, his father took good care to feed him. He took a gourd, a new fresh gourd . . . raised his hands to the sky and prayed, "God, is there nothing for you to give to this son of mine?" That gourd was filled with milk. That white son . . . drank the milk. [His father] took [him] . . . to be the servant of God. That is said to be how the English went away and learned. Arab and Dinka remained (ibid., 269).

As the brown child was also not treated well by his mother, his father took him and gave him to God. "The Arab came and found his education according to the word God had said to the woman, 'The [black] child you now favour will one day become the slave of my children.' [The Arab] found the horse . . . with [which] he went to capture . . . the descendants of his brother who was denied education by God. And when he captured them, he made them slaves" (ibid., 309).

Religiously devout as they are, the Nilotics are thus inclined to find spiritual rationalizations for their racial, cultural, and even economic subordination in the context of independent Sudan. In the following lyrics, the singer is painfully conscious of the indignities he has suffered, and attributes the hardships of urban labor to the inequitable distribution of resources among the races at the time of creation. He berates the ancestors who chose the gift of cattle rather than knowledge (ibid., 269, 305-9, 312-13).

God hates us for the things of the past
The ancient things he created with us in the Byre of
          Creation,
When he gave the black man the cow . . .
Leaving behind the Grain and the Book of his father . . .
Our curse goes to the elders of the original land;
The man who threw the Book away,
It is he who has given us into slavery.

In another song, the singer refers to the bad treatment the Dinka are receiving from the Arabs and contrasts it to the favored position of the black color of skin at creation, ultimately addressing his complaint to God,

> Our land is closed in a prison cell
> The Arabs have spoiled our land
> Spoiled our land with bearded [bren] guns . . .
> Is the black color of skin such [a bad] thing
> That the Government should draw its guns,
> The police pacing up and down
> Gunners causing dust to rise . . .
> Waving their bren-guns . . .
> Counting their [empty] shells
> Then saying, "One million shots
> Have not subdued the Ngok [Dinka]."
> Our case is in Court with the [powers] above
> The Court is convened between the clouds. . .
> [Our ancestral spirits] have a cause
> They seated the court and called God, . . .
> "God, why are you doing this?
> Don't you see what has become of the black skin?"[18]

R. G. Lienhardt analyzed the process by which the Dinka, who had taken their superiority for granted, came to accept a significant degree of inferiority. "The Dinka view of age-sets, based upon a cyclical notion of local history, begins to be displaced by a dynamic view of history, accompanied by a philosophy of progress, and with teleological overtones" (Lienhardt 1982, 89-90). While that shift may not explain the dynamic interplay between cultures, it begins to impose a dichotomy between the supposedly outmoded tradition and the highly valued incoming modernity. As Lienhardt explained, "'getting ahead' begins to be directed towards some distant, more universal end, defined in foreign terms," a form of society based on a foreign model rather than one conceived of by the Dinka (ibid).

With independence and redefinition of the national character to give prominence to Arab-Islamic culture, the Nilotics had to deal with yet another stereotype of racial, religious, and cultural concepts of development. In response to this new challenge, Southern resistance appears to be taking two forms, one religious and the other military. Both forms are mobilized for the redemption of a people who have endured more than they can withstand any longer.

During the seventeen-year war (1955-72) and extending into the present war that resumed in 1983, the conditions of upheaval, intense insecurity, and massive suffering from starvation and violent death have nudged Southerners increasingly toward religion in general and Christianity in particular as a source of salvation. Several factors account for this, among them a natural yearning for supernatural protection against an otherwise incomprehensible destruction; a search for alternative interpretations as the traditional belief system becomes discredited; a response to the Church as a source of material, social, and spiritual support for a people dispossessed by the state; and, not least, the need for a coherent competing modern religious identity with which to oppose the Arab-Islamic identity.

Ironically, while the traditional elders initially dismissed the Christian concept of everlasting life as a mere superstition, converts found the idea of both the perfection of Heaven and the doom of Hell most compelling. The traditional notion was that after death life continued in some ill-defined spiritual form. This left the threat of perishing into nothingness not adequately resolved, and it was precisely why the Nilotics remained in awe of death. As the number of converts increased and the work of the Christian mission spread, the optimistic view of the life hereafter began to take hold. The victory for the Christian doctrine is supported by the despair of the Dinka in the devastated world of modern Sudan.

Rev. Marc Nikkel, a Protestant missionary, made a study of the contemporary religious changes among the Dinka by analyzing a collection of religious songs composed to inculcate "the determination to survive by affirming that even out of suffering, positive elements are derived" (Nikkel 1991, 92). One song explicitly refutes Dinka fear of death as an end and sees it more in Christian terms as a transition to a better life.

> Death has come to reveal the faith.
> It has begun in our time and it will end in our time.
> You who fear the end of your life, do not fear death,
> For it only means that you will disappear from the face of
>   the earth.
> Who is there who can defend his life and leave death aside?
> We who live in the world, we are mere visitors upon the
>   earth (ibid).

The lamentation of the suffering in this world is contrasted with the hope in the everlasting salvation through God's supreme justice. Indeed, the belief of Dinka converts is perhaps an amalgam of hope for continued well-being in this world and redemption after death which Christianity promises.

> Let us comfort our hearts in the hope of God
> who once breathed life into the human body.
> His ears are open to our prayer;
> the Creator of man is alert to see!
> He reigns from his high throne;
> he sees the souls of those who die.
> Turn your ears to us! To whom else can we go for help?
> You are the only one!
> Let us be branches from the vine of your son!

> Jesus will come with the final word of judgment upon the
>   earth,
> He comes bearing the book of peace and the life of faith.
>   (ibid., 93)

The Nilotics of course have always turned to God and the spirits for protection at times of exceptional disasters; prophets have traditionally emerged under such circumstances. But as war and famine have disrupted society on a massive scale and traditional ways have been progressively undermined, more universalizing concepts that can address these problems are needed. According to the Christian missionary leaders, the Church is meeting the need, not only by offering that universal vision, but also by creating broader circles of identification and unity. The shift is now extending into discrediting the spiritual leaders of traditional society, some of whom are reported to be moving with the tide and joining Christianity.

In the process, traditional concepts are paradoxically being effectively mobilized to promote the new faith. Nikkel wrote: "Dinka tradition likens the diminutive stature of humankind to tiny black ants (*acuuk*) when compared with the greatness of (*Nhialich*), God Almighty. Known also for their single-minded industry, extraordinary strength, and swarming numbers, ants now provide a metaphor which Christians use to describe themselves as they work to build the Kingdom of God. For decades missionaries lamented the tepidity and lethargy of the Dinka church. Not so today." In a remarkably eclectic manner, Christian ideals of conversion converge with the politics of liberation struggle, soldiers mingling with other worshipers in a communion of the oppressed but determined fighters for freedom. Nikkel continued,

> Many discern the demise of the *jak* as a tangible victory in this double edged war. Spiritual triumph over "*shatan*" is perceived as a foretaste of victories yet to come, not least those of the SPLA over the Government of Omer el Bashir. Hope rises that the "New Sudan" might itself be healed, leaving behind the factional fratricide of recent years. Not without biblical precedent, Christians sometimes claim the prior victory. The SPLA itself is not unchanged by recent events, and indeed participates in them. Some commanders are now devout church goers, themselves leading in prayer. There is a growing band of commissioned evangelists nurturing the souls of young, cross toting, soldiers within the Movement. Spiritual and military warfare mingle. Soldiers with whom I conversed were toughened but temperate souls who crave an end to killing. Nonetheless, they are committed to the preservation of their people, their soil, their faith.[19]

Understandably, Nikkel is enthusiastic about the transformation toward Christianity which he sees unfolding. There is, however, more integration between tradition and incoming Christian influence than he sees or is predisposed to witness. It can indeed be argued that even within the framework of what he observes, the process may appear to undermine tradition, but it also empowers the people in a manner that ultimately ensures a sense of optimism and confidence in their ability to overcome tragedy, and this in turn ensures their survival as a people with a legacy and a destiny, both intertwined. The Church then becomes a modern tool for survival and paradoxically of continuity as well.

This is particularly visible in the way the Church provides a rallying ground for the displaced Southerners, especially in Northern cities. The clubs that the Church makes available to them provide religious instruction, offer literacy classes and other social services, and allow them to develop broader-based relationships and a sense of unity. Nikkel interprets this in terms of Dinka self-perception as having been orphaned and the moral call on the Church to provide the orphans with protection. The Dinka do, indeed, view the loss of their indigenous leadership, and worse, the destruction of their social order, as being orphaned. According to their traditional value-system, being an orphan is an exceptionally deprived condition, which imposes a strong moral obligation on the family and the leadership to provide appropriate emotional and material support. The welfare response of the Church therefore is within the cultural and moral values of the people.

> People are crying out all over the earth,
> "Lord, do not make us orphans of the land.
> Turn and look upon us, O Creator of humankind.
> Evil is fighting among us!
> The burdens tied upon our necks are impossible for us to
>   bear!" (Nikkel 1991, 98).

"Just as frequent is the sense of being cut off, orphaned, or neglected by the wider human community, and possibly even by God, the Creator himself. So alarming is this experience of an abandoned and dispossessed people that even the natural order finds voice to express its horror" (ibid). A song composed by a pastor from Bor follows the same theme:

> Pay attention to me you Lord of heaven and earth
> for the love of the person whom you created.
> The person who shoulders his spears alone,
> I am in the sinful land of Sudan
> The birds in the sky are surprised
> by the way I have been orphaned
> The animals of the forest
> are startled by my skeleton (ibid).

The Dinka appear to be seeing these conflicting emotions as reflected in the biblical prophecy in Isaiah 18, which has often been quoted by scholars as evidence of the Nilotic link with the biblical tradition.[20] There is a popular and increasing tendency for the people of the South to see in this chapter a prophetic universal statement of both their tragedy and their ultimate glory. For the Southerners, the optimistic prophecy in verses 6 and 7 is not only appealing, but also empowering, as it dramatizes both the level of devastation and the promise of salvation: "They shall be left together unto the fowls of the mountains, and to the beasts of the earth: and the fowls shall summer upon them, and all the beasts of the earth shall winter upon them." But then, "shall the present be brought unto the Lord of hosts . . . to . . . the Mount Zion."

The people believe, and they are reinforced in this by the Christian gospel, that they have suffered enough and that their salvation is now at hand. Ironically, while the source of this suffering for which they call on God to help is political, separation between the Church and the state is said to be honored in the Dinka religious songs. "In continuity with the CMS [Church Missionary Society] missionary prohibitions under Condominium rule for the separation of faith and politics among Christians, the songs of the Episcopal Church tend to provide a spiritual and theological vision, leaving specifically political issues to the genre of music composed within the Liberation Movement" (Nikkel 1991, 98). But here one must distinguish between the disciplined perspective from within the Church and the more popular spiritual view of God's comprehensive protection from tragedy, natural and manmade, economic and political, ultimately related to the war and the perceived injustice behind it. The tendency, which has been evolving for decades, to turn to the Christian Church as a potential source of redemption in the pressing circumstances of today's upheavals, has been articulated poignantly by observers since the dawn of independence. According to the Sandersons,

> The Missions offered, and the Churches embodied, doctrines and values which enabled Southerners effectively to challenge the Northern Sudanese claim to total superiority. Together with the skills that education had conferred, they also enabled the Southern response to transcend the sterile and obsolete objectives and the uncoordinated "tribal" basis of traditional Southern resistance. . . . Government policy, by developing in some districts along specifically Islamic lines as an administrative jihad (and for some months in 1965-6 as a frankly military jihad), doubtless helped to forge the links between Christian commitment and armed resistance. . . . Even in the Anglican Church, ideological resistance was evidently much stronger than its official policy of "loyalty," "co-operation" and "prayerful long-suffering" might seem to imply (Sanderson and Sanderson 1981, 125).

Marc Nikkel has also written insightfully about the contradictions of this destructive and yet potentially creative and regenerative process of alignment between tradition and Christian Western modernity:

A people struggling with great loss, with displacement, with the rapid erosion of ancient traditions, and of the structures of their society, cry out to their Creator. Remarkably, the Church in this setting has served as something of a preserver of traditional values even as it offered new opportunities. . . . Now, however, it is not the young and supple who choose to migrate and adapt to new values, but it is also the mature, the aged, the deeply rooted, who are forced to question long held assumptions as sections of traditional life are irreparably altered (Nikkel 1991, 99).

While Marc Nikkel's analysis of these religious changes among the Dinka reflects primarily a perspective from within the Church leadership, prudently emphasizing the spiritual aspect and keeping it separate from politics, the elite circles of the Christian South are promoting the idea that Christianity should be consciously cultivated as a pivotal element in the modern model of Southern identity that is competing with the Arab-Islamic model of the North. Like all sensitive issues involved in the conflict, this point of view is an essential ingredient in the hidden agenda of the war of visions.

It is now also becoming increasingly evident that the exercise of self-determination with the probability of secession is among the hidden agenda of most Southerners, notwithstanding the rhetoric of the leadership in favor of a new, united Sudan. But to have a choice to seek secession does not mean that it will necessarily be exercised—if appropriate conditions for unity are put in place. The Declaration of Principles (DOP) which the mediators of the Inter-Governmental Authority on Development (IGAD) presented to the parties in 1994 as a basis for the resolution of the Sudanese conflict can be combined into three main categories: self-determination as a fundamental and inalienable right; national unity as a desirable objective which should be given priority; and interim arrangements that formulate the basis and sustainability of unity, to be tested through a referendum at the end of the stipulated period. Since unity is an objective that should be given priority, there is an urgent need to formulate the principles or conditions upon which unity can be sustained. While there are many issues to be resolved, the issue of the relationship between religion (Islam in this case) and the state has emerged as the most controversial in the conflict. The focus is on the application of *shari'a* and the creation of an Islamic state in which women and non-Muslim Sudanese cannot enjoy equal rights as citizens of their own country.[21] As Abdullahi Ahmed An-Na'im observed:

At best, non-believers may be allowed to stay under the terms of a special compact which extremely restricts their civil and political rights. Believers who are not Muslims, mainly Jews and Christians, are allowed partial citizenship under Shari'a. . . . and are disqualified from holding any position of authority over Muslims. As such, [they] are disqualified from holding general executive or judicial office in their own country (An-Na'im 1987).

Needless to say, that cannot be an acceptable basis for national unity.

CONCLUSION

Religious intervention in the Sudan has followed three interactive models—one private, unorganized, and largely persuasive; another, more organized and government-sanctioned, but also private and in the context of separation of state and religion; and a third, sponsored and spearheaded by the government in a way that merged religion and the state. These patterns have not necessarily been sequential, although the general pattern appears to have progressively moved from the private and informal processes of early Islamization, through the Christian missionary activities, carried out in a context of separation of state and religion, to the postcolonial promotion of the Islamic agenda that has now culminated in the military Islamic regime of the National Islamic State, which is dedicated to the establishment of an Islamic state.

The response of the Dinka to the Islamic and Christian missionary interventions has been correlative to the method used. As a general principle, the persuasive, unofficial methods were more voluntarily accepted, although the Dinka were more selective in the aspects they adopted and integrated into their own religious belief-system. The coercive was more resisted, although when successful was more radical in transforming the converts. Conversion associated with incentives was also more effective, although the degree of acceptance varied with the proximity to the goods given or the services offered. Thus, while Christian missionary work was generally accepted as offering education and medical services, the elders who were not exposed to the education offered accepted the conversion of their children as part of missionary education without taking the spiritual aspect seriously; on the other hand, the children who were being educated were more engrossed in the religious dimension of their education and conversion. When coercion is combined with incentives, as was the case under the Mahdiya and the current Islamic regime, the response is a mix of general resistance by the society as a whole and opportunistic acceptance by individuals for material and social gains.

The challenge the religious agenda of the ruling National Islamic Front presents to the Sudan has become more than an isolated human rights issue; it is a core problem for national unity and the long-term prospects of nation-building. Traditionally, for the North, the appeal of the South lay in its weakness and underdevelopment, which made it a raw material to be molded, ideally into the Arab-Islamic pattern of the North rather than the Western Christian pattern of the colonialists. The stronger the South grows, the more the Muslim

Northerners feel challenged, and the stronger becomes their attachment to their religious identity (El-Affendi 1991, 44-45). The Muslim Brothers, who transformed themselves into the National Islamic Front in 1986 and who, in collaboration with Islamic elements in the army, seized power in June 1989, represent an extremist reaction to the secular challenge posed by the South in general and the SPLM/SPLA in particular.

As the South improves itself with education and develops a modern identity reinforced by Christianity, Western culture, and military strength, the emerging parity among the competing models makes the South too strong to disregard or to manipulate. But the more seriously the Southern grievances are considered, the clearer it becomes that they cannot be redressed within the Arab-Islamic framework of the status quo. As a result, the South begins to pose a real threat to the system: either the national framework is fundamentally restructured, or the South is decisively defeated and dominated, or the country risks disintegration. Sudan remains poised among these difficult choices. And with the realization that the needed compromises are difficult to make, the NIF regime becomes even more inclined toward adopting a hard line, hoping to break the back of the SPLM/SPLA, forcing Southern rebels to be more amenable to accepting far less than they are currently demanding. Experience, however, shows that the balance of power in the battlefield vacillates, with alternating equations in favor of and against both parties. The latest equation appears to favor the rebels, even though that could again change, as it has done before.

Which way the future of the Sudan will go remains the challenging question: To what extent is national unity, indeed the survival of the nation, compatible with the creation of an Islamic state? This question may sound rhetorical, but it poses serious issues on which the survival of the Sudan may depend.

Southern response to Islam in comparison with the response to the Christian mission confirms the conclusion that proselytization carried out coercively is apt to meet with resistance. Such intrusion is likely to be conceived as an invasion of the identity and the integrity of the targeted population and therefore a source of friction and even violent conflict. While communities can be coerced into submission to an alien religion, if overwhelmed and subjugated by the power of the aggressor, it is in the interest not only of peace, but also of the success of the religious mission, for the proselytizers to adopt persuasive strategies for spreading their religion. Alternatively, and to the extent that the creation of a religious state is a public policy priority, the consequences on the constitutional character of the state, including the right of self-determination for the South, must be recognized. Choices are bound to range among three options: a restructured, religiously neutral state framework; a loose coexistence in which religious, racial, ethnic, and cultural groups live and let live in mutual autonomy; or outright partition of the country along similar lines of identity.

NOTES

[1] U.N. Declaration on the Elimination of All Forms of Intolerance and of Discrimination Based on Religion or Belief, 1988, 125-29.

[2] Among the Northern Sudanese, the word *black* is never used to describe people, since it is considered insulting to call a freeman black, that being the color associated with the slave race.

[3] In his article "The Hadendowa," *Sudan Notes and Records* [hereafter *SNR*], vol. 20, no. 2, R. R. H. Owen observes a practice whereby the Hadendowa try to trace their ancestry to Arabia even if artificially. "An arabicized Hamitic tribe needs its *sheriffi* ancestor as much as a soap or tinnert lobster king needs his Norman blood. The origin of the Hadendowa, therefore, was on this wise" (184). In "The Rubatab," *SNR*, vol. 29, no. 1 (1936), 162-67, F. C. S. Lorimer also observes that the Rubatab "claim to be pure Abbassiun descended directly from Al Abbas, the uncle of the Prophet, and finding their race factor in the Beni Abbas branch of the Koraysh, the Prophet's own tribe" (162). However, this claim to Abbassid ancestry is denied by Harold A. McMichael in *A History of the Arabs in the Sudan* (Barnes and Noble 1967). For various genealogies claiming Arab descent from Arabia see also Yusuf Fadl Hasan, *The Arabs and the Sudan: From the Seventh to the Early Sixteenth Century* (Edinburgh University Press 1967), chap. 5.

[4] This point is invariably made by all studies on Northern Sudanese tribes, some of which have already been cited. For another example see Sandars 1935, 195-219. Sandars writes: "Like most Bega tribes, the Amarar have made a deliberate effort to forget their history to the time when they became Islamized. But although they have introduced a genealogy which they can trace back to the purest Arab blood they admit to being half-indigenous Bega: they have, however, by now eliminated all memory of their pre-Islamic history" (198). Their eponymous ancestor is allegedly "a man, an Arab of Kawahla stock, who came over and married one of the local women" (ibid.).

[5] For a historical overview of the Christian mission in the Southern Sudan at this early stage see Mohagoub Ahmad Kurdi, *The Encounter of Religion: An Analysis of the Problem of Religion in Southern Sudan,* Ph.D. diss., Temple University, June 1986.

[6] Quoted in Deng 1973b, 43.

[7] A common way to express willingness to die is to say that one has had children to continue the name. Chief Ayeny Aleu, determined to speak his mind, whatever the risks, said, "Let us die as long as we leave our children to continue our names" (Deng 1980, 47). And in the same vein, Chief Stephan Thongkol remarked, "I am a man who does not fear death. If I die, then I have children" (ibid.).

[8] Immortality through procreation is a widely shared value, not only in African traditional society, but also in Islamic culture. A. R. Radcliffe-Brown observed: "An African marries because he wants children. . . . The most important part of the 'value' of a woman is her childbearing capacity" (Radcliffe-Brown 1960, 230).

[9] The "e" in this *wei* is pronounced more sharply than the softer "e" in *wei* as "breath."

[10] The songs cited here also appear in Deng 1973a. I have made minor revisions in translation, partly to elucidate the meaning in this context.

[11] An elder articulated to me this dilemma when he said, "Educated youth have pushed us aside saying that there is nothing we know. Even if an elder talks of the

important things of the country, they say, 'There is nothing you know.' How can there be nothing we know when we are their fathers? Did we not bear them ourselves? When we put them in school, we thought they would learn new things to add to what we, their elders, would pass on to them. We hoped they would listen to our words and then add to them the new words of learning. But now it is said that there is nothing we know. This has really saddened our hearts very much" (Deng 1980, 286).

[12] These sentences were reduced on appeal. *Sudan Law Journal and Report* (1962), 83 (quoted in Deng 1995, 138).

[13] The motive behind the act was articulated by the government thus: "It is clear that the missionary organizations have directed most of the internal and external efforts against the national government. Their main objective has been to have the confidence in the Government shaken and the unity of the nation undermined. It became necessary, therefore, to pass an Act aiming at the regularization of the work of the missions" (cited in Deng 1973, 45n.41).

[14] The extracts cited here are also available in *Africans of Two Worlds* (Deng 1978), in which the raw material in *Dinka Cosmology* (Deng 1980) is reproduced in analytic form.

[15] For the story of the complicated marriage seniority of their mothers and their competition for power, see Deng 1986.

[16] Henderson, after explaining that "if the South, while remaining essentially Southern, could yet become an integral part of an independent Sudan it could help to bridge the inevitable gulf between Muslim and non-Muslim, Asian and African, white or brown and black, in the African future," goes on to say, "The Ngok Dinka, on the Bahr el Arab, had joined Kordofan Province at the reoccupation and had played precisely such a role as intermediaries between the Homr Baggara and the Dinka of the Bahr al Ghazal" (Henderson 1965, 164n†).

[17] For an account of slavery at the North-South borders, see Mohamud and Baldo 1987.

[18] From a collection by the author. First translated and quoted in Deng 1972 [1984], 150-51. Cited here with minor changes indicated by brackets.

[19] Marc R. Nikkel, *Link Letter* 8 (January 20, 1996).

[20] The Revised Version quoted by Professor E. E. Evans-Pritchard states:
Ah, the land of the rustling of wings, which is beyond the rivers of Ethiopia; that sendeth ambassadors by the sea, even in vessels of papyrus upon the waters, (saying) Go ye swift messengers, to a nation tall and smooth, to a people terrible from their beginning onward; a nation that meteth out and treadeth down, whose land the rivers divide (Evans-Pritchard 1940, 92).

[21] For a detailed discussion of the precise consequences of the application of *shari'a* in a modern nation-state for constitutional governance, criminal justice, international relations, and human rights, see, generally, An-Na'im 1990.

BIBLIOGRAPHY

An-Na'im, Abdullahi A. 1987. "Sudanese Identities," in *The Search for Peace and Unity in the Sudan*, edited by Francis Deng and Prosser Gifford. Washington: The Wilson Center.

———. 1990. *Toward an Islamic Reformation: Civil Liberties, Human Rights and International Law*. Syracuse: Syracuse University Press.

An-Na'im, Abdullahi A., and Francis M. Deng. 1996. "Expounding on the Principles," in *Their Brothers' Keepers: Regional Initiative for Peace in Sudan,* edited by Francis M. Deng. Addis Ababa: Inter-Africa Group.

———. "Self-determination and Unity: The Case of the Sudan," *Law and Policy* 18 (1996), 199-223.

Beshir, Mohamed Omer. 1968. *The Southern Sudan: Background to Conflict.* New York: Frederick A. Praeger.

Binagi, Lloyd A. 1984. "The Genesis of the Modern Sudan: An Interpretive Study of the Rise of Afro-Arab Hegemony in the Nile Valley, A.D. 1260-1826." Ph.D. diss., Temple University.

Cash, W. W. 1930. *The Changing Sudan.* London: Church Missionary Society.

Deng, Francis Mading. 1971. *Tradition and Modernization: A Challenge for Law among the Dinka of the Sudan.* New Haven and London: Yale University Press.

———. 1972. *The Dinka of the Sudan.* New York: Holt, Rinehart and Winston. New edition Prospect Heights: The Waveland Press, 1984.

———. 1973a. *The Dinka and Their Songs.* Oxford: Clarendon Press.

———. 1973b. *Dynamics of Identification: A Basis for National Integration in the Sudan.* Khartoum: Khartoum University Press.

———. 1978. *Africans of Two Worlds: The Dinka in the Afro-Arab Sudan.* New Haven and London: Yale University Press.

———. 1980. *Dinka Cosmology.* London: Ithaca Press.

———. 1982. *Recollections of Babo Nimir.* London: Ithaca Press.

———. 1986. *The Man Called Deng Majok: A Biography of Power, Polygyny, and Change.* New Haven and London: Yale University Press.

———. 1995. *War of Visions: Conflict of Identities in the Sudan.* Washington, D.C.: The Brookings Institution.

El-Affendi, Abdelwahab. 1990. "Discovering the South: Sudanese Dilemmas for Islam in Africa," *African Affairs* [Journal of the Royal African Society] 89 (July).

———. 1991. *Turabi's Revolution: Islam and Power in the Sudan.* London: Grey Seal.

Evans-Pritchard, E. E. 1940. *The Nuer.* Oxford: Clarendon Press.

Henderson, K. D. D. 1930. "Migration of the Missiriya into South-West Kordofan," *Sudan Notes and Records* 22, part 1, 49-79.

———. 1965. *Sudan Republic.* London: Ernest Benn Limited.

Herskovits, Melville. 1962. *The Human Factor in Changing Africa.* New York: Random House.

Howell, P. P. 1951. "Notes on the Ngok Dinka," *Sudan Notes and Records* 32, part 2.

Hutchinson, Sharon. 1980. "Relations between the Sexes among the Nuer," *Africa* 50, no. 4.

Johnson, Douglas, H. 1988. "Divinity Abroad: Dinka Missionaries in Foreign Lands," in *Vernacular Christianity: Essays in Social Anthropology of Religion Presented to Godfrey Lienhardt,* edited by Wendy James and Douglas H. Johnson. *JASO* Occasional papers, no. 7, 170-82. Oxford.

Kurdi, Mohagoub Ahmad. 1986. *The Encounter of Religion: An Analysis of the Problem of Religion in Southern Sudan.* Ph.D. diss., Temple University (June).

Lienhardt, Godfrey. 1961. *Divinity and Experience: Religion of the Dinka.* Oxford: Clarendon Press.

———. 1980. "Self: Public, Private. Some African Representations," *Journal of the Anthropological Society of Oxford* 11, no. 2, 69-82.

———. 1982. "The Dinka and Catholicism," in *Religious Organization and Religious Experience*, edited by J. Davis. ASA Monographs, no. 21. London and New York: Academic Press.

Little, David. 1995. "Belief, Ethnicity, and Nationalism," *Nationalism and Ethnic Studies* 1, no. 2 (Summer), 284-301.

———. 1996. "Tolerance, Equal Freedom, and Peace: A Human Rights Approach," Andrew K. Cecil Lecture on Moral Values in a Free Society, University of Texas at Dallas (November 11).

Malwal, Bona. 1981. *People and Power in Sudan*. London: Ithaca Press.

Mohamud, Ushari Ahmed, and Suleyman Ali Baldo. 1987. *The Dhein Massacre: Slavery in the Sudan*. London: Sudan Relief and Rehabilitation Association.

Nikkel, Marc R. 1991. "Aspects of Contemporary Religious Change among the Dinka," in *Sudan: Environment and People,* Conference papers, 90-100, Second International Sudan Studies, University of Durham (April 8-11).

———. 1996. *Link Letter* 8 (January 20).

Owen, R. R. H. 1937. "The Hadendowa," *Sudan Notes and Records* 20, no. 2, 147-208.

Radcliffe-Brown, A. R. 1960. "Introduction to the Analysis of Kinship System," in *A Modern Introduction to the Family*, edited by Norman Bell and Ezra F. Vogel. New York: The Free Press.

Sandars, G. E. R. 1935. "The Amarar," *SNR* 18, no. 2, 195-219.

Sanderson, Lillian Passmore, and Neville Sanderson. 1981. *Education, Religion and Politics in the Southern Sudan, 1899-1964*. London: Ithaca Press and Khartoum University Press.

Seligman, Charles G., and Brenda Z. Seligman. 1932. *The Pagan Tribes of the Nilotic Sudan*. London: G. Routledge & Sons.

U.N. Declaration on the Elimination of All Forms of Intolerance and of Discrimination Based on Religion or Belief: United Nations, Human Rights: A Compilation of International Instruments. 1988. New York: United Nations.

9.

MUSLIM PROSELYTIZATION AS PURIFICATION

Religious Pluralism and Conflict in Contemporary Mali

———————◆———————

Benjamin F. Soares

INTRODUCTION

Despite the long history of Islam in the region of West Africa that is the present-day Republic of Mali, it is only in the twentieth century that it has become the religion of the majority. This had hardly been the case at the time of the French conquest and the onset of colonial rule at the close of the nineteenth century. At that time, there were many in the region who were not Muslims—"animists," "pagans," or "unbelievers" in the different languages of their detractors. While perhaps the greatest waves of "conversion" by such people to Islam came during French colonial rule, there have been various efforts to convert non-Muslims to Islam and to eradicate certain social and religious practices deemed un-Islamic in the postcolonial period.[1] In this essay I begin by discussing the nature of religious pluralism in Mali, highlighting some of the practices that many Muslims find objectionable, and that, therefore, are a

Various parts of the research for this paper were funded by Fulbright-Hays, the Fulbright Program of USIA through the West African Research Association, the Wenner-Gren Foundation, and Northwestern University. An earlier version was presented to the American Anthropological Association Annual Meeting in 1995. I am grateful to Robert Launay, Hudita Mustafa, Anna Pondopoulo, and Diana Stone for comments on that version, and to Rosalind I.J. Hackett, John O. Hunwick, Robert Launay, Adeline Masquelier, Abdullahi An-Na'im, and Patrick Royer for comments and suggestions for the present version.

major source of tension, if not outright conflict, between Islam and Muslims, on the one hand, and—for lack of a better term—traditional religions and their practitioners, on the other. I then turn to consider the proselytization activities of one of Mali's most celebrated, contemporary Muslim religious leaders, examining the actual mechanisms of his campaigns to spread Islam among non-Muslims and to extirpate allegedly un-Islamic practices, most notably, spirit possession, as well as some of the intended and unintended consequences of such proselytization efforts. Such attention to religious pluralism and proselytization activities in this region of West Africa affords a significant opportunity for reflection on some of the complexity of the ways in which different social actors construe and reconstrue phenomena as "Islamic" and "un-Islamic."

RELIGIOUS PLURALISM

Religious pluralism is an important defining feature of the social landscape of contemporary Mali. Although estimates of the breakdown of Mali's population by religion are unreliable, Muslims may comprise between 70 and 90 percent and non-Muslims as much as 30 percent of the country's estimated nine million inhabitants (cf. Brenner 1993). There is considerable diversity in the religious discourses and practices of Muslims, as well as non-Muslims in the country. As far as the plurality of Islamic discourses and practices, there are basically three different conceptions of Islam: the Sufi, the anti-Sufi, and a third, incipient one, which has appeared in the context of an expanded postcolonial sphere and allows Muslims to identify with the broader Islamic community. Since at least the nineteenth century, a few Sufi orders (Arabic, *tariqa*), particularly the Qadiriyya and the Tijaniyya (including the Hamawiyya, a branch of the Tijaniyya), have been the main institutional forms for the practice of Islam in certain parts of the country. Mali has also been the site for important anti-Sufi activities, most notably by a loose group of self-styled "Sunnis"—locally known as Wahhabis[2] (a term they generally reject) who, since the 1940s, have sought to bring the practice of Islam in Mali closer to "correct" practices modeled on the presumed center of the Islamic world, the Arab Middle East. Most Malian Muslims, however, are neither formally affiliated with any of the Sufi orders nor especially enthusiastic about the anti-Sufis. In Mali, there is increasingly a more generally shared (though hardly uniform) sense of being Muslim and a commitment to Islam as a religion that has developed in the postcolonial period, which allows Muslims to imagine themselves as part of the global Islamic community.[3]

Some of the earliest known Arabic sources about West Africa from the eleventh century describe all sorts of practices deemed un-Islamic (see Trimingham 1962). Today, as in the past, certain individuals and groups, who call themselves Muslims, engage in a range of practices, which many, if not most, Muslim religious leaders and some laypersons in the country characterize unequivocally as un-Islamic. That is, most Malian Muslims, whether Sufi, anti-Sufi, or not, object to some of the social and religious practices of others (Muslims and non-Muslims) in the country.[4] "Spirit possession" is perhaps the most widespread (and familiar to outside observers) of these practices. It is practiced in various forms in villages, towns, and cities throughout Mali, as in many other Muslim societies in the broader region and beyond. Indeed, spirit possession is so prevalent in so many different Muslim societies that some scholars (e.g., Boddy 1989; Lewis 1986; Lewis et al. 1991) treat it as closely related to other Islamic discourses rather than as outside the realm of Islam or as forms of what is often called "popular" Islam. Without downplaying the influence of Islam on spirit possession, I want to point to the tensions between those who declare spirit possession un-Islamic and those who deny this as well as the long history of such tensions (see Masquelier 1993a).

Although the history of spirit possession in this part of West Africa is inadequately understood, it has had a long presence in this region.[5] Over the centuries, in a number of different Arabic texts Muslim scholars in the region have pointed to the practice of what we might today call spirit possession and mediumship.[6] In the nineteenth century, prior to the onset of French colonial rule, some European visitors to the region documented its existence (e.g., Raffenel 1856). In the early twentieth century, French colonial scholar-administrators collected ethnological and historical materials which suggested that certain Muslim leaders in the nineteenth-century Futanke state in Karta (in present-day western Mali) not only tolerated a form of spirit possession but even patronized those who organized it.[7] One of the leaders of the Futanke state is said to have sought out a renowned spirit medium for the treatment of an illness. Such patronage of spirit possession by the Muslim leader was, at the time, so controversial that some of the subjects objected, complaining that the ruler had become an "unbeliever" (Arabic, *kaffir*). That is, they effectively performed *takfir* (Arabic), declared that he ceased to be a Muslim. This was perhaps the most serious charge with which to challenge the legitimacy of his rule, and, as such, may have been a crucial factor in the power struggle that ensued in Karta prior to the French conquest (cf. Hanson 1996).

Although it is not possible to trace direct links between such reported instances and descriptions of spirit possession from the past and contemporary religious practices, we can say that today spirit possession is regularly practiced in a variety of forms throughout Mali (Colleyn 1988; Gibbal 1982, 1984, 1994; Malle 1985). In parts of Mali, many of those involved in spirit possession are organized into what are locally called "spirit societies" (*jine-ton* in Bamanakan) and "the dance of spirits" (*jine-don* in Bamanakan) (Gibbal 1982; Malle 1985),[8] the structure and organization of which are reminiscent of the Sufi orders (Lewis 1986, 102; Makris 1996). Like the Sufi orders, the spirit societies have a hierarchical structure in which spirit mediums—many of whom are women—are the leaders or organizers of the activities of the societies. For example, meetings and ceremonies are generally held only with the permission of the head spirit medium(s). The associates and followers of the mediums are generally in relations of subordination to them; that is, much like the adepts of Sufi orders are subordinate to Sufi leaders (*shaykhs*). Some spirit mediums are known for their considerable wealth and conspicuous consumption. In this way, they are not unlike some of the leaders of the main Sufi orders in the region, who are widely known for their ostentation and lavish lifestyles (see Soares 1996b). In addition, certain spirits in the pantheon are Muslim "saints" (Arabic, *wali*)—for example, Ahmad al-Tijani, the founder of the Tijaniyya—though not any recent saints from the immediate region.

It is important to note that people seek out the services of the spirit societies for many of the same reasons that they seek out practitioners of what can be called the Islamic esoteric sciences (Brenner 1985; Soares 1997a), that is, for good health, prosperity, or simply to make sense of the world (cf. Boddy 1994). In perhaps more cases than in the use of the specifically Islamic esoteric sciences, people seek out spirit societies and mediums for their therapeutic services. Indeed, this is how some leading spirit mediums spoke to me about their clientele. This may not be unrelated to the fact that even though most of those involved with spirit possession profess to be Muslims, the spirit societies usually maintain close ties with non-Muslim healers and diviners *(doma* in Bamanakan), for their knowledge of *bamanaya*.[9] In Bamanakan, Mali's most widely spoken language and increasingly its main lingua franca, *bamanaya* refers to the expert knowledge of the Bamana (or Bambara in French and in Arabic sources)—read non-Muslim—that includes practices involving blood sacrifice and the use of religious or power objects, as well as the use of plant-derived medicines for purposes of divination, protection against misfortune, and accumulation (cf. Bazin 1985; Soares 1997b; McNaughton 1988).

Many Malian Muslims readily assert that Islam and being Muslim are irreconcilable with spirit possession. Malian Christians (Catholics and Protestants) make similar statements about the incompatibility of Christianity and spirit possession. There are several kinds of objections that people have to spirit possession. Interestingly, the close association with non-Muslim healers is not among them. As in the nineteenth century case from Karta, many Muslims state that those who participate in spirit possession are effectively unbelievers. From this perspective, even though such people might call themselves Muslims or even act as such—through regular prayer, fasting during the month of Ramadan, and so forth—they are not "really" Muslims. This is because those who participate in spirit possession treat what they do in communicating and interacting with spirits (Arabic, *jinn*) as a religion (Arabic, *din*). In this way of thinking, since Islam is the only true religion, it necessarily follows that all people should give up spirit possession in all its forms.

For many Malian Muslims, one of the specific problems with spirit possession centers around questions of the sacrifice of animals during possession ceremonies. Specifically, the blood in animal sacrifice is spilled for spirits and not for God, not unlike the practices associated with non-Muslims in Mali. For this reason, many Muslim religious leaders and even laypersons in Mali condemn those involved in spirit possession for "association" or polytheism

(Arabic, *shirk*), labeling such people *mushrikun*, which translates somewhat loosely from the Arabic as idolaters. According to reported "Traditions" of the Prophet Muhammad, idolatry or polytheism is the greatest of sins (see Wensinck 1927). It is likely that Malians are drawing consciously or not upon such "Traditions."

Now I want to focus on some of the allegedly blamable practices known or at least suspected by some Muslims to occur during spirit possession. From the perspective of many Muslims, not only the spilling but also the use of the blood of a sacrificed animal is clearly forbidden. In spirit possession ceremonies, an animal is ritually sacrificed, according to the precepts of Islamic law. That is, a Muslim man wields the knife and utters "in the name of God." According to the Islamic legal texts used in this region as well as local practices and conventions, meat is only licit for consumption if sacrificed in such a manner (al-Qayrawani 1975, 297).[10] Since the meat of the sacrificed animal is prepared for a meal and nearly all those involved in spirit possession consider themselves Muslims, sacrifice according to Islamic legal precepts is taken for granted and generally unreflected upon. It is what happens during, or perhaps more accurately, after the sacrifice that is even more controversial. As the blood is flowing from the animal, someone, usually a spirit medium's assistant, catches some of the blood in a container, usually a calabash. Although this blood might be used in the confection of medicines, some of it may be used immediately for anointing. On some occasions, individuals might touch the fresh blood with the index finger of the right hand and put this finger in the mouth.[11] In some cases, this may be prelude to the onset of the dancing that accompanies possession by a specific spirit or spirits. In any case, the consumption of blood is unambiguously forbidden according to the locally used Islamic legal texts (al-Qayrawani 1975, 297). Moreover, nearly every Muslim in this context is able to articulate such a prohibition. The many Muslims who ultimately accuse those involved in spirit possession of worshiping things other than God because of such suspected blamable practices are attempting to anathematize them. As I will discuss below, many involved in spirit possession deny—sometimes quite vehemently—any un-Islamic behavior on their part.

To give some indication of the extent of the enmity toward spirit possession and its practitioners and the social pressures against them, I offer the following examples. Several Malian Muslims told me that if they happened to walk near a place where spirit possession was going on they would know from the distinctive and easily recognizable drum beats not to look and to pass by quickly. They explained that they had been instructed to do this from a very young age. One man pointed out that every step on the way to a spirit possession ceremony was quite literally a step toward hell. A friend, whom I had entreated to accompany me to spirit possession ceremonies, told me that he was unable to do so. This man, who fashions himself a very observant Muslim, worried that if he went to a ceremony he would need to fast for forty days afterward to purify himself.[12] A number of years ago, a prominent Muslim religious leader had been surprised to learn that spirit possession was occurring on a regular basis in a compound near his own. When he asked some people in his entourage why those in the neighboring compound seemed to drum so often, they replied that it was spirit possession. They were surprised by his question, having assumed all along that he would have been aware of what was going on, if only by the distinctive drum beats. The religious leader immediately sent someone to the compound to tell these neighbors that they should move elsewhere. They did so, relocating to a part of town away from his compound.

While these examples point to the pervasiveness of spirit possession, they also suggest that most Muslims acknowledge its existence in often close proximity. At the same time, many make conscious attempts to avoid spirit possession. If this seems to suggest an attitude of relative toleration, this is not always the case. The following is an example of a direct threat of violence against those involved in spirit possession. One man told me that when he was a young student of the Qur'an he and some of his peers learned that a woman involved in spirit possession had acquired a house near the compound where they were studying. He said that they were very unhappy to learn this and sought out the woman to inform her that if she ever engaged in spirit possession in the place in question that they would proceed to stone the house. The woman never moved into the house, and it was never used for spirit possession. Although the woman and her associates did not cease their activities, they did keep away from potential critics like these young men, thereby avoiding harassment and possibly even physical violence.[13]

If those involved in spirit possession have been able to act relatively freely in some villages and towns in Mali, there continues to be considerable conflict around spirit possession in many places. In some villages, certain inhabitants have actively sought to drive out those involved in spirit possession. The women who organized spirit possession in one village I know were compelled to leave. A man with a regional reputation for the specifically non-Islamic esoteric knowledge that he employed in divination and healing for himself and a range of clients told the women that what they did (organize a spirit society) was charlatanism. He insisted that they stop their activities or go elsewhere. In this case, the women seemed to have posed somewhat of a challenge to the man's authority as a ritual specialist. After unspecified threats, the women abandoned this particular village, though not their activities in spirit possession.

In some towns in Mali, some civil servants have been known to try to halt spirit possession activities for basically religious reasons. This has not always been easy, given that those involved in spirit possession have been able to secure a measure of protection from the Malian state, which asserts its secular nature regularly.[14] As an ostensibly secular entity, the Malian state is not permitted to intervene in the affairs of a particular religion. With spirit possession equated here with religion and having nearly the same status as Islam and Christianity, the state thus helps to guarantee the right to engage in religious practices like spirit possession. Although unable to officially ban spirit possession, some civil servants have taken advantage of their official roles to try to obstruct it. This has particularly been the case with a number of self-styled pious Muslim civil servants, who, in some cases, have employed administrative means to regulate spirit possession in areas under their jurisdiction. In many cases, such efforts have hampered, if not prevented, such activities. For example, local authorities often require costly permits for making noise, as is almost inevitable in the requisite drumming in most spirit possession ceremonies.

There are also a variety of other local and regional practices that are distinct from spirit possession, but which Muslim religious leaders find no less objectionable. Some of these are also "ritual" in nature and involve "spirits." For example, I attended the annual communal "visit" by the youth from a cluster of interrelated villages in western Mali with a protective female spirit, who is said to live in a cave adjacent to one of the villages. Although nearly everyone in this village professed to be Muslim and noted that their ancestors had been Muslims for at least a hundred years, people explained to me this "visit" was not Islamic. Some people—perhaps cautious when confronted by the inquisitive, visiting anthropologist—suggested that the "ritual" was all child's play. Others hinted that it was almost akin to the "folklorization" of the practices of non-Muslim ancestors (see Launay 1992). Still yet others told me that it all might look like play drumming, dancing, and refreshments, but it was actually quite serious. For these people, this annual ritual "visit" was an obligation; the villagers had to pay homage to this spirit, who had protected them in the past. To fail to do so might bring harm to them. In this case, many people find such "traditions" and/or "customs" inappropriate.

Thus far, most of the practices discussed have been those of people who consider themselves Muslims, even though many others find such practices at least objectionable if not explicitly un-Islamic, and, therefore, best renounced. At the same time, many other individuals and groups, who generally do not identify themselves as Muslims (or Christians for that matter), engage in local and regional "religious" practices or "traditions." Since such practices have long been in contact with Islam and Muslims, I am reluctant to use the term "indigenous."[15] In the past as well as in the present, it has not been uncommon for non-Muslim West Africans to use some of the signs and objects of Islam (Monteil 1924; Bravmann 1976, 1983; Launay 1992; Royer 1996). Even the above-mentioned ritual visit with the female spirit, which its practitioners do not see as an Islamic ritual, is actually tied to the Islamic lunar calendar. There are also many other practices explicitly anchored in allegedly non-Islamic knowledge, as is the case of *bamanaya*, with the manipulation of power objects, often through sacrifice. In contemporary Mali, many of the practices of non-Muslim healers and diviners, such as divination, blessings, and almsgiving, are actually quite similar in form to those of Muslims (cf. Bazin 1986).[16] *Bamanaya* is not, however, the only un-Islamic knowledge that people talk about or employ. Among many groups of people in Mali, but especially among those for whom Islamization is thought to be more recent, there is special knowledge, usually characterized as secret in nature, thought to be not only outside the realm of Islam but un-Islamic. For example, in Fulfulde, one of the most widely spoken languages in Mali, particularly by the Fulbe, there is the notion of *anndal balewal*, literally, black knowledge, which ritual specialists employ in ways analogous to ritual specialists in *bamanaya*.

In short, there is a wide range of religious practices, knowledge, "customs," "traditions," and so forth in Mali that many people find questionable, if not exactly un-Islamic, from explicitly and usually self-consciously *Muslim* perspectives. For this reason, we might say that the terrain was in some ways well-prepared for the organized campaigns against such activities, which got underway in the 1980s.

PROSELYTIZATION: PAST AND PRESENT

If some practices like spirit possession have a long history in Mali, the attempts by certain Muslims to get others to abandon such practices have perhaps an equally long history (Hunwick 1985). In the nineteenth century, there are numerous examples of Muslims objecting to some of the practices discussed in the above section. For example, a West African scholar from Timbuktu visiting North Africa addressed a treatise to the Muslim ruler in Tunis calling for the banning of spirit possession (Hunwick 1997). As part of the *jihad* he led in the nineteenth century throughout large parts of what is present-day Mali, Umar Tall destroyed the "idols" of some of his non-Muslim adversaries (Robinson 1985; Monteil 1924). Similarly, in the late nineteenth century, before his capture by the French, Samory, another important Muslim leader in this part of West Africa, also destroyed "idols" as a prelude to the construction of mosques:

> In each village where Samory was sovereign, he ordered the destruction of protective statues. He began to construct a mosque, even if rudimentary; he acted to support a priest *[imam]*, even if not a very learned one, in each mosque; he forced the chiefs of his subjects to send their children regularly to Quranic school (Gouilly 1952, 81).

It is significant that these images of West African Muslims destroying "protective statues" are actually quite similar in form to the motif of the prophet Muhammad's destruction of idols in Mecca at the beginning of his mission in 610. Indeed, this prophetic model is one upon which many Muslims throughout history have drawn (see, e.g., Fischer and Abedi 1990). Undoubtedly, those engaged in more recent proselytization in contemporary Mali have also looked to this model and its more recent West African imitators. Although many scholars have emphasized the often crucial role that Muslim saints and Sufis have played in the propagation of Islam before the twentieth century in such places as India, Indonesia, and sub-Saharan Africa (e.g., Levtzion 1979), the activities of such religious figures in the contemporary period have not received adequate attention. If proselytization by Muslims under French colonial rule in West Africa was quite commonplace (though largely unstudied for reasons that remain unclear) the study of such proselytization and its effects provides an important window on the anthropology and history of West African societies. I now turn to consider perhaps the most important of contemporary proselytization efforts in postcolonial Mali.

Over extended periods in the 1980s and the 1990s, Sidy Modibo Kane (1925-96), a prominent Malian Muslim religious leader, who was widely reputed to be a saint, undertook a series of long trips throughout the countryside in Mali (Soares 1996a, 1997b). It is reported that during these trips he converted thousands of non-Muslims and sometimes even whole villages to Islam and also worked to eradicate spirit possession and other purportedly un-Islamic practices. In all, he is said to have led such campaigns in nearly five hundred villages in Mali and many others in neighboring Côte d'Ivoire.[17] These proselytization efforts have been extensively commented on in Mali, not least because of their scope and range.

During his campaigns, Sidy Modibo, as the religious leader is commonly known, exhorted villagers to give up what he considered un-Islamic practices. While he found nothing objectionable in a minority of the villages he visited, he found at least one thing to combat in most places. He preached basically against three things he deemed either un-Islamic or incompatible with Islam. Here, I want to highlight Sidy Modibo's rhetoric, especially the tripartite categories he used to name that which he sought to eradicate. First, he inveighed against the use of *boli* and *basi*, "idols," that is, the plurality of non-Islamic power objects commonly employed in *bamanaya*.[18] Second, he condemned what he referred to as the *moonaankoobe*—which translates from Fulfulde (his first language) as "those who feign illness"—a commonly used term for those involved in spirit possession.[19] Alternately, he referred to such people in writing (in French and Arabic) as "people who practice the law of the jinn [spirits]." Third, he urged people to give up those "customs" (here using a word derived from the Arabic, *'adat*) that he claimed were incompatible with Islam and being Muslim. An example of such a custom is the social rule of some Malians that prevents bride and groom from cohabitating until a number of years after their actual marriage. It is striking how marked the categories used are. Most notably, "idols" for non-Islamic objects and "those who feign illness" and "the law of the jinns" for spirit possession unambiguously index the antipathy of Sidy Modibo—and many other Malians—for such objects and practices.

Sidy Modibo concentrated a considerable amount of his efforts among the country's non-Muslim rural population, particularly in some of those areas allegedly most resistant to Islamization in the past. In fact, he even went to some of the very places that were known for their firm and sustained opposition to the *jihad* led by Umar Tall in the nineteenth century. He spent time in the village, which the region's non-Muslims long considered "a holy town," according to one French colonial administrator, not least because it was "the principal boulevard of resistance in this land" against Islamization and the encroachment of Umar Tall's Islamic state (de Lartigue 1898). Unlike in earlier efforts to spread Islam in these same geographic areas, inhabitants from some of the villages invited Sidy Modibo to visit them. In many cases, he received the warmest of receptions.

Everywhere Sidy Modibo went, he proclaimed to people that their fortune would improve once they embraced Islam, if they were not Muslims, or once they renounced un-Islamic practices, if they already professed to be Muslims. In particular, he noted that those who had faced recurring drought would see better times if they did. When among people who considered themselves non-Muslims, Sidy Modibo and members of his large entourage actually implored villagers to relinquish their non-Islamic power objects and emphasized the pitfalls of not doing so. Sidy Modibo instructed members of his retinue to collect and count the objects, and careful records were kept of the numbers and provenance of the objects. In some cases, they destroyed these objects by fire immediately after collection; in other cases, they delivered some of them in sacks to the offices of the state-run media in Bamako, the capital city, ostensibly to publicize their meritorious activities.[20] Sidy Modibo taught non-Muslims the *shahada* (the Muslim profession of faith) and the ritual daily prayers. In many cases, a member of his entourage stayed behind to act as *imam* (prayer leader) and to instruct the villagers in prayer and Islam.

In those villages where the people professed to be Muslims, that is, in nearly half of the five hundred villages he visited, Sidy Modibo was not concerned with locating power objects. In his way of thinking, the existence of power objects here was not even a question—indeed it was inconceivable (cf. Soares 1997b). Instead, he was intent on discouraging the practice of spirit possession. This is because many Malians note that spirit possession is generally only present in those places in Mali where the people are Muslims.[21] In the many villages Sidy Modibo visited where spirit societies existed, he gave sermons against their practices. After doing so, he invited spirit mediums and their followers, almost all of whom were women, to renounce their practices before him. As part of the process of renunciation, Sidy Modibo placed his hands on the heads of spirit mediums. This he did to expel the spirits. Those women who agreed to this procedure usually emitted violent screams or deep moans—sounds that indexed the departure of the spirits inhabiting their bodies.[22] In many cases, such women required several days of rest to recover from what was an exhausting and trying experience of what might be called exorcism.

Even though these Muslim proselytization efforts in the 1980s and 1990s seem to be quite novel in Mali, particularly in their scale and scope, their techniques and strategies are not without precedent in this region. Al-Bakri's eleventh-century description of a West African ruler's conversion is in striking ways quite similar—in form and even in some of the details—to the contemporary campaigns. As he wrote, the ruler of Malel, presumably a Mande kingdom, had become Muslim after meeting a Muslim visitor to his kingdom:

> The king complained to this man about his people's sufferings [from prolonged drought]. He replied, "O king, if you only believed in God

almighty, acknowledged His unity and the mission of Muhammad, and believed in all the articles of faith, then I would pray on your behalf for relief from what you are suffering and for what has befallen you. Thus you could bring universal benefit upon the people of your country and thereby incite all your enemies and adversaries to envy." He persisted with him until he agreed to embrace Islam, and that in sincerity. . . . [Eventually, after the Muslim's prayers,] God enveloped [sic] the land with abundant rain. In consequence of this the king ordered the destruction of the idols and the expulsion of the magicians from his country (quoted in Trimingham 1962, 61-62).

Although some of the conditions facilitating the contemporary Muslim proselytization include Sidy Modibo's widespread reputation (Soares 1997b), he operated within a climate where many Malian Muslims are troubled by certain social and religious practices that they encounter, hear about, and often avoid. While many Malians praised the activities of Sidy Modibo on behalf of Islam, there was some opposition—overt and not so overt—to his proselytization efforts. In some cases, non-Muslims in certain villages refused to allow Sidy Modibo to visit. In other villages, after the departure of the religious leader, some presumed converts to Islam simply refashioned the objects they had surrendered and which had been destroyed by Sidy Modibo and members of his entourage. Moreover, some women involved in spirit possession were purposely absent from their villages during Sidy Modibo's visits.[23]

One must ask what the consequences of such proselytization have been. It is certainly the case that many Muslims in Mali continue to rely upon spirit possession, particularly, though not exclusively, for healing purposes. Despite the social pressure not to engage in spirit possession and the opprobrium surrounding it, and even such widespread and extensive campaigns against it, even some of those who do not dispute that spirit possession is unequivocally un-Islamic might, in some instances, be willing to engage with it. They do this, unremarkably, in often clandestine ways. This is particularly the case during personal crises such as serious illness. Thus, it is not uncommon for people who have been unable to find any effective treatment for serious illness— whether through the esoteric sciences of a Muslim religious figure, non-Muslim healers, or Western biomedicine—to seek out the therapeutic services of a spirit society and/or its medium. In some cases, a medium might organize spirit possession ceremonies for the purposes of treatment of a person who would ordinarily be very wary of spirit possession. I have observed self-consciously pious Muslims actually attending and participating in semi-public spirit possession ceremonies. In one case, this was because all other means of therapy had been tried to no avail. In another, a man purchased medicines from a spirit medium by indirect means; he relied on intermediaries so his dealings with the medium would not become public knowledge.

Very similar things can be said about sources of non-Islamic knowledge, as in *bamanaya* with its power objects, which Sidy Modibo also sought to eradicate.

Here too his efforts might have a limited effect because many Muslims in Mali continue to use and to rely upon the medicines and therapies of non-Muslim healers. They do so because many of these therapies are found to be efficacious, more affordable, readily available, and/or seemingly less risky than Western biomedicine. When asked about the use of such non-Muslim therapies, most Muslims are quick to note that the use of such "traditional" medicine is really no different from the use of other medicines also made by non-Muslims, particularly Western biomedicine. As long as such medicines are not tainted by illicit ingredients and practices, their use is permitted. In a sense, such things are only licit for these Muslims because they have been desacralized—at least from their perspective. But many Muslims also readily admit that it is difficult to determine with much precision whether such medicines are in fact licit, that is, made without contravening the precepts of Islamic law.[24]

As for those who are actively involved in spirit possession, and are not simply appealing to it in times of crisis, many are unwilling to forego their interaction with the spirits despite the social pressures they face. They do not necessarily see a contradiction between spirit possession and being Muslim.[25] But they are fully aware that many other Muslims do see them as irreconcilable. For this reason, many do try to hide their involvement in spirit possession from disapproving friends, neighbors, and relatives, and often go to great lengths to do so. Similarly, disapproving relatives might keep their social distance from kin involved in spirit possession. For example, I know a particularly renowned spirit medium who told me that since she was a child she has had a close relationship with the spirits, as other women in her family have had. As a young woman, she married a Muslim cleric, and, over the years, he grew unhappy about her involvement in spirit possession. He finally told her that she would have to decide between the spirits or marriage to him. She decided to choose the former, and they were divorced. Since that time, she has worked as a medium and healer, establishing a regional reputation and acquiring considerable capital. Needless to say, her continued involvement in spirit possession is the source of considerable embarrassment to some of her relatives, particularly those who are Muslim clerics.

All of this points to the fact that many of those who participate in spirit possession are embattled, whether in the daily interactions with fellow Malians or the rather extraordinary encounters with a celebrated Muslim religious leader like Sidy Modibo committed to stamping out spirit possession. It is perhaps the case that those involved in spirit possession are even more embattled than "traditional" healers given the professionalization of African medicine, which the Malian state has promoted. With few exceptions, spirit possession adepts are unable to counter the rather pointed criticism they receive from the many Muslims, who charge them with un-Islamic behavior. When Sidy Modibo went to see one of Mali's most renowned spirit mediums, he asked her directly about her allegedly un-Islamic practices. In response, she categorically denied doing anything illicit in nature. As evidence of her own piety as well as probity, this particular spirit medium indicated to her potential critics—including Sidy Modibo—that she conducts her spirit possession sessions in Arabic, that is, the language of the Qur'an. As further proof, teachers of the Qur'an not only live in but also teach in her own compound, where she organizes her activities—perhaps a good example of what some have called "debating Muslims" (see Fischer and Abedi 1990). On the whole, most spirit mediums and their followers, however, are unwilling or unable to stand up so directly to critics like Sidy Modibo. One spirit medium I know told me that her activities in spirit possession were not in any way un-Islamic. She explained that one man, who was a descendant of the prophet Muhammad, had consulted her for healing and had been effectively cured.[26] Needless to say, such "evidence" is unlikely to convince many Malians of the merits of spirit possession and, more specifically, her activities, which many condemn outright, even without direct knowledge of them.

One of the ironies is that the postcolonial Malian secular state, which often associates itself with Islam (Soares n.d.) and might even have encouraged "conversion" to Islam (Soares 1996a), in other instances helps to guarantee the right to engage in religious practices that are abhorrent to the majority, including spirit possession, in overwhelmingly Muslim towns and villages. Although spirit possession has remained popular, those involved in spirit possession keep a fairly low profile. In some cases, they have even been forced to modify their practices. For instance, while those involved in spirit possession might in some cases have a tradition of not convening during the month of Ramadan, in other cases it seems that this "tradition" might be a strategy to avoid too much attention from potential critics, including those part of or close to the civil service. When funds are not available for costly permits required for drumming in urban areas, those involved in spirit possession might meet and try to summon the spirits in publicly less obtrusive ways. For example, they can convene without noisy drumming—though many complain that such techniques are much less efficacious. In spite of the opprobrium and considerable pressure they face from such "modernizing"—not to mention secularizing—actors, many people continue to embrace "traditional" religious practices, spirit possession, and so forth. If some practice their allegedly un-Islamic religious traditions openly and defiantly, many others do so much more discreetly. In the end, such "traditional" religious practices may indeed be transformed, as they are increasingly relegated to private or at least semi-public venues, that is, out of the view of some of their critics.

Although Sidy Modibo's proselytization efforts might not be the direct cause of such developments, he undoubtedly profited from a general climate of hostility to spirit possession and other such "un-Islamic" religious practices and traditions. At the same time, his proselytization has also been important in focusing attention on what so many Malian Muslims find objectionable, but paradoxically not so objectionable that they will not have recourse to them if de-sacralized, and, if not de-sacralized, at least in time of crisis or covertly.

Notes

[1] Islamization under French colonial rule in West Africa is still not properly understood. For a French colonial perspective, see Cardaire 1954. For recent studies, see Harmon 1988; Launay 1992; and Launay and Soares 1999. I have discussed the anthropological debates about "conversion" elsewhere. See Soares 1995.

[2] *Wahhabis* and the *Wahhabiyya* are the terms used to describe the community formed in Arabia by Muhammad b. 'Abd al-Wahhab (d. 1787), whose doctrines were adopted and propagated by the House of Sa'ud of present-day Saudi Arabia. During the French colonial period, administrators applied the terms *Wahhabi* and the *Wahhabiyya* to "reformist" Muslims and anti-Sufis in West Africa, and this terminology continues to be used. Anti-Sufis, so-called Wahhabis, in Mali have received considerable scholarly attention. See, for example, Kaba 1974; Hamès 1980; Amselle 1985; Triaud 1986; Niezen 1990; Brenner 1993; and Soares 1997a. On Saudi activities in Africa, see Schulze 1993.

[3] I have developed this theme elsewhere. See Soares 1997a, n.d.; cf. Brenner 1993; Launay and Soares 1999.

[4] I am unable to address here the issue of anti-Sufis accusing Sufis of un-Islamic behavior. See the references in note 2 above.

[5] The form of spirit possession that emerged under French colonial rule among the Songhay of West Africa captured in Jean Rouch's film, *Les maîtres fous*, is possibly the most familiar to Western scholars. On the history of spirit possession among the Songhay, cf. Olivier de Sardan 1984; Stoller 1995. See also Makris 1996 for a discussion of the history of spirit possession in the Sudan.

[6] Such documentation of spirit possession was almost without exception a prelude to the denunciation of such practices as un-Islamic. For an example from the fifteenth century, see Hunwick 1970.

[7] See Centre des Archives d'Outre-Mer, Aix-en-Provence, France, 75 APOM 5/6, Robert Arnaud, "Du commandement chez les Diawaras. Histoire d'une tribu guerrière du Soudan," 30 June 1918, "Note sur une pratique Fétichiste en usage chez les Diawara." The rest of this paragraph is based on this source.

[8] Most of what follows concerns this form of spirit possession.

[9] On the subject of healers in Mali, see Brunet-Jailly 1993 and Diakité 1993.

[10] See the discussion of "sacrifice" in chapter 29 of al-Qayrawani, a text from the Maliki school of Islamic jurisprudence, that is widely used in West Africa.

[11] For a discussion of similar practices in the Sudan, see Boddy 1989 and Makris 1996.

[12] It is interesting to compare this with the rules for "expiation" in al-Qayrawani (1975, 167-69).

[13] For a discussion of the harassment of some of those involved in spirit possession in neighboring Niger, see Stoller 1989; Vidal 1990; and Masquelier 1993a, 1993b.

[14] This is interesting to compare with rule under the Mahdists (1885-98) in the Sudan, when a form of spirit possession was suppressed. See Makris 1996, 167.

[15] For a general critique of ethnological views of "paganism" and a discussion of some of the connections between Islam and other religious traditions in this part of West Africa, see Amselle 1990. For a very interesting study along these lines based on recent ethnography in Mali, see Zobel 1996. See also Matory 1994.

[16] This is without mentioning reported, though unconfirmed, cooperation and collaboration between such non-Muslims and Muslim religious leaders, for example, in healing or in "cleansing" a town of malevolent spirits.

[17] This information comes from a list of villages visited by the Muslim religious leader in the present author's possession.

[18] Sometimes the religious leader's entourage used the French word (*fétiches*) and, other times, words in Bamanakan such a *boli* and *basi*, "power objects." On such terminology, see Hackett 1996. For a discussion of some of these issues for contemporary Benin, see Elwert 1995.

[19] See *moonaade* in DNAFLA 1993. Needless to say, spirit possession adepts do not embrace such language.

[20] Members of the entourage informed me that the state-run media in turn sent the objects to the National Museum in Bamako. This may have been in response to a 1985 Malian law protecting the "national cultural heritage" (*patrimoine culturel national*). See Jonckers 1993, 87 n.4.

[21] In other words, they do not consider all forms of "possession" in Mali to be spirit possession.

[22] As I have noted elsewhere (Soares 1997b), I learned such details from Sidy Modibo's entourage.

[23] It is important to note that there are no known cases in which those involved in spirit possession successfully blocked a visit by the religious leader.

[24] It is not clear, however, what role the increased professionalization of indigenous medicine has already had in this realm. On the professionalization of African medicine, see Last and Chavunduka 1986.

[25] Recent discussions of "religious diversification" (Aguilar 1995), plural practices in a Muslim society (Lambek 1993), "syncretism" (Stewart and Shaw 1993), and reconsiderations of "conversion" (Royer 1996) are all relevant here.

[26] If this is another example of "debating Muslims," the power differentials involved in such debates are more manifest here.

BIBLIOGRAPHY

Aguilar, Mario I. 1995. "African Conversion from a World Religion: Religious Diversification by the Waso Boorana in Kenya," *Africa* 64, 5:525-44.

Amselle, Jean-Loup. 1985. "Le Wahabisme à Bamako (1945-1985)," *Canadian Journal of African Studies* 19, 2:345-57.

———. 1990. *Logiques métisses*. Paris: Payot.

Bazin, Jean. 1985. "A chacun son Bambara," in *Au coeur de l'ethnie: Ethnies, tribalisme et Etat en Afrique*, edited by Jean-Loup Amselle and Elikia M'Bokolo, 87-127. Paris: La Découverte.

———. 1986. "Retour aux choses-dieux," in *Corps des dieux*, edited by Charles Malamoud and Jean-Pierre Vernant. *Le Temps de la Réflexion*, 7:253-73.

Boddy, Janice. 1989. *Wombs and Alien Spirits: Women, Men, and the Zar Cult in Northern Sudan*. Madison: University of Wisconsin Press.

———. 1994. "Spirit Possession Revisited: Beyond Instrumentality," *Annual Review of Anthropology* 23:407-34.

Bravmann, René A. 1976. *Islam and Tribal Art in Africa*. Cambridge: Cambridge University Press.

———. 1983. *African Islam*. Washington: Smithsonian.

Brenner, Louis. 1985. "The 'Esoteric Sciences' in West African Islam," in *African Healing Strategies*, edited by B. du Toit and I. H. Abdalla, 20-28. Buffalo: Trado-Medic Books.

————. 1993. "Constructing Muslim Identities in Mali," in *Muslim Identity and Social Change in Sub-Saharan Africa*, edited by Louis Brenner, 59-78. Bloomington: Indiana University Press.

Brunet-Jailly, Joseph, ed. 1993. *Se soigner au Mali: Une contribution des sciences sociales*. Paris: Karthala and ORSTOM.

Cardaire, Marcel. 1954. *L'Islam et le terroir africain*. Koulouba: Institut français d'Afrique noire.

Colleyn, Jean-Paul. 1988. *Les Chemins de Nya: Culte de possession au Mali*. Paris: Éditions de l'École des Hautes Études en Sciences Sociales.

de Lartigue, Lt. 1898. "Notice historique sur la région du Sahel," *Bulletin du Comité de l'Afrique française, Renseignements Coloniaux*, 4:69-101.

Diakité, Djigui. 1993. "Quelques maladies chez les Bamanan," in *Se soigner au Mali: Une contribution des sciences sociales*, edited by Joseph Brunet-Jailly, 25-48. Paris: Karthala and ORSTOM.

DNAFLA. 1993. *Lexique (Fulfulde-Français)*. Bamako: Ministère de l'Education Nationale.

Elwert, Georg. 1995. "Changing Certainties and the Move to a 'Global' Religion," in *The Pursuit of Certainty*, edited by Wendy James. London and New York: Routledge.

Fischer, Michael M. J., and Mehdi Abedi. 1990. *Debating Muslims*. Madison: University of Wisconsin Press.

Gibbal, Jean-Marie. 1982. *Tambours d'eau: Journal et enquête sur un culte de possession au Mali occidental*. Paris: Le Sycomore.

————. 1984. *Guérisseurs et magiciens du Sahel*. Paris: A. M. Métailié.

————. 1994. *Genii of the River Niger*, translated by Beth G. Raps. Chicago: University of Chicago Press.

Gouilly, Alphonse. 1952. *L'Islam dans l'Afrique Occidentale française*. Paris: Larose.

Hackett, Rosalind I. J. 1996. *Art and Religion in Africa*. New York: Cassell.

Hamès, Constant. 1980. "Deux aspects du fondamentalisme islamique: Sa signification au Mali actuel et chez Ibn Taimiya," *Archives de sciences sociales des religions* 50, 2:177-90.

Hanson, John H. 1996. *Migration, Jihad, and Muslim Authority in West Africa*. Bloomington: Indiana University Press.

Harmon, Stephen A. 1988. *The Expansion of Islam among the Bambara under French Rule: 1890 to 1940*. Ph.D. diss., University of California, Los Angeles.

Hunwick, John O. 1970. "Notes on a Late Fifteenth-Century Document concerning 'al-Takrur,'" in *African Perspectives*, edited by C. Allen and R. W. Johnson, 7-33. Cambridge: Cambridge University Press.

————. 1985. *Shar'ia in Songhay*. London: Oxford University Press for the British Academy.

————. 1997. "Black Slave Religious Practices in the Mediterranean Islamic World." Paper presented to the Summer Institute, *Identifying Enslaved Africans: The 'Nigerian' Hinterland and the African Diaspora,* York University.

Jonckers, Danielle. 1993. "Autels sacrificiels et puissances religieuses: Les Minyan (Bamana-Minyanka, Mali)," in *Fétiches II: Puissance des objects, charme des mots*, edited by Albert de Surgy. *Systèmes de pensèe en Afrique noire* 12: 65-101.

Kaba, Lansiné. 1974. *The Wahhabiyya*. Evanston: Northwestern University Press.

Last, Murray, and G. L. Chavunduka, eds. 1986. *The Professionalisation of African Medicine*. Manchester: Manchester University Press.

Lambek, Michael. 1993. *Knowledge and Practice in Mayotte: Local Discourses of Islam, Sorcery, and Spirit Possession.* Toronto: University of Toronto Press.

Launay, Robert. 1992. *Beyond the Stream: Islam and Society in a West African Town.* Berkeley and Los Angeles: University of California Press.

Launay, Robert, and Benjamin F. Soares. 1999. "The Formation of an 'Islamic Sphere' in French Colonial West Africa," *Economy and Society.* In press.

Levtzion, Nehemia, ed. 1979. *Conversion to Islam.* New York: Holmes and Meier.

Lewis, I. M. 1986. *Religion in Context: Cults and Charisma.* Cambridge: Cambridge University Press.

Lewis, I. M., Ahmed Al-Safi, and Sayyid Hurreiz, eds. 1991. *Women's Medicine: The Zar-Bori Cult in Africa and Beyond.* Edinburgh: Edinburgh University Press.

Makris, G. P. 1996. "Slavery, Possession and History: The Construction of the Self among Slave Descendants in the Sudan," *Africa* 66, 2:159-82.

Malle, Youssouf. 1985. "Le culte de possession en milieu bamanan: Le 'Jine-don' dans le district de Bamako: Etude clinique du 'Jiné-bana.'" Mémoire, fin d'études, Ecole Normale Supérieure, Bamako (Mali).

Masquelier, Adeline. 1993a. *Ritual Economies, Historical Mediations: The Poetics and Power of Bori among the Mawri of Niger.* Ph.D. diss., University of Chicago.

———. 1993b. "Narratives of Power, Images of Wealth: The Ritual Economy of Bori in the Market," in *Modernity and Its Malcontents,* edited by J. Comaroff and J. Comaroff, 3-33. Chicago: University of Chicago Press.

Matory, J. Lorand. 1994. "Rival Empires: Islam and the Religions of Spirit Possession among the Oyo-Yoruba," *American Ethnologist* 21:495-515.

McNaughton, Patrick. 1988. *The Mande Blacksmiths: Knowledge, Power, and Art in West Africa.* Bloomington: Indiana University Press.

Monteil, Charles. 1924. *Les Bambaras de Ségou et du Kaarta.* Paris: Larose.

Niezen, Ronald. 1990. "The 'Community of the Helpers of the Sunna': Islamic Reform among the Songhay of Gao (Mali)," *Africa* 60, 3:399-423.

Olivier de Sardan, Jean-Pierre. 1984. *Les sociétés songhay-zarma (Niger-Mali).* Paris: Karthala.

al-Qayrawani, 'Abdullah b. Abi Zayd. 1975. *Al-Risala.* Edited and translated by L. Bercher, 6th ed. Algiers: Editions populaires de l'armée.

Raffenel, Anne. 1856. *Nouveau voyage dans le pays des Nègres,* vol. 1. Paris: Napoléon Chaix.

Robinson, David. 1985. *The Holy War of Umar Tal.* Oxford: Clarendon Press.

Royer, Patrick Yves. 1996. *In Pursuit of Tradition: Local Cults and Religious Conversion among the Sambla of Burkina Faso.* Ph.D. diss., University of Illinois, Urbana-Champaign.

Schulze, Reinhard. 1993. "La da'wa saoudienne en Afrique de l'Ouest," in *Le radicalisme islamique au sud du Sahara,* edited by René Otayek, 21-35. Paris: Karthala.

Soares, Benjamin F. 1995. "The Sufi, the Migrant, and the State." Paper presented to the Annual Meeting of the American Anthropological Association, Washington.

———. 1996a. "A Contemporary Malian Shaykh," *Islam et Sociétés au Sud du Sahara* 10:145-53.

———. 1996b. "The Prayer Economy in a Malian Town," *Cahiers d'études africaines* 36, 4:739-53.

————. 1997a. *The Spritual Economy of Nioro du Sahel: Islamic Discourses and Practices in a Malian Religious Center*. Ph.D. diss., Northwestern University.

————. 1997b. "The Fulbe Shaykh and the Bambara 'Pagans': Contemporary Campaigns to Spread Islam in Mali," in *Peuls et Mandingues: Dialectiques des constructions identitaires*, edited by Mirjam de Bruijn and Han van Dijk, 267-80. Paris: Karthala.

————. n.d. "The Public Sphere of Islam and a Cancelled Christian Crusade in West Africa." Unpublished manuscript.

Stewart, Charles, and Rosalind Shaw, eds. 1993. *Syncretism/Anti-Syncretism*. New York: Routledge.

Stoller, Paul. 1989. *Fusion of the Worlds: An Ethnography of Possession among the Songhay of Niger*. Chicago: University of Chicago Press.

————. 1995. *Embodying Colonial Memories: Spirit Possession, Power, and the Hauka in West Africa*. London and New York: Routledge.

Triaud, Jean-Louis. 1986. "'Abd al-Rahman l'Africain (1908-1957), pionnier et précurseur du wahhabisme au Mali," in *Radicalismes islamiques*, volume 2, edited by O. Carré and P. Dumont, 162-80. Paris: L'Harmattan.

Trimingham, J. Spencer. 1962. *A History of Islam in West Africa*. London: Oxford University Press.

Vidal, Laurent. 1990. *Rituels de Possession dans le Sahel: Exemples peul et zarma du Niger*. Paris: L'Harmattan.

Wensinck, A. J. 1927. *A Handbook of Early Muhammadan Tradition*. Leiden: E. J. Brill.

Zobel, Clemens. 1996. "Les génies du Koma: Identités locales, logiques religieuses et enjeux socio-politiques dans les monts Manding du Mali," *Cahiers d'études africaines* 36, 4:625-58.

10.

RADICAL CHRISTIAN REVIVALISM IN NIGERIA AND GHANA

Recent Patterns of Intolerance and Conflict

——————◆——————

Rosalind I. J. Hackett

INTRODUCTION

The primary goal of this essay is to examine patterns of religious resurgence, together with the changing nature of proselytization, in Nigeria and Ghana today. I am especially interested in the more radical, revivalist, viz., evangelical/pentecostal/charismatic, developments occurring within Christianity since the 1970s, which, as I will show, account for a great deal of the religious intolerance exhibited in recent times. Nigeria, in particular, has become transformed from a model of relative religious tolerance to a country with a reputation for repeated outbreaks of religious violence, some with extremely serious loss of life and destruction of property (see Ibrahim 1991 and Udoidem 1997 for an overview).[1] There is already a good body of scholarship on Islamic revivalist movements (Westerlund 1992; Umar 1993; Kukah 1993),[2] so I only mention these in connection with the activities of the Christian groups. These religious developments lend themselves to the type of multidimensional analysis which is a hallmark of the present project on proselytization. In the latter part of the essay I discuss briefly areas of conflict management and resolution.

Both Ghana and Nigeria achieved political independence from Britain in 1957 and 1960 respectively. They have experienced similar patterns of missionization and civilian/military governance. Nigeria has a far larger Muslim presence (perhaps 60 percent) compared to the dominance of Christianity in Ghana (60 percent).[3] The main focus will be on Nigeria, however, and its recent history of increasing religious tensions between Muslims and Christians, with relevant comparisons and contrasts made with the Ghanaian situation. The chapter is written using the lens of a scholar of religion, notably one with strong interests in the social and cultural aspects of religion, and more specifically its ambiguous influences in the area of politics and human rights. As someone interested in the media and popular culture, I have made heavy use of the local print media, notably religious publications, as well as the electronic media, for these are more revealing of key figures and events, as well as of prevailing sentiments and mobilizing beliefs (see Hackett 1998).[4]

A major theoretical assumption of this essay, as I understand it to be for the whole project, is that religion is no mere epiphenomenon but that the metaphors and symbols of its discourse concern the mediation and transformation of power (cf. Marshall 1995). In fact, Gustavo Benavides maintains that central to any ideological system labeled as "religion" is "the problem of difference, or to be more precise, the creation of difference: its absolute maintenance, its absolute overcoming, and the paradoxical formulations that result from the attempts to deal with the tension between ideology and difference" (Benavides 1989, 5, cited in Ilesanmi 1995). For too long, many Western and African scholars, perhaps because of personal and/or professional bias, have failed to do justice to the religious variable in contemporary African affairs (Atanda et al. 1989, ix). Some scholars of religion have not helped matters by favoring a decontextualized and ahistorical view of religion, or one so clouded by confessionalism as to be heuristically hampered.[5] But the religious riots that have occurred in Nigeria since 1980, beginning with the Maitatsine movement, have necessitated and elicited analytic responses from all quarters, not least the academic.[6]

Islam was already well established in the northern regions of Ghana and Nigeria (it came into northeastern Nigeria in the eleventh century) by the time Christianity took firm root in the coastal areas (around the middle of the nineteenth century). Prior to that, indigenous religious traditions, with their paramount religio-political rulers and complex pantheons of local and regional deities, characterized the religious landscape. Mutua (1996 and elsewhere in this volume) argues rightly that there is no level playing field when it comes to the marketplace of religions in Africa. As non-proselytizing, non-competitive systems, which constitute such an integral part of their respective cultures, the local, indigenous religions lose out. There is no gainsaying the loss of status of these religious traditions to the "imperial" or "imported" religions of Islam or Christianity. They suffer particularly at the hands of the charismatic and pentecostal movements which are the focus of this essay.[7] Furthermore the political exploitation of indigenous religions is evident, whether it is the absence of official "holy days" or representatives on government committees, or the appropriation of their "traditional" values and practices—such as libations and ancestrally sanctioned communities—for constructing a civil religion (Olupona and Hackett 1991). It bears noting, however, that in many parts of West Africa, there are numerous, multiform examples of the capacity of these religions to transform and adapt. We should not forget, for example, the influence that traditional beliefs and practices continue to exert through the ongoing domestication and inculturation of Islam and Christianity into the lives of many Africans (cf. Sanneh 1983).[8] Nonetheless, the traditional religions have lost serious ground, and are generally not viewed as political players except through the mediumship of their traditional rulers (who for the most part are now Christian or Muslim). Even though the political nationalism of the 1950s and 1960s benefited traditional religion (Kalu 1989, Awolalu 1989), more recent attempts to revitalize indigenous cults and universalize their belief and value systems are generally limited and/or short-lived in their appeal (Hackett 1991). Revivals of traditional religious activity linked to cultural developments, such as occurred with the renewed interest in the arts of Vodun in the Republic of Benin, may be affected or curtailed by political and religious changes.

As stated above, despite the many interesting issues posed by such religiously pluralistic contexts as Nigeria and Ghana, I will be concentrating on contemporary developments in Christianity. This is in part because these developments have been the focus of my recent research, and as a way of viewing and explaining changes in intra- and interreligious relationships, as well as between religion and the state. Some of these changes have occurred with disastrous consequences, as will be shown for Nigeria.

RELIGIOUS RESURGENCE

It has been clear for some time now that there has been a resurgence of religious activity in both Nigeria and Ghana in recent years.[9] In Nigeria, this has been accompanied by a marked politicization of religion (Williams and Falola 1995, Hunwick 1992, Ibrahim 1989, 1991, Akinrinade and Ojo 1992, Usman 1987). This resurgence, I maintain, is attributable in large part to the growth in numbers and popularity of the Christian charismatic and pentecostal movements, which have become a major force over the last three decades. (About these, more below.) Arguably there has also been a general pluralization and diversification of religious options, whether indigenous or exogenous in origin (cf. Hackett 1989). This is not peculiar to this area—it is part of globalizing cultural forces—but there is no doubt that the religious innovation and creativity of Ghanaians and Nigerians have facilitated this development. Their renowned mobility, whether for trade, vacation, or educational purposes, is also a factor in accounting for the range of religious interests. So too is the explosion in media and information technologies.

Statistically, the newer Christian charismatic movements might not appear as a dominant group, but their influence far exceeds their demographic status. Since they are dynamic and have multimedia organizations, they penetrate areas beyond the parameters of the conventional "church." Their strong evangelistic outreach is fueled by a conversionist ideology and facilitated by the latest in church growth techniques. I would venture to say that there is not a Christian church in Ghana or Nigeria today that has not been confronted by the wave of revivalism. While only a few have resisted these changes (such as the recalcitrant Anglican bishop in the Warri Diocese in southern Nigeria, whose diocese tried to impeach him some years ago), most incorporate them, and some embrace them wholeheartedly.

Brief mention should be made of the origins of these movements, since their present complexity can be confusing in terms of nomenclature and institutional boundaries. For example, in Ghana, *pentecostal* refers to the older churches of this type (dating from the 1930s and often of Western provenance), while *charismatic* is applied to the newer (post 1970), locally generated movements and ministries whose focus is healing, prosperity, and experience.[10] In Nigeria, however, *pentecostal* is more commonly used as a form of self-designation for these revivalist movements, connoting the centrality of the Holy Spirit in all church affairs. *Charismatic* has tended to be used to describe those revivalist movements within the churches, such as the Roman Catholic Church. However, as a label it is gaining wider currency and so it is my preferred term to describe this new type of spiritual and independent African church. *Fundamentalist* is inapplicable as a general label despite the presence of teachings on scriptural inerrancy. Furthermore, this label is generally resented by most Christians, for its associations with more extreme Muslim factions (at least as they get portrayed via some print and broadcast media). The nondenominational evangelical movements, such as the Scripture Union and the Student Christian Movement, which flooded the schools in the 1940s from Britain, with their emphasis on personal salvation, a strict Bible-centered morality, and soul-winning, laid the foundations for the later charismatic movements. It has been the livelier, spirit-filled, and empowering worship of the charismatics which has revitalized, and to some extent revolutionized, Christianity in these areas (as it has too in many parts of Latin America and Asia) (cf. Martin 1990).

Briefly, there are a number of factors which help explain the growth of these movements in Nigeria and Ghana. The political trajectories of both countries, failed civilian governments, and unpopular, longstanding military regimes have entailed many frustrations. Religious organizations have provided outlets for expression and action—but more cathartic and veiled, rather than of a directly critical nature (cf. Marshall 1991). Economically, Ghana and Nigeria have gone through hard times with Structural Adjustment Programs and falls in commodity prices, whether oil or gold. "Only God can save us" is a common refrain. Marxist observers and skeptical journalists have pointed fingers at the money-making activities of the churches, and the conspicuous salvation/ consumption lauded by some of the more flamboyant leaders.[11] The gospel of prosperity which characterizes the majority of these "new generation churches," or "newbreed churches" as they are sometimes popularly called now, is an obvious draw in hard times. But the benefits of the organizational skills they impart and the social networks they offer should not be downplayed. Their progressive, goal-oriented attitudes attract the youth, disillusioned with the empty moral claims of their elders and leaders. Those churches with more holiness origins (often stemming from the Apostolic Faith Mission—a U.S.-based church that was active in Nigeria as early as the 1930s), such as W. F. Kumuyi's Deeper

Life Bible Church, have a much more stringent moral outlook, but still (or because of this) attract large numbers of members.

From a sociocultural perspective, the charismatic movements constitute highly motivated and mobilizing communities—in large part because their membership is dominated by the youth and urban elites. In trying to reshape the lives of their members along biblical lines, they can be somewhat merciless toward "traditional" and "ancestral" cultural beliefs and practices. They can be disruptive of families in their quest for converts and avoidance of the unsaved. There are very ambivalent attitudes toward women—at one level they may enjoy greater participation and leadership opportunities in God's army; at another level, the conservative moral stance of these movements can stigmatize and demonize women.

"FORWARD EVER, BACKWARD NEVER": COMMISSION, COMMITMENT, AND CONVERSION

Now I want to examine more closely the proselytizing goals and techniques of these newer Christian movements. Despite their fears of modernist and secularist tendencies, the charismatics have readily learned and adopted the modern technologies and skills needed to propagate their message on a mass scale (cf. Lawrence 1989).[12] They have easily cornered the market, as the mainline churches have tended rather to put their money into schools or hospitals (cf. Gifford 1991, 100-101). Their multimedia approach to evangelism means that they do not just preach in churches or over the airwaves, but they also are driven to exploit human encounters both privately and in public places such as buses and taxis, markets, offices, hospitals, schools, and prisons. Mass healing crusades at sports stadia or revival grounds are a hallmark of these movements. Their texts circulate and their gospel music rings out. Their car stickers bedazzle and their sermon tapes are sought after. Their ideology is potentially democratizing and anti-elitist. Anointing and spiritual empowerment frequently override theological training or the charisma of office. Heroic and charismatic figures do rise up to provide the necessary leadership and mediation of power. But the fluid dynamism of the Spirit is deconstructive of the Church as an encrusted, Western tradition. Here the agency is local, the goals and connections are global (raising doubts and fears about expected allegiances to family, ethnic group, and nation), and the source is perceived as nothing short of cosmic and transcendental.

What distinguishes these movements is not their denominational labels and heritage, it is rather their commitment to a "full gospel," Bible-centered, not forcibly, but leaning toward, literalist, religious orientation (Hackett 1993). They readily distinguish between those who subscribe to such a worldview— often referred to as "born-again"—and those who do not. The latter may be disparagingly labeled as "dead Christians" or "unsaved." Such exclusivism, together with a theodicy generally given to externalization, leads easily to a demonization of the Other. In the past, the Other was the "pagan," of whom few remain. The conversion of nominal Christians and "pagans" is far less dramatic and challenging than that of a Muslim.[13] Former Muslims may in some cases choose to retain one of their Muslim names to advertise their conversion.[14] Mission work in the Muslim-dominated northern areas is sometimes sponsored by those in the south, or by groups which actually operate there (cf. Ojo 1997).[15] Christian activity is not new in these areas—churches like the Evangelical Church of West Africa and the Church of Christ in Nigeria (former mission-related organizations) have longstanding experience in this regard. But it is the newer groups who employ more aggressive and less diplomatic proselytizing techniques in order to commandeer religious public space and converts.[16] The Muslim stronghold of Kano rejected violently and bloodily the 1991 attempts of the German evangelist Reinhard Bonnke to subvert the crescent with the cross (Hock 1996, 315-28). His Christ for All Nations crusade throughout Africa is provocative to say the least—"from the Cape to Cairo" is the war cry, with claims that Africa will be the most Christian continent on earth by the time their famous big tent is erected in Cairo at the end of the century (Gifford 1987, 1993).

Educational institutions serve as important sites of proselytization, and often of conflict (see Hackett, in press; Ibrahim 1991, 132f.).[17] While religious organizations and proselytization were banned temporarily in schools and colleges above primary level following the 1987 riots in Kafanchan and other places in Kaduna State, this was not enforced beyond the northern states. The evangelical and charismatic movements have long realized the potential of targeting the youth. Hence, many school and college campuses in both Ghana and Nigeria are overwhelmed with religious groups seeking the souls of the young.[18] The competing and distracting cacophony of the situation may be overlooked by parents and some more sympathetic administrators, who would prefer that their wards become religious zealots rather than raging Marxists or nefarious drug dealers. Beyond the obvious moral expectations people have of religion, we should not underestimate the role of the campuses as seed beds for nurturing potential members as well as future leaders and movements (see Ojo 1988).

FROM SAVING SOULS TO SAVING FACE

Let us look at how and why the proselytizing tactics of the charismatics are perceived as increasingly militant and provocative by other religious organizations and governments alike. Rev. Father Dr. Matthew Kukah—the General Secretary of the Council of Catholic Bishops in Nigeria and a well-known, outspoken voice on religious and political affairs—rightly observes that this more confrontational stance is a recent development (1993, 226; see also Udoidem 1997, 179-80). Kukah characterizes this new exclusivist, not just rejuvenating, approach as a "collision course" with Islam (1992, 196). While one could point to the sheer competitiveness of Nigeria's (and Ghana's to a lesser extent) religious scene as well as the millennialist beliefs adding urgency to the evangelistic enterprise, many Christians would rather single out two paradigmatic events—the acrimonious national debates in Nigeria over the attempt by revivalist Muslims to establish a federal *Shari'a* court of appeal in 1979 during the drawing up of the new constitution, and the decision of the Babangida government to join the Organization of Islamic Conference (OIC) in 1986. This unannounced decision fueled conspiracy theories of Muslim domination for the Christian sector of the population (see especially Akinrinade and Ojo 1992), as well as theories of manipulation and politicization of religion by government and unpatriotic oligarchs (Usman 1987).[19]

There has always been some element of distrust between Muslims and Christians over each other's political agenda. This is linked in part to the division of the "national cake" as well as territory—the notion of the "Muslim North" for example. But the physical destruction of churches as well as loss of life that occurred during the 1987 riots further inflamed Christian feelings and seemed to tip the balance. While leading churchmen from the Roman Catholic and Anglican churches were vocal in their criticism of unfair governance, it was the increasingly dominant charismatic church leaders who became the strongest advocates of a more "politically active" Christian response. They criticized Christians in authority for "not using their wealth and positions the way Muslims are using theirs."[20] They lamented the perceived marginalization of and discrimination against Christians in the north of Nigeria in particular.[21] They objected to government money being used to build mosques. Kukah suggests that the mounting fervor can also be attributed to the disputations between these new generation churches and the older, mainline churches (1993, 226).[22] The latter may challenge the registration of the newer churches or their inclusion in church or government councils.[23] But the new generation churches owe no obeisance to ecclesiastical parents or to international partners. They can act independently, and do so at times with impunity, fueled by their critical, exclusivist stance. In other words, any type of intra-religious tension—and there is plenty among the various Muslim groups at the present time also (see, for example, Sulaiman 1993, Westerlund 1992, Ryan 1996)—can heighten the climate of religious intolerance and competitiveness.

The charismatics view Islam as their biggest obstacle to a "truly Christian" Nigeria. They see a connection among Islam, occult forces, and power mafias at the highest level (Marshall 1993, 237-40, Takaya 1989/90). This is well illustrated by the headlines (and articles) of the popular Christian magazine *Today's Challenge,* published by the Evangelical Church of West Africa in Jos: "Fighting against the Forcible Islamisation of Nigeria" (1987, vol. 1), "Muslim Fanatics on Rampage" (1995, vol. 1), and "Is Islam Lawlessness?" (1995, vol. 3). The current editor, Obed Bassau Minchakpu, is fond of condemning the "satanic schemings . . . of the devil and his agents masquerading as muslim fundamentalists" (1996, vol. 1, 19).[24] The discourse of the revivalists may incite the desired response by omission just as by inclusion. The report by the activist Christian Association of Nigeria (CAN) on the Kaduna riots in 1987 makes virtually no reference to the atrocities committed by Christians.[25] Likewise, Gaiya (1997, 52-53) is critical of *Today's Challenge* in fueling Christian intolerance of Muslims with its biased reporting. He highlights the failure of the widely read magazine to recognize the insensitive provocation caused by Christians with their elaborate and expensive advertisements in Kano in 1991 for the Bonnke crusade, especially following the government refusal to allow the South African Muslim preacher Ahmed Deedat to come to Nigeria.

A longstanding area of tension between Christians and Muslims has been incursions into Muslim-dominated territory.[26] This stems from a general disagreement over religious freedom. For example, in *Religious Disturbances in Nigeria,* the study produced in 1986 by the National Institute for Policy and Strategic Studies at Kuru, it was reported that

> the remote causes of the incident lay in the longstanding uneasy relationship between the Christians and the extremist Muslim groups. On the Muslim side there seems to be a belief that Christian churches and institutions are mushrooming in predominantly Muslim areas. The Muslims would like to curb that development. The Christians on their part feel that their constitutional right of freedom of worship is being denied them (31).

The land issue does not go away. In a northern city like Kano, Muslims have made it clear that churches can only be erected in officially designated areas. Attempts to purchase land or renew leases for church purposes or rebuild churches are generally blocked.[27] There are plenty of stories circulating also about mosques being built alongside churches to ensure parity, or Christians protesting government or company sponsorship of mosques in official compounds or in the workplace.

Because of limited and declining resources, and unpredictable access to them, numbers take on an importance, and it is the more vocal and radical Christians and Muslims who have realized this.[28] In this regard, a Christian publication rationalizes the competitive proselytization of recent times as follows:

> We are not surprised that these riots came at a time when certain powerful religious leaders were showing great interest in the religious composition of the country. Only last year, a respected Moslem religious leader claimed that 85% of Nigerians are Moslems. He later changed that claim to 80% and finally this year reduced it to 70%. Evidently, Islam is losing ground fast and therefore is in need of a jihad to reverse the trend. Christians naturally become the victims of such a jihad, the Islamic losses are considered to be the result of conversion to Christianity (TEKAN 1987, 59, cited in Ahanotu 1992, 40).

The enthusiastic and forceful proselytizing tactics of the newer Christian groups have naturally provoked a series of angry and at times violent responses from their Muslim counterparts.[29] As indicated above, their techniques are more penetrating and threatening to other groups than more conventional, controlled, and time-honored methods of proselytization based on diplomacy and mutual respect.[30] For example, welfare work by Christians has long been permitted in many northern areas. But when Christians openly vaunt the number of "Alhajis" they have converted, some Muslims react violently, as they did in Kumasi, Ghana, in 1996.[31] Even some Christians have drawn the line at circulating audio cassettes from Muslim converts to Christianity, while others are prepared to put their money behind more public and institutional statements such as the Converted Muslims Christian Ministry, with its headquarters in Kumasi and another branch in the north.[32] More generally, Muslims object to the continuing use by Christians of the word *crusade* and their agenda to Christianize the North (see Sanni 1983, 42; Westerlund 1992, 91). For example, in the words of the Council of Ulama in their response to the 1987 Kafanchan riot (Bello 1987, 48), "the fire of the Crusades has been rekindled, we are witnessing once again Christian intolerance and barbarism." They accuse the army of being a "Crusader force" for defending Christians and persecuting Muslims (ibid., 49), and the police and the judiciary of injustice in letting one of the "prime movers" (Rev. Abubakar Bako) of the "carnage in Kafanchan" escape. More significantly for the focus of this essay, they blame the breakdown in harmonious relations on "those Christians who, spurred by extreme fanaticism and intolerance, have adopted opposition to Islam, as a way of life, indeed as their religion" (ibid.).

It is the electronic media which increasingly constitute one of the key sites of interreligious communication and, potentially, conflict (see Hackett 1998). In fact, it is claimed that FRCN radio reports of the 1992 riots in Zangon-Kataf fueled riots in Kaduna, over one hundred miles away, not only informing Muslims but inciting them to action.[33] More generally though, it is the Christian use of high-tech public-address systems for evangelizing and preaching at open-air crusades that angers Muslims for the way that it encroaches on Muslim space. People are still talking about how the German evangelist Reinhard Bonnke's powerful equipment could carry his message right into people's homes which were far from the revival site. Likewise television and radio can be watched and heard in privacy and cannot be controlled. The community is incidental to conversions and healing—all the individual has to do is put his or her hand on the television, pronounce the prescribed words, and make a personal commitment. The content is also perceived as subversive in the eyes of Muslim authorities—instead of appealing to doctrine as part of the proselytizing process, the new evangelists are offering what every human being craves: health and wealth. The spectacle of the crippled walking and the downtrodden raised up has become a powerful icon of the Christian revivalists—Western or not. The popularity of Pat Robertson's 700 Club, with its conservative Christian reading of news and events, together with the TV drama

"Another Life," is not limited to the Christian community. In Jos, due to general popular demand, the programs were reinstated despite objections from the Plateau State Television authorities.[34] In Ghana, the newly created FM radio stations, while constitutionally secular, feature a lot of religious broadcasting, especially in the morning hours, by local charismatic preachers, or by radio hosts who are obviously Christian. Their style of preaching and music has wide appeal, to the extent that no radio station could survive without them.

Not wishing to be outdone by the Christians, by the early 1980s Muslims had stepped up their use of the electronic and print media to communicate the tenets of their faith.[35] The late Sheikh Abubakar Gumi, a leading Islamic scholar, anti-Sufi campaigner, and educational and juridical reformer, made regular use of the media in the 1980s and early 1990s (see Loimeier 1997, 184-85). In the southern part of Nigeria, Muslim prayer vans and preachers became more active in the business of conversion, and more Muslim magazines and newspapers were in evidence to counteract the Christian bias of the media.[36] Southern Muslims are trying to persuade Muslims further north to put their money into supporting television programming, for example, during Ramadan.[37] Muslims have frequently complained about the appearance of American evangelists on television as evidence of continuing Western imperialism, and about the anti-Muslim bias of the media in the south in particular.[38] In some northern states they have banned such programs or arranged for alternative (Muslim) broadcasts on other stations in the state. In Kano the transmission from Kaduna to Kano was cut because the Nigerian Television Authority (NTA) was broadcasting Christian programs.[39] Foreign evangelists are indeed less evident today, but their materials and disciples still circulate freely.[40]

Nigeria now has observer status only with the Organization of Islamic Conference, but new mosques may still bear the hallmarks of Libyan or Saudi Arabian funding, causing resentment among Christians about outside funding that Muslims can tap into and fueling fears of the Islamization of Nigeria. Likewise, the Nigerian government's decision in 1997 to join the Developing 8 (D8)—an economic alliance of developing nations—provoked another outcry from Christians because of the predominantly Muslim character of the alliance and its avowed solidarity with the OIC.[41] Religious affiliation was removed from the recent Nigerian census, but that does not mean that religion has disappeared from the political scene.[42] Political appointments are closely monitored by both sides.[43] Christians were very offended by Sheikh Gumi's claim in 1987 that no Nigerian Muslim would ever accept a non-Muslim president.[44] The issue of discrimination and marginalization at this level became a matter of public discourse again in June 1997 following a report that the New York City Council was making efforts to get Nigeria sanctioned for persecuting its Christian population.[45]

The Ghanaian government keeps a firm hold on religious groups (it banned the Jehovah's Witnesses and Mormons for a time, and reputedly "eliminated" a leading evangelist some years ago). It has tried to do this through registration requirements and restricted religious broadcasting. However the growth of FM radio stations has provided new outlets, in addition to the pulpit, for some charismatics to voice their criticism (albeit oblique) of the present government—particularly in terms of its compromises with other religious groups. The somewhat arbitrary action of Rawlings's government in welcoming the leader of the Nation of Islam, Louis Farrakhan, on two occasions (1994 and 1996), and according him an inordinate amount of television air time and diplomatic treatment, was resented by many Ghanaians. Many attributed it to political manipulation, while others speculated as to the secret "Islamizing" intentions of the government.

The trends and tensions described above are not unique to West Africa, but adding these often intolerant, divisive, and militant attitudes that we have seen developing over the last decade to the configuration of local political and economic problems of both Ghana and Nigeria at the present time makes for a potent, volatile mix.[46] The task of integrating religious difference and sublimating discord requires more constructive efforts than either the Nigerian or Ghanaian governments have shown. Official condemnations of religious intolerance are common, and widely reported in the media, but it has been left to individuals and religious and nongovernmental organizations to actively engage the issues.[47] In this regard, I would like to highlight the work of two individuals, Evangelist James Wuye and Imam Muhammad Nurayn Ashafa, who are joint founders and coordinators of the Muslim/Christian Youth Dialogue Forum in Kaduna, northern Nigeria. Wuye is an Assemblies of God pastor and assistant secretary of CAN, Kaduna; and Ashafa runs the Centre for Islamic Propagation out of the Ashafa Islamic Bookshop. Together they have transformed and channelled their respective (traumatic) experiences of religious violence into a program of promoting interreligious understanding between Muslim and Christian youths in Northern Nigeria. Since the youth on both sides are often the flash points in any potential conflict situation, their grassroots efforts over the last couple of years have borne fruit. They have received training in conflict resolution and trauma management in Britain and South Africa respectively. Together they have authored a manuscript detailing their partnership and points of contact and departure, as well as the narrative of religiously motivated violence in Nigeria. It is entitled *The Pastor and the Imam Responding to Conflict* (Ashafa and Wuye 1999). They are now trying to involve senior lawmakers and public officials in their work and find funding to expand their programs over a wider area.

CONCLUDING REMARKS

Religious tensions, notably between Christians and Muslims, and occasionally escalating to violence, have regrettably become part of the Nigerian scene over the last two decades. While the outbreaks of violence have been confined to the north, Nigerians have been privy to the narrative of events and the wars of words of national religious leaders through media coverage. Ghana, too, has experienced some incidents of religious unrest. It is always keeping a watchful eye on developments in Nigeria. In this essay, I have argued that the growing militancy of the newer, more radical Christian groups—fueled by the power of the Spirit and revival—has contributed in a significant way to the climate of tension and suspicion. That is not to deny the configuration of factors at play in a country as complex as Nigeria—any analyst is challenged when trying to unravel the web of political, social, economic, ethnic, cultural, and religious factors in any particular context.

It goes without saying that political and economic reform in Nigeria would provide a conducive backdrop for more harmonious interreligious relations, but I would like, in closing, to point to specific areas which I consider particularly instrumental in the promotion of religious tolerance. The media stand out as primary forums for information and dialogue. Compared to other African countries, for example, Nigeria and Ghana are blessed with a vibrant and lively press (although both have experienced attempts by government to curb press freedom in recent years). As the electronic media sector expands in both countries it becomes imperative that they are sensitive to their roles in building respect rather than resentment, and that the various constituencies are fairly represented in terms of air time or coverage.

Educational institutions, notably the universities, could do more to nurture an informed and sensitive dialogue on religious tolerance, one involving all parties (see Olupona 1989).[48] The schools have a responsibility not just to ensure that the respective groups receive the religious education of their choice (which is officially part of the curriculum in both Nigeria and Ghana) but also to see that all students receive education about other religious orientations. The government should be seen to manage openly, promptly, and efficiently (which it has frequently been criticized of not doing in Nigeria), but not be embroiled in, religious affairs (cf. Crow and Nwankwo 1996, 173). This is especially important at the onset of unrest, given that it is often only a minor incident (a local publication, a communal dispute over meat slaughtering, or an aggressive banner) that triggers wider conflict. The establishing of commissions to investigate Christian-Muslim conflicts may be one such path to take (although they have not always fared well in Nigeria). Just like the declarations on religious tolerance that emerge frequently from politicians and religious leaders, they carry little weight or legitimacy if the individuals or the structures are popularly perceived (and/or known) as unjust or illegitimate.

Because of their political history, the majority of Nigerians are sensitive to issues of discrimination—notably pertaining to ethnicity, and to the overt or covert manipulation of religion. Religious affiliation, while played down at the national level in more recent times, still gets debated at the more popular level. These issues would generally not get discussed in terms of international human rights standards but rather in terms of the constitution, and national and state quotas. For example, the non-establishment clause in the Nigerian constitution is generally interpreted to mean the support (certainly not antipathy toward), rather than privileging, of religious organizations.[49] But this has become a source of controversy and mobilization for the more radical groups. Extremist Muslim groups view the secularist clause as evidence of a Western (Christian) conspiracy to deny Muslims their rights and identity (see Westerlund 1992, 83-85). For some of the more militant Christians in Nigeria, the ready acceptance of the separation of "church and state" and retreat to a more privatized religious life has, in their opinion, weakened Christians politically (cf. Casanova 1994). Hence the clarion call in many of the charismatic Christian magazines to see politics less as a "dirty business" and more as a religious calling.[50] But moving into the public sphere should be accompanied not by a sense of anger and revenge, but rather by a responsible concern to seek mutual understanding and see positive (religious) values restored in a nation weakened by "moral bankruptcy." There are any number of calls by scholars and religious leaders to focus on the shared resources of the country's religious traditions to build rather than divide and destroy (see, e.g., Okafor 1997 and Abubakre et al. 1993).

So, despite the negative effects of the trends adumbrated in this account, there is a general sense that religion is desirable (as articulated in moral terms) in the lives of individuals and the national community (in fact, necessary to public well-being, argues Ilesanmi 1995, 1996; see also Mozia 1989). The majority of Ghanaians and Nigerians would readily defend the inviolability of religious freedom, adding that any government, whether civilian or military, would interfere with that at their peril.[51] That does not exclude an awareness and real fear of the excesses of religion (the Maitatsine movement of the 1980s with the massacre of over four thousand Nigerians is all that needs recalling here [see Christelow 1985, Kastfelt 1989]). Nigerians and Ghanaians know enough about events in Iran and Sudan to keep arguing about the merits of a tolerant, multi-religious state.[52] The volume of texts—primarily local—that has been produced on religious conflict in Nigeria is quite remarkable and indicative both of popular concern, as well as of the key, yet multifaceted, role religion plays in the lives of Nigerians (see Hackett, forthcoming).

But the last two decades have unfortunately seen the resurgence and emergence of religious groups and individuals with ambitions and ideologies that seem to override the parameters of tolerance. Furthermore, as I have shown, their proselytizing tactics can be coercive and discriminatory. Nigeria has come off worse because of its larger population, more equally balanced Muslim and Christian populations, a history of religion being manipulated by political hegemonies, and a continually worsening economic and political situation. As stated earlier, a series of repressive military governments has rendered religious forms of expression expedient in defending rights and territory. So there is every evidence that radical revivalist groups will continue to flourish in Nigeria, because theirs is a discourse of empowerment in a situation where survival has become paramount. But whether they will garner the necessary support to pursue their militant aims from a people tired and fearful of interreligious strife seems less likely now than it might have five years ago.

NOTES

[1] In fact, Nigeria was chosen as one of the countries to be studied as part of the overall Religion, Nationalism, and Intolerance Project directed by Professor David Little at the United States Institute of Peace. A joint conference on Nigeria and the Sudan was held in 1991. I am currently incorporating the proceedings into an updated manuscript entitled *Nigeria: Religion in the Balance* to be published by the U.S. Institute of Peace.

[2] See also "Many Voices of Islam," *Newswatch* (Lagos) (October 10, 1988), 20-25.

[3] Ghana Evangelism Committee, *National Church Survey* (Accra, 1989), 13. See also, Ryan 1996, 82. Statistics on Nigeria are far harder to come by. Religion was excluded from the 1992 census.

[4] Portions of my 1998 article on the use by pentecostal and charismatic groups of modern media technologies may be found in the present chapter, notably the section on the background to and characteristics of these movements.

[5] This critique is also strongly delivered by Simeon Ilesanmi (1995, 106; 1996) as part of his wider argument that religion plays a decisive role in the Nigerian political sphere. Achille Mbembe (1988, 16-17) rightly observes that contemporary Islam south of Sahara has received more appropriate academic attention than Christianity, which was left to the prevailing anti-intellectualism of the theologians.

[6] This is well evidenced in the wide range of materials assembled by the department of Islamic Studies at the University of Bayreuth, under the leadership of Professor Jamil Abun-Nasr together with Dr. Roman Loimeier as part of their Islam in Africa project. A number of the sources for this essay were found in their "Materialsammlung Islam in Afrika" with its strong focus on Nigeria, and for which I am grateful.

[7] Archbishop Professor Benson Idahosa, who, until his sudden death in June 1998, headed possibly the largest pentecostal organization in Nigeria, was renowned for his confrontations with traditional religious authorities, whether the Oba of Benin or the convener of conferences of witches (see Hackett 1993). He also purportedly built his lavish palace on the grounds of a traditional religious shrine in Benin City which he had destroyed after having been attacked by thugs hired by a cartel of local traditional religious specialists (*Church Times* [May 28, 1993], 8).

[8] We should never downplay the diversity which is disguised by the concepts "Islam" and "Christianity," nor the agency of Africans in the spread and transformation of these religions. Work has recently started on an African Christian Biography Project, led by Dr. Jon Bonk at the Overseas Ministries Study Center, which aims to document the many contributions of Africa's church leaders which are frequently ignored in Western church-history reference books.

[9] For a journalistic rendering of the "rise of religion" in Nigeria and the brewing of "schisms," see "Selling the Message of God," *ThisWeek* (February 8, 1988).

[10] It should be noted that several Ghanaian evangelists were in fact trained in Nigeria. This is less and less the case as they set up their own Bible colleges and seminaries (e.g., as in the case of Mensa Otabil and his International Central Gospel Church).

[11] For a scholarly critique of these churches in the southern African context, see Paul Gifford, *The New Crusaders: Christianity and the New Right in Southern Africa* (London: Pluto Press, 1991).

[12] Interestingly, many of the church growth techniques derive from the Korean mega-churches—notably from Pastor Yonggi Cho's Yoido Full Gospel Church in Seoul. The latter's numerous publications are readily found in Nigerian and Ghanaian church bookshops. See Hackett 1996.

[13] Kukah (1992, 205n.19) cites G. O. Moshay, *Who Is This Allah?* (Ibadan: Fireliners International, 1990) as a particularly visceral example of a Christian attack on Islam. For examples of triumphalist conversion accounts, see "Muslim Fanatic Converts to Christianity," *Today's Challenge* 1 (1995): 15, 21 and "From Islam to Christ," ibid., 29-30. Interestingly, both accounts are about other locations than Nigeria, viz. Indonesia and an unnamed country, perhaps India or Sri Lanka.

[14] For example, Rahman George together with the surname. In Ilorin there is a convert by the name of Akewu gba Jesu, meaning one who has read the Qur'an but still believes in Jesus. Information from H. O. Danmole, Birmingham, August 21, 1997.

[15] On a recent visit (June 1997) to Jos in central Nigeria, I was informed that several of the charismatic organizations had pulled back from the North and settled in Jos—already a long-established missionary base—because of the interreligious tensions.

[16] For example, Calvary Ministries (CAPRO), an indigenous missions agency in Jos and possibly the largest of all charismatic mission agencies in Africa (information from Matthews A. Ojo), describes its recent book—*Battle Cry for the Nations*, ed. Timothy O. Olonade (Jos: CAPRO Media Services, 1995)—as "a conscious attempt to provoke the church to harness all her resources to rescue the unreached millions from the grips of idolatry and Islam."

[17] The perceived Western Christian character of Nigeria's schools has always been a sensitive issue. Sanni and Amoo wrote their book *Why You Should Never Be a Christian* (1987) "to check the forceful conversion of Muslim students to Christianity."

[18] At Obafemi Awolowo University, Ile-Ife, for example, the sports stadium has been popularly renamed the Jesus Stadium because of the nightlong vigils and prayer meetings held there by the numerous campus Christian groups. At the University of Ghana, Legon, officials debated in 1996 the overuse of university buildings by Christian groups and excessive religious activity of students (personal communication, Kofi E. Agovi, July 1996).

[19] Ojo (1988, 188-89) notes that it was a charismatic student organization, the Christian Students' Social Movement of Nigeria (CSSM), that was especially vocal against the OIC decision. Its opposition to international Islam was evident in earlier hostile references to OPEC.

[20] Interview with Ambassador Jolly Tanko Yusuf, "Fighting against the Forcible Islamisation of Nigeria," *Today's Challenge* 1 (1987), 16-19.

[21] Marshall (1993, 239) reports that the Pentecostal Fellowship of Nigeria at its National Conference in 1991 specifically addressed the Muslim threat and the need for more Christian political participation.

[22] Although Kukah does suggest (1995, 227) that there was a (temporary?) reduction in the attacks by pentecostalist and charismatic Christians in particular on other churches. Some of these hostile (particularly anti-Catholic) positions derived from overseas (U.S.) inspirational literature.

[23] For several years the Christian Association of Nigeria (CAN) has campaigned to serve as a gatekeeper for church registration with the government. It sees this as a way of curbing the excessive proliferation and commercialization of the "newbreed"

or "mushroom churches." CAN's cause was given a boost in late 1996 when a number of "mystic and fetish-like items" were recovered from some adventist churches in Onitsha following the torching of these churches by angry mobs believing them to be the site of ritual killings. Earlier, in September 1996, a decapitated body was found at an Owerri pentecostal church together with human skulls and other "suspicious" paraphernalia. The ensuing riots resulted in the destruction of other "newbreed" churches. The events occasioned a number of vehement criticisms by mainline church leaders of this "toxic waste of America" and "pentecostal witchcraft," and dismissals by leading charismatic leaders of such unchristian activities (*The Week* [December 9, 1996]).

[24] As an example of a fictional account that disparages Muslims, see Tsado 1986.

[25] CAN Kaduna 1987. CAN was formed in the 1960s in northern Nigeria as a protest movement to challenge the proselytizing activities of Ahmadu Bello, the Sardauna of Sokoto (Ahanotu 1992, 192n.123). Kukah (1993, 260) situates it earlier, in 1948. It has become a powerful lobbying group, despite its internal differences. Radical elements, for example, wanted to form a political party in the Third Republic (Ahanotu 1992, 38).

[26] See, for example, Sanni 1983. Christians have complained about the restricted building of churches or even the dismantling of them as well as stoning of their gospel teams in the North. See Chukwulozie 1986, 182 (Appendix III, "Press Conference on the Position of New Life for All on Government Restriction of Religious Preaching Read by Its National Chairman, Rev. Luther D. Cishak, in Jos on June 27, 1984").

[27] Rev. Dr. Isaac Laudarji, senior pastor, ECWA church, Kano, personal communication, July 3, 1997. See also Crow and Nwankwo 1996, 173.

[28] See "Who Really Are the Majority?" *Today's Challenge* 6 (1986), 4-7, 32. Some Christians like to cite the local government elections during the Babangida era, when Christians won in Muslim areas. This was attributed to a greater effort on CAN's part to field candidates, but also to perhaps greater numbers of Christians than previously supposed or Muslim preferences for Christian candidates. Rev. Dr. E. O. Oyelade, personal communication, Ile-Ife, June 18, 1997.

[29] Prior to the Muslim-Christian conflict at the College of Education in Kafanchan in March 1987, which then spread to Kaduna, the Muslims had objected to the Christian students' erection of a banner saying "Welcome to Jesus Campus" as part of their Mission '87. The banner was removed (CAN Kaduna 1987, 84). The same report also contains a reference to the banning of house preaching. Eventually it was the derogatory interpretation of Muhammad's prophethood by guest evangelist Rev. Abubakar Bako, a former Muslim, during his revival address, that inflamed the sentiments of the Muslim Student Association. The ensuing clashes between Muslim and Christian students led to serious rioting, loss of life, and destruction of property, which then spread to neighboring cities such as Kaduna and Zaria. (For a Muslim interpretation of events, see the special issue of *Radiance* 8 [1987], the magazine of the Muslim Students Society.)

[30] For instance, a cartoon in *Al-Madinah* 1, no. 1 (September 1995), 7, mocks the Christian evangelist who tries to get the passengers of a bus to close their eyes "in Jesus' name"—even the bus driver!

[31] The 1996 Christian/Muslim clashes in Kumasi (an important commercial center in the middle of Ghana) were purportedly sparked off by an evangelist preaching at an open-air crusade that he had converted large numbers of "Alhajis." Information from Kwabena Asamoah-Gyadu, Birmingham, March 17, 1997.

[32] Converted Muslims Christian Ministry produces literature such as *The Qur'an in Light of the Bible?* by Ahmed K. Adjei (Kumasi: CMCM Publications, 1994).

[33] Matthews A. Ojo, personal communication, Ile-Ife, July 2, 1997. Cf. also Kukah 1993.

[34] Information from Umar Danfulani, Bayreuth, February 21, 1997.

[35] This was in part because the Muslim Students Society (MSS), originally founded in 1954 to counter the influence of the Christian evangelical student groups such as the Student Christian Movement (SCM), began to develop more radical and proselytizing tendencies in the 1970s, and allegedly received literature and funding from Iranian Muslims to challenge the secularism of the Nigerian state (Williams and Falola 1995, 177-79).

[36] For example, *Hotline* magazine, published by Alhaji Sani Kontagoro; *The Reporter* published by Major-General Shehu Musa Yar'adua; the *New Nigerian* and "Gaskiya ta Fi Kwabo" newspapers, owned by the Federal Government (see Minchakpu 1995, 9). In addition, there are the magazines of the Muslim Students Society, *al-Muezzin* (the Trumpet) and *Al'Ilm* (the Knowledge).

[37] Information from Professor H. O. Danmole, Birmingham, August 21, 1997.

[38] See Akintola 1995, 12-14. He cites, among other things, the use of derogatory terms to describe Muslims, and the playing of gospel music during Ramadan.

[39] Elder Saidu Dogo, secretary of the Christian Association of Nigeria, Kaduna, interview, July 2, 1997. He also spoke of CAN's campaign to have the NTA employ Christian newscasters in Kaduna.

[40] In fact, the Abacha government (1995) banned foreign Christian preachers from visiting the country for security reasons. This was interpreted as further evidence of the government's attempts to Islamize the country (see Minchakpu 1995, 9). Oyelade dates the restrictions on foreign Christian missionaries to much earlier, in 1983 (1994, 66). It seems not to have been enforced in any noticeable or lasting way.

[41] See "Drums of Discord" and "Shifting Centre," *The Source* (June 30, 1997).

[42] For instance, moves by the Nigerian government to introduce French as the second national language in Nigeria were publicly criticized by the Islamic Group of Nigeria. The national president contended that Arabic would be a more suitable choice given the number of Arabic speakers in Nigeria and neighboring countries and the fact that it is the official language of the Organization of Islamic Countries and the World Assembly of Muslim Youths, of which Nigeria is a full member. See *The Guardian* [Nigeria] (June 20, 1997).

[43] See Oyelade 1994, 69-70; see also the CAN publication, *Leadership in Nigeria*, which analyzes the religious breakdown of political appointments at state and federal levels.

[44] Interview with Sheikh Muhammad Gumi, "The Dirge," *Africa Events* (1987), 48-51.

[45] There was an interesting rebuttal of this by a journalist in the *Sunday Vanguard* (June 29, 1997, 7), who, using concrete examples, argues rather the contrary—that Christians dominate Nigerian politics and that neither the OIC nor D8 are Islamic organizations. In fact, this whole issue is guaranteed to elicit divergent opinions depending on the respondent's religious affiliation, location, educational status, and political knowledge.

[46] Interestingly, not all observers agree that Nigeria's dire economic straits are a recipe for interreligious tension. Rev. Fr. Professor Joseph Kenny points out that in

the period after Abacha came to power in 1993, there were no serious outbreaks of religiously related violence. Interview, Ibadan, June 27, 1997.

[47] Arguably, the type of dialogue fostered by nongovernmental organizations seems to have generated more harmony, perhaps because of the lower expectations and fewer stigma attached to such groups. There have been several academic efforts. See, for example, Dr. C. S. Momoh's National Association of Religious Tolerance, launched in 1987 with a seminar on religious tolerance and later followed by the publication of four impressive volumes of *Nigerian Studies in Religious Tolerance* (Momoh et al. 1988). The Nigerian Association for the Study of Religions published a volume in 1984, entitled *Religion, Peace and Unity in Nigeria*, edited by Sam Babs Mala and Z. I. Oseni. Until his sudden death in 1996, Mala was one of the key figures in Christian-Muslim dialogue in Nigeria. A more substantial volume appeared in 1993 with the financial support of then-president Babangida—*Studies in Religious Understanding in Nigeria,* edited by R. D. Abubakre et al. A seminar entitled "Inter-faith Dialogue between Christians and Muslims in Nigeria" was organized by the Africa Leadership Forum in Jos in October 1994. The conference jointly organized by Obafemi Awolowo University, Ile-Ife, and the Council for the World's Religions (U.S.) in Ife in December 1989, entitled "Religion and Peace in a Multi-Faith Nigeria," was later published (see Olupona 1992). Religious organizations, such as the Roman Catholic PROCMURA (Project for Christian-Muslim Relations in Africa), based in Nairobi, and the Lutheran Church, have sponsored various types of seminars and conferences on Muslim-Christian relations in Nigeria. I am less familiar with Muslim initiatives, apart from the conferences on Muslim/Christian Dialogue organized by the International Islamic Federation of Student Organizations (IIFSO).

[48] It was the Department of Religious Studies at the University of Ibadan that began the teaching of Islam in such a context. Even though the Muslim scholars departed to the Department of Arabic and Islamic Studies over the years, the teaching of courses on Islam persists, thanks to Rev. Fr. Professor Joseph Kenny. Similar courses have now spread to Catholic and other seminaries. The Universities of Jos and Ilorin, with their equal compositions of Christian and Islamic scholars and courses, provide an important statement of the need for mutual understanding. In the secondary school system, Islam, Christianity, and traditional religions are generally taught as part of social studies. Beyond that, religious education becomes more bifurcated in terms of Christian and Islamic Studies. There have been complaints from both Muslim and Christian parents in some areas of the country about discrimination or the absence of courses for their children.

[49] 1979 Constitution of the Federal Republic of Nigeria, chapter 1, section 10, and *The Constitution of the Federal Republic of Nigeria* (Promulgation) 1989, No. 12. Section 11 of the latter states: "The Government of the Federation or of a State shall not adopt any religion as State religion." Pending the promulgation of the Constitution written by the Constitutional Conference in 1995 and subsequently approved by the head of state, the government observes some provisions of the 1979 and 1989 Constitutions. The decree suspending the 1979 Constitution was not repealed, and the 1989 Constitution has not been implemented.

[50] Ironically, some would argue that it is the rise in Christian militancy and self-defense (predominantly through the agency of the activist Christian Association of Nigeria) since 1992 that is serving as a check and balance on Muslim extremist activities.

[51] In fact, a report by the Political Bureau (constituted by the Babangida government) stated in 1987 that Nigerians want a political system of government that will ensure religious freedom. The report further claimed that "in most of these contributions the case was consistently made that Nigerians are a religious people and that to whatever creed they belong, they all desired to live in peace and worship in peace" (186). Cited in Minchakpu 1995, 6.

[52] For example, "The Blood-Bath We Must Avoid," *The Analyst* 3, no. 5 (September-October 1988), 5; "Religion in Africa: A Time Bomb?" *African Concord* (March 18, 1988), 6-7.

BIBLIOGRAPHY

Abubakre, Razaq D., et al., eds. 1993. *Studies in Religious Understanding in Nigeria.* Ilorin: Nigerian Association for the Study of Religions.

Ahanotu, Austin. 1992. "Muslims and Christians in Nigeria: A Contemporary Political Discourse," in *Religion, State and Society in Contemporary Africa,* edited by Austin Metumara Ahanotu, 11-70. New York: Peter Lang.

Akinrinade, Olusola, and M. A. Ojo. 1992. "Religion and Politics in Contemporary Nigeria: A Study of the 1986 OIC Crisis," *Journal of Asian and African Affairs* 4 (Fall): 44-59.

Akintola, Lakin. 1995. "Who Is a Fanatic?" *Al Madinah* 1, no. 1 (September): 10-18.

Ashafa, Ustaz Muhammad Nurayn, and Evangelist James Movel Wuye. 1999. *The Pastor and the Imam Responding to Conflict.* Lagos: Ibrash Islamic Publications.

Atanda, J. A., Garba Ashiwaju, and Yaya Abubakar, eds. 1989. *Nigeria since Independence: The First Twenty-Five Years.* Volume 9, *Religion.* Ibadan: Heinemann.

Awolalu, J. O. 1989. "Traditional Religion in Nigeria: A Liturgico-Cultural Viewpoint," in Atanda 1989, 9:25-40.

Bello, Omar. 1987. "The Dirge," *African Events* (August): 48-51.

Benavides, Gustavo. 1989. "Religious Articulation of Power," in *Religion and Political Power,* edited by Gustavo Benavides and M. W. Daly. Albany: State University of New York Press.

CAN (Christian Association of Nigeria) Kaduna. 1987. *Kaduna Religious Riots '87.* Kaduna: CAN Kaduna Publicity Committee.

Casanova, Jose. 1994. *Public Religions in the Modern World.* Chicago: University of Chicago Press.

Christelow, Allan. 1985. "The 'Yan Tatsine Disturbances in Kano—A Search for Perspective," *The Muslim World* 75, no. 2 (April): 69-84.

Christian Association of Nigeria (CAN). N.d. *Leadership in Nigeria.* C.A.N. Publicity Northern Zone.

Chukwulozie, Victor. 1986. *Muslim-Christian Dialogue in Nigeria.* Ibadan: Daystar Press.

Crow, Melissa, and Clement Nwankwo. 1996. "Before 'Things Fall Apart' in Nigeria," in *Vigilance and Vengeance: NGOs Preventing Conflict in Divided Societies,* edited by Robert I. Rotberg. Washington, D.C.: Brookings Institution.

Gaiya, Musa A. B. 1997. "The Press and Religious Politics in Nigeria: The Role of *Today's Challenge," Jos Studies* 7, no. 1 (June): 50-58.

Gifford, Paul. 1987. "African Shall Be Saved: An Appraisal of Reinhard Bonnke's Pan-African Crusade," *Journal of Religion in Africa* 17, no. 1: 63-92.

———. 1991. *The New Crusaders: Christianity and the New Right in Southern Africa*. London: Pluto Press.

———. 1993. "Reinhard Bonnke's Mission to Africa: And His 1991 Nairobi Crusade," in *New Dimensions in African Christianity*, edited by Paul Gifford. Ibadan: Seter.

Hackett, Rosalind I. J. 1989. *Religion in Calabar: The Religious Life and History of a Nigerian Town*. New York: Mouton de Gruyter.

———. 1991. "Revitalization in African Traditional Religion," in *African Traditional Religions in Contemporary Society*, edited by J. K. Olupona, 135-48. New York: Paragon House.

———. 1993. "The Symbolics of Power Discourse among Contemporary Religious Groups in West Africa," in *Religious Transformations and Socio-Political Change*, edited by L. Martin, 381-401. Berlin: Mouton de Gruyter.

———. 1996. "New Directions for African and Asian Charismatics," *Pneuma* 18, no. 1 (Spring): 69-77.

———. 1998. "Charismatic/Pentecostal Appropriation of Media Technologies in Ghana and Nigeria," *Journal of Religion in Africa* 28, no. 3: 258-77.

———. In press. "Conflict in the Classroom: Educational Institutions as Sites of Religious Tolerance/Intolerance in Nigeria," *Brigham Young Law Review*.

———. *Nigeria: Religion in the Balance*. Forthcoming. Washington, D.C.: US Institute of Peace.

Hock, Klaus. 1996. *Der Islam-Komplex*. Hamburger Theologische Studien 7. Hamburg: LIT.

Hunwick, John O., ed. 1992. *Religion and National Integration in Africa: Islam, Christianity, and Politics in the Sudan and Nigeria*. Evanston, Ill.: Northwestern University Press.

Ibrahim, Jibrin. 1989. "The Politics of Religion in Nigeria: The Parameters of the 1987 Crisis in Kaduna State," *Review of African Political Economy* 45, no. 6: 65-82.

———. 1991. "Religion and Political Turbulence in Nigeria," *The Journal of Modern African Studies* 29, no. 1: 115-36.

Ilesanmi, Simeon. 1995. "The Myth of a Secular State: A Study of Religious Politics with Historical Illustrations," *Islam and Christian-Muslim Relations* 6, no. 1: 105-17.

———. 1996. *Religious Pluralism and the Nigerian State*. Athens, Ohio: Ohio University Press.

Kalu, Ogbu U. 1989. "Religions in Nigeria: An Overview," in Atanda 1989, 9:11-24.

Kastfelt, Niels. 1989. "Rumours of Maitatsine: A Note on Political Culture in Northern Nigeria," *African Affairs* 88, no. 350: 83-90.

Kukah, Matthew Hassan. 1992. "The Politicisation of Fundamentalism in Nigeria," in *New Dimensions in African Christianity*, edited by Paul Gifford, 183-206. Nairobi: All Africa Conference of Churches.

———. 1993. *Religion, Politics and Power in Northern Nigeria*. Ibadan: Spectrum Books.

———. 1995. "Christians and Nigeria's Aborted Transition," in *The Christian Churches and the Democratisation of Africa*, edited by Paul Gifford, 224-38. Leiden: E. J. Brill.

Lawrence, Bruce B. 1989. *Defenders of God: The Fundamentalist Revolt against the Modern Age*. San Francisco: Harper & Row.

Loimeier, Roman. 1997. *Islamic Reform and Political Change in Northern Nigeria.* Evanston, Ill.: Northwestern University Press.

Mala, Sam Babs, and Z. I. Oseni, eds. 1984. *Religion, Peace and Unity in Nigeria.* Ibadan: Nigerian Association for the Study of Religions.

Marshall, Ruth. 1991. "Power in the Name of Jesus," *Review of African Political Economy* 52: 21-37.

——. 1993. "'Power in the Name of Jesus': Social Transformation and Pentecostalism in Western Nigeria 'Revisited,'" in *Legitimacy and the State in Twentieth Century Africa.* London: Macmillan.

——. 1995. "'God Is Not a Democrat': Pentecostalism and Democratisation in Nigeria," in *The Christian Churches and the Democratisation of Africa*, edited by Paul Gifford, 239-60. Leiden: E. J. Brill.

Martin, David. 1990. *Tongues of Fire: The Explosion of Christianity in Latin America.* Oxford: Blackwell.

Mbembe, Achille. 1988. *Afriques Indociles: Christianisme, Pouvoir et Etat en Socété Postcoloniale.* Paris: Karthala.

Minchakpu, Obed Bassau. 1995. "An Islamic Manifesto?" *Today's Challenge* 3: 8-9.

——. 1996. "Religion and Politics in Nigeria," *Today's Challenge* 1: 6-9.

Momoh, C. S., C. O. Onikpepe, and Victor Chukwulozie, eds. 1987, *Nigerian Studies in Religious Tolerance.* Lagos: Centre for Black and African Arts and Civilization and National Association for Religious Tolerance.

Mozia, M. I. 1989. "Religion and Morality in Nigeria: An Overview," in Atanda 1989, 9:168-83.

Mutua, Makau Wa. 1996. "Limitations on Religious Rights: Problematizing Religious Freedom in the African Context," in *Religious Human Rights in Global Perspective*, edited by J. D. van der Vyver and J. Witte Jr., 417-40. The Hague: Martinus Nijhoff.

National Institute for Policy and Strategic Studies. 1986. *Religious Disturbances in Nigeria.* Kuru.

Ojo, Matthews A. 1988. "The Contextual Significance of the Charismatic Movements in Independent Nigeria," *Africa* 58, no. 2: 175-92.

——. 1997. "The Dynamics of Indigenous Charismatic Missionary Enterprises in West Africa." Paper presented at a conference entitled "African Initiatives in Christian Mission," University of South Africa, January 13-17.

Okafor, F. U., ed. 1997. *New Strategies for Curbing Ethnic and Religious Conflicts in Nigeria.* Ibadan: Spectrum Books.

Olupona, Jacob K. 1989. "The Dynamics of Religion and Interfaith Dialogue in Nigeria." A Keynote Address presented at the Council for the World's Religions and Obafemi Awolowo University Conference on Religion and Peace.

——, ed. 1992. *Religion and Peace in a Multi-Faith Nigeria.* Ife: The author.

Olupona, Jacob K., and Rosalind I. J. Hackett. 1991. "Civil Religion," in *Religion and Society in Nigeria*, edited by Jacob K. Olupona and Toyin Falola, 265-81. Ibadan: Spectrum.

Oyelade, E. O. 1994. "Politics and Religion in Nigeria: A Christian Perspective on Dialogue," *The Bulletin of the Henry Martyn Institute of Islamic Studies* 13, no. 3/4 (July-December): 62-75.

Ryan, Patrick. 1996. "Islam in Ghana: Its Major Influences and the Situation Today," *Orita* 28, no. 1/2 (June and December): 70-84.

Sanneh, Lamin O. 1983. *West African Christianity: The Religious Impact*. London: Hurst.

Sanni, Ishaq K. 1983. "Who Really Are the Fanatics?" *Al Ilm* (June-September).

Sanni, Ishaq K., and Dawood Ayodele Amoo. 1987. *Why You Should Never Be a Christian*. Ibadan: Iman Publications.

Sulaiman, Muhammad Dahiru. 1993. "Shiaism and the Islamic Movement in Nigeria 1979-1991," *Islam et Sociétés au Sud du Sahara* 7 (novembre): 5-16.

Takaya, Bala J. 1989/90. "The Kaduna Mafia and the Church in Nigeria," *Bulletin of Ecumenical Theology* 2, no. 2/3, 1:6-15.

TEKAN (The Fellowship of Churches of Christ in Nigeria). 1987. *Toward the Right Path for Nigeria*. Jos: TEKAN.

Tsado, Jacob. 1986. "Counterfeit Christmas: The Story of a Fake Messiah," *Today's Challenge* 6: 12-13.

Udoidem, Sylvanus I. 1997. "Religion in the Political Life of Nigeria: A Survey of Religious-Related Crises in Nigeria since Independence," in Okafor 1997, 152-83.

Umar, Muhammad Sani. 1993. "Changing Islamic Identity in Nigeria from the 1960s to the 1980s: From Sufism to Anti-Sufism," in *Muslim Identity and Social Change in Sub-Saharan Africa*, edited by L. Brenner, 154-87. London: Hurst and Co.

Umechukwu, Panta O. J. 1995. *The Press Coverage of Religious Violence in Nigeria*. Enugu: Ugovin Publishers.

Usman, Yusufu Bala. 1987. *The Manipulation of Religion in Nigeria: 1977-1987*. Kaduna, Nigeria: Vanguard.

Westerlund, David. 1992. "Secularism, Civil Religion, or Islam? Islamic Revivalism and the National Question in Nigeria," in *Religion, State and Society in Contemporary Africa*, edited by Austin Metumara Ahanotu, 71-101. New York: Peter Lang.

Williams, Pat, and Toyin Falola. 1995. *Religious Impact on the Nigerian State: The Nigerian Predicament*. Aldershot, UK: Avebury.

11.

RELIGIOUS FRAGMENTATION IN KENYA

—————◆—————

Hannah W. Kinoti

On 30 April 1997, the Kenyan dailies carried an item entitled "Pastoral Letter from Church and State Co-operation on Development" (*East African Standard* 1997, 11; *Kenya Times* 1997, 3; *Daily Nation* 1997, 29). The committee of bishops and lower-ranking clergy that published that advertisement claimed to represent some 291 denominations spread over the nine districts of Nyanza Province. This province is the home of the second largest ethnic community in Kenya, the Luo. There is a small minority of other ethnic groups in the province. The advertisement was a rejoinder against "other" Christians in the Luo community who were critical of this group of churches for fraternizing with political elements in the country. For our purposes this implies that there are other denominations or religious groups besides the 291 mentioned. Some of the "other" denominations are the historical mission-founded denominations including the Roman Catholic Church, the Anglican Church, and Seventh-day Adventists.

A closer look at the sociocultural and religious scene of Nyanza indicates that for an ethnic group otherwise fairly homogeneous culturally and even politically, religion is the one thing that subdivides the Luo community into small sections. Clans and families have been split up to such an extent that some "Christian denominations" have as few as one hundred members, complete with the hierarchical church government common to most churches worldwide. Usually the membership of such small denominations coincides with the extended family and growing children become members automatically. However, upon moving out of the family group, the youth may drift to other religious groups or may start their own denominations.

The exact number of religious groups in Nyanza is unknown as new ones continue to emerge. Although Nyanza is reputed to have the highest number of religious groups, the picture in the rest of the country, especially Central and Western Provinces, is not very different. Kenya has some forty-two ethnic groups with an estimated population of thirty-two million people and an estimated six thousand religious groups. The exact figure is unknown due to a number of factors. Research and documentation lag far behind the religious situation in Kenya. The government does not seem to have adequate machinery to monitor new religious groups that are constantly in the making. Some of the groups are not even aware of the requirement for registration by the Registrar of Societies. Furthermore, de-registration of groups does not guarantee their cessation. In recent years the government has been reluctant to register certain groups, on the grounds that they may be a threat to peace and security. But there are many groups that do not give up for what they consider unfounded government fears.

Religious diversity is not new among Kenya's indigenous peoples. The society is characterized by ethnic entities, each of which traditionally lays claim to a comprehensive way of life and religion as part of that way of life. The religious expressions of the different indigenous peoples were never uniform, but then they did not run into thousands! It is to be noted, however, that traditional African societies do not have a word for religion. In other words, traditionally "religion" has not been a distinct department of life which one can enter and leave at will. Religion has been an integral part of everyday life, a life nevertheless "sanctified" in both simple and elaborate ritual (Zuesse 1979). The traditional African sociocultural environment enabled individuals to define their identity, and gave them a large measure of dignity and confidence as they progressed along the ritual path of life and as they participated in the daily round of activities. For the individual person the most important rituals were centered in the home. What Louis Leakey says about the Gikuyu of Central Kenya is true of other ethnic groups. He maintains that belief in God was the fundamental basis of life. "Religion held each family together, united the inhabitants of every village, bound together the inhabitants of the various villages of a territorial unit and gave the cohesion that was essential to their mutual security" (Leakey 1977, 16-17). Indeed, according to Leakey's informants, the wrath of God visited and punished people when the inhabitants of different villages became too independent of one another. God "persisted in punishing them until they became united once more by joint acts of public worship and sacrifice" (ibid.).

God's rules were also believed to be specific on matters of personal and public morality as well as in inter-ethnic relations among neighboring ethnic groups. Religious beliefs militated against the hatred and the anarchy that are so easily fueled in present-day society. This more or less homogeneous and integrated situation was suddenly and rudely interrupted by colonialism—the political, cultural, and economic subjugation of African society by Western powers (Cowan et al. 1965; Tignor 1976; Rosberg and Nottingham 1966). In the case of Kenya it was the British colonial power.

The thesis of this chapter is that in the last hundred years, ever since the entry of Christian missionaries into Kenya, human rights in terms of freedom of conscience have been greatly undermined. The Kenyan indigenous population has been subjected, without due respect to its religious heritage, to a great deal of pressure to decide for Jesus, Allah, and lately, Asian deities. In the context of rapid social change, spiritual insecurity is one of several insecurities the African society is suffering. The most affected institution of society is the family, notably the youth. Within the memory of some, the family has shifted from being a bulwark of support and the central point of reference and identity for an individual to becoming irrelevant in matters of religion.

RELIGIOUS DIVERSITY IN KENYA: AN OVERVIEW

In 1920 the borders of what then came to be known as the Kenya Colony and Protectorate of the British Empire were placed on the map. The main port along Kenya's coastline, Mombasa, had been placed on the world map as Manfasa in about 1150 by Adrisi, a geographer who lived in Sicily. Egyptian, Arab, Indian and Chinese traders are said to have had trade links with the East African coastal peoples since around 3580 B.C. The Indian name for Mombasa was Mumbai-sa ("quite like Mumbai"—Mumbai was the name for Bombay; the distance between them by sea was only 1,760 miles). In 1331 Ibin Battuta, a renowned West African traveler, visited Kenya's coast and recorded in his writings that the people of Mombasa were pious Muslims. By 1500 Mombasa was importing cloth from India (Maggoye 1986).

In spite of these early contacts Kenya had with the outside world, Islam did not penetrate Kenya's hinterland and Asian religions do not seem to have been a package with trade. Inland communities enjoyed their tribal religions or world views until the turn of the twentieth century when Kenya was colonized along with other African countries. The Portuguese had attempted to introduce Christianity in the sixteenth century, and the Catholic faith flourished in the coastal region for a hundred years. However, in 1631 Muslims massacred several hundred Christians, and by 1729 Arabs had regained control of Mombasa. In 1890, after the first wave of the modern era of missionaries had begun, Catholic missionaries found only fifty Goans in Mombasa (Barrett et al. 1973, 30).

The evangelization of Kenya and Africa needs to be seen against the background of changing conditions in Europe and America in the eighteenth and nineteenth centuries. In Europe the Industrial Revolution brought about rapid expansion of industrial cities with corresponding expansion of urban population and resulting social problems. The Church was aroused to the urgent need for missionary work among the urban population, and this was much encouraged by the evangelical revival movement, which addressed itself to social reforms on a voluntary basis. So missionary work had been going on in Europe and America before attention was turned to Africa. This was the period of the slave trade. Moving stories by explorers and traders about human misery under the slave trade and of the "Dark Continent" which was "ignorant" of the Gospel aroused much interest. Though some missionary societies preceded colonial powers, on the whole, missionary activities coincided with the scramble for and partition of Africa by European powers.

In Kenya the missionary entered with the trader, the settler, and the administrator. They were all empire builders. At first, however, missionaries were not interested in Kenya. Some were interested in reaching Galla country, lying to the north of Kenya and south of Ethiopia, where an ancient Christian civilization was supposed to be found. Others were interested in Uganda, the "cradle of the Nile," and the railway from Mombasa to Kisumu was built in 1901 in order to open the way to Uganda. However, failure to reach Galla and the completion of the railway to Kisumu in 1901 together with the protection accorded by the British colonial administration meant that Kenya became rapidly settled. Between 1906 and 1916 there were fourteen different missionary groups operating in different parts of the country and running schools. Two late arrivals raised the number to sixteen in the mid-1930s, so that an observer who surveyed the scene concluded that there was no need for more societies or more missionaries (Groves 1955, 187; Barrett et al. 1973, 33-34). Competition for influence in the African countryside was inevitable, especially as the missionary groups differed in backgrounds and were not altogether sympathetic with each other.

A United Missionary Conference held in June 1909 had discussed the embarrassing problem of Christian disunity among missions working in Kenya (Mungeam 1978, 153-61). Church Missionary Society (C.M.S.) delegate J. J. Willis read a paper entitled "The Desirability of a Common Native Church" (1909) in which he urged the formation of a single native church in British East Africa (Kenya) (ibid., 153).[1] Even then Rev. Willis warned that the effort was doomed to failure due to three main reasons: First, the Protestant church had gone too far since the Reformation toward individualism. In Willis's words:

> From some points of view one may well be tempted to save further time by at once giving up the question as, for the present at least, insoluble. From the time of the Reformation onwards, the tendency of the Protestant Church has been towards disintegration. The Great doctrine of individual right as of private judgment has been so developed as to threaten to destroy all authority and all regard for antiquity, and to split up our Protestant Christianity into a thousand mutually independent, and often antagonistic sects. And so far every effort to reunite them has ended in *failure*. Where so many earnest, thoughtful, and prayerful efforts have failed, it may well seem presumption and mere waste of time on our part, to repeat the same attempt, with the prospect it may be of a similar failure (ibid., 153).

Second, the missionaries already working in Kenya represented churches separated by major differences: "When we think of the differences between Presbyterian and Episcopalian, between Quaker and Seventh-day Adventist, and the all but impossibility of ever reconciling them in this world, we may pause appalled at the hopelessness of any attempt to reconcile such extremes" (ibid.). Third, Willis regretted that the missionaries were not free agents and could not act without involving and compromising societies and churches which they represented. He saw the best they could do was to maintain friendly relations while carrying on the work each had started.

One might wonder why the missionaries bothered to discuss the matter of unity at all, but the Lambeth Conference of the Anglican Communion had just met and had expressed the need for "effective and visible co-operation" between the workers in the mission field. The missionaries in Kenya did make concrete steps to cooperate by establishing the Alliance but did not entirely eliminate competition and a certain amount of antagonism over spheres of influence.

Western education in colonial Kenya was initially entirely in the hands of Christian missions as the colonial government was slow in getting involved. When Africans began to appreciate the value of Western formal education, parents sent their children to any mission school because their priority was education over denominationalism. Missionaries, on their part, used education as a strategy in their double mission to evangelize and to civilize. School and church were places people went to in order to practice Christianity. Depending on which schools children had attended, families begun to discover that different members of the same family belonged to different denominations. Sometimes that trend of things proved dysfunctional in terms of family relations. This has been compounded by the increasing proliferation of Christian groups.

MISSIONARY METHODS AND SOCIAL TRANSFORMATION OF KENYAN SOCIETY

The colonial era of missionary enterprise on the whole targeted the youth in order to fulfill the double mission of evangelizing and civilizing. The general assumption that Africans were at the bottom of the evolutionary ladder of civilization and that missionaries had the mandate from God to uplift the African gave them a rare impetus to work. In this one respect the missionaries were united. Theirs was an outlook which "denied any culture of value in Africa" (Hastings 1976; Fortes and Dieterlen 1965, 31; Cowan et al. 1965, 4-5) and held that "everything in non-Christian religions was evil" (Vidler 1961, 252). It was an outlook which believed in the utter superiority of Western culture. Africa, by contrast, was the "Dark Continent," ignorant of the way of salvation and civilization. Missionaries had a Gospel to preach and a lifestyle to commend. Their ultimate message, from their point of view, was the "freedom of Christ's empty tomb." It implied freedom from the ignorance of past centuries, from slavery to malign spirits, from barriers to human progress imposed by tribal custom, and from restraint from social and economic life imposed by untamed natural forces (Murray-Brown 1972, 41).

To the missionaries, the slavery of the African under the European in the West Coast, and the Arab in the East Coast, was but an outward manifestation of the real dire yoke from which the African had to be freed. A few missionary reports can be cited by way of illustration. Writing in 1917, Parlo, a Catholic pioneer missionary with the Consolata Mission, described Gikuyu life as he had judged it in 1902 as "essentially deplorable, barbarous, inhuman." According to Parlo, "every moral principle in which our civilization glories and which our religion commands is . . . simply reversed" (Cagnolo 1933, 257). Parlo explains that the "crude reality" of the conditions which the missionaries found became "the basis and impulse of all the extensive civilizing missionary work, which has been carried out in subsequent years" (ibid., 254).

At the 1909 United Missionary Conference already referred to, an African Inland Mission (A.I.M.) missionary, W. P. Knapp, is on record as saying that "only the enemy of righteousness could have been responsible for the customs and superstitions of these natives [the Gikuyu among whom he was a missionary]." Knapp cited some Gikuyu customs which he recommended should be actively "deprecated" because, in his opinion, "there are many social and domestic customs which could never be associated with decent living to say nothing of Christian living" (Mungeam 1978, 166-68, 171-203).

In a book significantly entitled *Beyond the Kikuyu Curtain*, Helen Virginia Blakeslee, another A.I.M. missionary among the Gikuyu, from 1911 to 1954, gives her description of the land in which she was evangelizing: "Kikuyu land . . . has been dominated by the prince of darkness for past ages. The flooding of the district with the light of the gospel has revealed the hidden things of darkness, the character and source of every evil tribal custom" (Blakeslee 1956, 7). Naturally for Blakeslee, conversion to Christianity for a young girl who was torn between home and mission station was simply a decision to "leave the paths of the Agikuyu to take the path of God" (ibid., 34).

Arthur Barlow of the Church of Scotland Mission among the Gikuyu concluded a report on the peculiarities of the Gikuyu, who had "a religion of a kind, though it be ignorant and perverted," by saying: "Such are the characteristics of the people whom the Church of Scotland Mission, with missions from other churches, is working to win for the Kingdom of Christ and assist to advance in the scale of humanity" (Barlow 1923, 29).

Before giving the highlights of missionary civilizing/proselytizing work we can note one or two pertinent comments by missionaries who were active in the mission field. Barlow continues in his article on the Gikuyu by observing: "Civilization has come upon them with a rush since the first white men came amongst them. Many influences are now extended upon them which are changing their ideas and their manner of life for good and for evil" (ibid.). Likewise Cagnolo, writing in 1933, states that "a good number of families, Christian or merely emancipated from barbarous customs, have adopted a standard of living with lodgings, diet, and manner which border on the civilized" (Cagnolo 1933, 258).

THE MAKING OF "KUSOMA" CHRISTIANS

Referring specifically to the Scottish missionaries who built a mission center at Thogoto (the name is a corruption of *Scotland*), Jomo Kenyatta's biographer, Jeremy Murray-Brown, describes them as "Christian Zealots pursuing the best ideals of Western Society at that time: order and obedience; the team spirit, courage and self-sacrifice; pride in tradition and in the wearing of uniforms, cleanliness, punctuality and honesty, respect for . . . women" (Murray-Brown 1972, 46).

Barlow described the general missionary objective in education: "The aim of Christian Education among a primitive people must always be to develop mind and character rather than the impart of information" (Barlow 1923, 31). The missionaries set to work to instill discipline in every aspect of life for the moral uplift of the mission boys. Murray-Brown (1972, 47) quotes Dr. Arthur, a C.M.S. doctor who spearheaded the fight against female circumcision, in part as saying:

> Drill and physical jerks helped "promote order and obedience." The Boys' Brigade . . . with uniforms provided by well-wishers in Scotland, was "a bracing influence." The first thing the boys received on returning from holidays was a good scrubbing before they were issued clean shirts: "they looked so nice, fresh and clean when we assembled for a game of football . . . which was played . . . for moral benefit . . . to stiffen the backbone of these boys by teaching them manliness, good temper and unselfishness—qualities amongst many others that have done so much for a Britisher" (ibid.).

As Murray-Brown observes, hymns and prayers, indoor games and football were all meant "to turn the old savage Adam into the purposefulness of the new Christian. And above it all floated the Union Jack, a symbol of the earthly power which made this work of God possible" (ibid.).

Missionaries from other mission societies were performing similar operations wherever they were working. The A.I.M. was at first keen on sole evangelism, but a pioneer missionary, Willis Ray Hotchkiss, who had arrived in 1895 found the A.I.M. policy unsatisfactory. When he returned to the country six years later he joined the Friends Africa Industrial Mission to teach carpentry, brickmaking, and farming. These skills were vital for the "elite" Christian community destined to separate from surrounding heathenism, as oil and water separate. To give another example, J. J. Willis, the C.M.S. missionary already mentioned, wanted to give elite education to sons of Luo chiefs. The Luo thought they were outwitting him by sending him, at Maseno School, only youth who were social rejects. When after fifteen years Maseno mission boys began to replace Luo traditional rulers as the new ruling class in colonial Kenya, Luo children began to flock to school in large numbers. Indeed, Western education turned out to be the most popular missionary method, especially when combined with Western medicine and evangelism (Barrett et al. 1973, 33).

This method however, succeeded in producing what has come to be known as *Kusoma* Christianity. (*Kusoma* is a Swahili word meaning "to learn" or "to be educated.") For several decades such Christians, known as *asomi*, the "educated ones," were characterized not so much by an inner Christian piety (though some were truly converted), but by an outward appearance of Western dress (initially calico cloth for women and khaki drill shorts for men; white shorts and shirts were particularly popular among the Luo), some acquisition of the European "magic" of reading and writing (enough to enable the new class of colonial "elite" among the African underdogs to follow simple written instructions), square-shaped houses in place of the common African round-shaped dwellings (to admit light for the purposes of reading the Bible), and new "Christian" names (Oliver 1952, 214; Oduyoye 1977, 69).

The new African Christians who emerged were a mixture of many things. Many were alienated from their families due to the prohibitions imposed on them by the missionaries. Many became unsure of themselves. Going out to evangelize their own people as catechists or evangelists they had to confine themselves to what missionaries had taught them directly or the missionary tradition of the respective missionary society. Inevitably, denominationalism was perpetuated in the spirit of rivalry and competition—sometimes leading even to hostility. This was aggravated when members of the same family converted to different denominations. Constrained in a straitjacket as they were under colonial subjugation and yet not being of low intelligence as Africans were supposed to be (Leys 1924), some reacted through religious schisms and renewals. Others found respite in formalism, and others still became Christian in name only. Evidently, however, most became hypocritically loyal to missionary teachings—their resentment and even regret being only admitted in confidential conversations. To give an example, a retired church minister interviewed by Gathii (1966) spoke of missionary strong-arm policies when he said:

> Missionaries confused fundamental theology with superficiality. When the Church was under them they taught us "loyalty, loyalty, loyalty" without realizing that the elders they appointed to assist them would have anything to contribute. They called us pagans and compelled us to leave behind our former customs and beliefs. We were confused and did not realize that we might have retained some of the things.

Pioneer "mission girls" also regret that they should have been rendered so inadequate to teach their own children. One, for instance, confesses that they "chastise" themselves when they realize belatedly that giving a child a Bible to read is no substitute for parental guidance. Another explains that they stopped teaching their children because the only knowledge they had and which they might have passed on to their children was the "tribal" cultural heritage which they were advised was not good.

Carey Francis was a prominent missionary educator who was headmaster of two leading mission schools, Maseno and Alliance high schools respectively. Francis complained about the ridiculous length to which formalism went:

> Sunday after Sunday we say, "I admit that God is our Father" . . . a vast majority of those who say so leave it at that, and it has never occurred to them that they were meant to do anything else . . . the answer to every problem of conduct is "Pray!" . . . The average heathen would say to be a Christian meant to have one wife, to read, not to drink or work on Sundays. The average Christian would say the same but would add: "to pray to God." I doubt whether ten percent would say anything about Jesus Christ. One of our best boys (at Maseno) told me how . . . he gave away his testament as soon as he was baptized. He had received his "name"; what more use was the Book? It is a pretty common attitude (Greaves 1969, 36-37).

A study carried out on Church discipline in one of the Church denominations in Kenya led to the conclusion that the people had hurried to modern secularism never having met Christ (Gathii 1966, 47).

Some observers of the whole missionary enterprise within the context of colonialism have questioned the real worth of the transformation being effected in individuals and families in the name of Christianity. Oliver (1952, 213-14) sees the industrial education, which was aimed at enabling African Christians to adopt certain new economic and social standards, as lifting the Africans out of their own society only to enmesh them in European economic enterprise. This was certainly the case because the colonial land policies, native labor policies, heavy taxation, and restrictions on the growing of cash crops were deliberate moves to impoverish the Africans without distinguishing whether they were Christian or pagan (Leys 1924, 184-85, 298; Ross 1927, 99). In an annual report on one district in Central Kenya, H. E. Lambert, the district commissioner regretted that "individualism is the most obvious political trend . . . and it has developed . . . with such rapidity that it constitutes the most serious threat to the structure of society based not long ago on its very anti-thesis" (File LAMB/1/6, University of Nairobi Archives). Lambert suggested that Europeans had a duty to help the natives to return to "some sort of social stability" since "it was our own infringement of his social system which removed him from the position of equilibrium he had achieved for himself before our advent" (ibid.). Generally the European employers in Kenya preferred to employ "raw" Africans from the "bush" rather than "mission boys" because according to popular belief in their circles the former were reliable (Turnbull 1962). The anthropologist Colin Turnbull recorded his observations of Kenya from his visit during the colonial period. He found that after all the civilizing work white settlers asserted "with surprising frequency that they would never employ Christian 'boys' because they are so unreliable; they lie and steal and cause trouble. . . . [They] prefer to draw their staff 'from the bush,' where 'the native is unspoiled'" (ibid., 27).

Reference can be made to the disillusionment expressed by those who directly received Christian missionaries' proselytization and colonial subjugation. Writing in 1938 out of political grievance, Kenyatta laments:

> Religious rites and hallowed traditions are no longer observed by the whole community. Moral rules are broken with impunity, for in place of unified tribal morality there is now . . . a welter of disturbing influences, rules and sanctions, whose net result is only that a Gikuyu does not know what he may or may not, ought or ought not to do or believe but which leave him in no doubt at all about having broken the original morality of his people (Kenyatta 1938, 251).

African Independent Churches (variously referred to as African Initiated Churches and African Instituted Churches) began to break away from mission Christianity in a bid to inculturate the Gospel in African culture and to break loose from white missionary domination. These churches broke away and continue to do so in circumstances of felt oppression and disillusionment. The government, both colonial and post-colonial, has persistently disapproved of these churches' attempts to assert African rights to self-determination. These rights encroach on politics, which is a sensitive issue in Kenya. For instance, John Owalo, who initiated the Nomiya Luo Church in 1914, had changed allegiance from Church of England to Islam, then to the Roman Catholic Church before the visionary experience that led to his quest for "a place to feel at home." Nomiya is Luo for "I was given," meaning, "I was given God's Word." When he was taken to task by the colonial authorities for his activities, he retorted: "Leave me to preach. I am preaching to Africans, not to whites." In 1927 Dini ya Roho (Holy Ghost Church) broke away from the American Friends African Mission, and its leaders began preaching against foreign religious leadership and calling for the expulsion from Kenya of the American missionaries.

Even though African religion had been denied or regarded as ignorant and perverted, it was an integral part of African culture which had given Africans the equilibrium Lambert and others recognize existed. The ongoing proselytizing took its toll on the people in terms of loss of dignity and confidence, and a definite decline in morality.

NAIROBI AND ITS HISTORICAL ROOTS OF DIVERSITY

Kenya, as already noted, has a reputation for religious pluralism, and Nairobi, its capital city and hub, explains this pluralism. Major world religions to be found in Nairobi include Christianity, Islam, Hinduism, Sikhism, Jainism, and

Judaism, each preserving many elements of its sociocultural origins, little altered through centuries of history. In Nairobi, Christianity is the most fragmented, with Catholic, Anglican, and Protestant groups sharing adherents with a fast-growing number of African Independent Churches which are movements of schisms from and renewals within the older, mission-related Christian churches. In recent years, Nairobi has also become host to an ever-increasing number of new religious movements, some of which display elements of Pentecostalism, Eastern mysticism, African culture, or a blend of two or more of these elements.

FOUNDATIONS OF RELIGIOUS PLURALISM IN NAIROBI

Religious pluralism in Nairobi can be attributed to the following four factors.

1. FAST INFLUX OF RACES AND COLONIAL APARTHEID POLICY

Nairobi is a cosmopolitan city, and from the very beginning of its relatively short history its population has been multiracial and multiethnic. In 1899, the Uganda railway line, under construction from the coastal town of Mombasa, reached the swampy plain by the Nairobi River. Within three months the line was open for public transport to and from the Kenya coast. Although there was already an existing safari camp since 1890, the influx of newcomers was such as to warrant it being described in 1900 as a "tin-pot mushroom township," and "the most lawless dangerous spot in Africa." Nairobi was fast settled by a European colonial community which included soldiers, settlers, traders, hunters, colonial administrators, and missionaries—all Christians by classification. Of the thirty-two thousand workers imported from India for the construction of the railway line, sixty-seven hundred stayed in Kenya permanently. The majority settled in Nairobi and included Muslims, Hindus, Parsis, Sikhs, and Jains (Barrett 1982, 432-33).

European and Asian Settlements

Nairobi began as a colonial urban center. The initial settlement conformed to the colonial policy of apartheid, according to which European and Asian urban subsystems were to develop separately in specially segregated areas. Accordingly, by 1912 Nairobi's population consisted of 2,235 Europeans living on 2,700 acres of the higher, more picturesque parts of the municipality, and 4,300 Asians (mostly Indians) crowded in a "noisome squalid ghetto" of no more than 7 acres in the Indian Bazaar on either side of Nairobi River (Leys 1924, 286-87).

Through the years of the colonial era both communities proceeded to build their places of worship—cathedrals, churches, and chapels in the "European" area; mosques and temples in the "Asian" area. Segregation was not a cause of religious diversity, but it served to underline the differences. The apartheid conditions had the effect of heightening parochial differences among the Asians themselves, so that they became politically divided along religious lines. In 1906 they had formed the Nairobi Indian Association in order to fight for civic rights. The association aimed at strengthening ties between Gujarat Hindus, Punjab Hindus, Muslims, Goans, and Sikhs. However, when India was partitioned in 1947 the rift between Muslims and Hindus in India affected the relations between the two communities living in Kenya. Meanwhile, political representation in the Legislative Council in Kenya was on racial lines. Indian Muslims began to complain of the Hindu majority in the Legislative Council. When they were granted a separate religious representation by the governor, Sir Philip Mitchell, the Sikhs also agitated for a separate electorate (Nazareth 1981, 104, 109). These beginnings of differentiating the Indian community along religious lines have persisted to the present, becoming more complex. Thus, for instance, Nairobi has Punjab Muslims, Punjab Sikhs, and Punjab Hindus.

Sprawling African Settlements

Burgeoning Nairobi also had an African population, officially not recognized but there anyway. Rosberg and Nottingham (1966, 23) observe that from the start Nairobi "was laid out to accommodate a European and Indian population, not an African one." African railway workers were provided for in the railway quarters, where they lived in dormitory barracks which were inadequate in terms of privacy and decency, with wages below subsistence level (Frost 1978, 9). The rest of the African population lived in unplanned ghettos in various parts of the municipality. The initial African population in Nairobi was ethnically diverse. Among the early arrivals with the railway were Sudanese and Somali soldiers, Somali and Swahili traders, Digo and Nyamwezi porters, as well as Baganda, Nandi, and Maasai camp followers (Rosberg and Nottingham 1966, 23). By 1921 there were already eight African settlements with rather telling place names such as Mombasa (the coastal town), Kaburini (by the graveyard), Kariokor (the depot for African carrier corps during the First World War), Kileleshwa, Kibera (a ghetto for Sudanese and Somali Muslims), Pumwani (a resettlement site which was thought to be large enough to accommodate all the Africans likely to migrate to Nairobi in the foreseeable future, but which contained 3,996 people living in 317 houses ten years later), and Pangani.

Pangani could be singled out as a good example of ethnic diversity with the attendant religious diversity. In 1890 it was already a safari camp with a nucleus of Kikuyu and Kamba settlers who had been converted from their indigenous religions to Islam by their Swahili acquaintances. By the end of the First World War it had become definitely a Muslim village, but it contained three separate mosques for Kikuyu, Kamba, and Luo Muslims respectively. In 1938 it had 293 household heads, 247 being Muslim, 12 Christian, and 34 "pagan" (that is, adherents of African indigenous religions). Inhabitants of Pangani had come from twelve different Kenyan ethnic groups and the rest from Uganda, Tanganyika (Tanzania), Abyssinia (Ethiopia), Nyasaland (Malawi), Zanzibar, Belgian Congo, Italian Somaliland, Sudan, Madagascar, and Mozambique (Rosberg and Nottingham 1966, 357). It can hardly be doubted that Pangani had a good variety of religious traditions. Pangani was demolished in 1938, and its inhabitants were dispersed to other parts of Nairobi and its environs, including Ongata Rongai and Karai in Kikuyu division of Kiambu district (Maingi 1987, 1, 133). As can be expected, wherever new settlements have occurred new religious groupings have formed.

2. COMPETITION AMONG EARLY CHRISTIAN MISSIONARIES

Competition and even hostility among the various missionary groups were inevitable. Apart from the fact that each desired maximum influence over the Africans, the missionary groups differed in their backgrounds, their theologies, and their traditions. Christian converts who had been evangelized in the rural areas and had then gone to Nairobi in search of livelihood had no common Christian tradition to pursue except the one each had been schooled into. It is quite feasible that the twelve Pangani Christians in 1938 could have belonged to several if not twelve different denominations.

Religious apartheid was also present in the missionary scene, notably among the Protestant churches. For instance, the Scottish missionaries who evangelized the Kikuyu belonged to the Church of Scotland. In Kenya they established Church of Scotland missions which made up the Presbyterian Church of East Africa. St. Andrews Church in Nairobi belonged to the Church of Scotland, being organized and controlled from Edinburgh and conducting its services in English for a European congregation. Also in Nairobi were two Church of Scotland mission churches, St. John's Pumwani and Bahati Martyrs Church. Both congregations were entirely Kikuyu and their services were held in the Kikuyu language (Frost 1978, 178). In the Anglican community, the bishop of Mombasa was understood to be bishop of two churches, one being the (European) Church of England in Kenya and the other being African "missionary congregations." In the early 1940s the European congregation at St. Mark's in Parklands deprived African servants of the opportunity of holding Swahili worship services on Sunday afternoons on the grounds that "they [the Europeans] would have to sit in the same seats on the following Sunday morning" (Frost 1978, 176). Africans in the European areas who wished to worship would have to commute to the Eastlands (the least attractive part of the town) where native churches were to be found. Colin Turnbull is not a little sarcastic after describing the immorality of the white urban population when he says:

> And in the midst of this great centre of civilization in heathen Africa the Church (one for each denomination) raises its steeple and calls the faithful to worship—white this side, black that—or, better still, it calls them at separate times, or even gives them, with Christian generosity, separate

buildings so that nobody can accuse them of discrimination (Turnbull 1962, 28-29).

3. AFRICAN GRIEVANCES AND THE RISE OF INDEPENDENT CHURCHES

The rise of African Independent Churches and other religious movements in Africa has attracted much attention in scholarship (see Barrett 1968, 1971; Martin 1974). Kenya has its large share of them and in Nairobi they make a major contribution to the religiously diverse landscape.

The colonial transformation of African society in Kenya brought with it many upheavals. Africans had grievances over land alienation, forced labor, inadequate wages, missionary patronage and condemnation of African culture, colonial education policies, and poor urban living conditions (Kinoti 1983, 96-114; Njeri 1984, 40-53; Tignor 1976; Ross 1927). A number of the churches which broke away from missionary control from as early as 1914 did so in order to manage their own educational programs and spiritual affairs. Those churches apparently perceived religious independence to be the basic solution to the total situation of outside domination and lack of self-determination. Subsequent to the first break-aways many more schismatic and renewal movements have followed. In 1972 Nairobi's religious scene included thirty-four African independent churches and groups. Today the number would be nearer one hundred.

4. DIVERGENT ISLAMIC TRADITIONS

A study by Maingi on Islam in Nairobi between 1900 and 1963 concludes that sectarianism is one of the most salient characteristics of Islam in Nairobi, that all Muslim sub-groups are represented in Nairobi, and that Islam in Nairobi is organizationally fragmented both along ethnic and sectarian lines (Maingi 1987, xi, 246, 250).

The first major split occurred after the death of the Prophet Mohammed over his succession. It produced the Shia, who favored succession by heredity, and the Sunnis, who did not. The Shia were further split into the "Seveners" and the "Twelvers" after the death of Iman Jafar in A.D. 765. They followed his two sons Ismail and Al-Kazim respectively. The "Seveners" were further split at the death of Al-Mustansir in 1094, the majority following his son Nizar and others his brother Mustali. Meanwhile the Sunni had developed into four schools of thought (*Madhabib*) namely, *Shafi'i*, *Malik*, *Hanafi* (constituted by Asian Sunni Muslims), and *Hanbali*.

During the eighth century, Arab and Persian Muslims entered the coastal towns of Kenya and developed Islamic Swahili culture. In turn, the Swahili transmitted Islam to the interior peoples wrapped up in Swahili culture and had established settlements in Nairobi (Mji wa Mombasa and Pangani) before the railway brought in the Asians. However, one of the features of this Swahili Sunni Islam was its reflection of the Lamu social class distinctions between *waungwana* (civilized high class) and *washenzi* (uncivilized). Like the Christian missionaries, they tried to impose culture in the name of religion. Their converts soon rebelled and this explains the presence of the three mosques mentioned at Pangani. Nairobi African Islam was therefore fragmented on ethnic lines, such as Swahili, Nubian, Somali, Kikuyu, Kamba, and Luo.

When the Asian Muslims entered the scene they came as Shia or Sunni. Among the Shia were the Ismailis, the Bohra, and the Ithna' ashari. There are also small groupings made from the Kuchi, the Halai, and the Akai. All these are basically closed groups along ethnic sectarian lines. The Punjab Sunni Islam is, on the other hand, accommodating and has encouraged other Asian Sunni groups to cooperate in building mosques. It has also been largely responsible for building up Sunni Islam in Nairobi. These are the features of Islam that lead Maingi to conclude that Nairobi does not have a "Muslim community" in the strict sense of the word.

I conclude this section by observing that these foundations have served to promote more and more fragmentation. Future prospects can be expected to be extremely complex, if not chaotic. Currently Nairobi has numerous new religious movements.

CURRENT FRAGMENTATION OF KENYAN SOCIETY ALONG RELIGIOUS LINES

AFRICA THE PLACE FOR MISSION: KENYA AS GATEWAY

In his book *Battle for Africa*, Brother Andrew of Open Doors International speaks for many when he says, "To many people in the Christian world, it seems that the word *Africa* almost automatically evokes the word *missionary*." He says the two words have frequently been associated in literature and church lore throughout history. Perhaps Brother Andrew is not aware that he speaks for other religions also. As far as Christianity is concerned, anyhow, he expresses some disappointment which is probably shared by many who value Christianity not as a simple Gospel of Jesus Christ but as an ideology among other ideologies in the perpetual struggle for sociopolitical control.

> Africa is the most familiar mission field in the world. Over the past hundred years it has had the attention of more foreign missions than any other single area. It is a great irony that this missionary-saturated continent should be the part of the world most completely vulnerable to an anti-Christian revolution! (Andrew and Conn 1977, 53).

The revolution in reference here is the socialist ideology which Andrew says has attracted African countries as they have gained political independence from their former colonial masters. Since the author is addressing a Western audience, he makes the real reason for a renewed effort on Africa explicit:

I am going to urge you in this book to join in the battle for Africa, but admittedly not for any lofty or unselfish motive. We who sit in comfortable lands thousands of miles away from Africa must get involved in the fight for our *own* survival's sake. What does Africa have to do with us? Everything! A revolution has come to Africa, and if it overwhelms that continent it will move on to a closer battleground. Its ultimate target is you (Andrew and Conn 1977, 17).

With the Cold War over or subsided, the next major enemy is Islam, and the battle for "souls" rages on. It is not clear what hidden agenda there are in current proselytization activities. What is apparent, however, is that so many are hopping into Africa and that the African soul is as exploitable as it has always been. Two years ago a Hindu missionary confided to me that he regretted that Hindus in Kenya have been complacent and did not commend Hinduism to Africans before Christianity disrupted African society. This missionary is a prolific writer and has already translated the Vedas into English for local consumption. He has also produced fifty tracts for free distribution to schools and colleges. The battle for Kenya involves Christianity, Islam, and Eastern religions. Indigenous peoples are not consulted.

Kenya is evidently a gateway into Africa, and for many a contemporary missionary Kenya is the first port of call and the initial testing ground. Many do not move on after landing in Kenya. Rather, they establish their headquarters for Africa and for the region in Nairobi or some other Kenyan location. By way of illustration, the Raja Yoga movement of the Brahma Kumaris, founded in 1936 in India, has Nairobi as its headquarters for Africa. As a New Age movement and with the driving motto, "Remember—Now or Never," Raja Yoga, through its Brahma Kumaris World Spiritual University (BKWSU) is committed to the global mission of preparing humanity for the imminent New Golden Age (when Lord Shiva comes as destroyer/purifier) by raising soul-consciousness through "complete yogic science." The Brahma Kumaris are very active in unobtrusive ways and a growing number of Kenyans are finding the movements that promote peace attractive (Nasimiyu-Wasike and Waruta 1994, 94-95).

Ananda Marga movement established its first mission after India in Kenya in 1968. By 1989 it was running fifty nursery schools with about five thousand children each year. These are children of the poor section of Kenyan society. Ananda Marga are influencing children and young people for tomorrow through the path of Tantric yoga. This is another New Age movement committed to "change the world and do so immediately." It is an esoteric movement with visions of a golden age when "society will be run by *sadripas*—those physically fit, mentally strong and spiritually elevated"—the Ananda Marga (Salvadori 1989, 142).

According to Andrew Walker, who followed closely the British Restoration movement, the movement followed spontaneously on the heels of British Pentecostalist/charismatic movement, which itself split into two factions. Within two years of the split one faction, Restoration One (R1), began missionary work "even before they had properly established their British churches." Bryn Jones and David Mansel went to Kenya in 1971 "where they pioneered a new church." They returned the following year and made contact with the president. Their "missionary work" is reported to have resulted in miracles of healing. "Feeling they had an entree into Kenya with their relationships with government officials and the President himself, R1 decided to raise money in various projects designed to help the Kenya tribes be self-supporting" (Walker 1988, 105). The number of aid workers and missionaries on development projects has been quite significant, particularly in the face of worsening living conditions for many Kenyans over the last two decades.

POST-INDEPENDENCE PROSELYTIZING

Kenya attained political independence from Britain in 1963. Christianity was the dominant religion. African religion was never given active support except that traditional healers could from then on practice more openly. African religion has continued to influence Christianity, notably through many of the African Instituted Churches. Although freedom of worship is enshrined in Kenya's Constitution, African religion continues to experience discrimination in two ways. "Nativist" religious groups do not get registered, seemingly in the interest of law and order. If these religious groups register as "Christian" or "Church," they seem to be advised to say nothing about African forms of worship in their constitutions. When later they attempt to introduce traditional elements of worship such as animal sacrifice, the government intervenes, claiming that those innovations were not spelled out in the constitution of the Church. This was the experience in 1987 of a "church" that registered itself as the Evangelistic Gospel Church of the Holy Morning Star.

On the whole, groups that might be described as belonging to the category of African Religion experience a number of disadvantages. They are to be found among the poorer and less educated or illiterate peasantry. Since the majority of the local community has converted to other religions, they give the impression of being remnants of the past. Children who may belong by virtue of being born of practicing parents end up abandoning the religion as they acquire some education and enter the modern sector of life. As they are regarded as unprogressive, and have no access to modern means of communication, they remain somewhat isolated. As such they do not proselytize but may attract individuals seeking "a place to feel at home." Overtly or otherwise they are intimidated into assuming Christian or Jewish (Old Testament) descriptive names. Tent of the Living God and the Kenya African Sabbcrynssk of Soi Praying and Healing Church can be cited as examples. The former is more politically inclined, and the latter teaches that salvation is not through Jesus Christ but through the ancestors.

There are in Kenya "nativist" religious groups whose existence could be attributed to youth disaffection, at various levels, with mainstream society.

The Rastafari is pan-African and in spite of its counter-cultural features it endeavors to recapture the lost dignity of African peoples. By far the main feature drawing youth from the historical mainline churches is the Pentecostalist/ charismatic restoration movement. From about the early 1970s the Pentecostal/charismatic movement reached Kenyan schools through itinerant preachers, and the youth were ready to exercise "charisma" in their local denominational churches. But these churches were and continue to be closed to youth leadership. The liberating effect of the Holy Spirit seems to have given impetus to the youth to launch out on their own, and some charismatic churches came into being as a result. Others, such as the End Time Messengers (Branhamites), were advised to have no association with denominations. (Catholic charismatics have remained in the church but there are tensions.) In some instances the charismatic renewals have strongly criticized the older, mainline churches. Many of these newer outer groups meet in cinema and civic halls, school classrooms, or tents.

Jehovah's Witnesses in East Africa were registered as a religious organization in Kenya in 1962. In 1972 there were thirty-four foreign missionaries working in Kenya. They were declared banned by the government in April 1973. The ban has since been lifted, and they now rank among the most active evangelists in Kenya. They walk in twos for door-to-door evangelism and sales of their publications, *Awake* and *The Watch Tower*, at highly subsidized costs. Many people are suspicious of Jehovah's Witnesses for not preaching the message of salvation through Jesus Christ, even though they spread a comforting message of the imminent God's Kingdom on earth. The refusal of Jehovah's Witness proselytizers to pray with even those they preach to compounds people's suspicion of the movement. The mainline churches caution their followers against association with Jehovah's Witnesses. The Charismatics and Pentecostalists also have nothing to do with this movement. The same is true of the Mormon Church, which is a relatively new arrival in Kenya. Mormonism seems to attract the more well-to-do section of Kenyan society. Some of the issues raised by the older churches, and by parents, can be summarized as follows:

First, the majority of youth has found new loyalties in the itinerant preachers and mass crusaders who leave behind cassettes and literature which the youth consume wholesale. Intellectual exercise is out, but the word of the "master" ("apostle" or "brother") is "gospel truth." Further, the doctrines of discipling (variously referred to as "shepherding" or "covering") inhibit freedom for the individual. A disciple is dependent on a discipler (a personal socio-spiritual keeper) for decisions even on personal matters. Some relationships are sealed in covenants where one vows to submit totally to the shepherd. These loyalties to person and fellowship take priority over family loyalties and attendant responsibilities. Those earning salaries commit large portions of their income to their church over and above their family commitments.

Second, the dispensation doctrines have created a state of frantic evangelism before the return of Christ at the end of this millennium. The only agenda is evangelism and church-planting. Some students are abandoning academic studies in order to devote time and preaching to the "unreached" peoples. Kenyan families invest heavily in the education of their children.

Third, the real motives of street and itinerant preaching have been questioned. Some ministries are becoming businesses.

THE MISSIONARY ENTERPRISE OF EASTERN RELIGIONS

Until about two decades ago, Eastern religions were confined to the Asian populations in Kenya's urban areas. Currently there is a Hindu mission in Kenya founded by a professional Asian journalist. He is a prolific writer and is reaching many young people in schools and colleges through his tracts. The Hindu Mission to Kenya is committed to provide a workable philosophy of life.

A number of movements active in Kenya would fall under the umbrella of New Age. They are movements committed to promoting peace, to environmental improvement, and to unified religion. Among movements active and attracting young people are Ananda Marga, Nichiren Buddhism, Raja Yoga, Transcendental Meditation, Sathya Sai Baba, and the Hare Krishna. Some deny they are religious, and proselytizing is done in an unobtrusive way. Some of them are millennial and also working to beat the millennialist deadline at the end of this century.

Rev. Sun Myung Moon has an active center in Nairobi which proselytizes under the clandestine name The Association for Education and Development. Many young people have joined this church in search of educational development without realizing what it really stands for. The year 1993 saw the visit of Mrs. Moon to Nairobi, where she proclaimed that she and her husband were the true Parents fulfilling the Completed Testament Age which Christ failed to fulfill. Her audience was mostly Christian. Since her visit, Sun Myung Moon has openly declared himself to be the Christ—or perhaps more precisely, Christ of the Second Advent. (Alternately, he is described as Lord of the Second Advent—meaning that Christians or the world should not await the second coming of [Jesus] Christ.)

ISLAMIC PROSELYTIZING

As indicated in a preceding section, Islam in Kenya is diverse, following ethnic lines and schools of thought. In recent years the growing number of new mosques in areas where there were previously none indicates there is a certain amount of proselytizing going on. This is clearly spearheaded by the Ahmadiyya movement, which uses literature to criticize Christianity and explain the Islamic faith. This movement is not approved by Sunni Islam. However, research into the movement indicates that the majority of converts are drawn from Sunni Muslims (Martin 1974). It would seem, as Martin hypothesizes, that the main objective of the concerted attacks on Christianity is to win other

Muslims, especially Sunnis. Islamic fundamentalism, though not as pronounced in Kenya as Christian fundamentalism, is further contributing to the Islamic expansion in Kenya.

CONCLUDING REMARKS

Fragmentation is clearly not an overstatement of the Kenyan religious scene even though religious pluralism is a contemporary global phenomenon. Clearly in-depth research is needed to establish the extent to which the proselytizing activities of various groups generate fragmentation and may be a threat to social order, a negative influence on the family, and a subversion of individual freedom of conscience.

This chapter has given a bird's-eye view of religious pluralization in Kenya, especially in Nairobi, but has not exhausted the list of movements clamoring for a catch from the same pool, the Kenyan population. Numerous groups are now actively proselytizing in Kenya, including the Mormons and the Bahais. Some of these groups, such as the Jehovah's Witnesses, seem to be more duty-bound to walk the streets and knock at doors in residential areas. One "church," Scientology, claims to be the "world's fastest growing religion" and shows an address in Thika town in Kenya as one of its global mission centers, though this town can hardly be considered a cosmopolitan place. Mainline Christianity in Kenya today no longer fits the description as an "ideological arm" of the state, as Aaron Gana (1997, 223) aptly described the Church in colonial Africa. The Catholic Church and some Protestant churches, notably the Church of the Province of Kenya (Anglican), the Presbyterian Church of East Africa, and the Methodist Church in Kenya have spearheaded the movement for democracy while maintaining their nonpartisan stand. The more conservative arm of the Protestant churches continues to be committed to the biblical injunction to obey the government of the day. This difference in outlook is yet another factor that renders the troubled youth vulnerable to escapist alternatives.

NOTE

[1] The paper by Willis is reproduced in full by Mungeam (1978) and occupies pages 153-60 plus the first six lines of page 161. A further six lines on page 161 summarize responses to the paper by other delegates and the adoption of some three resolutions.

BIBLIOGRAPHY

Andrew, B., and C. P. Conn, 1977. *Battle for Africa*. Old Tappan, N.J.: Flemming H. Revell Company.

Barlow, A. R. 1923. *Kikuyu: 1898-1923 Semi Jubilee Book of the Church of Scotland Mission, Kenya Colony*. Edinburgh.

Barrett, D. B. 1968. *Schism and Renewal in Africa: An Analysis of Six Thousand Contemporary Movements*. Nairobi: Oxford University Press.

———. 1971. *African Initiatives in Religion: Twenty-One Studies from Eastern and Central Africa*. Nairobi: East African Publishing House.

———. 1982. *World Christian Encyclopedia: A Comparative Study of Churches and Religions in the Modern World A.D. 1900-2000*. Nairobi: Oxford University Press.

Barrett, D. B. et al., eds. 1973. *Kenya Churches Handbook: The Development of Kenyan Christianity, 1498-1973*. Kisumu: Evangel Publishing House.

Blakeslee, H. V. 1956. *Beyond the Kikuyu Curtain*. Chicago: Moody Press.

Cagnolo, C. 1933. *The Akikuyu: Their Customs, Traditions, and Folklore*. Nyeri: Consolata Mission Press.

Cowan, L. G., et al., eds. 1965. *Education and Nation Building in Africa*. New York: Praeger.

Crouch, M., ed. 1993. *A Vision of Christian Mission: Reflections on the Great Commission in Kenya 1943-1993*. Nairobi: NCCK.

Fortes, Meyer, and Germaine Dieterlen, eds. 1965. *African Systems of Thought*. London: Oxford University Press.

Frost, R. A. 1978. *Race against Time: Human Relations and Politics in Kenya Independence*. London: Rex Collings Ltd.

Gana, A. 1997. "The African Political Crisis and the Church in Africa," in *Vision for a Bright Africa: Facing the Challenges of Development*, edited by G. Kinoti and P. Kimiyu. Kampala and Nairobi: IFES Anglophone Africa and AISRED.

Gathii, H. W. 1966. "Church Discipline: A Contemporary Problem of the Church in Kikuyu," Department of Philosophy and Religious Studies, Makerere University College.

Gifford, P., ed. 1992. *New Dimensions in African Christianity*. Nairobi: AACC.

Greaves, L. B. 1969. *Carey Francis of Kenya*. Rex Collings. London.

Groves, C. P. 1955. *The Planting of Christianity in Africa*. Vol. 14, *1914-1954*. London: Lutterworth Press.

Hastings, Adrian. 1976. *African Christianity: An Essay in Interpretation*. London: Chapman.

Kinoti, G. K. 1994. *Hope for Africa and What the Christian Can Do*. Nairobi: AISRED.

Kinoti, H. W. 1983. "Aspects of Gikuyu Traditional Morality." Ph.D. diss., University of Nairobi.

———. 1988. "Religious Pluralism in Nairobi and Its Environs." Paper read at a conference on Urban Growth and Spatial Planning of Nairobi, Nairobi.

———. 1992. "African Morality: Past and Present," in *Moral and Ethical Issues in African Christianity: Exploratory Essays in Moral Theology*, edited by J.N.K. Mugambi and A. Nasimiyu-Wasike. Nairobi, Kenya: Initiatives Publishers.

———. 1993. "The Challenge of the New Age Movement and Oriental Mysticism," in *Mission in African Christianity*, edited by A. Nasimiyu-Wasike and D. W. Waruta. Nairobi: Uzima Press.

———. 1994a. "Inter-Religious and Inter-Faith Dialogue," in *Cast away Fear: A Contribution to the African Synod*, edited by A.B.T. Byaruhanga-Akiiki et al. Supplement to *New People*, no. 29 (March-April). Nairobi: Comboni Missionaries.

————. 1994b. "Intra- and Inter-denominational Conflicts: The Phenomenon of New Religious Movements," in *Conflict Resolutions, Reconciliation, and Peace Making*. Kampala: Association of Theological Institutions in Eastern Africa (ATIEA) Staff Institute.

————. 1995. "New Religious Movements and the Youth: Challenges in Pastoral Counseling," in *Caring and Sharing: Pastoral Counseling in the African Perspective*, edited by D. Waruta. Nairobi: ATIEA.

————. 1997a. "The Church in Reconstruction of Our Moral Self," in *The Church and the Reconstruction of Africa: Theological Considerations*, edited by J.N.K. Mugambi. Nairobi: AACC.

————. 1997b. "Inter-Religious and Intra-Religious Dialogue." A series of five lectures delivered at ATIEA Staff Institute, Mukono, Uganda.

Lambert, H. E. File LAMB/1/6. Jomo Kenyatta Memorial Library. University of Nairobi.

Leakey, L.S.B. 1977. *The Southern Kikuyu Before 1903*. 3 volumes. London: Academic Press.

Leys, N. M. 1924, *Kenya*. London: Hogarth Press.

Maggoye, M. O. 1986. *The Story of Kenya: A Nation in the Making*. Nairobi: Oxford University Press.

Maingi, A. N. 1987. *The Diversity Factor in the History of Islam in Nairobi 1900-1963*. M.A. thesis, University of Nairobi.

Martin, E. R. 1974. *Certain Aspects of the Ahmadiyya Movement in East Africa*. Ph.D. diss., University of Nairobi.

Mawani, P.I.V. 1975. *The Jamat Kharna as a Source of Cohesiveness in Ismaili Community in Kenya*. M.A. thesis, University of Nairobi.

Mungeam, G. H. 1978. *Kenya: Select Historical Documents 1884-1923*. Nairobi: East African Publishing House.

Murray-Brown, J. 1972. *Kenyatta*. London: George Allen and Unwin Ltd.

Nasimiyu-Wasike, A., and D. W. Waruta, eds. 1994. *Pastoral Care in African Christianity: Challenging Essays in Pastoral Theology*. Nairobi: Uzima Press.

Nazareth, J. M. 1981. *Brown Man Black Country: On the Foothills of Uhuru*. New Delhi: Tidings Publications.

Njeri, P. 1984. *The Akorino Churches: A Study of the History and Some of the Basic Beliefs of the Holy Ghost Church of East Africa 1926-1980*. M.A. thesis, University of Nairobi.

Odinga, O. 1967. *Not Yet Uhuru: The Autobiography of Oginga Odinga*. London: Heinemann Educational Books.

Oduyoye, M. A. 1997. "The Church of the Future in Africa: Its Mission and Theology," in *The Church and Reconstruction in Africa: Theological Considerations*, edited by J.N.K. Mugambi. Nairobi: The All Africa Conference of Churches.

Oliver, R. 1952. *The Missionary Factor in East Africa*. London: Longman.

Rosberg, C. G., and J. Nottingham. 1966. *The Myth of Mau Mau: Nationalism in Kenya*. Nairobi: East African Publishing House.

Ross, W. M. 1927. *Kenya from Within*. London: Frank Cass.

Salvadori, C. 1989. *Through Open Doors: A View of Asian Cultures in Kenya*. Nairobi: Kenway.

Tignor, R. L. 1976. *The Colonial Transformation of Kenya: The Kamba, Kikuyu and Maasai from 1900 to 1939*. Princeton, N.J.: Princeton University Press.

Turnbull, C. 1962. *The Lonely African*. New York: Simon and Schuster.

Vidler, A. R. 1961. *The Church in an Age of Revolution*. Baltimore: Penguin Books Ltd.

Walker, A. 1988. *Restoring the Kingdom: The Radical Christianity of the Home Church Movement*. London: Hodder and Stoughton.

Zuesse, E. M. 1979. *Ritual Cosmos: The Sanctification of Life in African Religions*. Athens, Ohio: Ohio University Press.

12.

ISLAMISM IN ALGERIA

The Risks and Prospects of Inter-Islamic Proselytization

——————◆——————

Chabha Bouslimani

INTRODUCTION

How should we interpret the expansion of an Islamist movement in the course of the 1980s in Algeria, and the radicalization from 1992 onward of armed groups who appeal to God's law to impose on the state and society their conception of the Sunna (Tradition of the Prophet) as the fundamental element of their political legitimacy?

The first point to note is that Islam, the state religion according to Article 2 of all the Algerian Constitutions (1976–1989–1996), represents one of the principles of the ideological plan of Algerian nationalism. Yet, the precise role of Islam is contested among various factions in the country. Second, these contestations are among Sunni Muslims, who constitute 90 percent of the population—it is Sunni Islam that strongly influences the minds, culture, and social relationships of the Algerian people.[1] But as noted later, there is a clear Shi'a influence on the present Islamist groups in Algeria, primarily because of events in Iran since 1979. Even allowing for this recent trend, however, it is clear that the religious battles in this country are not about a conflict between Muslims and non-Muslims. Rather, they are about the divisions among Sunni Muslims themselves over interpretation of the Qur'an and the Sunna, and associated institutions. There are also significant disagreements among these about strategies and approaches to achieving the objectives of various groups and factions.

If behind the ensemble of "Islamist groups" is hidden a proliferation of anonymous tendencies which are difficult to discern, their overriding shared characteristic is to extol the total destruction of a political system judged to be

291

"impious" and therefore "illegitimate," with a view to installing a theocratic state on the basis of the model of the state the Prophet established in Medina (Western Arabia) in 622. They all seek to establish an "Islamic state" which will strictly enforce *Shari'a* on all aspects of public and private life, though there may be little agreement among Islamist groups about the precise *Shari'a* principles they seek to enforce.[2] Is it appropriate in this context to speak of proselytization in the general sense of the term? Certainly in the case of political and terrorist groups. On the other hand, the imprecision of the terminology engenders an amalgamation of the two notions—fundamentalism and integrism—that we shall try to distinguish after a brief overview of the salient facts of Algerian history.

ISLAM IN ALGERIAN HISTORY

Algeria today is to all appearances characterized by a monolithic religious landscape. Sunni Islam, of the Maliki School, is dominant. In 1987, there were no more than 50,000 Roman Catholics, compared to 900,000 in 1962, and 7,000 Protestants out of a total population of 21 million. The Jewish community is equally small in size.[3] Before becoming Muslim, Algerians worshiped their indigenous deities. They then converted to Christianity. The Berbers inhabiting the Maghreb (North Africa) were influential because of their adoption of Donatism, propounded by the bishop of Carthage as a reaction against Rome.[4] It was also in Hippo (present-day Annaba) where one of the fathers of the church, Saint Augustine, lived and developed his teachings. During that Christian era, disagreements crystallized the particularities of communities, giving birth to churches refusing the Chalcedonian doctrine on the nature of Christ.[5]

Algeria was completely Islamized by the eleventh century after the conquest of Okba BenNafi and the withdrawal of the Byzantine Christians. The success of Islam in the Maghreb, despite Berber irredentism and the disappearance of Christianity, are questions which have not been sufficiently addressed. The historian André Miquel argues that Islam provided a response to two problems—theological and sociopolitical. The various responses given by the leaders and founders of heretical movements and the Eastern Churches to the problem of the nature of Christ tended to underline, in the face of the official teachings of Constantinople, the uniqueness of the godhead. This being the case, Islam was therefore viewed, Miquel claims, as being the inheritor of the Eastern conception of the divine. On the sociopolitical scene, the tensions between the Berbers and the Romans, then the Byzantines, notably the struggles against taxes and work in the Roman villas, accelerated Arab ascendancy over Berber peoples who were claiming egalitarianism. A cultural and geopolitical transformation thus occurred. But Islam did not succeed in effacing the original traditions, though it was within the context of Islam and through the Arabic language that those other traditions were accessed.

The first dissensions within the heart of Islam attained a particular intensity in the Maghreb where the Khariji secession and the Shi'i revolts contributed to the establishment of local states. With the coming of Islam to the region, the religious conflicts began to center around issues of descent: Shi'ism was violently opposed to the Sunni position on the organization of power, but nonetheless shared with Sunnism respect for the Qur'an. The Khariji challenged historically both Sunni orthodoxy and Shi'i teachings. Their first representatives (the Ibadites) founded the Tahert kingdom in Algeria.

The Ibadites continued to survive through their rituals in the valley of the Mzab, but did not advocate violence. The Shi'ia imposed their authority on Algeria and Egypt with the Fatimid dynasty (tenth century); Sunnism would be restored through another Berber dynasty, the Almoravids (twelfth century), who went on to conquer Andalucia. The Arab troops, which were originally composed of nomadic groups, spread Islam in the towns, while Christianity had only reached the larger urban areas. The large Sufi brotherhoods, which emerged from the towns of Algeria, reinforced their authority in those rural areas which sustained a popular Islam centered on saints' cults. These brotherhoods (Senoussia, Tidjaniyya, and Rahmania) played an important role in the nineteenth century under French colonial rule which watched over them closely, or banned them (Ageron 1964, 62).

This historical overview aims to recall the complexity of religious, cultural, and ethnic identity in Algeria, with its multiple centers of historical power. In the Maghreb, the particularities are expressed through different types of Christianity and of independence, which sought to acquire local churches from Rome. The rivalries over succession within the Prophet's family gave rise to Chasm, which in turn concealed radical sociopolitical movements—a spirit of revolt, puritanism, egalitarianism, which were also preponderant traits of Berber culture. Indeed, these claims took on Shi'i forms, from Kharijism to the chronic insurrections of certain brotherhoods. This background of contradictory influences remained unclear in the collective conscience and historical memory. Nonetheless, it is a key element, albeit unexplored, of Algerian historical and cultural experience.

From 1830 onward the French conquest and the prohibitions on the Arabic language, Qur'anic instruction, and theological education, as reported by R. Algeron, served to limit the role of the Ulama (doctors of the *Shari'a*) (Leca and Vatin 1975, 31). Popular and mystical Islam was tolerated, but closely supervised—imams were placed under the tutelage of the French authorities. Furthermore, the annual pilgrimage to Mecca was forbidden. The colonial system closed the doors on a population in perpetual poverty. It also served to constrain the elites, whether through cultural assimilation without political rights or citizenship, or by causing them to resort to violence (Mérad 1967, 430). Yet the urban and rationalist Islam of the Ulama experienced a revival in the 1920s and 1930s with the reformist movement, which was developing in Algeria as it was elsewhere in the Arab world. This Islamism gave form to nationalist claims by taking root in the regions which had constituted the traditional bastions of resistance. Its appeal to the youth can be explained by its political impact and not its religious discipline. According to the same author, the young reformists admired the Turkey of M. Kemal as much as the Arabia of Ibn Seoud.[6]

FUNDAMENTALISM OR INTEGRISM?

The fundamentalist movements which denied the popular roots of political decision-making were by no means a novel phenomenon on the contemporary scene. In the case of Islam itself there were traditions of austerity and fundamentalist reactions imposed by Chasm or by Wahhabism.[7] In the case of the Maghreb, some Berber dynasties, such as the Almoravids, who were particularly fundamentalist, swept into the kingdom of Cordoba, casting anathema on books and philosophy. In this respect, the appearance of a fundamentalist phenomenon in Algeria is situated on a historical continuum and must therefore be seen as connected to religious trends which at regular intervals proscribed luxury and urban civilization and preached submission to dogma and banned all moral freedom. As a cultural product, the Islamist movement is also a reaction against the modernist project of the independent Algerian state.

At this point, the inflation of terminology on Islamism calls for some more precision. Fundamentalism signifies literally the return to original Islamic sources. The reinterpretation of Tradition was the guiding force of Reformist Islam in the nineteenth century throughout the region. In Algeria, following on from the Egyptian reformers, Muhammed Abduh and Rashid Rida, the Reform movement manifested itself in the teachings of Ibn Badis, who opposed the Ulama tradition—guardians of the transmission of religious knowledge—at the beginning of the century. Ibn Badis insisted on the necessity of the foundational value of the Qur'an and the Sunna, but accorded little importance to eschatological questions. He illustrated well the profound mistrust of the Salafiya with regard to the Kalam, which was considered as a source of divisions in the community.[8] The Algerian Islamist movement, in particular the Islamic Salvation Front (FIS), and the different associations it emerged from, drew on the thought of the Egyptian Muslim Brothers of Hasen El Banna, who also urged a return to the original sources, and not to Ibn Badis. Fundamentalist opposition hinged on the problems of interpretation from these sources, and the means of struggle—whether by ballot boxes or by bullets.

But the difference is in fact centered not on the return to the origins, as is too frequently assumed, whether implicitly or explicitly—it is rather between the political movement and the armed groups. In Algeria, the armed groups, just as the political parties, proclaim the Tradition of the Prophet and the Sunna; the nuances emerge over whether to be open to other religions, Christianity, for example, or whether to withdraw into oneself. There is also disagreement over relations with other cultures, and about how to respond to perceived persecution or aggression by the outside world. Some even called for the assassination of Christians, the departure of foreigners, while others denounced such stands on the grounds that Religions of the Book were to be respected. All of this, together with the fact that some groups initially condemned democracy before later embracing it, complicates the question of definition. Finally, we should not overlook the non-negligible role of social class differences among the militants.

From the outset of independence in 1962, various conflicts set the Islamists at odds with the state; they acted clandestinely during the 1970s, while openly advertising their project of "re-Islamizing" the state and Algerian society. But it was the economic crisis of the 1980s, and the attendant identity crisis, as well as the international context, which provided the movement with its strength and mystique. But why of all the Maghrebian societies was it Algeria which descended into violence—when the standard of living had so rapidly progressed and where the numbers of highly educated people remained so high?

ISLAM AS NATIONAL IDEOLOGY

From 1954 onward, the motto of the FLN (National Liberation Front), which affirmed the primacy of armed struggle and the independent state, was "the restoration of the sovereign and democratic Algerian State within the framework of Islamic principles" (Declaration of 1 November 1954). Islam was also integral to the ideological plan of Algerian nationalism after independence, as all the basic texts of the FLN attest. Furthermore, it constituted one of the sources of the legitimacy of power, in the same way as economic development or history.

But if Islam was the religion of the state, the political community went beyond the Muslim community, as Leda and Vatin have analyzed: non-Muslim Algerians were entitled to vote. At a more ideological level, setting aside Marxism and liberalism, the successive FLN platforms claimed that Islam was compatible with socialism.[9] So the National Charter of 1976 recalls that the construction of socialism can be identified with the blossoming of Islamic values. This compromise was summarized in the famous formula of President Boumédiène: "Algerians do not want to go to paradise on an empty stomach."

The Islamist political movement (with all its factions and groups) which became a major force by the early 1990s was largely influenced in the 1970s by the Egyptian Muslim Brothers. It organized itself around the El-Qiyam Association and the humanist Muslim magazine, before it approached the Khomeini networks or became activist, as did Abassi Madani, the leader of the Islamic Salvation Front, who initially began his campaign for the "restoration" of *Shari'a* to end the nation's moral decline through a "charitable" organization called Da'wa. When political parties were legalized in 1989, a controversy erupted between the Islamists who wanted to establish a political party and those like Mahfoud Nahnah, who preferred to keep the status of the Da'wa as a social association. Those who supported the establishment of a political party prevailed, as illustrated by the results of the general elections of 1992, when the army seized power instead of allowing the second round of elections which the Islamic Salvation Front was clearly going to win.

Some Islamist students who belonged to the El-Qiyam ("Values") Association had conducted campaigns since Algerian Independence for the integral submission of the state to the precepts of Islamic *Shari'a*: closing of shops at the times of prayer; exclusion of non-Muslims from public service; restrictions on the schooling of girls (which is compulsory in Algeria), as well as on their public outings and freedom to work. Using aggressive tactics and physical violence, the state banned, for example, the sale of alcohol and sought to control the behavior of young, unmarried couples on several occasions, but then withdrew those measures.

"Every party, every regime, every leader who is not based on Islam is illegal," proclaimed a magazine of Muslim humanism in 1965 which had assumed the mantle of reformism, while apparently distancing itself from the fundamentalist tendencies of El-Qiyam. This publication was edited by an intellectual, R. Bennabi, the director of higher education. Another individual, R. Benaissa, influenced the diffusion of Shi'ism in Algeria in the 1960s and 1970s, when he was advisor to the head of state for religious affairs.

Closer to the Muslim Brothers of Egypt, the El-Qiyam Association, which claimed a membership of five thousand people, was initially disbanded by a prefectural decree of 28 September 1965, and definitively banned by a ministerial decree on 1 March 1966. During the 1970s there were several clashes in the universities: in April 1979, some Islamist activists sprayed some young women with hydrochloric acid, gravely injuring them. These acts of violence against women occurred periodically. Elsewhere, the official press was regularly concerned with the status and activities of small integrationist groups and over the circulation of cassettes disseminating the sermons of the Sayed Qutb, the Egyptian leader of the Muslim Brothers.[10]

The state tried to contain this dispute but from time to time cracked down on Islamist and Communist students who challenged the university. It retained exclusive control over people's religious lives, places of worship, naming of imams responsible for sermons at the mosque, as well as the content of these sermons. Theological education and conferences on Islamic thought were also controlled by the state. The Islamists ended up obtaining in 1979 the freedom to preach in some of the mosques in the capital, other than on Fridays, the weekly day of congregational prayer. It was in one of these mosques that Ali Benhadj, one of the primary leaders of the Islamic Salvation Front, exercised his preaching talents—the virulence of which succeeded in draining off several hundreds of young people.

The monopoly of the state on the administration of religious affairs and its authoritarian management of social relations caused a faction of the Islamists to resort to a more fundamentalist type of Islam, and led to the development of clandestine radical groups, such as that of Mustapha Bouali, who created resistance groups between 1981 and 1986, when he was finally killed by state security forces. Rebellions against the state as well as the consensus that the latter sought to establish became evident at the moment of the agrarian revolution in 1973 when the religious brotherhoods—which had already supported the coup d'état in 1965 against President Ben Bella—tried to thwart the nationalization of lands and their redistribution to the peasants. The proposed Family Law bill (to enact Islamic *Shari'a* principles), though repeatedly rejected, nonetheless revealed the weight of the Islamists and the balancing act that the state sought to perform.

WOMEN AS THE FOCUS OF TENSIONS

The promulgation of the Family Law bill constituted one of the most important controversies since independence. This bill's original pilot studies were done in 1966 and 1976 by the minister of Religious Affairs and of Justice, proposed to the National Assembly, and then put on the shelf. In 1981 a group of former *moudjahidate* (women fighters in the war of national liberation) organized a protest to stop the vote; they obtained the agreement of the president to withdraw the project in January 1982. In June 1984, another project—which differed little from the preceding one—was adopted by the National Assembly; women called for its abrogation on the grounds of its nonconformity with the Constitution; others demanded its amendment to eliminate the requirement of a guardianship for women to conclude a marriage, the dowry, and to guarantee the right to the conjugal home following a divorce. In this way, the statute became an ideological battleground which pushed women into the background, for the very identity of Muslim society was said to be at stake.

The subordinate status of women was constantly linked with the word of God and *Shari'a*, such as the various groups interpreted the Qur'an and the Sunna. The Algerian Constitution of 1976 recalls (article 39) that all citizens are equal before the law in terms of rights and responsibilities, and proscribes any discrimination based on sex, race, or work. Article 41 guarantees women all political, economic, social, and cultural rights. The Constitution of 23 February 1989 (article 31) affirms that fundamental freedoms and human and civil rights are guaranteed for all Algerians—men and women alike. The contradictions evoked by these arrangements stemmed from the fact that it was impossible to question a statute founded on the rules of the *Shari'a*, without being charged with apostasy (for a Muslim to repudiate his or her Islamic faith, which is a capital crime under *Shari'a*). The Islamist argument for a return to the sources was the primary method of the Salami reformists, who wanted to free juridical thought from later interpretations. They also wanted to erase the distance between the Qur'anic ideal and *Shari'a* objectives, on the one hand, and social practice and current jurisprudence, on the other. Feminist discourse was therefore attacked by the Islamists, because, according to them, it distanced itself from *Shari'a*. The equality claimed by the feminists did not correspond to the status of women understood by Islamists to be required by them according to the verse "women have rights equivalent to their obligations and in conformity with practice" (Qur'an, chap. 2 [al Baqara], v. 228). While feminists take democracy and human rights as the framework of their claims, Islamists base their position on the religious definition of the status of women, and its consequent notions of rights and duties.

The claims made by women centered on the rights of individual women in both the family and public contexts. Feminists are seeking the complete revision of the Family code, which followed the Maliki School view of *Shari'a* (as stated in its standard text, *Mukhatasar al-Khalil*), which places serious restrictions on unmarried as well as married women. The revisions demanded by feminists are supported by gender equality under Algerian constitutional provisions and legislation, but these principles of equality were put into question by society. In particular, feminist demands for equality were opposed by the Islamic Salvation Front in 1989, when Abassi Madani, the leader of the movement, proposed to women that they should stay at home to bring down unemployment.

In reality, this was a social and anthropological debate that moved onto the political stage as the result of actions by the Islamists and certain, more secular, groups of feminists. The Islamists found the political space all the more favorable since social behavior either publicly or privately had not changed as rapidly as the economic structures or urbanization of Algerian society in thirty years. Finally, the Islamist discourse was powerfully represented by women who belonged in large numbers to Islamic associations. Whether students, professionals, or housewives, some tens of thousands of young women joined the ranks of the radical fundamentalist Islamists. However, the lack of interest or concern by the state about debates about women's rights encouraged Islamist violence against leading feminists and individual women in public life or whose lifestyle was deemed by terrorist groups as un-Islamic.

DEMOCRACY AND PROSELYTIZATION

The Islamist movement, with all its confused tendencies, enjoyed its peak in 1989 and 1990, the period of political democratization and the advent of the multiparty system. The single-party state of President Boumédienne's regime prioritized the construction of the state and its ideology, and that of President Chadli ben Jadid (1979-92) emphasized the primacy of the economy to broaden its social base. In practice, however, these policies heighten social inequality. Moreover, with the fall in oil prices in 1986 and the reduction in state revenues, the government was unable to meet social needs. As a result of these factors, there was a severe political crisis in October 1988 which led to the installation of the multiparty system as the official policy of the state, followed by the legalization in 1989 to regulate the establishment and functioning of political parties, including Islamist parties. But these developments, in turn, resulted in economic, social, and cultural shock for the society and the state. On the social level, urbanization and the ruralization of towns, youth unemployment (65 percent of the population was twenty-five years old or younger), and the freezing of many jobs in the public sector contributed to heightening a sense of national crisis.

Taking advantage of their having become established in charitable organizations and the fragmentation of a civil society still in the process of formation, the Islamists managed to control the social and political sphere through their mobilizing efforts to recruit and manipulate the poor population of the country's cities. The Islamist campaigns to capture a mass following were conducted through several types of "charitable" associations: preaching and proselytizing organizations (established in the universities, and in the popular areas around the Da'wa); collective prayer associations along the lines of the brotherhoods and popular religion; and the "proselytizing" associations seeking to propagate the ideological and political message of the Islamists among preaching activities, control of professional and political associations, social organizations, and so forth.

As noted earlier, the ideological reference points of these Islamist movements were either Egyptian, Iranian, or even closer to the conceptions of the Indo-Pakistani Mawduudi, and Wahhabism. Saudi Arabia supported the latter movement because of its hostility to Algerian socialism. What distinguished the political movement from the other associations was its desire to constitute a counter-elite of an Islamic state founded on *Shari'a* and by a "democracy" judged to be compatible with Islam. But the literate and university group used the same methods to propagate its ideas: cassettes, publications, tracts. Members frequently passed from one organization or one trend to another. All the associations developed their mobilizing themes around the family code, religious education, social justice, and the illegitimacy of the state.

The Islamic Revolution in Iran favored the constitution of international networks linked by Algerian students. In Afghanistan, hundreds of young Algerians from poor areas left as volunteers, while others, sometimes the same ones, participated in the war in Bosnia, a veritable hub of proselytization. In 1991, the Algerian government had to denounce officially the attitude of Iran and Saudi Arabia—both were accused of financing Algerian Islamists. Movements such as Da'wa and the FIS were rooted in the frustration of the urban youth of Algeria, who were excluded or marginalized by the official policies of 1967-79. Islamists also attracted many professionals who also lacked purpose and future hope. With the opening up of democratic processes in 1989, the FIS began to mobilize in all the large cities in the country, engaging in activities that were meaningful and relevant to local communities because of its knowledge of the social terrain of the country as a whole.

Strengthened by its victory in the municipal elections of June 1990 with 54 percent of the vote, the FIS became more radical and stepped up its pressure on society. In the interests of its municipal administration, it created militants to control morals, cancel shows, close cultural centers, and forbid bathing on the beaches. The Islamist activists, especially the Da'wa, had previously carried out intensive voluntary work in the hospitals, offered educational support in the mosques, and organized collective marriages and circumcisions for the benefit of destitute people. By distributing food, medication, and clothes they were able to propagate the wearing of clothes judged to conform more to tradition and disclose a new lifestyle particularly for children, who in turn pressured their parents into accepting these new practices. The dynamism of the Islamists was also evident in the distribution of brochures, books, and cassettes in the streets and through the channels of the informal economy. All of these activities reinforced their proselytization efforts. Although, as noted earlier, the majority of Algerian Islamists, and the public at large, identify as Sunni Muslims, there is an increasingly strong Shi'i influence, especially among the militant Islamists. The decline in the number of conversions from Sunni to Shi'i Islam during the 1980s and the re-conversions back to Sunnism can be explained for the most part by the outbreak of the Iran-Iraq conflict and the dislocation of certain networks, notably the imprisonment of pro-Iranian militants in Syria. However, some armed groups continued to practice a determined Shi'ism, imbued with a cult of sacrifice, a disdain for life on earth, and violence which targeted the total destruction of the Algerian state and lifestyles deemed to be un-Islamic.

On the political level, these Shi'i groups refused all electoral legitimation, and they threatened to kill voters. Their emirs (princes or leaders) combined military command and a religious authority purportedly infallible. An essential consequence flowed out of this infallibility—the populace owed blind obeisance, for the emir was never wrong and could not sin. An imam in the Shi'i, not Sunni, sense of the term does not have to accept the consensus of the community, for he is himself of quasi-divine emanation. It was in this way that numerous emirs, whose jurisdiction extended over the various urban and suburban districts, were able to decree a multitude of *fatwas* to legitimate their actions. They judged that whosoever strayed from the straight path through an error could no longer return to the faith and therefore deserved death by decapitation, thereby excluding entry into paradise. In their struggle against the state, these groups did not spare women and children. On the contrary, they seemed deliberately to target women and children in their attacks on unarmed civilian populations. Shi'i theology and history were taken as justification for the violent elimination of dissent. And the Shi'i institution of temporary marriage *(muta)* became general practice in these groups and was used to legitimize the frequent kidnaping of women.

CONCLUSION

The decision of the Algerian government to legalize a more moderate Islamism following the constitutional amendment of November 1996 and the modification of the electoral law to ban the creation of religiously based parties were attempts to safeguard against the spread of radicalism. But can one distinguish between radical and moderate Islamism, or from mere extremism irrespective of any religious affiliations? Following that change in government policy, the so-called moderate Hamas movement (which came out of the Da'wa) quite simply changed its acronym to become the Movement for Society and Peace (MSP). Wavering between defensive and repressive legislation, the state cannot respond to social questions generally characterized by lack of moderation given the economic, cultural, social, and structural adjustment crisis. Such policies cannot eliminate radical Islamic fundamentalism, which erodes the very core of society. Instead, the forced moderation of the leaders of some movements, without addressing underlying causes of violent radicalism among the angry and frustrated youth, simply encourages young militants to resort to armed struggle.

As can be seen from the case of Algeria, intra-religious proselytization (among different Muslim factions in this case) can be as violent and destructive as interreligious proselytization. While some exceptionally vicious violence was perpetrated on Christians in Algeria, the vast majority of the more than 100,000 victims of violence since 1992 were unarmed civilian Muslims. The sort of proselytization that can be observed in the case of Algeria is not based on a tradition of critical reflection. Rather, it is a reflection of a constant search, among different political movements, for an imaginary symbolic unity of the community. Only an analysis of the multiplicity of religious orientations will permit a much more precise evaluation of proselytization in such situations.

The failure of FIS to transform itself into a peaceful political movement while retaining its control over its followers reveals the more fundamental question of defining Islam as an ideological and social force in Algeria. The present situation in that country may allow for continuation of the debate about the cultural and intellectual heritage of Islam, thereby clearing the way for the possibilities of multiplicity of understanding the textual sources of Islam. The Sunni tradition of the Algerian public may also be more conducive to political solutions to religious conflict in the country. But these possibilities have not yet been realized in practice, at least not in a sufficiently sustainable manner.

NOTES

[1] Sunnism accords a central place to Law *(fiqh)*, the science of jurisprudence. The Maliki School, one of the four great schools of Islamic law, founded by Malik ibn Anas (who died in 795) dominates throughout North Africa (the Maghreb). This school is founded on consensus *(Ijma)*, especially local consensus.

[2] The term *Shari'a*, mentioned several times in the Qur'an (chap. 45 *(al-jathiya)*, v. 18; chap. 42 *(al-shura)*, vv. 13 and 21; chap. 5 *(al-ma'ida)*, v. 48) came to signify the law of divine origin revealed by God and known by all human beings, even those who claim to follow this law as established by divinities which do not exist (chap. 42, v. 21). This law is the "way" which opposes the passions of the ignorant (chap. 45, v. 18).

But the actual evolution of *Shari'a* as a comprehensive system of law and ethics was the product of human interpretation and application over several centuries after the Prophet's death. For an overview of the sources and development of *Shari'a* see Abdullahi Ahmed An-Na'im, *Toward an Islamic Reformation: Civil Liberties, Human Rights and International Law* (Syracuse University Press, 1990), chap. 2.

³ The displacement of Algerian Jews dates back to the Crémieux which offered them French nationality in 1870. They numbered 140,000 in 1954 according to R. Ageron (1964, 62).

⁴ Donatism is a fourth-century heresy which led to a religious schism in the church of Africa. It was propounded by Bishop Donat, who denied any value to sacraments administrated by unworthy or so-deemed bishops. His main opponent was Augustine.

⁵ The Council of Chalcedon (451) acknowledged only one nature of Christ, a divine nature, and so declared a heresy the monophysism surviving under another lessened form in some Oriental churches.

⁶ The Wahhabism of Ibn Abdal Wahhab (1703-92) integrated into its doctrine dynastic interests and Islamic legitimation. This integrationist tendency with an internationalist vocation gave an initial impetus to the formation of preaching associations all around the Arab world.

⁷ For the reformers, *Salaf* were the men of the first three generations of Islam. *Salafi* is someone who refers to those first generations, and *salafiya* is the reformist movement which grew out of the thought and action of Muhammad Abduh. *Kalam* is the philosophy of religion which utilized dialectical argumentation to combat philosophy using its own techniques.

⁸ The association of Muslim Brothers created in 1929 enjoyed great success in the 1950s and 1960s. (This frame of reference is to the exclusive authority of the Revelation as ideal Constitution of the community and social justice.)

⁹ In 1968, for example, the minister of Religious Affairs justified in the name of Islam the agrarian revolution, the struggle against obscurantism and charlatanism by alluding to the brotherhoods and the El-Qiyam association (African Revolution no. 282, July 1968). For the ideological content of socialism see also the Declaration of Boumédiène, 5 July 1965; for Islam as state religion, consult the texts of the Congress of Soummam, August 1956 (el moujahid 4 1962), the Charter of Tripoli of 1960, and the Charter of Algiers 1964, and the National Charter of 1976.

¹⁰ Sayed Qutb (1906-66) was imprisoned by Nasser and hanged in 1966. The Islamists referred to two of his texts: *Ma'Alim Fi Tariq* (*Milestones*) and *Fi-Zilal Qur'an* (*In the Shadow of the Qur'an*).

BIBLIOGRAPHY

Ageron, R. 1964. *Histoire de l'Algérie contemporaine*. Paris: Presses Universitaires de France.

Leca, J., and J. C. Vatin. 1975. *Algérie politique, institiutions et régime*. Paris: CNRS.

Mérad, A. 1967. *Le Réformisme musulman en Algérie de 1925 à 1940*. The Hague: Mouton.

CONTRIBUTORS

Abdullahi Ahmed An-Na'im is professor of law at the Emory University School of Law and Fellow of the Law and Religion Program at Emory. After obtaining his first degree in law (LL.B. Honors) from the University of Khartoum in 1970, he studied at the University of Cambridge (England) where he received an LL.B. degree with honors and a diploma in criminology (1973), and earned the Ph.D. in law from the University of Edinburgh, Scotland (1976). He is the author of several books and some thirty articles and chapters on Islamic law, human rights, and constitutionalism. He is the author of *Toward an Islamic Reformation: Civil Liberties, Human Rights and International Law;* editor of *Human Rights in Cross-Cultural Perspectives: Quest for Consensus; Human Rights in Africa: Cross-Cultural Perspectives* (with Francis Deng); and *The Cultural Dimensions of Human Rights in the Arab World* (in Arabic).

Tshikala K. Biaya earned the Ph.D. in history of Africa, University of Laval, Quebec, Canada. He co-edited *L'Afrique Revisite* and has published many articles in scholarly journals.

Chabha Bouslimani is an Algerian journalist currently based in France.

Francis M. Deng graduated with a law degree from Khartoum University and pursued post-graduate studies in the United Kingdom and the United States, where he obtained a doctorate from Yale Law School in 1968. After many high-level diplomatic, professional, and academic appointments, Dr. Deng joined the Brookings Institution in Washington, D.C., in 1989 as senior fellow and helped establish the African Studies branch of the Foreign Policy Studies program, which he heads. In 1992, Ambassador Deng was named by U.N. Secretary-General Boutros Boutros-Ghali as his Special Representative on internally displaced persons worldwide. Dr. Deng has authored or edited over twenty books in the fields of law, conflict resolution, human rights, anthropology, folklore, history, politics and two novels. His latest Brookings publications include *Human Rights in Africa: Cross-Cultural Perspectives* (1990); *Conflict Resolution in Africa* (1991); *The Challenges of Famine Relief: Emergency Operations in the Sudan* (1992); *Protecting the Dispossessed: A Challenge for the International Community* (1993); *War of Visions: Conflict of Identities in the Sudan* (1995); *Sovereignty as Responsibility: Conflict Management in Africa* (1996); *Masses in Flight: The Global Crisis of Internal Displacement*, co-authored with Roberta Cohen (1998); *The*

Forsaken People: Case Studies of the Internally Displaced, co-edited with Robert A. Cohen (1998); and *African Reckoning: A Quest for Good Governance*, co-edited with Terence Lyons (1998). His first book, *Tradition and Modernization: A Challenge for Law among the Dinka of the Sudan* (1971), won the 1972 Heskovits Award for the best book published the year before. *Human Rights in Africa: Cross-Cultural Perspectives,* co-edited with Abdullahi Ahmed An-Na'im, was the 1990 winner of the Excellence in Publishing award sponsored by the Association of American Publishers.

Farid Esack is a South African Muslim theologian who works in South Africa, Pakistan (Islamic theology), the United Kingdom (Qur'anic hermeneutics), and Germany (biblical hermeneutics). Dr. Esack is a commissioner on gender equality, serves on a number of development, media, academic, and interfaith boards as a director and/or advisor. His publications include *But Moses Went to Pharaoh; The Struggle;* and *Qur'an, Liberation and Pluralism.* He has also published widely in academic journals on gender, liberation theology, interfaith relations, religion and identity, and Qur'anic hermeneutics.

Rosalind I. J. Hackett is Lindsay Young Professor at the University of Tennessee, Knoxville, where she teaches in religious studies and anthropology. She taught for several years in Nigerian universities before gaining the Ph.D. from the University of Aberdeen, Scotland, in 1986. She has published three books and numerous articles on religion in Africa. She is currently working on a study of religious conflict in Nigeria for the U.S. Institute of Peace.

Hannah W. Kinoti is associate professor of religious studies and teaches in the University of Nairobi, where she obtained the Ph.D. She is a former chair of the Department of Religious Studies. She obtained her B.A. and Dip.Ed. at Makerere University in Uganda. She has contributed several chapters in the series on African Christianity published in Nairobi. She has held a one-year fellowship at Harvard Medical School, Department of Social Medicine.

J. Paul Martin has been the executive director of Columbia University's Center for the Study of Human Rights since its foundation in 1978. He is also co-director of the human rights and humanitarian affairs concentration in the master's degree in international affairs. In addition to his writings on rights and religion, he directs the Center's four-year-old training and research program on religion and religious freedom for nongovernmental organizations and religious leaders from Eastern Europe, a program funded by The Pew Charitable Trusts. Dr. Martin also writes on and organizes human rights education programs for human rights nongovernmental organizations in Africa.

Makau Mutua was educated at the University of Nairobi, the University of Dar-Es-Salaam, and at Harvard Law School, where he obtained a doctorate of juridical science degree in 1987. He is an associate professor of law at the State University of New York at Buffalo School of Law, where he teaches international human rights, international business transactions, international law, and human rights, gender, and culture. He is the director of the Human Rights Center at SUNY Buffalo. Professor Mutua has published numerous scholarly and popular articles and written human rights reports for the United Nations and leading NGOs. Previously, Professor Mutua was the associate director at the Harvard Law School Human Rights Program and director of the Africa Project at the Lawyers Committee for Human Rights. He serves as the chairman of the Kenya Human Rights Commission and sits on the boards of several international organizations and academic journals.

Lamin Sanneh received the Ph.D. in Islamic history at the University of London. He taught at Harvard University for eight years before moving to Yale University in 1989 to become the D. Willis James Professor of Missions and World Christianity. He has been actively involved in Yale's Council on African Studies. He is an editor-at-large of the ecumenical weekly *The Christian Century,* and serves on the editorial board of several academic journals. He is the author of over a hundred articles on religious and historical subjects, and of several books, including *The Jakhanke Muslim Clerics: A Religious and Historical Study of Islam in Senegambia; West Africa Christianity: The Religious Impact; Translating the Message: The Missionary Impact on Culture,* now in its eighth printing; *Encountering the West: Christianity and the Global Cultural Process; The Crown and the Turban: Muslims and West African Pluralism; Piety and Power: Muslims and Christians in West Africa;* and *The American Factor in West Africa Christianity, 1770-1890: A Study in Antislavery and Antistructure* (forthcoming from Harvard University Press).

Benjamin F. Soares, an anthropologist, has been a National Science Foundation-NATO postdoctoral fellow at the Ecole des Hautes Etudes en Sciences Sociales, Paris, and is currently a postdoctoral fellow, the Committee on Human Development, the University of Chicago.

J. D. van der Vyver is I. T. Cohen Professor of International Law and Human Rights at the Emory University School of Law, was professor of law and dean of the faculty of law, Potchefstroom University for Christian Higher Education, and ad hominem professor of law at the University of the Witswatersrand, Johannesburg, South Africa. He has written more than two hundred law review articles on a wide range of subjects, notably human rights, and is the author of several books and monographs, including *Introduction to Legal Science**, co-authored with F. J. van Zyl (2d edition 1982); *The Juridical Function of State and Church: A Critical Analysis of the Doctrine of Sphere Sovereignty** (1972); *Human Rights** (1974); *The Protection of Human Rights in South Africa** (1975); *Seven Lectures on Human Rights* (1976); *The Law of Persons and Family Law**, co-authored with D. J. Joubert (3d edition 1991); *The Republic of South Africa Constitution Act** (1984); and *Reformed Christians and Social Justice* (1988).

Harry Winter, O.M.I., has been a member of the Catholic religious order known as the Missionary Oblate of Mary Immaculate since 1957. Currently he serves as one of three directors of the Oblate Center for Mission Studies based in Washington. A member of the American Society of Misology, he specializes on reference tools for missiologists and published recently *Oblate Missiologists* (Oblate Center for Mission Studies, Washington, D.C.), a study that includes the work of Archbishop Marcello Zago, O.M.I., recently named Secretary of the Congregation for the Evangelization of Peoples by the pope.

---

*Books written in Afrikaans.

INDEX

Abboud, General Ibrahim, 208
Abot, Deng, 212
Achebe, Chinua, 173
adaptation, processes of, 37–38
Adija, Loth, 214, 215
Afghanistan, 299
Africa: civilization clash due to invasion by Christianity and Islam, 171–74; as "Dark Continent," 270, 272; pre-colonial, 84–89. *See also specific topics*
African Charter on Human and People's Rights, 183
African Christian Democratic Party, 140
African Christians, number of, 176
African church, 170
African countries: ideological divide between Muslim, socialist, and secular, 109–18
African culture(s): banned by colonial state and church, 178; government banning of, 178; "vital compatibility" between and Christianity and, 181
African Independent Churches, 277, 281
African Inland Mission (A.I.M.), 273, 274
African Instituted Churches, 284
African Muslim Party, 140
African philosophy, 184 n.8; rehabilitation of, 183–84
African religion(s), 148, 184 n.7, 185 n.12; banned by colonial state and church, 178; as communal and non-universalist, 172; do not try to convert or remake the other, 172; intentional displacement of, 170; intersection with Islam and Christianity, 166, 169–70; purity of, 170; and the state, 169–70; suppression of, 171–78; vilification and demonization of, 170, 172–74, 184 n.8. *See also* traditional religions
African religious beliefs, 34, 198–201

African religious ontology, 185 n.10
Africans: conception of religion, 172; subjugated to messianic traditions, 170; viewed as "primitive," 172
agency, 6, 7
Aina, Tade Akin, 10
Akamba, 179–80
Akot, Chief Albino, 209
Al-Bakri, 237–38
al-Fakhrí, 88, 89
al-Kánemí, Muhammad, 90
al-Ka'ti, Mahmúd, 86, 87
al-Nemery, Jaafer Mohammed, 112, 113
al-Sa'dí, 'Abd al-Rahmán, 85
Algeria, Islam in, 291–92, 300–301; and democracy and proselytization, 298–300; fundamentalism *vs.* integrism in, 294–95; history of, 292–94; as national ideology, 295–97; and women as focus of tensions, 297–98
Algerian Constitutions, 110, 291, 297
Algerian students, international networks linked by, 299
Allah, 65–67, 69, 70
Amos Group, 157
An-Na'im, Abdullahi Ahmed, 112, 221–22
Ananda Marga, 283
Anaya, S., 16
Andrew, B., 282–83
Anglophone countries in Africa, 125, 128, 129, 133
Angola, 113, 114; Constitution of, 113, 114, 137; MPLA Draft Constitution of, 116, 134; MPLA-Workers' Party, 113
animism, 172, 185 n.17, 200, 228
anti-Semitism, 42
apartheid policy, colonial, 278–80
apostasy, 15
Arabization, 194–98, 206, 207; history of, 194